CREATION, USE, AND DEPLOYMENT OF DIGITAL INFORMATION

CREATION, USE, AND DEPLOYMENT OF DIGITAL INFORMATION

Edited by

Herre van Oostendorp
Utrecht University

Leen Breure
Utrecht University

Andrew Dillon
The University of Texas

Routledge
Taylor & Francis Group
New York   London

First published by Lawrence Erlbaum Associates, Inc., Publishers
10 Industrial Avenue
Mahwah, New Jersey 07430

Transferred to digital printing 2010 by Routledge

Routledge

270 Madison Avenue
New York, NY 10016

2 Park Square, Milton Park
Abingdon, Oxon OX14 4RN, UK

Cover design by Kathryn Houghtaling Lacey

Library of Congress Cataloging-in-Publication Data

Creation, Use, and Deployment of Digital Information, edited by Herre van Oostendorp,
  Leen Breure, and Andrew Dillon.
  ISBN:978-0-8058-4587-7

Includes bibliographical references and index.

Contents

Contributors

Chapter 1

Herre van Oostendorp
Institute of Information and Computing
  Sciences
Utrecht University
Padualaan 14, 3584 CH Utrecht
The Netherlands
Fax +31 30 2513791
e-mail herre@cs.uu.nl

Leen Breure
Institute of Information and Computing
  Sciences
Utrecht University
Padualaan 14, 3584 CH Utrecht
The Netherlands
Fax +31 30 2513791
e-mail leen@cs.uu.nl

Andrew Dillon
School of Information
SZB 564
1 University Station D7000
University of Texas
Austin, TX 78712-1276
USA
Fax 512 471 3971
e-mail adillon@ischool.utexas.edu

Chapter 2

Gregory Crane
Department of Classics
Tufts University
107 Inman Street
Cambridge, MA 02139
USA
e-mail gcrane@emerald.tufts.edu

Chapter 3

Leen Breure
Institute of Information and Computing
  Sciences
Utrecht University
Padualaan 14, 3584 CH Utrecht
The Netherlands
Fax +31 30 2513791
e-mail leen@cs.uu.nl

Chapter 4

Jacco van Ossenbruggen
CWI Amsterdam
Kruislaan 413, P.O. Box 94079
1090 GB Amsterdam
The Netherlands
Fax +31 20 592 4199
e-mail Jacco.van.Ossenbruggen@cwi.nl

Lynda Hardman
CWI Amsterdam
Kruislaan 413, P.O. Box 94079
1090 GB Amsterdam
The Netherlands
Fax +31 20 592 4199
e-mail Lynda.Hardman@cwi.nl

Chapter 5

Jan-Herman Verpoorten
Institute of Information and Computing
Sciences
Utrecht University
Padualaan 14, 3584 CH Utrecht
The Netherlands
Fax +31 30 2513791
e-mail janherm@cs.uu.nl

Chapter 6

Joske Houtkamp
Institute of Information and Computing
Sciences
Utrecht University
Padualaan 14, 3584 CH Utrecht
The Netherlands
Fax +31 30 2513791
e-mail joske@cs.uu.nl

Chapter 7

Hermi Tabachneck(-Schijf)
Institute of Information and Computing
Sciences
Utrecht University
Padualaan 14, 3584 CH Utrecht
The Netherlands
Fax +31 30 2513791
e-mail hermi@cs.uu.nl

Chapter 8

Herre van Oostendorp
Institute of Information and Computing
Sciences
Utrecht University
Padualaan 14, 3584 CH Utrecht
The Netherlands
Fax +31 30 2513791
e-mail herre@cs.uu.nl

Nina Holzel
Institute of Information and Computing
Sciences
Utrecht University
Padualaan 14, 3584 CH Utrecht
The Netherlands

Chapter 9

Peter Foltz
Department of Psychology
New Mexico State University
Las Cruces, NM 88003
USA
Fax +1 505 646 6212
e-mail pfoltz@crl.nmsu.edu

Adrienne Y. Lee
Department of Psychology
New Mexico State University
Las Cruces, NM 88003
USA
Fax +1 505 646 6212
e-mail alee@crl.nmsu.edu

Chapter 10

Cilia Witteman
Faculteit der Sociale Wetenschappen
Radboud Universiteit Nijmegen
Postbus 9104, 6500 HE Nijmegen
The Netherlands
Fax +31 24 3612776
e-mail c.witteman@ped.kun.nl

Nicole Krol
Faculteit der Sociale Wetenschappen
Radboud Universiteit Nijmegen
Postbus 9104, 6500 HE Nijmegen
The Netherlands
Fax +31 24 3612776
e-mail N.Krol@ped.kun.nl

Chapter 11

Eleonoor ten Thij
Institute of Information and Computing
Sciences
Utrecht University
Padualaan 14, 3584 CH Utrecht
The Netherlands
Fax +31 30 2513791
e-mail eleonoor@cs.uu.nl

Chapter 12

Robbert-Jan Beun
Institute of Information and Computing
Sciences
Utrecht University
Padualaan 14, 3584 CH Utrecht
The Netherlands
Fax +31 30 2513791
e-mail rj@cs.uu.nl

Rogier van Eijk
Institute of Information and Computing
Sciences
Utrecht University
Padualaan 14, 3584 CH Utrecht
The Netherlands
Fax +31 30 2513791
e-mail rogier@cs.uu.nl

Chapter 13

Lidwien van de Wijngaert
Institute of Information and Computing
Sciences
Utrecht University
Padualaan 14, 3584 CH Utrecht

The Netherlands
Fax +31 30 2513791
e-mail lidwien@cs.uu.nl

Chapter 14

Ronald Batenburg
Institute of Information and Computing
Sciences
Utrecht University
Padualaan 14, 3584 CH Utrecht
The Netherlands
Fax +31 30 2513791
e-mail ronald@cs.uu.nl

Pascale Peters
Faculteit Sociale Wetenschappen
Utrecht University
Postbus 80140, 3508 TC Utrecht
The Netherlands
Fax 030 2534405
e-mail C.P.Peters@fss.uu.nl

Chapter 15

Mary Dyson
Department of Typography and Graphic
Communication
The University of Reading
2 Earley Gate, Whiteknights
P.O. Box 239
Reading RG6 6AU
United Kingdom
Fax +44 (0)118 935 1680
e-mail m.c.dyson@reading.ac.uk

Chapter 16

Andrew Dillon
School of Information
SZB 564
1 University Station D7000
University of Texas
Austin, TX 78712-1276
USA
Fax 512 471 3971
e-mail adillon@ischool.utexas.edu

Chapter 1

Introduction to Creation, Use, and Deployment of Digital Information

Herre van Oostendorp
Leen Breure
Utrecht University

Andrew Dillon
University of Texas

This book is about designing, using, and deploying digital information and digital information systems. It presents research outcomes from the perspective of research in *information science,* broadly construed, a term used now to cover a range of theoretical and practical approaches to information studies.

The far-reaching digitization of society provides the directive for research in information science. Information science is concerned with themes on the intersection of information and communication technology (ICT), on the one hand, and the individual and society in a broad sense, on the other hand. Of special importance is the process of creation of digital content. It comprises important topics such as authoring, information mapping, visualization and 3-D models, and automatic content publishing, with special attention to mechanisms for personalizing the presentation of digital information. (See further, for instance, Stephenson, 1998, for a broad orientation on Web-oriented publishing research in Europe.) Apart from these technological issues, the accessibility of information has become a necessary condition for participating in economic, cultural, and societal processes, both for individuals and for organizations. Digital networks span the world, making a large part of human communication independent of time and place. Information has become the most important production factor and, as such, increasingly determines the functioning of individuals and the structure of organizations. All this has drastically altered the relationships among companies and between companies and their customers, affecting the contact between government and citizen as well.

This continuing computerization of society reveals ever more clearly that problems are often not inherent in the techniques, but rather appear in their application. Consequently, it is not only the computer experts and technicians that determine what conditions digital systems must satisfy (Van Oostendorp, 2003), but also the users and the organizations in which they work. The issues involved are too complex to lend themselves to merely ad hoc, practical solutions. Not only does the usability of systems or programs need to be improved (Dix, Finlay, Abowd, & Beale, 2004), but the efficient and strategic use of the total of information sources and information technology needs to be taken into account as well.

To be able to handle information successfully, the user must possess appropriate knowledge, consisting of concepts, rules, and experiences. Knowledge engineering (Schreiber et al., 2000), in the sense of creating knowledge from data, documenting best practices, and creating wide accessibility of specific expertise, is one of the most important strategies for competition and survival in a world market that seems less and less predictable. It is not surprising, then, that much use of ICT appears to be directly connected to forms of knowledge engineering (Davenport & Prusak, 1998). Thus, a tight interconnection of information and knowledge is evolving. Increasingly, organizations are becoming aware that this knowledge can be systematically documented and internally shared (cf. for instance Ackerman, Pipek, & Wulf, 2002).

Three areas of interest based on this view are: (a) the life cycle of information: the creation, design, implementation, exploitation (deployment), evaluation, and adaptation of content; (b) the cognitive and communication processes: interaction aspects, usability, use, and engineering of knowledge; and (c) the deployment of information within organizations and the policies concerning digital information. The approach (see Fig. 1.1) whereby such a life cycle is placed within a human (individual, organizational, and societal) context is typical for the information-science methodology followed in this book.

PURPOSE

Corresponding to aforementioned three areas of interest, the purpose of this book is to present results of scientific research on: (a) how digital information has to be designed, (b) how artifacts or systems containing digital content should maximize usability, and (c) how context can influence the nature and efficiency of digital communication. Notions from these three different areas are presented in this book.

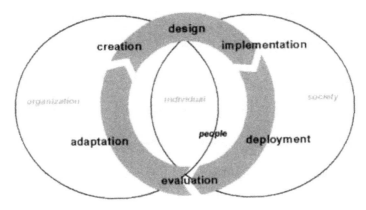

FIG. 1.1. Life cycle of information in a human context.

FOCUS

The focus of the current book is, thus, on digital information. It is treated from three perspectives, outlined in the following sections.

Creating Electronic Publications

In Part I, the complexity of technical choices and alternatives met by designers and writers when they have to integrate content, functionality, and layout into one particular design is described. Chapters 2 through 6 provide supporting information for those who are working on the area of creating electronic publications.

Using Digital Information and Digital Systems

In Part II, chosen technical alternatives are discussed in view of their acceptability or usability for end users. More fundamentally, however, it is important to understand how users process complex multimedia information and how we can support users, for instance, when they have to make complex decisions, as with decision support systems, or when distance or tele-learning are involved. Chapters 7 through 11 discuss cognitive psychological research on these processes and pay attention to usability issues.

Deploying Digital Information

It is important to consider the relation between information needs and media choice of users. Furthermore, it is important for designers to know in what context, and for what purpose, users will apply the information systems that are designed. The relation between context and deployment of ICT means is treated in Part III.

GLOBAL CONTENT OF THE BOOK
AND OVERVIEW OF CHAPTERS

Creating Electronic Publications

In Part I, five chapters present information on how electronic documents can be realized, and the complexities, alternatives, functions, and restrictions are treated. In chapter 2, Crane argues that, in a digital environment, digital documents should be able to interact with each other and this document-to-document interaction stands at the core of true digital publication. We are only now beginning to explore what new forms and functionality digital publications will assume. From this perspective, Crane presents a discussion of how digital primary sources such as Plato or Shakespeare and reference works for the humanities should be designed. A central topic in chapter 3, by Breure, is the idea of cross-media publication, that is, the process of reusing information across multiple output media without having to rewrite it for distinct purposes. On the basis of concepts from genre theory (cf., e.g., Toms & Campbell, 1999), Breure presents the outline of an editorial system capable of (re)producing text fragments in new contexts. Van Ossenbruggen and Hardman (chap. 4) discuss digital document engineering techniques that are important for reusability and tailorability of digital documents. They stress the importance of describing the content of a document separately from the description of its layout and other stylistic characteristics. However, in current tools, this is merely a syntactic separation. They explore in their chapter the requirements for semantic-driven document engineering. Chapter 5 by Verpoorten also concerns the reuse of digital content involving educational content and educational software. The development of educational ICT is often expensive and time consuming. Reuse of digital content is often difficult because much domain expertise and practical experience of educational designers is required. Verpoorten describes in chapter 5 an approach that enables an easy reuse of digital content for different applications. Chapter 6 by Houtkamp discusses characteristics of the representation and display of 3-D models of buildings, and some characteristics of the observer that influence the affective appraisal of the building that is modeled. It is argued that more insight into and control of the cues is needed in the representations that are responsible for triggering a certain affect (or even emotion). Only then is it possible to effectively engineer the affects of observers.

Using Digital Information and Digital Systems

Part II contains five chapters on how human beings process information and how technical solutions can satisfy human restrictions. Chapter 7 by Tabachneck(-Schijf) sketches contributions from cognitive psychology to examine how constructing a multimedia presentation, for example, in Microsoft PowerPoint, rests on complex cognitive processes such as multiple representations and mental models. Van Oostendorp describes in chapter 8 a study on collective problem solving in a computer-supported collaborative working (CSCW) environment. More specifically, he shows the positive influence of adding a chat box and making explicit the role of participants with icons on group problem solving. On a more general level, it is assumed that these added features help to construct an accurate—in this case, shared—mental model, and thereby facilitate information processing, causing the improvement in performance. With more and more information available in digital form, it becomes critical to present that information in a pedagogically effective manner. In chapter 9, Foltz and Lee discuss the development of new adaptive training systems, focusing on research on automated assessment of essays, by means of applying the latent semantic analysis technique (Landauer, Foltz, & Laham, 1998). Witteman and Krol discuss in chapter 10 what a knowledge engineer has to do when the aim is to build an intelligent information system, that is, when the goal is more ambitious than simply storing facts in a database that may be queried. Such a system supports the generation of new knowledge from knowledge elements about the domain of application stored in its knowledge base, complemented with inference rules that allow well-founded conclusions, given data provided by the user. The perspective of this chapter is to provide a methodology that may improve the chances of success of building an effective knowledge-based system. Ten Thij elaborates in chapter 11 on the design and use of an online expert center, aimed at providing students educational resources to help them learn how to write. She focuses on how collaboration between students, in the context of an online community support system (Preece, 2000), can assist feedback processes, thereby enhancing writing processes.

Deploying Digital Information

Part III treats in four chapters the context in which digital information processing and deployment takes place. The goal of chapter 12 by Beun and Van Eijk is to discuss theoretical principles that drive a conversation between a user and a computer. They focus on the feedback process that regulates the repair of communication flaws caused by conceptual disparities between a computer system and its user when using particular terms in a communication language. The goal of chapter 13 (Van de Wijngaert) is to provide a framework that explains why some technologies are successful—in the sense of the individual's decision to use a certain technology—and others not. This framework is centered on the notion that there are needs of individuals on the one hand, and costs on the other hand. When a (positive) balance between both is found, the application is chosen and used successfully. This framework is illustrated by the success (or failure) of electronic supermarkets. Batenburg and Peters present in chapter 14 an overview of research on the impact of telework on organizations and society, since the 1990s, with an empirical focus on the Dutch situation. They introduce a theoretical framework—also useful for other countries—focused on explaining why telework has been embraced by some employers and employees but not by others. Dyson synthesizes in chapter 15 experimental research on reading text from screen focusing on how reading is affected by specific typographic variables and reading speed, and how the mechanics of reading on screen (i.e., scrolling) relate to the reading task. It provides recommendations on the design of digital documents.

In the concluding chapter, chapter 16, Dillon outlines a broad view of what is meant by *information* and questions many of our implicit assumptions about what we are doing when we claim to be engaged in information work. In doing so, he presents a general perspective on the problem of understanding (digital) information, what it is, and how digital deployment complicates the issues for us in designing and using it.

APPROACH

The authors in this book come from different disciplines: science, arts, psychology, educational sciences, and computer science. We are convinced that, to present an overall view on the problem area of designing digital content and using information systems, a multidisciplinary approach is necessary. This team of authors provides such an approach. Additionally, together the chapters present a representative idea of what a focus on information science has produced at Utrecht University and at the University of Texas, involving multidisciplinary faculties engaged in the major problems of information science. For us, this implies the interrelated study of psychological, social, and technological factors (see Fig. 1.1) that play a role in the development, use, and application of ICT.

WHY THIS VOLUME?

It is essential that the perspectives we mentioned and the scholars from these different fields join together to understand and fully exploit the new possibilities of ICT. It is important for designers to become aware of human and contextual constraints. Only then can the design process of designers and information processing and communication by end users in a digital environment be improved. And it also goes the other way around. It is instructive for social scientists to see where, in the complex design process, decisions are made that could influence the resulting use, understanding, and even emotions evoked by the resulting systems. We aimed to create a balanced view. Even more concretely, while preparing our university courses we noticed that a textbook that contains the aforementioned ideas was, unfortunately, lacking. We hope this book fills that gap.

ACKNOWLEDGMENT

We are very grateful to Henriette van Vugt for her very accurate and quick editorial assistance. Without her help this book would not have been realized.

REFERENCES

Ackerman, M., Pipek, V., & Wulf, V. (Eds.). (2002). *Sharing expertise: Beyond knowledge management.* Cambridge, MA: MIT Press.

Davenport, T., & Prusak, L. (1998). *Working knowledge: How organizations manage what they know.* Cambridge, MA: Harvard Business School Press.

Dix, A., Finlay, J., Abowd, G. D., & Beale, R. (2004). *Human–computer interaction* (3rd ed.). Harlow, England: Pearson Education Limited.

Landauer, T. K., Foltz, P. W., & Laham, D. (1998). An introduction to latent semantic analysis. *Discourse Processes, 25,* 259–284.

Preece, J. (2000). *Online communities: Designing usability, supporting sociability.* Chichester, England: Wiley.

Schreiber, G., Akkermans, H., Anjewierden, A., De Hoog, R., Shadbolt, N. R., Van de Velde, W., & Wielinga, B. (2000). *Knowledge engineering and management: The CommonKADS methodology.* Cambridge, MA: MIT Press.

Stephenson, G. A. (1998). Electronic publishing resources on the Web. *Computer Networks and ISDN Systems, 30,* 1263–1271.

Toms, E. G., & Campbell, D. G. (1999). Genre as interface metaphor: Exploiting form and function in digital environments. In *Proceedings of the 32nd Hawaii International Conference on Systems Sciences (HICSS '99)* (pp. 1–8). Los Alamitos, CA: IEEE Computer Society.

Van Oostendorp, H. (Ed.). (2003). *Cognition in a digital world.* Mahwah, NJ: Lawrence Erlbaum Associates.

Part I

CREATING ELECTRONIC PUBLICATIONS

Chapter 2

In a Digital World, No Book
Is an Island: Designing Electronic
Primary Sources and Reference
Works for the Humanities

Gregory Crane
Tufts University

Although electronic publication has become common, almost all of it adheres to forms optimized for print. In an electronic environment, electronic documents interact with each other and this document-to-document interaction stands at the core of true electronic publication. Although technologies such as XML and the Semantic Web provide methodologies by which documents can more effectively interact, we are only now beginning to explore what new forms and functionality electronic publications will assume. This chapter takes its examples from the primary sources for cultural heritage, but the issues are general.

Many digital collections now exist and support intellectual activity of various kinds for differing audiences, but most of these mimic forms developed for print. Servers provide PDF and HTML versions of print publications. These publications may be searchable, but they are often designed for reading offline. The digital environment contributes—and contributes substantially—by speeding physical access. This is not a trivial advantage; even if the physical document is available in the local library and the round trip from work area to stacks is only a few minutes, the minimum transaction costs for checking 10 documents during a day is substantial.

In a digital environment, documents interact not only with their readers but also with each other. Automatic citation linking, which converts textual references into links, represents only one method whereby electronic publications talk to one another. Digital libraries manage large bodies of electronic documents. The concept of the digital library is still fluid and evolving: One could view Google as a digital library system for the web as a whole or restrict digital library to more tightly controlled systems such as the Association for Computing Machinery's digital library of its own publications (http://portal.acm.org) or more decentralized, but still managed, collections such as the U.S. National Science Digital Library (http://nsdl.org). Nevertheless, all of these systems add value to their individual component documents, with each providing services that make their collections as a whole greater than the sum of their parts.

Digital library systems challenge authors to create documents that interact with machines as well as with people. The implications of this are profound, because multiple systems already mediate between electronic information and the perceptible materials—audio as well as video—presented to the human audience. We need to reexamine the ways in which we create publications in the light of our growing ability to serve a broader variety of materials (geospatial, sound, video, etc.) to wider audiences than print publication could ever reach.

Emerging technologies will allow us to get more out of traditional document types. Simple information retrieval has already changed the ways in which we interact with textual materials. A great deal of research is being devoted to the automatic analysis of relatively unstructured source materials; in the case of intelligence analysis, the sources of information may be quite diverse (e.g., intercepted phone transmissions) and the authors less than enthusiastic about communicating their ideas to a broad audience. Progress is being made in such areas as automatic summarization, topic detection and tracking, automatic cataloguing, machine translation, and other areas of document-understanding technologies. But however successful such technologies may be with unstructured material, the more useful structure already inherent in the source document, the less uncertainty and the better subsequent systems can perform.

New common languages for data and document structures such as XML and the Semantic Web are emerging, with increasingly expressive standards and guidelines for various domains. This chapter concentrates on research done with primary sources for cultural heritage, because these resources often raise broader challenges than conventional scientific publications. Most publications are secondary source materials that are not themselves of interest but serve as a means to some other end. They are containers of information and ideas with which we conduct our real work and from which we extract the main points as quickly as possible. They should be as short and succinct as possible, and the more we can filter them for those points of interest to us, the better. Such documents constitute the vast majority of all academic publications and may not warrant the investment of complex formatting.[1] Furthermore, most documents of this sort cluster around a small number of structural prototypes, with abstracts, tables of contents, chapters, and a relatively closed set of similar architectural patterns.

CHARACTERISTICS OF PRIMARY SOURCES

Primary materials are, however, qualitatively different. Editors of culturally significant materials already in the print world developed elaborate knowledge structures that can be translated into powerful digital resources.

First, primary sources are of "persistent value," a phrase used to describe materials that hold their value over time. Most publications in medicine and other rapidly moving fields decline in value very rapidly, as the state of knowledge moves on and new results supersede old. A description of London written in the 19th century is also out of date, but its value lies precisely in the fact that it preserves details about the city that no longer exist. Indeed, its value as a historical source increases as the physical and social forms of the city evolve over time. Likewise, as medical and scientific publications drift out of date, they can become themselves primary sources to historians of science, but they thus serve a different audience with its own interests.

Second, primary sources can attract immense scholarly labor. A copy editor may devote several weeks to a monograph. The scholar Charlton Hinman, however, spent years painstakingly comparing different printed copies of Shakespeare's First Folio, identifying minute changes that the printers made as they noticed errors during their work (Hinman, 1963). Scholars devote years of labor to the creation of an authoritative scholarly edition for a single important text. A single canonical document may generate thousands of book-length studies, as well as a rich suite of commentaries, specialized lexica, bibliographies, and other research tools. In an electronic environment, such scholarly resources can include databases that go beyond print: Martin Mueller (2000), for example, created a linguistic database for the 250,000-word corpus of archaic Greek epic by disambiguating the automatically generated morphological analyses from the Perseus digital library. The automatically generated analyses made the subsequent disambiguation task feasible, though laborious. The resulting tool opens up new avenues of research.

---

[1]Consider for example the online proceedings of "Human Language Technologies 2001" (http://www.hlt2001.org). Although this conference summarized much of the most advanced work on text analysis, its proceedings were published as simple PDF files. No search engine, much less automatic summarization, named entity extraction, or other technology, is associated with the site.

Third, because primary sources can retain their value over long periods of time and because they attract substantial reference tools, collections of primary sources can serve as highly intertwined systems, in which the components interact closely. Classics proved a useful field in which to explore such systematic effects because classicists evolved consistent conventions of citation and nomenclature that have in some cases remained stable for centuries. Thus, text citations from a 19th-century commentary (e.g., "Hom. Il. 3.221") can be converted automatically into links that point to the same line of Homer's *Iliad* (book 3, line 221) that the commentator viewed a century before. The system is not perfect—the 19th-century edition may differ from that of the editions currently in use—but the overall effect is impressive. One Greek–English lexicon (Liddell, Scott, Jones, & McKenzie, 1940) that we placed online contains 220,000 links to the circa 5,000,000-word corpus of classical Greek in Perseus. Overall, we have mined more than 600,000 hard links within the 15,000,000-word Perseus Greco-Roman collection.

Not all disciplines have shown such consistency in naming. Shakespearean scholarship has a long history and substantial research of persistent value took place in the 19th century. Shakespearean editors, however, regularly renumber the lines of the plays. Thus, "3.2.211" points to different sections of the play depending on which edition is used. Where authors provide short text extracts as well (e.g., "now is the winter of our discontent") and where we have identified a string as a quote, we can locate the phrase in an arbitrary edition with a text search. We can apply various computational techniques to align two online editions of a work (Melamed, 2001), creating a reasonable conversion table between different systems of lineation. Nevertheless, the lack of a consistent reference scheme substantially complicates the task of managing Shakespearean scholarship. Sensing the problem, one publisher even claimed rights over its line numbers, although its lineation was largely based on counting line breaks in the First Folio (Hinman, 1968).

In an electronic environment, publications can constitute semi-autonomous systems that interact without human intervention—the books in an electronic library should be able to talk to one another, and the extent to which this conversation between books can take place provides one measure for the extent to which an electronic library fulfills the potential of its medium. Consider one relatively straightforward example. A reader selects a word in an online text, prompting the text to query an online dictionary for an entry on that word. The text also informs the dictionary what author and work the reader is examining. The dictionary then highlights those definitions that are listed for this particular author. The text can also pass the citation for the precise passage (e.g., Thuc. 1.38). The dictionary can then check whether the relevant dictionary entry discusses this particular word in this particular passage. Because our large Greek lexicon cites almost 10%

of the words in some commonly read authors and the 10% disproportionately represent odd or difficult usages, the automatic filtering can have substantial benefits. Thus, very simple document-to-document communication can tangibly enhance ultimate human interactions.

CHALLENGES OF WORKING WITH PRIMARY SOURCES

The previous advantages also raise problems that all publications must ultimately address.

First, documents only interact insofar as they share common structures. Primary sources do not conform to modern conventions of publication. We must take them as we find them and adapt ourselves to their peculiarities if we are to study them properly. Consider the problem of the early modern English in which Shakespeare wrote. Spelling had not been standardized. Besides *Shakespeare*, for example, we find *Shakespere, Shakespear, Shakspeare, Shackespeare*, and a dozen other references—Shakespeare even spelled his own name differently at different times (Shakespeare, Evans, & Tobin, 1997). Regularization of spelling would certainly help retrieval (consider the problem that *I* can designate the pronoun or "eye"), but modern spelling can have unexpected consequences. Modern English distinguishes between *cousin* and *cozzen*, but the opening of the non-Shakespearean play *Woodstock* spells each word identically, emphasizing a pun made on the two (Rossiter, 1946).

Idiosyncrasies extend to the organization of documents. Many important sources are reference works with formats far more complex than articles and monographs. City directories are an important historical source that can be converted into databases much more useful than their print sources, but, even when the apparent structure appears simple, such conversion is often complex. Professionally edited lexica are crucial sources of information and can serve as knowledge sources for computational linguists, but they often contain inconsistencies that defy regularization. The Text Encoding Initiative (TEI) defined two separate forms of dictionary entry: the flexible <*entryFree*> that could accommodate the vagaries of human practice and the stricter <*entry*>, which prescribes a more regular form to which only new dictionary entries could regularly adhere (Sperberg-McQueen & Burnard, 1994).

Second, if no document should be an island, then we need to see each document that we publish as one node in a larger, growing network. Hard as it may be to understand how our publication interacts with the resources currently available, we need to anticipate as much as possible how our publications can interact with data and services that may emerge in the future.

The citation scheme to which classicists have adhered shows how good design can pay dividends generations later and in systems that earlier scholars could scarcely have imagined. Investing in the most generic possible conventions raises the chances that our work will work well in future environments: Such conventions include not only citation schemes but also tagging guidelines (such as the TEI) and well-established authority lists.

Those publishing humanities resources may well avoid cutting-edge structures. Linguistics, for example, may have radically changed the way we view language, providing us with substantive insights beyond those available in older philological approaches. But linguistic theories have proven complex and fluid, with radically different ideas competing with one another and little consensus. If a humanist had designed a research lexicon or grammar around one of the more appealing theories current in linguistics in 1980, the reference work would now have relatively little appeal. Nevertheless, judicious use of emerging ideas can in fact lay the foundation for publications of broad appeal. George Miller's *WordNet* semantic network (Fellbaum, 1998), for example, is based on a few well-established relationships. Although informed by progressive thought from the cognitive sciences, it is not tied too closely to any one paradigm.

The greatest problems that we face as we develop a network of interoperating publications may be social and political. Where the greatest print libraries have been able to provide scholars in at least areas with essentially self-sufficient collections, no one group will soon be able to aggregate all the content and services needed for any one subject. In classics, the Perseus Project has assembled a useful core of resources that supports some research and learning activities. Perseus contains a relatively small set of source texts and its strengths lie in the integration of heterogeneous, but thematically linked, resources. The *Thesaurus Linguae Graecae* (Pantelia, 1999) contains a far more comprehensive collection of Greek source texts, but it does not contain the lexica, grammars, commentaries, and language technologies (such as morphological analyzers or document comparison functions) found in Perseus. Users cannot, at present, interact with both systems at once. It is not impossible for Perseus and the *Thesaurus Linguae Graecae* (*TLG*) to federate their systems—each collection is connected to the fast Internet 2 network and bandwidth is not a problem. Perseus and *TLG* servers could exchange hundreds of transactions before generating for the user a composite page in real time. Nevertheless, such federation would, at the moment, require a conscious decision by two separate projects, with special programming. Such mutual alliances may work for a small number of projects, but useful sources can materialize in many places and in many forms. We need to design documents that can self-organize with the least possible human labor. Bigger systems will require more labor, but they must be scalable: We can, for example, manage an increase in size by a factor of 1,000,000 if we require only six times as much labor.

Various technologies are emerging that will make federation of data more transparent. The Open Archives Initiative (OAI; Suleman & Fox, 2001) and the FEDORA Object Repository (Staples & Wayland, 2000) provide two complementary approaches to this problem. The OAI is easily implemented and easily accepted: Repositories generally exchange catalogue records (although the model is designed to be extensible). The FEDORA model focuses on the digital objects and is better suited to supporting more fine-grained exchanges of data, but the technical requirements are higher and the political issues more challenging. Organizations such as the National Science Digital Library (http://www.nsdl.nsf.gov) are emerging to provide the social organization needed for diverse institutions to share their data. Humanities funders such as the Institute for Museum and Library Sciences are fostering similar collaborations.[2] Nevertheless, we will not for some time have a clear model of how digital publications that we create and store in particular archives will interact with other resources over time.

Third, we need to consider the implications of digital publication when we develop collections. Canonical works that are intensely studied constitute logical beginnings to a collection of electronic documents. They have large audiences. They are also often relatively easy to publish online. Novels may be long, but their formatting is usually straightforward. Plays are more complex but individuals can use, with moderate effort, optical character recognition to proofread and format collections of plays.

Nevertheless, electronic publication may derive much of its value because it integrates documents in an overall network of complementary resources. In my own work, I have found myself stressing the conversion of dense reference works into databases as early as possible. Grammars, encyclopedias, glossaries, gazetteers, lexica, and similar publications provide the framework that makes electronic reading valuable. These resources are, however, very expensive and difficult to place online. One cannot effectively apply optical character recognition to a 40-megabyte Greek–English lexicon where millions of numbers in citations are core data. And even if one has a clean online transcription, it can take substantial programming skill, domain knowledge, and labor to capture desired semantic and morphological information. At some point, others may create such resources

---

[2]A recent funding call from IMLS solicited "projects to add value to already-digitized collections as a demonstration of interoperability with the National Science Foundation's National Science Digital Library Program. Added value may include additional metadata, development of curriculum materials, or other enhancements to increase the usefulness of the collection(s) for science education. There are no subject limitations on collections, but applicants should explain how the materials could be useful for science education. Contact IMLS for more information."

and the social and technical infrastructure will allow us to federate our work with theirs, but the developer of a new collection probably cannot predict how and when, if ever, his or her materials will be able to take advantage of such external resources. Thus, even if we view federation as probable, if not inevitable, we need to plan for the short and medium terms.

Fourth, assuming that we have created a digital resource and followed a common form (e.g., TEI guideline tags), there are many levels of acceptable effort. A 1,000,000,000-word document with no formatting at all can be TEI conformant if it has a proper TEI header, which can be a very simple catalogue entry. Or a TEI-conformant document can contain parse trees that encode the morphological analysis of every word and the syntactic structure of every sentence. Someone placing a work online may choose to include raw page images, page images with uncorrected but searchable optical character recognition output, lightly proofread optical character recognition output, or professionally keyed, tagged, and vetted editions. It may take $10 worth of labor to convert a book to "image front/optical character recognition back" format, but $1,000 worth of labor to create a well-tagged version where 99.95% of the keystrokes accurately reflect the original—a difference of two orders of magnitude in the cost. We need to decide when the benefits justify this extra investment.

One taxonomy (Friedland et al., 1999) describes five levels of tagging:

1. Fully automated conversion and encoding: To create electronic text with the primary purpose of keyword searching and linking to page images. The primary advantage in using the TEILite DTD at this level is that a TEI header is attached to the text file.
2. Minimal encoding: To create electronic text for keyword searching, linking to page images, and identifying simple structural hierarchy to improve navigation.
3. Simple analysis: To create text that can stand alone as electronic text and identify hierarchy and typography without content analysis being of primary importance.
4. Basic content analysis: To create text that can stand alone as electronic text, identify hierarchy and typography, specify function of textual and structural elements, and describe the nature of the content and not merely its appearance. This level is not meant to encode or identify all structural, semantic, or bibliographic features of the text.
5. Scholarly encoding projects: Level 5 texts are those that require subject knowledge, and encode semantic, linguistic, prosodic, or other elements beyond a basic structural level.

These five levels of tagging involve increasing amounts of effort and expertise. The first four are reasonably well defined and describe the basic analysis of the content. The authors of this taxonomy (Friedland et al.) were librarians who had successfully created substantial digital collections. The fifth level is far more open-ended, delineating the point at which the authors felt that their work, as librarians, ended and where specialized editorial work began.

Those publishing primary materials in the humanities could well use an established taxonomy that describes various categories of scholarly editing. Canonical works of literature, whose language is the object of concerted and sustained study (e.g., Shakespeare or Sophocles), should have accompanying databases of morphological and syntactic information that reflect multiple possible interpretations and have been carefully edited. On the other hand, it is not clear whether such resources for the complete works of Dickens would be justifiable: The corpus of Dickens' works is much larger than that of Shakespeare or Homer, although Dickensian scholarship and teaching do not—at present—pursue questions that would benefit from such resources. Research and teaching can, of course, evolve to exploit new technological resources and each generation of scholars seeks new avenues of research with which to distinguish itself from its predecessors. A neophilological movement, exploiting the possibilities of computational linguistics, may seem far-fetched to some, but the very unconventionality of such an approach could attract attention from ambitious junior faculty. An editor of Dickens might then choose a cautious strategy, creating a database of syntactic analyses (e.g., a tree bank) for several widely read novels and then use this as a training set that would support automatic analysis for the rest of Dickens' work. Such automatic analysis, though imperfect, would probably be enough to suggest possible new areas of research. Subsequent scholars might edit the automatic analyses or decide that the automatic analyses were perfectly serviceable for their purposes. Or teachers and researchers could find little use for the syntactic data. Because those studying 19th-century novels have never had such a resource, we cannot predict how they might exploit it. Nor would the response to such a resource over a relatively short period of time (e.g., 5–10 years) necessarily indicate its long-term value. Substantive new research directions can take a generation or more to establish themselves. A generation ago, editors had fairly clear ideas of what sorts of materials they would assemble and roughly how their final work could take shape. Current editors cannot assume continuity or even linear rates of change.

Editors need to decide how far automatic processes can take them where their scarce labor should begin. This was alluded to previously when it was suggested that automatically generated syntactic parses might be perfectly serviceable for much, if not all, work. Editors must make a difficult cost–benefit decision, based on where technologies stand and where they might evolve: They must decide where the investment of their time advances the teaching and research of their audiences.

Some materials contain many discrete references to the world. Named entities include dates, people, places, money, organizations, physical structures, and so on. If a system can recognize the dates and places within a document, it can, for example, automatically generate timelines and maps illustrating the geospatial coverage of a document or a collection of documents. We have, in fact, implemented such automatic timelines and maps to help users visualize the contents of Perseus, its individual collections, and the documents within them. We have found that we can identify dates with reasonable accuracy. Place names from the classical world and even modern Europe are relatively tractable. The automatic analysis of U.S. place names is much harder, because not only are there dozens of Springfields scattered around the eastern United States, but some states have multiple towns with the same name (e.g., the various Lebanons in Virginia). Associating a particular Springfield or Lebanon in a given state with a particular place on a map is complex. The automatically generated maps are noisier than the automatically generated timelines. The editor thus needs to decide whether to edit the automatic analyses, making sure that each place name in a publication is linked to the proper place in the real world, and, of course, annotating those instances where we cannot establish the physical referent. Such disambiguation requires access to large authority lists, of which library catalogues are the most common example.

TYPICAL REDESIGN CHALLENGES

The previous examples point to a broader question. Scholarship and information technology, like science and instrumentation, evolve together. Just as scientific instruments such as the sextant and the slide rule no longer occupy the roles that they once did, forms of scholarly publication are also subject to evolution. The hand-crafted concordance, for example, is now obsolete as a scholarly enterprise and the keyword-in-context is one function of text search and visualization. Likewise, other reference works may continue to play a major role, but, like the textual apparatus, may undergo drastic change. Consider the following examples.

Designing a Lexicon

Students of classical Greek have long had access to a strong lexicon. Between 1843 and 1940, Henry George Liddell, Robert Scott, Henry Stuart Jones, and Robert McKenzie, in collaboration with many others, produced nine editions of the Greek–English lexicon commonly known as LSJ (for Liddell–Scott–Jones; Liddell et al., 1940). This work in turn was based on an earlier

German lexicon, the *Handwörterbuch der grieschischen Sprache* of Franz Passow (1786–1833), which was itself the result of more than one generation: The 5th edition appeared between 1841 and 1857, years after Passow's death, under the direction of Valentin Christian Rost and Friedrich Palm.

Nevertheless, the very richness of this reference work generated problems. No comprehensive revision has been undertaken since 1940; supplements, instead, appeared in 1968 (Liddell et al., 1968) and 1996 (Liddell, Glare, & Thompson, 1996). The lexicon was simply too massive and the cost of revision was prohibitive. Nor was it clear that a simple revision would be appropriate. Lexicography in general and our knowledge of Greek have evolved since the 19th century when the lexicon was designed. The coverage of LSJ is also fairly narrow: Whereas 220,000 citations point to fewer than 5,000,000 words included in the Perseus Greek corpus, another 220,000 point to more than 65,000,000 words of Greek in the *Thesaurus Linguae Graecae* and not in Perseus (Pantelia, 1999). Thus, 50% of the citations point to less than 8% of the current online corpus of literary Greek. The situation for intermediate students of Greek is even worse. The standard student lexicon is a largely mechanical abridgement of the 7th edition of the (then still only) Liddell–Scott lexicon and appeared in 1888 (Liddell & Scott, 1888). If researchers rely on a lexicon completed just after the fall of France, students of classical Greek thus commonly rely on a dictionary first published when Winston Churchill was a schoolboy.

A Cambridge-based team has begun work on a new *Intermediate Greek Lexicon*. Although initial plans envisioned a conventional print resource, electronic tools have allowed the lexicon staff to design the intermediate lexicon work as an extensible foundation for a more general lexical resource that could ultimately replace LSJ. The electronic medium raises further questions. The sheer effort of typesetting earlier editions of the lexicon was massive: Publication (1925–1940) of LSJ 9 took longer than the revision of the content itself (1911–1924). The text of LSJ 9 is now in TEI-conformant XML form and could (if this were considered worthwhile) be edited incrementally and constantly updated. Alternately, new entries can be created and distributed as they appear, an approach that opens up new ways to organize labor. Thus, lexicographers could concentrate initially on individual subcorpora (e.g., the language of Homer, Plato, or Greek drama) or on terms of particular significance (e.g., *hubris*). Without the constraints of the printed page, articles could have multiple layers; a scholar could, like Helen North (1966), produce a monograph-length study of *sôphrosunê* (conventionally rendered "moderation" or "self-control"), developing this to the lexicon as a publication worthy of tenure or promotion. Instead of scattering more modest notes on Greek lexicography in sundry journals, scholars could submit a steady stream of contributions that would appear faster and be more widely accessible as parts of the lexicon.

Substantial as such changes could be, emerging language technologies raise even more fundamental questions. Would the interests of teaching and research within a discipline with a strong lexicographic tradition be better served if we set aside the problem of creating new dictionary entries and concentrated instead on developing a suite of linguistic databases and analytical tools? A new intermediate Greek lexicon (IGL) covering a corpus of 5 million words might take 10 years of labor. English computational linguistics is highly developed and it is often hard to use English tasks to project the labor required for non-English work, but Chiou, Chiang, and Palmer (2001), analyzing the creation of a tree bank of Chinese, reported that a human being could manually create dependency trees for circa 240 words in 1 hour of labor. The use of a rough parser that attempts to generate as many initial trees as possible can substantially increase the speed of this process (Chiou et al., 2001, reported a speed-up from 240 to more than 400 words per hour). Such speeds could produce up to 10,000 parse trees in a week, meaning that the same 10 years of labor devoted to the creation of hand-crafted entries could produce a tree bank for something approaching 5 million words. The tree bank would not provide the same lexical support as a dictionary, but it would provide a wealth of grammatical and syntactic data: Students could ask which words depended on which and study the overall structure of the sentence in ways that are not now feasible. Those conducting research could then ask more sophisticated questions about a word's selection preferences (e.g., semantic relationships such as the fact that *to climb out of bed* is a valid idiom in English but not, for example, in German) or subcategorization frame (the fact that a given verb tends to take the dative rather than the accusative). A linguistic database that could support broad sets of queries might arguably constitute a larger contribution to teaching and research than a traditional lexicon that was more polished but could not serve as the basis for such broad linguistic analysis.

A tree bank does not preclude, although it may postpone, systematic human lexicographic analysis. Ten years of labor that included the creation of a tree bank could, however, yield results comparable to 10 years of traditional effort: Automatic processes can speed the production of parse trees, and the existence of the tree bank can speed the production of dictionary articles. Even if the 10 years of labor produce a tree bank and no finished articles, the tree bank can address the much larger problem of studying the broader corpus of Greek: The tree bank can provide a training set for automatic systems that scan the remaining 95% of Greek literature. Even if the tree bank delays the immediate goal of providing a finished lexicon for a key subset of Greek, it may thus have a major impact on how we study and read Greek as a whole.

Deciding between a traditional lexicon or an intermediate tool such as a tree bank is difficult because the value of a linguistic database, even if it seems theoretically clear, depends in part on the willingness with which the scholarly community will embrace it. The more advanced the new instrument, the greater the amount of time the community may need to learn how to use it. Semantic analysis of Greek remains a fundamental tool for most of those who use Greek texts. Few students of Greek, however, have a background in computational linguistics or are currently prepared to evaluate the results of imperfect automatic analysis, even where the precision of such results is high and well defined. As historians of science know, the acceptance of new instrumentation and theory depends on social as well as intellectual factors.

New Variorum Shakespeare Series

The American Horace Howard Furness published the first volume of the *New Variorum Shakespeare* (*NVS*) series in 1871 (Shakespeare & Furness, 1871), continuing a tradition that had begun in England but that had produced no new volumes in half a century. The series continues now under the direction of the Modern Language Association. Its format, though not unaltered, closely resembles that established by Furness and its purpose remains the same: Each *NVS* edition is designed "to provide a detailed history of critical commentary together with an exhaustive study of the text" (Hosley, Knowles, & McGugan, 1971, p. 1). Ideally, anyone studying a play by Shakespeare would be able to learn from the *NVS* edition the main ideas advanced throughout the history of scholarship.

Daunting as it may have been to Furness, Shakespearean scholarship increased dramatically during the 20th century. In the past generation, increased institutional demands for publication have stimulated an explosive growth of Shakespearean scholarship, as faculty publish for tenure and promotion. Few, if any, practicing Shakespearean scholars could claim a comprehensive knowledge of the publications on any one play, much less Shakespeare as a whole. In this regard, at least, Shakespearean scholars understand the plight of their colleagues in fast-moving areas of scientific and medical research. The labor required to produce an *NVS* is now staggering. Major plays such as *Hamlet* require teams of scholars and years of labor. And where scholarly fields still reward those who create foundational tools such as variorum editions, early modern English studies has shifted more toward theory and different categories of edition.

The problem of, and one possible approach to, providing "an exhaustive study of the text" was already mentioned. Most Shakespearean scholars are, however, more interested in critical opinion than in the history of the text. They want to understand as quickly as possible the most important ideas relevant to a play, a passage, or some particular topic (e.g., stage history). Although more than a decade has passed since the last *NVS* edition (Shake-speare & Spevack, 1990) was published, the *NVS* editorial board has been aggressively seeking out new authors and laying the groundwork for new editions. It might be possible to establish a stream that published one or two editions a year.

Even if the publication stream could approach two *NVS* editions per year, that would still mean that each edition was revised once roughly every 20 years, with the average *NVS* volume taking 10 years. Ten years is a very long time in contemporary Shakespearean studies, as it is in many fields. New critical approaches can rise and fall within a decade. Moreover, an exploratory survey of one recent Shakespearean journal (the *Shakespeare Quarterly*) revealed that around 50% of the secondary sources cited were less than 10 years old. And, of course, even if editors could provide yearly updates, Shakespearean criticism sustains such diverse interests that few, if any, individual editors could adequately address the needs of this community as a whole.

Still, the pace of Shakespearean scholarship is not as swift or demanding as AIDS research, bio-engineering, or similarly active (and heavily funded) areas and older work remains significant. A new *NVS* edition is a blessing, whereas an older *NVS* remains a useful instrument for previous scholarship. Nevertheless, other paradigms exist by which fields track developments for their constituents. The Max-Planck-Institut für Gravitationsphysik in Potsdam publishes *Living Reviews in Relativity*, an electronic journal in which authors of review articles can update their reviews over time (http://www.livingreviews.org/). Other approaches, however, draw more heavily on such language technologies as document clustering, automatic summarization, and topic detection and tracking. It would be easy to list the many ways in which the needs of Shakespearean scholars differ from those tracking bioterrorism (Hirschman, Concepcion, et al., 2001) or changes in the drug industry (Gaizauskas, 2001), but the underlying strategies behind such systems are general and can be adapted to the needs of scholars.

We can thus imagine a new *NVS* that tracked scholarly trends on Shakespearean scholarship. Such a system may not yet be feasible: Too many humanities publications are not yet available online and the technology is still evolving. Nevertheless, a new editor undertaking to produce an *NVS* edition is planning an information resource that will not appear for another 5 years or more and is thus, whether consciously or not, betting on the shape of things to come. A series that can, after 140 years, still consider itself the "new" variorum has an inherently long-term perspective. The *NVS* has consciously adapted its practices to respond to changing information resources: The 1971 handbook described how the series would no longer provide "type-facsimiles" of the First Folio because the Hinman Facsimile

(Hinman, 1968) edition was widely available (Hosley et al., 1971, p. 1). The changes provoked by 21st-century technology are likely to prove far more substantive.

CONCLUSION

Digital libraries are the natural home for publications of persistent value and in digital libraries the books talk to each other. These document–document interactions allow the system to customize the information presented to end users. We have, however, only just begun to design documents to support sophisticated document-to-document interactions. We are years, if not decades, away from establishing stable conventions for truly electronic publication. Those publishing in rapidly moving fields may feel little need to design documents that support as-yet undeveloped services in future digital libraries. The present situation is, however, challenging for those who are creating publications with projected life spans of decades or even centuries. The previous examples suggest the extent to which we no longer know how to design such basic document types as dictionaries and scholarly editions. We urgently need more research, development, and evaluation of best practices and models.

But if the future stays both exciting and unclear, one old principle of library science—indeed, a principle that informs the dawn of Western philosophy—remains fundamental. Machine translation, automatic summarization, question answering, clustering, and similar technologies are emerging, but all benefit immensely if documents refer clearly and unambiguously to particular objects. Thus, if our documents associate a reference to *Washington*, with its referent *Washington, DC* versus *George Washington the president*, higher order processes will be much more efficient (e.g., clustering systems would know up front that two documents were focused on George Washington rather than the capital of the United States). Much of Plato focuses on the problem of defining key terms such as *virtue* or *good*, but even Plato's interlocutors realized that particular references to particular things could be highly precise. Library scientists and particular domains have established authority lists by which we can connect particular references to particular objects: The *Getty Thesaurus of Geographic Names* provides "tgn,7013962" as a unique identifier for Washington, DC, the Library of Congress provides "Washington, George, 1732–1799" for President George Washington. On a practical level, we can engineer systems today that help authors and editors connect references to people, places, and things with their precise referents. Although we cannot predict what systems will emerge, we do know now—and have known for generations—that clarity of reference and document structure is important and feasible.

REFERENCES

Chiou, F., Chiang, D., & Palmer, M. (2001). Facilitating treebank annotation using a statistical parser. In *Proceedings of the first International Conference on Human Language Technology Research, HLT 2001* [Online]. Available: http://www.hlt2001.org/papers/hlt2001-26.pdf

Fellbaum, C. (1998). *WordNet: An electronic lexical database.* Cambridge, MA: MIT Press.

Friedland, L., Kushigian, N., Powell, C., Seaman, D., Smith, N., & Willett, P. (1999). *TEI text encoding in libraries: Draft guidelines for best encoding practices (Version 1.0)* [Online]. Available: http://www.indiana.edu/~letrs/tei

Gaizauskas, R. (2001). Intelligent access to text: Integrating information extraction technology into text browsers. In *Proceedings of the first International Conference on Human Language Technology Research, HLT 2001* [Online]. Available: http://www.hlt2001.org/papers/hlt2001- 36.pdf

Hinman, C. (1963). *The printing and proof-reading of the first folio of Shakespeare.* Oxford, England: Clarendon Press.

Hinman, C. (1968). *The first folio of Shakespeare: The Norton facsimile.* New York: Norton.

Hirschman, L., Concepcion, K., et al. (2001). Integrated feasibility experiment for biosecurity: IFE-Bio. A TIDES demonstration. In *Proceedings of the first International Conference on Human Language Technology Research, HLT 2001* [Online]. Available: http://www.hlt2001.org/papers/hlt2001-38.pdf

Hosley, R., Knowles, R., & McGugan, R. (1971). *Shakespeare variorum handbook: A manual of editorial practice.* New York: Modern Language Association.

Liddell, H. G., Glare, P. G. W., & Thompson, A. A. (1996). *Greek–English lexicon.* Oxford, New York: Oxford University Press, Clarendon Press.

Liddell, H. G., & Scott, R. (1888). *An intermediate Greek–English lexicon, founded upon the 7th edition of Liddell and Scott's Greek English lexicon.* Oxford, England: Clarendon Press.

Liddell, H. G., Scott, R., Jones, H. S., & McKenzie, R. (1940). *A Greek–English lexicon.* Oxford, England: Clarendon Press.

Melamed, I. D. (2001). *Empirical methods for exploiting parallel texts.* Cambridge, MA: MIT Press.

Mueller, M. (2000). Electronic Homer. *Ariadne* [Online], *25.* Available: http://www.ariadne.ac.uk/issue25/mueller/intro.html

Pantelia, M. (1999). *The thesaurus linguae graecae. 2002* [Online]. Available: http://www.tlg.uci.edu

Rossiter, A. P. (1946). *Woodstock, a moral history.* London: Chatto & Windus.

Shakespeare, W., Evans, G. B., & Tobin, J. J. M. (1997). *The Riverside Shakespeare.* Boston: Houghton-Mifflin.

Shakespeare, W., & Furness, H. H. (1871). *A new variorum edition of Shakespeare.* Philadelphia: Lippincott & Co.

Shakespeare, W., & Spevack, M. (1990). *Antony and Cleopatra.* New York: Modern Language Association.

Sperberg-McQueen, C. M., & Burnard, L. (1994). *Guidelines for electronic text encoding and interchange.* Providence, RI: Electronic Book Technologies.

Staples, T., & Wayland, R. (2000). Virginia dons FEDORA: A prototype for a digital object repository. *D-Lib Magazine* [Online], *6.* Available: http://www.dlib.org/dlib/july00/staples/07staples.html

Suleman, H., & Fox, E. A. (2001). A framework for building open digital libraries. *D-Lib Magazine* [Online], *7.* Available: http://www.dlib.org/dlib/december01/suleman/12suleman.html

Chapter 3

Reuse of Content and Digital Genres

Leen Breure
Utrecht University

REUSE OF CONTENT

The Problem of Reusability

One of the fundamentals of the present information society is cross-media publishing, which refers to the process of reusing information across multiple output media without having to rewrite it for distinct purposes. Given a repository with information stored in a media-independent way, a smart publishing system can deliver it concurrently on different platforms without much human intervention. This strategy of create once, publish everywhere, going back to Ted Nelson's famous Xanadu project (founded 1960) and restated by contemporary authors (Tsakali & Kaptsis, 2002) seems to be the logical answer to the demands of the still-growing range of output devices, as Web PCs, WAP phones, handheld PDAs, and TV set-top boxes. It requires that digital information be well structured, divided into relatively small components, and enriched with metadata, thus improving identification and retrieval for reuse and allowing adaptation and personalization through rule-based aggregation and formatting. Such information that is decomposed, versatile, usable, and wanted will be referred to as *content*. Reuse is attractive to maximize the return of investment. However, most of the strategies to achieve that purpose require special, highly controlled procedures for creating content. This chapter explores an alternative approach for reusing existing content that has not been created explicitly for reuse. It is based on the natural controlling mechanism of genre, which appears to direct a great deal of our content production.

Reuse of information has become the Holy Grail of content engineering, partly because of the multiplicity of media, and partly because different publication contexts share (almost) the same information elements. Reuse forms the core of database-driven applications, like e-business portals, online news sites, and virtual art exhibitions. Database publishing is a proven technology relying on content components that are independent, homogeneous, and structured according to strict rules, which allows simple reordering for different purposes with varying forms of presentation. In a comparable way, these conditions can also be met for certain types of text, like technical documents in industry. The same component may be used in different products, which leads to a natural repetition of documentation fragments in product manuals. Such a process can be made more efficient and sophisticated by systematic information markup, which has been an important motivator for adopting SGML and, more recently, XML, in enterprise content management.

Successful projects involve the automatic creation of product training documents (Day, Liu, & Hsu, 2001), and the publication of technical manuals in different languages, where text writing is severely controlled and massive updates are run automatically (Honkaranta & Tyrväinen, 2001; Priestley, 2001; Skipper, 1999; Terris, 2001). This type of reusability requires careful planning and a high degree of control over authoring. Self-contained components are a key prerequisite: Each unit must stand on its own and not depend on other parts of the documentation to render it useful. In addition, authors should strictly adhere to style guides to produce uniform texts. If SGML or XML is used, a schema-driven editor is recommended to enforce a valid content structure. Information that is reused should preferably be referenced by means of hyperlinks, and not copied from one context to another ("reuse by reference" as opposed to "reuse by value"; Garzotto, Mainetti, & Paolini, 1996).

Current Research: Architecture and Methodology

A great deal of research on the reuse of content is concerned with the architecture of such components and of dedicated content authoring and managing systems. One of the best-documented recent examples is IBM's DITA (Darwin Information Typing Architecture), an XML-based, end-to-end architecture for authoring, producing, and delivering technical information. It consists of a set of design principles for creating "information-typed" modules at a topic level and for using that content in delivery modes such as online help and product-support portals on the Web (http://www-106.ibm.com/developerworks/xml/library/x-dita1/).

Unfortunately, the creation of the majority of valuable content is beyond such strict control as found in the publication of technical manuals. At the same time, some form of reuse may be still worth considering, because the production process is labor intensive. For example, the production effort in multimedia applications can be reduced considerably by reusing pictures and movie clips with minor modifications, which may require cloning and manual alteration. This is similar to plain reuse of textual content, which is far less easy than it looks, as we all may have experienced when we tried to insert apparently ready-made fragments from previous publications into a new one and ended up rewriting a considerable part. Plain copying is reuse by value, which leads to less efficient strategies than the reuse by reference described earlier. Modified versions cannot be updated automatically because copy and source are not linked in a structural manner.

In spite of apparent disadvantages, there is room for computer-assisted reuse strategies applicable to content that has not been explicitly created for reuse. It comes down to recycling, allowing for more human intervention in the editorial process. Research on this type of reuse methodology is to be found under different headings, like:

- Document assembly: recycling documents, adding structure to existing heterogeneous content (Glushko & McGrath, 2002; Lehtonen, 2001).
- Virtual documents: querying heterogeneous sources, coupled with intelligent computer interpretation and a special editor for manual refinement of the document prescription and the transformation rules (Paradis, Vercoustre, & Hills, 1998); restructuring existing documents and reuse of fragments (Rekik, Vanoirbeek, Falquet, & Nerima, 2002).
- Hypermedia applications: reusing multimedia content modified in some respect (Garzotto et al., 1996); template-based multimedia assembly, at which the designer specifies patterns (Nanard, Nanard, & Kahn, 1998).

These publications show domain-specific shades in methods and techniques, but, generally speaking, there seems to be no way around reducing the relative "chaos" in heterogeneous documents to a well-structured set of identifiable fragments, as in disciplined strategies for creating reusable content from scratch.

THE CASE OF ONLINE NEWS

Online News as a Genre

This chapter falls into the category of methodological research on reusing existing publications. It intends to formulate a strategy, together with some concepts of software tools that support the editorial process in which reuse plays an important role. The application domain is online news. In order to solve the apparent chaos of heterogeneous documents, it conceives content as a product of established communication patterns. Content is usually created purposefully, in a specific situation, in response to certain requirements, and intended for a known audience. Communication patterns determine the integration of content with form (i.e., structure and presentation) and communicative function. Arbitrary examples may illustrate this point: A news story, an article in an encyclopedia, teaching material, tourist information—all of them show recurrent patterns. This view is widely supported by genre theory, which emphasizes genre as based on a rather stable combination of content, form, and function. Genre theory has its roots in linguistic, literary, and social disciplines, but has been recently applied to internet publications as well. However, up to now research on digital genres has been hardly connected with content engineering (exceptions are Paré & Smart, 1994; Vaughan & Dillon, 2000; Watters & Shepherd, 1997). The present chapter is motivated by the assumption that content engineering can benefit from a statistical analysis of genre characteristics to find regularities in the combination of content, form, and function that could help to tune editorial software.

Genre: Content, Form, Function

The current online version of the *Encyclopaedia Britannica* (2004) defines *genre* as "a distinctive type or category of literary composition, such as the epic, tragedy, comedy, novel, and short story." This notion rests on a widespread superficial usage of genre that refers mainly to some characteristic combination of content and form. This rather vague concept should be distinguished from well-defined scientific variants, elaborated in the genre theories of the 19th and 20th centuries, which emphasized function and purpose next to content and form. Eriksen and Ihlström (2000) defined a *genre* as an abstraction over a class of recurrent communicative events (Berkenkotter & Huckin, 1995; Orlikowski & Yates, 1994). The triplet <content, form, function> is a characteristic of modern genre theories.

Situated genre theories (Bazerman, 1988; Berkenkotter & Huckin, 1995; Miller, 1984; Swales, 1990) show that such peculiarities in content and form are more than traditions kept alive. They are the appropriate reactions to recurrent communicative situations in a certain discourse community. Genre structures influence communication by creating shared expectations about the form and content of the interaction, thus easing the burden of production and interpretation (Erickson, 1999). Genre can thus be conceived as "an institutionalized template for social interaction" (Orlikowski & Yates, 1998). In their social life, people master an effective use of established genres, for example, as a framework for scholarly and organizational communication. Students are trained to communicate their scientific results in compliance with a discipline's methodology and professional practices. A letter with a specific function, like a request or a recommendation, has to stay within the constraints of that genre, reckoning with accepted communicative forms and phrases.

The majority of the genre theories have evolved around printed publications, and reflect, therefore, the limitations of traditional media. Digital communication is characterized by a far greater degree of interactivity. Studies on digital genres emphasize in particular the third component in the triplet <content, form, function>. Here, function shifts to functionality, that is, the options offered to the user for manipulating content and its display. Along this line, the concept of genre is used for a better understanding of the required functionality of digital documents.

Digital Genres

Crowston and Williams (1997) were among the first to realize the importance of the genre concept for analyzing communication on the internet. They noted that the Web was an excellent place for studying the development of genres, because of its easy access and its inherent capabilities of experimentation, freedom of structuring, and interactions between many communities. The authors were particularly interested in studying how the adoption of a new communication medium, the Web, was leading to the adaptation of existing genres and the emergence of new ones. Choosing the individual Web page as the unit of analysis rather than Web sites, they identified 48 different genres with distinct characteristics in a randomly selected sample of 1,000 Web pages (e.g., well-known reproduced genres like article, book, column, concert review, report, and testimonial, and many adapted genres and a minor portion of new ones like FAQ, file directory listing, home page, order form, and server statistics).

Shepherd and Watters (1998) coined the term *cybergenre* to denote digital genres and did a survey (Shepherd & Watters, 1999) similar to that of Crowston and Williams (1997), but on a higher level of abstraction and with a sample of much smaller size (96 Web sites were randomly selected). Their purpose was studying content, form, and function of Web documents and they identified only six different genres (home page, brochure, resource, catalogue, search engine, and game). Because the design of this survey differed in several respects from that by Crowston and Williams, Shepherd and Watters (1999) tried to map their results onto the former genre list to make results more comparable. With some reservation, they concluded that the Web might have changed considerably in 2 years' time.

Such observations lead to the question of how stable digital genres are, in particular with regard to the rapid advance in new technologies. Shepherd and Watters (1998) shared the conclusion by Yates and Sumner (1997), that, in spite of the apparent evolution driven by technological factors and changing functional requirements, the notion of genre still provides a certain degree of stability and fixity. The combination of content and form "provides a familiar and strong metaphoric reference for users that transcends changes in functionality" (Shepherd & Watters, 1998).

Watters and Shepherd (1997) emphasized the role of genre in the evolution of user interface for the internet, thus shifting attention to the technical functionality of electronic documents. Normally, a program's user interface is designed with a specific user group in mind and with regard to specific goals and tasks. However, Web usage is fuzzier. The actual goals and tasks may vary considerably. The constraints of a particular genre thus provide a familiar combination of content and functionality.

This idea of genre as interface metaphor was further elaborated by Toms and Campbell (1999). A document provides various visual cues that enable users to grasp its form, purpose, and function quickly. Correct identification occurs when these cues are consistent with those defined by its genre. One can imagine that, recognizing the genre, the user "loads" a framework of expectations, which helps him or her to interpret the document and facilitates a particular kind of use. The effect of genre on user expectation was also confirmed by Dillon and Gushrowski (2000), who examined more than 100 personal home pages and asked subjects to select those elements that they thought should be included in any good personal home page. They found a broad agreement as to what a home page should contain. Following this line, Vaughan and Dillon (2000) supposed that genre can drive comprehension, and tested whether an information space for newspapers that was in accordance with genre conventions improved user performance. They found that generic conventions contributed to greater efficiency. Genre-related expectations do have a basis in cognitive processes, resulting, among other things, in better speed and navigation performance. For Web designers, these results indicate the importance of incorporating the audience's prior knowledge and experience with a genre.

Problems with Genre

No matter how useful the genre concept may be for getting a better grip on the multitude of forms in Web publishing, it seems difficult to make it directly useful to content design. Like any other form of design in information technology, it demands clear definitions and requirements, and these are not yet provided by genre studies. The precise definition of a genre is problematic, and a widely accepted taxonomy of genres is still lacking. We may easily agree on the core characteristics of well-known genres, but there will be always a large gray zone. Any classification is subject to discussion:

What may be right in one survey may be not appropriate in another. Existing taxonomies are often bound to specific fields, where they function quite well.

As a result, the fuzziness of genre classification makes measuring difficult. The lack of commonly accepted genre categories becomes problematic in research that pertains to random samples from the Web. Sometimes genres are identified by careful coding of predefined features (Orlikowski & Yates, 1994), or they may be described conceptually on basis of characteristics in form and purpose (Crowston & Williams, 1997). To summarize: The genre concept is particularly useful where its theoretical framework is concerned. It helps to understand content, form, and function in relation to the communicative context of a discourse community, but it needs a more operational definition to make it applicable to content engineering.

Bridging the Gap: Genre and Content Engineering

The attractiveness of the genre concept lies in the fact that it covers the problematic aspects of content reuse, such as context, purpose, function, form, and structure. Connecting genre with content engineering (in this case restricted to online news) requires that genre qualities be mapped onto a news engineering model. We may conceive a news story as a template with slots holding news topics. A topic is (ideally) a self-contained news story fragment describing a news item (subject), that is, an event, or certain aspects of an event, like background, motivations, plausible explanations, persons involved, and so on. A particular genre imposes constraints on the set of topics that fit the slots. These constraints are used in queries that retrieve topics from the news repository, in other words, they are the slots' properties. They can be grouped by the aforementioned core aspects of genre: content, form, and function. Because content has various shades of meaning, I prefer here a slightly different and more precise formulation: The constraints comprise three aspects of content itself, namely, subject, form, and function, as shown in Fig. 3.1.

The three aspects of content are:

1. Subject: The subject of a specific news story and, therefore, of the topics contained, is determined by the stream of events forming the news of the moment. Subjects can vary in granularity and be subdivided into smaller items. The collection of subjects may be ordered as a tree (subject tree); in the context of the Semantic Web many initiatives are being developed to describe such trees. In a simple form, it consists of a set of nested XML elements, describing a theme.

2. Form: A subject can be dealt with in different ways, varying from a factual account in hard news to a more interpretative one in an opinion news-

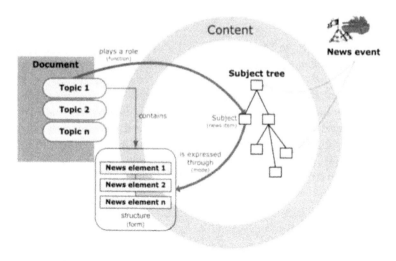

FIG. 3.1.   Mapping genre concepts onto the content-engineering domain.

paper. From the point of view of subject matter, we may call this the *mode* of presentation. It relies on phrasing and textual structure and therefore pertains to the generic aspect of form. In terms of content engineering, it relates to the elements that compose the topic (internal topic structure): factual information, quotes, statements attributed to persons, interpretations, and so forth.

3. Function: A third class of constraints regards the communicative function a topic in its entirety plays in clarifying an item, for example, explaining background, providing details or comments by the local government, and so on. *Role* is a more adequate term. This constraint describes the rhetoric relationship that exists between the topic (i.e., the news story fragment) and the subject. Function implies purpose and has, for that reason, a strong influence on form: An author creates or composes what he or she needs.

Restating the Problem of Reusability

The model described previously helps to restate reusability in terms of genre and to formulate some hypotheses. Topics are reusable if they meet the constraints of the slots. Subject will be dictated by the stream of news events, but genre will have influence on the mode of presentation and may "attract" certain topics that fulfill specific rhetoric roles at the expense of others. For example, news messages for mobile devices must be short and may leave few space for topics that elaborate a news item or offer multiple explanations. Provided that the subject is the same, we expect that reuse of content within the same genre will be easier and more successful than between different genres, because of stable conventions. For example, hard news fragments will fit in rather well with cover stories of daily newspapers, but may need some revision and addition for an opinion magazine (i.e., more interpretative text), and an even more thorough restructuring for a news encyclopedia. (Compare studies in popularization of scientific research; Goldman & Bisanz, 2002.)

Test Material: CNN and CNN for Students

These postulated generic characteristics of online news, mode (form) and role (function), should be further tested empirically. In the present chapter I confine myself to the former category (i.e., form) and analyze differences in topic structure in two samples of online news stories, closely related as far as genre and subject matter are concerned, namely about terrorism and the prelude to the Iraq war: one from CNN (http://www. cnn.com/) and the other from the educational counterpart, CNN for Students (formerly CNNfyi: http://fyi.cnn.com/fyi/). CNN for Students (CNNfS) is an educational Web site with news for students and resources for teachers, created in cooperation with Harcourt. It provides stories written by CNN journalists, working in collaboration with teachers, that are appropriate in vocabulary and content for middle and high school students. Each story is linked to a lesson plan or a shorter "discussion/activity." The Web site refers to accompanying educational TV programs. Teachers' resources include educational calendars, teaching tips, and the latest news and issues in education.

I gathered the material (12 new stories from each) during 2002, following headline news about terrorism (Bali bombing, Al Qaeda, Bin Laden) and the alleged threats from Iraq. The news stories from CNNfS fall into two categories: Some are from the regular CNN Web site, others are specifically written for students. Only the latter category is included in the sample. In a comparison with regular CNN news, the CNNfS stories stand out because of their shorter text length and concise formulation, but still look like hard news. Both obviously belong to the genre of online news. The questions to be answered are: (a) Are both sets part of a single genre or of two different subgenres? and (b) are there any traces of information reuse?

Research Method

The news stories are published in HTML and as such (because of a lack of semantic markup) not suitable for a quantitative analysis of distinct elements. For that purpose, they need to be coded in XML in a manner that matches the research questions, which requires a detailed modeling of on-line news in advance. Therefore, the research method breaks down into the following steps (as depicted in Fig. 3.2):

1. Modeling the news genre by means of:

• A conceptual model for documenting the structure of these news sto-ries as conceived within this project, preferably in terms of objects because of the object-oriented nature of current information technology. UML is a well-known modeling language for object-oriented computer applications, but now gets to be used more and more in high-level content modeling as well (Carlson, 2001; Conallen, 1999; Jensen, Møller, & Pedersen, 2001; Routledge, Bird, & Goodchild, 2002; Ståhl, Jankko, & Oittinen, 2002). A UML-class diagram defines types of objects and their relations, without as-sumptions about physical encoding, which is also applicable to content com-ponents being objects too.

• A markup model: The conceptual model offers an overview only. It needs to be translated into a set of tags to be used in actual markup, defined in a so-called DTD (document type definition). Several XML industry stan-dards exist for news encoding. Perhaps one of them has been used in the production stage of the sampled material, but this markup will have gotten lost in the HTML version published on the news Web site. So, if we gather material directly from the Web site there is no way to relate the conceptual model to the original, detailed structuring of the news texts. This leaves a top-down approach only. The DTD to be used is to be derived solely from the aforementioned conceptual model.

2. Tagging the online news samples: Preparing the test set for analysis by adding XML tags to the news stories according to the DTD and validating the results against the DTD.

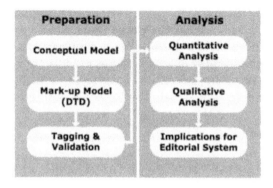

FIG. 3.2. Research method.

3. Quantitative analysis of the tagged content: counting elements and words in order to get some genre-sensitive metrics. Once texts are tagged according to DTD-comprising tags that highlight genre-specific features, frequency counts of the occurrence of these tags help to describe a genre in an exact manner. How is the genre actually structured? Which tags are used and how frequently? How is text distributed over different parts? What differences exist between the samples?

4. Qualitative analysis: answering the aforementioned question by examples. What happens to content, in concrete terms, when it moves from one genre to an other?

5. Practical implications: specifying guidelines for setting parameters of a content-engineering system that supports genre-specific retrieval, composition, and editing. I am not concerned with any system in particular, but confine myself to a conceptual level. One may think of a commercially available XML database, with a dedicated XML editor coupled, which allows retrieving and browsing content components in a genre-specific manner.

MODELING NEWS

The Structure of News Texts

The structure of newspaper content and online news has received ample attention from various angles, but high-level comprehensive models, preferably object-oriented models (for hypermedia, cf. Garzotto, Mainetti, & Paolini, 1995; Meghini, Rabitti, & Thanos, 1991; Nguyen, Wu, & Sajeev, 1998; see Fig. 3.3) or e-business models (Carlson, 2001), are still lacking. Nevertheless, there are contributions in that direction, coming from three major areas: discourse analysis, XML news vocabularies, and studies on online news.

Discourse Analysis. In the 1980s, Van Dijk (1988) described the typical "installment structure" of news discourse: The most relevant things come first in headline and lead, followed by details and some background information in the first part of the article, followed by minor details and digressions in the second part. Nowadays, this hierarchy is even more applicable in a hasty Web society where news is read from screen. His analysis of macro- and microstructures and of the cognitive processes involved in news comprehension is helpful for the design process as well, but does not yet yield a model in a technical sense. Moreover, differences between conventional newspapers and online news must not be overlooked.

At about the same time, rhetorical structure theory (RST) was developed, originally as part of studies of computer-based text generation (Mann & Thompson, 1987, 1988). RST is intended to describe the coherence of texts (independent of the lexical and grammatical forms) and deals

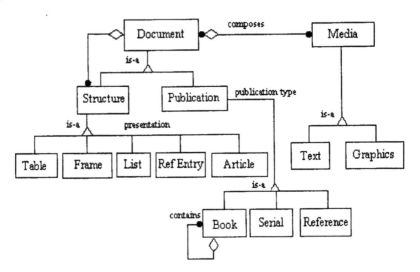

FIG. 3.3. Example of an object model for multimedia documents. From "Object-Oriented Modeling of Multimedia Documents," by T.-L. Nguyen, X. Wu, and S. Sajeev, 1998, available: http://www7.scu.edu.au/programme/docpapers/1852/com1852.htm.

with relations between text spans, which may have different roles, mostly that of nucleus or satellite. Rhetorical relations are defined functionally, in terms of the effect the writer intends to achieve by presenting such text spans. It has been used for analyzing news broadcasts (Noel, 1986) and for modeling multimedia content, such as the generation of news programs (video sequences) from digital archives (Lindley, Davis, Nack, & Rutledge, 2001). Recently, it received an extension in the form of cross-document structure theory (CST), which attempts to characterize the relationships that exist between pairs of sentences that come from one or more documents in a cluster of topically related articles (Radev, 2000; Zhang, Blair-Goldensohn, & Radev, 2002). It has been developed with a view to automatic news summarization (e.g., NewsInEssence) and provides extensive coding schemes for semantic relationships between news fragments. Both approaches are certainly valuable, but more applicable to a concrete level of specific news stories rather than to generalizations over genre.

XML News Vocabularies. The Web has boosted the requirement for automatic handling of news content. News is a commodity that is exchanged and sold through content syndication channels and regularly updated news feeds (e.g., content providers such as Moreover). This requires markup, currently in XML, not only for structuring the news story itself, but also for adding metadata that describe news resources. Sender and receiver have to agree on matters like protocol, envelope (identifying a segment of information), header (the metadata about a news item), and the structure of the content of the item itself (Dumbill, 2000). This has given rise to various XML vocabularies, that is, standardized sets XML tags, which, of course, reflect an underlying model of online news (e.g., NITF, XMLNews, NewsML, and PRISM). Some of them, like NewsML, come with a genre taxonomy for news (current, background, feature, opinion, etc.). They provide precise documentation, including DTDs. Drawbacks from my point of view are their strong emphasis on administrative metadata and their relatively low level of modeling: DTDs tend to be lengthy and do not provide a comprehensive conceptual overview. As far as the coding of the body of the news item, the markup is mainly aimed at retrieval (location, event, different types of names, etc.).

Electronic Newspapers and News Portals. The boom of online news and the challenge printed editions have to face have become the subject of a wide range of studies on electronic newspapers and news portals (for an introduction, see Bierhoff, Van Dusseldorp, & Scullion, 1999; Gates, 2002; Watters, Shepherd, & Burkowski, 1998). Particularly, Scandinavian research has focused on the structure of online newspapers in comparison with their printed counterparts. Some of the models presented come close to what I am looking for. Saarela, Turpeinen, Puskala, Korkea-Aho, and Sulonen (1997) described an object model of hypermedia newspapers, focusing, however, more on multimedia components than on text. Ståhl et al. (2002) followed a UML approach in modeling the cross-media publication process with an emphasis on the behavioral aspects, rather than on the structure of news content itself. Working from a genre perspective, Ihlström and Eriksen studied the evolution of three Scandinavian news sites from 1996 to 1999 (Eriksen & Ihlström, 1999, 2000; Ihlström, 1999). They elaborated the genre of online news in terms of content, form, and rationale. Originally conceived as "electronic newspapers" with a lot of material copied from the printed editions, these Web sites established a distinct role with an increasing emphasis on the immediate presentation of hard news (next to theme sections on soft news not directly related to current affairs). "Key content is hard news, and an important goal is to provide this as fast is possible" (Eriksen & Ihlström, 1999).

Conceptual Model

In spite of a good deal of useful material from different angles, I have not found a ready-made model that suits my purposes. Constructing my own, I started with XML news vocabularies that emphasize the news story, particularly NITF (news industry text format) and the related standard XMLNews (originally designed as a subset of NITF). This resulted in a UML-class diagram representing an object-oriented generalization about the basic structure defined by these standards, however, leaving out many details (see Fig. 3.4).

The structure proposed should not be considered as complete and usable in all circumstances without any modification, but rather as a template for similar models in specific projects allowing for modification, extension, and fine tuning.

A few comments on the main components of Fig. 3.4 are as follows:

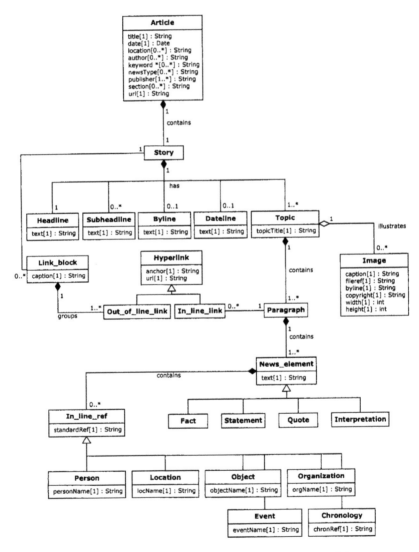

FIG. 3.4. UML class diagram of an online news article.

1. The object `Article` contains properties with metadata pertaining to the entire document. As usual in UML–XML transitions, many XML elements become object properties, for example, NITF divides a news article into head and body sections, where the head contains a number of tags for metadata. The properties of `Article` are only a subset of the list defined in news vocabularies, and may require considerable extension depending on the amount of metadata actually administered.

2. The objects contained by `Story` are the text fragments as displayed to the reader. Headline and subheadlines are self-evident; `Byline` is used for the statement about authors, `Dateline` for the date and location where the story was created.

3. `Topic` and the dependent objects, in particular, `Paragraph`, are central in the present analysis. Currently, most (but not all) online news sites follow the convention of short paragraphs separated by white space, mostly containing one long or a few short sentences. A topic is a set of these paragraphs about the same subject.

A short paragraph usually contains an elementary statement, but longer paragraphs may comprise several news elements. The model takes this into account by introducing the composition `Paragraph/News_element`. In practice, in the short-paragraph layout (as with CNN and CNNfS) news elements coincide with paragraphs. To reveal structure, I have divided news elements (i.e., paragraphs) into subclasses that represent the mode information expressed in:

- `Fact`: The most concise manner of communicating news events is by means of facts, a simple statement on what has happened, for example: "Germany has launched a huge security operation as the country braces for mass demonstrations against the visit of President George W. Bush" (CNNfS, May 21, 2002).

- `Quote`: Direct speech is a truthful but also lengthy way of stating news: " 'I can confirm to you that I have received a letter from the Iraqi authorities conveying its decision to allow the return of the inspectors, without conditions, to continue their work,' Annan said in announcing the news" (CNN, September 17, 2002).

- `Statement`: Indirect speech comes close to citation, but stands midway between quotes and fact as far as form goes: "The International Atomic Energy Agency said Tuesday it was ready to send inspectors to Iraq as soon as the U.N. Security Council gives the go-ahead" (CNN, September 17, 2002).

- `Interpretation`: This is the least objective formulation, reflecting the journalist's opinion, inference, or conclusion, and occurs more frequently in soft news and in opinion newspapers: "Gore's speech appeared to have energized some Democrats who have privately been voicing concerns about the Bush approach" (CNN, September 27, 2002).

If paragraphs are short, as in most cases, classifying into one of these categories is relatively easy, however, even then it is not always indisputable. Mixed forms occur, which demand making choices and sticking to a disciplined and consistent coding strategy. The paragraph's overall structure may hold a clue, or one has simply to cut the knot. A few examples are:

- Fact with an embedded quote fragment: "Iraq's letter to the United Nations offering to allow the return of weapons inspectors 'without conditions' is being met cautiously by some world leaders and outright skepticism by President Bush" (CNN, September 17, 2002).
- Interwoven fact and statement: "Zachary Abuza, a security analyst who has written extensively on al Qaeda, said the meeting was convened by Hambali—who is said to be the operations chief of Jemaah Islamiyah" (CNN, November 9, 2002).
- Combination of quote and statement: " 'We can see it from their Web sites, that al Qaeda views this as a major target for disruption and recruitment and for conducting terrorist attacks,' Wolfowitz added, saying that the Bali attack had been a wake-up call for the Indonesian government and people in the war on terrorism" (CNN, November 8, 2002).

4. XML news vocabularies provide a variety of tags for referencing persons, locations, objects, and so on occurring in a paragraph. Their frequency could be considered as a measure for the degree of detail and may be relevant for differentiating between genres (these elements have not been brought into the current study yet). If used, markup should include standard names for the entities referred to in the text. This requirement is modeled by the superclass In_line_ref having an attribute standardRef. The subclasses hold the text fragments themselves.

5. Images are difficult in the sense that it may not be fully clear how they are related to parts of the story (they could even be associated with the article as a whole). For the sake of content management, linking to topics seems to be useful. The image caption offers some guidance on how to code.

6. Hyperlinks are used relatively sparingly in the body of the news story. Typically, they are added to the end of a paragraph ("full story," "main points," "more reaction," etc.). This kind of usage is represented by the class In_line_link. Most prominent are the blocks of links referring to

other, related resources for further reading. They form an integral part of the news article and are included in the model as Link_block.

Markup Model and Tagging

The DTD has been derived from the conceptual model, but considerably simplified for fast and convenient encoding (see Fig. 3.5). The tag set has been tuned to the current research purposes. Only a part of the model described has actually been used (article with a minimum metadata, topics, images, paragraphs as classified, and leaving inline markup for bold, italics, and hyperlinks as it is). Notice that some object attributes in the conceptual model, like title and author, have become separate elements in the markup model.

```
<!ELEMENT article (title, source, author?, date, headline,
     subheadline?, subhead?, topic*)>
<!ATTLIST article id NMTOKENS #REQUIRED>
<!ENTITY % bodytext "(#PCDATA | b | i | a)*">
<!ELEMENT b (#PCDATA)>
<!ELEMENT i (#PCDATA)>
<!ELEMENT a (#PCDATA)>
<!ATTLIST a href CDATA #REQUIRED>

<!ELEMENT title (#PCDATA)>
<!ELEMENT source (#PCDATA)>
<!ELEMENT author (#PCDATA)>
<!ELEMENT date (#PCDATA)>
<!ELEMENT headline (#PCDATA)>
<!ELEMENT subheadline (#PCDATA)>
<!ELEMENT subhead %bodytext;> <!-- the 'lead' -->

<!ELEMENT topic (topictitle, (image | fact | statement |
quote |
     interpretation)*)>
<!ATTLIST topic id NMTOKENS #REQUIRED>
<!ELEMENT topictitle (#PCDATA)>

<!ELEMENT image (img, caption?)>
<!ELEMENT img EMPTY>
<!ATTLIST img src CDATA #REQUIRED>
<!ATTLIST img border NMTOKEN #IMPLIED>
<!ATTLIST img width NMTOKEN #IMPLIED>
<!ATTLIST img height NMTOKEN #IMPLIED>
<!ELEMENT caption (#PCDATA)>

<!ELEMENT fact %bodytext;>
<!ELEMENT statement %bodytext;>
<!ELEMENT quote %bodytext;>
<!ELEMENT interpretation %bodytext;>
```

FIG. 3.5. DTD used for CNN and CNNfS.

ANALYSIS AND RESULTS

Quantitative Analysis

The topic structure has been analyzed in both sets of news stories by count-ing (by means of an XSLT style sheet) the tags of topic, fact, statement, quote, and interpretation, and their length in characters. This shows the distribution of text over the different classes. The data obtained are shown in Fig. 3.6.

Comparison of the means (see Fig. 3.7) over the different categories of news elements showed that CNN articles contained somewhat more facts, $t(df = 22) = 1.82$, $p < .08$, than CNNfS articles, and concerning the quotes, there is a strong significant difference, $t(df = 22) = 4.47$, $p < .001$. The other differences were nonsignificant due to the standard deviations.

article	1	2	3	4	5	6	7	8	9	10	11	12	1..12
CNN													
Facts	1090	236	905	1578	2836	1504	930	1687	2144	1446	347	681	15384
Statements	524	2005	1570	818	2852	3504	776	1276	660	1564	722	2649	18920
Quotes	3087	2158	1512	1986	2063	1423	1246	1837	1500	1489	439	237	18977
Interpretation	137	0	121	176	0	315	0	103	0	397	0	0	1249
	4838	4399	4108	4558	7751	6746	2952	4903	4304	4896	1508	3567	**54530**
CNNfS													
Facts	1391	435	502	1909	1938	0	540	502	661	375	597	427	9277
Statements	0	1349	274	243	2093	1981	1706	1326	1448	928	471	972	12791
Quotes	508	0	816	461	901	1608	0	0	0	516	0	0	4810
Interpretation	0	0	231	0	0	0	152	0	0	0	458	170	1011
	1899	1784	1823	2613	4932	3589	2398	1828	2109	1819	1526	1569	**27889**

CNN   CNN for Students

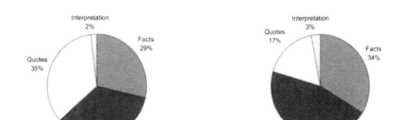

FIG. 3.6.   Distribution of text over classes of news elements.

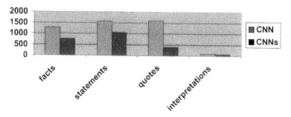

FIG. 3.7.   CNN–CNNfS: Mean number of characters for each class.

Because of the strong difference in article length between CNN and CNNfS, means = 4,544 and 2,324 characters, respectively, $t(df = 22) = 4.06$, $p < .001$, a relative measure was also computed, that is, the number of characters per type of information was divided by the length of the article. Thus, a measure expressing the relative contribution of each category to the length of the article was derived. Figure 3.8 shows the mean relative measurement (proportion) per category. When corrected or differences in length, it appeared that in only one category was there a strong significant difference between CNN and CNNfS: The mean proportion of quotes was higher in CNN than in CNNfS, $t(df = 22) = 3.04$, $p < .01$; the other categories showed no significant differences.

Summarizing, CNN articles contain more seen facts and quotes than CNNfS articles, but they are also longer. When corrected for differences in length (articles from CCNfS are about 50% shorter), we only see a differ-

mean proportion characters per category

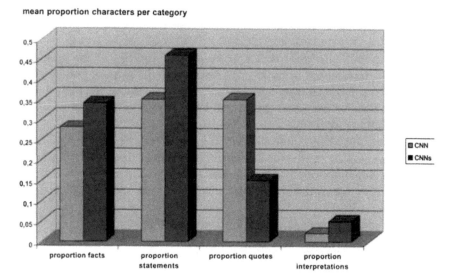

FIG. 3.8.   CNN–CNNfS: Mean proportion of characters for each class.

ence in mean number of quotes: CNN articles contain relatively more quotes than CNNfS articles. The main difference is that CNNfS articles contain absolutely and relatively fewer quotes compared to CNN articles.

The educational context seems to have enforced a concise briefing. One way of accomplishing this is telling simply what has happened, by using facts and interpretations. This, however, is not what has actually been done. The journalists appear to have stuck to their professional code and to the matching genre conventions of objective communication, and preferred a combination of facts and statements, rather than space-consuming quotes. Judging by this similarity in the mode in which news subjects are expressed, one single genre seems most plausible: For the most part, the same kinds of elements (facts, etc.) are used. Admittedly, the news genre comprises more than this single aspect of mode, but we may conclude that the genre mechanism seems to have enforced enough regularity to allow reuse of text fragments. But can we indeed trace any reuse?

Qualitative Analysis

Perhaps more clarifying than the bare statistics is what happened to content itself. Are there any examples of content that was clearly reused? The categories of text analyzed do not run in parallel on both Web sites, and apparent reuse cannot be indicated, but among the 12 stories at least two pairs are comparable. The first example is about Blair's speech in parliament when he presented the dossier about Iraq's weaponry (the numbers refer to the articles, of which the quantitative data are listed in Fig. 3.6):

• At CNN the story (#2) consists of four topics: (a) the speech itself, mainly represented by quotes, (b) reaction in the form of quotes from Iraq and from CNN's European political editor, (c) more detailed statements about the dossier's main points, and (d) a fact and a statement about the parliament's debate.

• The CNNfS counterpart (#3) is more than 50% shorter. It comes with only two topics: (a) shortly introducing the matter through a pithy quotation and a fact about the 50-page file and (b) political reactions from the White House and Iraq with concluding remarks—a mixture of all four categories.

The second pair deals with the explosions on Bali:

• The CNN story (#5) has three topics: (a) about the explosions themselves, mixing facts with statements from officials, followed by (b) speculations about responsible terrorists (following roughly the same pattern) and (c) the Australian victims, a topic beginning with facts about Australian casualties, and concluding with quotes and statements from spokesmen.

- The related article at CNNfS (#8) is about one third the length of the CNN article and has three topics: (a) brief information on the explosions (statement plus fact), (b) reactions from governments (statements), and (c) a single concluding factual paragraph.

CNNfS stories seem to have been specially written for educational purposes. There is no evidence of literal reuse. Although the material for comparison is scarce, the examples discussed give some clues to how a certain subject is treated in the distinctive context of both genres. There is an overlap in subjects, but for obvious reasons some news items are left out (e.g., details about the Iraq dossier, the Australian victims). Where the subject is the same, like "explosions" and "political reactions," the document's slots seem to have different functions: In the CNN stories bare details are to be provided, whereas the equivalent slots in the educational stories required summarization and aggregation while omitting many quotes. The material gathered does not offer ample opportunity to investigate the editorial procedures followed; a better understanding would require interviews with the journalists involved or more insight into the editorial production process.

CONCLUSIONS: IMPLICATIONS
FOR AN EDITORIAL SYSTEM

As mentioned at the beginning of this chapter, the majority of valuable content is created without strict procedures that enable reuse. This raises the question of whether it is possible to better exploit natural controlling mechanisms such as genre, which seems to be a dominant feature in almost all cultural artifacts. In spite of the prevalence of the genre phenomenon, the concept itself is not immediately applicable to the domain of content engineering due to its origin in nontechnical sciences and its lack of precise definitions. One way to overcome this is a statistical analysis of genre characteristics, which could provide a profile for content retrieval and content authoring. In the same way a word processor uses a style checker that proposes alternative formulations, it could use a genre checker coupled with a content management system to produce a set of text fragments suitable in the current editing context.

In order to implement such a strategy, the following steps need to be taken:

1. Label the components of a genre text in a precise and unambiguous way (create a conceptual model).
2. Translate the conceptual model into a tag set (defined in a DTD) and tag the texts in compliance with this DTD.

3. Analyze how the genre components are actually used (create a statistical genre profile).

4. Create an editorial environment that can use such a genre profile. This requires not only an XML editor with a plug-in that checks text for compliance with the profile, but also an editor that has access to an underlying content management system, in which additional text fragments are stored.

Conceptual Model and DTD

As for the first step in the preceding list, one may not expect one size to fit all. As with all document modeling, it may be handy to start with a reference model like the one defined earlier and modify it as required. The important point is to follow a model-based approach and to report about it. The same goes for the DTD.

Statistical Genre Profile

To create a genre profile, one has to know how the constraints of a specific genre influence the way authors select and use the components. To observe this interplay between genre and content, I have studied the composition of news stories from CNN and from CNNfS. Without getting engaged in a fundamental discussion on what exactly constitutes a genre and what would be a sufficient discriminator for (sub)genres, based on the findings one could consider the CNNfS sample as a subgenre within online news. It deals with roughly the same subject matter, in the same manner as the main genre, but shows some dissimilarities due to differences in audience and purpose. Because the CNNfS Web site frequently refers to regular CNN news stories, we may conclude that distinction in intellectual level and didactic structure are not given high priority. But length proved to be an outstanding constraint. We have no inside information about the real procedures followed, but the analysis of the material gathered allows the formulation of a rationale. Apparently, the articles in the present CNNfS sample have been specially written for that Web site and were meant as short introductions to current events. Above all, these texts had to be short, which required a stronger and more deliberate selection of content. Rather than straightforwardly telling what had happened through a concise mixture of facts and interpretations, authors gave preference to the structure of regular news stories and chose a more objective combination of facts and statements, omitting quotes to gain space.

The analysis in the foregoing sections helps to create a genre profile showing constraints in selection and use of elements:

• Selection: Having defined a conceptual model, the distribution of text across classes of elements can be calculated. Distribution can be turned into rules for checking whether a given text expresses a subject in a genre-specific mode (see Fig. 3.1). In the case of hard news, the predominance of facts and quotes or statements provides the familiar feeling of objective information about events.

• Use: Qualitative analysis of parallel news stories highlights the division of elements over text slots: what elements will go into the head, the body, and the tail of a news story. Unfortunately, the samples analyzed did not allow solid conclusions for the current genre, but this does not alter the method. The conceptual model used allows the discourse structure to be expressed in terms that are not only descriptive, but also directly related to the engineering of content.

Editorial Environment

How can all this be put into practice? At least three different scenarios are conceivable. All of them presuppose content that is well marked with tags indicating type of elements and subject matter:

1. Guided authoring: The editorial system may show to what degree the text edited complies with the defined genre profile and come up with suggestions for suitable content fragments, retrieved from the repository (just like an XML editor showing which tags are allowed in a certain context).

2. Guided transformation: An existing text may need to be transposed to a related (sub)genre, like a news story from CNN to a CNNfS article. In such a case the system will suggest possible ways of alteration. After a choice has been made, it can look up alternative text fragments for substitution. For example, if a text contains relatively too many facts, it may search for equivalents in the form of statements or quotes about the same subject.

3. Automatically filling open slots: Many genres enforce a global pattern in the composition of elements. That is why news stories look alike, even if they differ in many details. This pattern can be captured in a template, as a frame with open slots. Each slot must refer to a specific subject (news item in my example, see Fig. 3.1) and specify which types of elements are eligible. Rhetorical Structure Theory can be helpful in modeling such templates. Next, as a proposal the system may fill the slots with suitable text fragments. Additional rules, for example, with regard to ranking, may refine such a procedure. Finally, the (human) editor can make a definitive selection.

As far as daily routine in content production is concerned, the weak point of these options is the gap between the current word-processing technology restricting markup to the usage of styles (which are not simply to be transformed into XML markup), and professional XML editors that do not yet equal the ease of use of popular word processors. To make these scenarios successful, markup has to be added almost automatically without much effort from the user. Admittedly, XML editors already come with more user-friendly variants, mostly designed as XML-form editors, but customizing is quite labor intensive. A new generation of XML editors may bring a shift in mainstream content production. A regular document will be directly encoded in XML and new built-in technologies like Smart Documents (in the XML-based Office 2003 suite) will enable easy embedding of program logic (written in Visual Basic, C, or C++), additional user interface controls, and rules like the ones discussed earlier. This changing perspective makes these scenarios less academic than they may look on first sight.

REFERENCES

Bazerman, C. (1988). *Shaping written knowledge: The genre and activity of the experimental article in science.* Madison: University of Wisconsin Press.

Berkenkotter, C., & Huckin, T. N. (1995). *Genre knowledge in disciplinary communication: Cognition/culture/power.* Hillsdale, NJ: Lawrence Erlbaum Associates.

Bierhoff, J., Van Dusseldorp, M., & Scullion, R. (1999). *The future of the printed press: Challenges in a digital world.* Maastricht, The Netherlands: European Journalism Centre.

Carlson, D. (2001). *Modeling applications with UML: Practical e-business applications.* Boston: Addison-Wesley.

Conallen, J. (1999). Modeling Web application architectures with UML. *Communications of the ACM* [Online], *42*(10). Available: http://www.cs.toronto.edu/km/tropos/conallen.pdf

Crowston, K., & Williams, M. (1997). Reproduced and emergent genres of communication on the World-Wide Web. In *Proceedings of the thirtieth annual Hawaii International Conference on System Sciences (HICSS '97)* [Online]. Available: http://crowston.syr.edu/papers/genres-journal.html

Day, Y. F., Liu, P., & Hsu, L. H. (2001). Transforming large-scale product documents into multimedia training manuals. *IEEE MultiMedia, 8,* 39–45.

Dillon, A., & Gushrowski, B. (2000). *Genres and the Web: Is the personal home page the first unique digital genre?* [Online]. Available: http://memex.lib.indiana.edu/adillon/genre.html

Dumbill, E. (2000). *XML in news syndication* [Online]. Available: http://www.xml.com/pub/a/2000/07/17/syndication/newsindustry.html

Erickson, T. (1999). Rhyme and punishment: The creation and enforcement of conventions in an on-line participatory limerick genre. In *Proceedings of the 32nd Hawaii International Conference on System Sciences (HICSS '99).* [Online]. Digital Library IEEE. Available: http://csdl.computer.org/comp/proceedings/hicss/1999/0001/02/00012005.pdf

Eriksen, L. B., & Ihlström, C. (1999). In the path of the pioneers: Longitudinal study of Web news genre. In *Proceedings of the 22nd Information Systems Research Seminar in Scandinavia, Finland* [Online]. Available: http://iris22.it.jyu.fi/iris22/pub/EriksenIhlström.pdf

Eriksen, L. B., & Ihlström, C. (2000). Evolution of the Web news genre: The slow move beyond the print metaphor. In *Proceedings of the 33rd Hawaii International Conference on System Sciences (HICSS 2000).* [Online]. Digital Library IEEE. Available: http://csdl.computer. org/comp/proceedings/hicss/2000/0493/03/04933014.pdf

Garzotto, F., Mainetti, L., & Paolini, P. (1995). Hypermedia design, analysis, and evaluation issues. *Communications of the ACM, 38*(8), 74–86.

Garzotto, F., Mainetti, L., & Paolini, P. (1996). Information reuse in hypermedia applications. In *Proceedings of the seventh ACM conference on hypertext* (pp. 93–104). New York: ACM Press.

Gates, D. (2002). *The future of news: Newspapers in the digital age* [Online]. Available: http://www.ojr.org/ojr/future/1020298748.php

Glushko, R., & McGrath, T. (2002). *Patterns and reuse in document engineering* [Online]. Available: http://www.idealliance.org/papers/xml02/dx_xml02/papers/03-04-01/03-04-01.pdf

Goldman, S. R., & Bisanz, G. L. (2002). Toward a functional analysis of scientific genres: Implications for understanding and learning processes. In J. Otero, J. A. León, & A. C. Graesser (Eds.), *The psychology of science text comprehension* (pp. 19–50). Mahwah, NJ: Lawrence Erlbaum Associates.

Honkaranta, A., & Tyrväinen, P. (2001). *Possibilities and constraints for managing and reusing information content of structured documents: The case of operation and maintenance manuals* [Online]. Available: http://www.cc.jyu.fi/~ankarjal/IRIS24.pdf

Ihlström, C. (1999). *Navigation in large Web sites: Three cases of internet news publishing.* Unpublished master's thesis, Gothenburg University, Gothenburg, Sweden [Online]. Available: http//www.hh.se/staff/caih/texts/Ihlstrom_IA7400.pdf

Jensen, M. R., Møller, T. H., & Pedersen, T. B. (2001). Converting XML data to UML diagrams for conceptual data integration. In *Proceedings of the first international workshop at CaiSE*01 on Data Integration over the Web (DIWeb)* [Online]. Available: http://www.cs.auc.dk/~mrj/publications/diweb.pdf

Lehtonen, M. (2001). *Document assembly with XML structured source data* [Online]. Available: http://www.cs.helsinki.fi/u/mplehton/pub/xml2001.pdf

Lindley, C. A., Davis, J. R., Nack, F., & Rutledge, L. (2001). *The application of rhetorical structure theory to interactive news program generation from digital archives.* Amsterdam: Centrum voor Wiskunde en Informatica.

Mann, W. C., & Thompson, S. A. (1987). *Rhetorical structure theory: A theory of text organization* (Report No. ISI/RS-87-190, pp. 1–81). Los Angeles: University of Southern California, Information Sciences Institute.

Mann, W. C., & Thompson, S. A. (1988). Rhetorical structure theory: Toward a functional theory of text organization. *Text, 8,* 243–281.

Meghini, C., Rabitti, F., & Thanos, C. (1991). Conceptual modeling of multimedia documents. *Computer, 24*(10), 23–30.

Miller, C. R. (1984). Genre as social action. *Quarterly Journal of Speech, 70,* 151–167.

Nanard, M., Nanard, J., & Kahn, P. (1998). Pushing reuse in hypermedia design: Golden rules, design patterns and constructive templates. In *Proceedings of the ninth ACM Conference on Hypertext and Hypermedia: Links, objects, time and space-structure in hypermedia systems* [Online]. Available: http://doi.acm.org/10.1145/276627.276629

Nelson, T. H. *Project Xanadu* [Online]. Available: http://xanadu.com

Nguyen, T.-L., Wu, X., & Sajeev, S. (1998). Object-oriented modeling of multimedia documents. *Computer Networks* [Online], *30*(1–7). Available: http://www7.scu.edu.au/programme/docpapers/1852/com1852.htm

Noel, D. (1986). *Towards a functional characterization of the news of the BBC World News Service.* Wilrijk, Belgium: Universiteit Antwerpen, Universitaire Instelling Antwerpen.

Orlikowski, W., & Yates, J. (1994). Genre repertoire: The structuring of communicative practices in organizations. *Administrative Science Quarterly* [Online], *39*. Available: http://ccs.mit.edu/papers/CCSWP166.html

Orlikowski, W., & Yates, J. (1998). *Genre systems: Structuring interaction through communicative norms.* [Online]. Cambridge, MA: MIT Press. Available: http://ccs.mit.edu/papers/CCSWP205/

Paradis, F., Vercoustre, A.-M., & Hills, B. (1998). A virtual document interpreter for reuse of information. *Lecture Notes in Computer Science, 1375*, 487–498.

Paré, A., & Smart, G. (1994). Observing genres in action: Towards a research methodology. In A. Freedman & P. Medway (Eds.), *Genre and the new rhetoric* (pp. 146–155). London: Taylor & Francis.

Priestley, M. (2001). DITA XML: A reuse by reference architecture for technical documentation. In *Proceedings of the 19th annual International Conference on Computer Documentation* [Online]. Santa Fe, NM: ACM Press. [Online]. Available: http://doi.acm.org/10.1145/501516.501547

Radev, D. R. (2000). *A common theory of information fusion from multiple text sources, step one: Cross-document structure* [Online]. Available: http://www-personal.umich.edu/~zhuzhang/CST/

Rekik, Y. A., Vanoirbeek, C., Falquet, G., & Nerima, L. (2002). *Reusing dynamic document fragment through virtual documents: Key issues in document engineering* [Online]. Available: http://www.lgi2p.ema.fr/~multimedia/ihm99/articles/rekik.rtf

Routledge, N., Bird, L., & Goodchild, A. (2002). UML and XML schema. In X. Zhou (Ed.), *Conferences in Research and Practice in Information Technology: Vol. 5. Proceedings of the 13th Australasian Conference on Database Tehcnologies (ADC 2002)* [Online]. Melbourne, Australia. Available: http://titanium.dstc.edu.au/papers/adc2002.pdf

Saarela, J., Turpeinen, M., Puskala, T., Korkea-Aho, M., & Sulonen, R. (1997). Logical structure of a hypermedia newspaper. *Information Processing and Management, 33*, 599–614.

Shepherd, M., & Watters, C. R. (1998). The evolution of cybergenres. In *Proceedings of the 31st annual Hawaii International Conference on System Sciences (HICSS '98)* [Online]. Digital Library IEEE. Available: http://csdl.computer.org/comp/proceedings/hicss/1998/8236/00/82360097.pdf

Shepherd, M. A., & Watters, C. R. (1999). The functionality attribute of cybergenres. In *Proceedings of the 32nd Hawaii International Conference on System Sciences (HICSS '99)* [Online]. Digital Library IEEE. Available: http://csdl.computer.org/comp/proceedings/hicss/1999/0001/02/00012007.pdf

Skipper, M. (1999). *Reuse and reality: A journey from ideal concept to real world implementation* [Online]. Available: http://www.infoloom.com/gcaconfs/WEB/granada99/ski.htm

Ståhl, H., Jankko, T., & Oittinen, P. (2002). Modelling of publishing processing with UML. *Graphic Arts in Finland* [Online], *31*. Available: http://www.media.hut.fi/GTTS/GAiF/GAiF_PDF/GAiF2002_3-2.pdf

Swales, J. (1990). *Genre analysis: English in academic and research settings*. Cambridge, England: Cambridge University Press.

Terris, J. F. (2001). *Re-use, re-purpose, re-package* [Online]. Available: http://www.idealliance.org/papers/xml2001/papers/html/04-01-04.html

Toms, E. G., & Campbell, D. G. (1999). Genre as interface metaphor: Exploiting form and function in digital environments. In *Proceedings of the 32nd Hawaii International Conference on System Sciences (HICSS '99)* [Online]. Digital Library IEEE. Available: http://csdl.computer.org/comp/proceedings/hicss/1999/0001/02/00012008.pdf

Tsakali, M., & Kaptsis, I. (2002). *Cross-media content production and delivery: The CONTESSA project* [Online]. Available: http://contessa.intranet.gr/public/e-2002-214-CONTESSA-paper-final.doc

Van Dijk, T. A. (1988). *News as discourse*. Hillsdale, NJ: Lawrence Erlbaum Associates.

Vaughan, M. V., & Dillon, A. (2000). Learning the shape of information: A longitudinal study of Web-news reading. *Proceedings of the fifth ACM Conference on Digital Libraries*, 236–237. San Antonio, TX.

Watters, C. R., & Shepherd, M. A. (1997). *The role of genre in the evolution of interfaces for the Internet* [Online]. Available: http://net97.dal.ca/970326-03/

Watters, C. R., Shepherd, M. A., & Burkowski, F. J. (1998). Electronic news delivery project. *Journal of the American Society for Information Science, 49*(2), 134–150.

Yates, S. J., & Sumner, T. R. (1997). Digital genres and the new burden of fixity. In *Proceedings of the 30th Hawaii International Conference on System Sciences (HICSS '97)* [Online]. Digital Library IEEE. [Online], Available: http://csdl.computer.org/comp/proceedings/hicss/1997/7734/06/7734060003.pdf

Zhang, Z., Blair-Goldensohn, S., & Radev, D. R. (2002). *Towards CST-enhanced summarization* [Online]. Available: http://www-personal.umich.edu/~zhuzhang/CST/

Chapter 4

From Syntactic- Toward Semantic-Driven Document Transformations

Jacco van Ossenbruggen
Lynda Hardman
CWI Amsterdam

The large amount of Web content that currently needs to be designed, authored, and maintained has made the need for document-engineering technology clear to Web developers. Terms such as *structured document, style sheet,* and *document transformation* were once considered technical jargon used only by SGML zealots. After the success of HTML (W3C, 2000), CSS (Bos, Lie, Lilley, & Jacobs, 1998), XML (Bray, Paoli, & Sperberg-McQueen, 1998), XSLT (Clark, 1999), and related specifications, however, they have become fundamental and well-known ingredients of everyday Web design.

Following the mantra "separation of content from presentation," these document-engineering techniques have revolutionized document processing in terms of longevity, reusability, and tailorability of electronic documents (Van Ossenbruggen, 2001). By stressing the importance of describing the content of a document separately from the description of its layout and other stylistic characteristics, the document-engineering approach brings many well-known advantages:

- It provides Web sites with the flexibility to modify the look and feel of their presentation, without the need to change the content.
- It enables reuse of the same content in different contexts, by flexibly using different layout and styles when appropriate.
- It makes volatile content (such as stock quotes and weather forecasts) and "legacy" database content available on the Web.

- It protects content from rapid changes in the presentation technology. Even in the first 10 years of the Web, we have already seen, for example, various versions of (X)HTML, the introduction of Java and JavaScript, style sheets, and plug-ins.

The short history of the Web can be split into three generations. First-generation Web content was manually authored, often using layout-oriented HTML editors that did not support the separation of content from presentation. Second-generation Web content already benefits from the advantages in document engineering sketched earlier. At the time of this writing, the majority of the HTML pages on the Web had been automatically generated. Many Web sites use a combination of document templates that are automatically filled in with content stored in databases, and structured XML documents that are transformed and styled into HTML using XSL and CSS style sheets on the user's request.

Ideally, the advantages of second-generation Web content would apply not only to HTML pages, but also to other types of content. In practice, however, much of today's multimedia and 2-D or 3-D graphics content is still manually authored, with all of the associated drawbacks. This is a direct result of the inherently text-centric assumptions underlying current document-engineering models. To develop second-generation Web content for nontextual information, new models and tools need to be created for multimedia applications. This is the topic of the next section, which discusses multimedia document transformations and their role in the design of Cuypers, the transformation engine developed by our research group at CWI.

The limitations of the current document-engineering approach, however, go beyond text versus multimedia. A more fundamental problem is that the separation of content from presentation in current tools is merely a syntactic separation. Structured documents define their content in terms of their XML syntax, document transformations convert the syntax of the content into the syntax of the presentation, and style sheets are merely a collection of rules that assign style properties to specific syntactic elements of the presentation. All knowledge about the semantics, the intended meaning of the content, is either absent or implicit. Current, syntax-driven, document-engineering tools are insufficient for applications that require automatic processing based on the semantics of the content.

The next, third-generation, Web is more commonly known as the Semantic Web (Berners-Lee, Hendler, & Lassila, 2001). The Semantic Web is devoted to making the semantics of Web content explicit and to developing tools for processing these semantics. Whereas usage scenarios in the Semantic Web literature often focus on using explicit semantics for improved searching and retrieval services on the Web, the remaining sections focus on presentation of retrieval results by employing explicit semantics in the current document-engineering chain.

MULTIMEDIA DOCUMENT TRANSFORMATIONS

The on-demand generation of multimedia Web presentations from content stored in multimedia databases has—at least in theory—the same advantages as the on-the-fly generation of HTML pages on the current, second-generation, Web. In practice, however, current models and tools are inadequate for all but the most trivial multimedia presentations, for a number of reasons:

1. Conveying order: An important characteristic of text formatting is that the overall order of a presented text is usually determined by the lexical order of the main text in the source document. The main job of the formatter is to break the source text up into separate lines and pages. The precise results depend on well-understood algorithms (Knuth, 1986) and style properties such as font size, hyphenation rules, and margin sizes. Independent of the chosen style, the basic order of the text flow will, in general, remain unchanged. In multimedia, however, the order of the presentation is not conveyed through text flow. Instead, the temporal layout and, to a lesser extent, the spatial and navigational layout are the key mechanisms for ensuring a user perceives the information in an appropriate sequential arrangement. In addition, for multimedia documents, we do not have commonly accepted formatting procedures that, controlled by well-understood style parameters, map the source document to a layout that indeed conveys the "right" order.

2. Expressing temporal behavior: At the basis of every multimedia tool lies a model for describing the presentation's temporal synchronization and orchestration, which determine when the media items play. In the current document-engineering chain, however, the very notion of time is nonexistent. As pointed out earlier, the temporal order of a multimedia presentation conveys a major part of the narrative of the presentation. But even if the presentation respects the correct temporal order, incorrect timing and out-of-sync presentation can still significantly undermine the user's correct understanding of the intended semantics.

3. Resource limitations: Despite being limited by page boundaries, current text-formatting models assume an unlimited area on the screen or on paper into which they can render the text. If a word does not fit on this line, it will fit on the next, if a line does not fit on this page, it will fit on the next page, and so on. For online presentations, it is often possible to add scroll bars when text becomes larger than the browser window. In many multime-

dia presentations, the notion of a scroll bar or "next page" often does not exist or is undesirable. The space available for the renderer is then strictly limited, for example, all media items for a given scene need to fit within a given screen size.[1]

4. "Fallible" style and transformation rules: Current style and transformation rules are assumed to be always correct, and the result of applying the rules is passed on to the rendering engine, which is expected to always be able to render the text according to the style properties specified by the rules. In multimedia, this assumption does not hold.[2] Due to the often strict resource limitations of multimedia, a chosen layout may work for a given set of inputs, but not for the next. In that case, it should be possible to detect that the results of applying a style or transformation rule consume more than the available resources. Subsequently, the application of that rule should be prevented and, instead, an alternative rule should be applied.

We have explored these issues and implemented an alternative document-transformation strategy in our multimedia engine Cuypers (Van Ossenbruggen, Geurts, Cornelissen, Rutledge, & Hardman, 2001). In the Cuypers transformations depicted in Fig. 4.1, the specification of the temporal behavior of the presentation is as important as the visual layout. After the media items have been selected (step 1 in the figure), a high-level, but explicit, semantic model is required that can be used to determine (step 2) the logical order and grouping of the material in the presentation. Some of our current prototypes deploy explicitly defined relations such as "the content in A is evidence for the content in B" or "the content in A prepares the user for understanding the content of B," and other relations borrow from rhetorical structure theory (Mann, Matthiesen, & Thompson, 1989). Still others derive the logical order from the available metadata (Little, Geurts, & Hunter, 2002; Rutledge et al., 2003). In step 3, layout and resource constraints such as maximum screen size and bandwidth resources may be explicitly specified, characterizing the user's device according to the notion of a delivery context (W3C, 2001b). Finally, every transformation rule will explicitly fail if it results in a presentation that violates the constraints (step 4) specified by the delivery context. In that case the system will backtrack to

---

[1]Even for text, there are sometimes strict limits, such as page limits in many scientific publications. These cases are also not supported by current tools. For example, it is not possible to write an XSLT or CSS style sheet that will guarantee to format the text of this chapter within the page limit established by the editors.

[2]This is another assumption that does not always hold, not even in the text-only case. When style rules produce undesired results, the document-engineering approach often falls apart. To get the desired layout, authors are forced to tweak the style rules (potentially introducing undesired results in other parts of the document, or in other documents) or to tweak the content (breaking the separation of content and presentation).

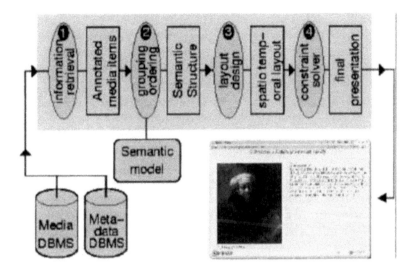

FIG. 4.1. Transformation steps (represented by ellipses) and the intermediate data structures (represented by rectangles) in the Cuypers architecture. (Image courtesy Rijksmuseum, Amsterdam.)

apply alternative rules, a process that is repeated until a set of rules is found that meet the specified constraints. This constraint-driven approach to document transformations allows us to generate not only synchronized multimedia presentations automatically, but also different presentations targeted to devices with different resources from a single transformation sheet. (For more detailed information about the Cuypers engine, see Van Ossenbruggen et al., 2001; Van Ossenbruggen, Geurts, Hardman, & Rutledge, 2003; Geurts, Van Ossenbruggen, & Hardman, 2001; Geurts, 2002; and Martinez, 2002.)

TOWARD SEMANTIC-DRIVEN TRANSFORMATIONS

Although our current implementation of the Cuypers engine addresses many of the multimedia-related issues discussed in the previous section, it still suffers from the syntax–semantics dichotomy. To introduce this problem and related research questions, we use an example multimedia presentation. To answer these questions, we revisit the basic assumptions underlying the document-engineering approach and contrast them with the assumptions underlying the graphic-design approach.

Internal dependencies in document design need to be taken into account to produce an internally coherent design. For example, the choice of an appropriate background color depends on the foreground color and vice versa. External dependencies need to be taken into account to balance the interests of the various parties involved. For example, the design decision of a content provider to style a presentation using the provider's company color scheme may conflict with the color preferences of a colorblind user. Such internal and external dependencies remain implicit in the current document-engineering models and tools, but can only be taken into account through explicit encoding of their semantics.

Example: Text Versus Media Semantics

Whereas readers use visual clues (like the indentation at the start of a paragraph, or the vertical white space that separates sections) for interpreting a text, the semantics of a text document are, to a large extent, conveyed by its textual content in a way that is independent of the chosen layout. Part of the semantic relations among the sections of this chapter, for example, are explicitly stated in the text by using phrases such as: "In the third section, we discuss this topic more extensively. . . ." Other relations are implicit, and it is up to the human reader to establish what those relations are. Most of these explicit and implicit relations are independent of the chosen layout. They do not change, for example, when the publisher decides to switch from a single to a multicolumn layout style or vice versa.

In contrast with text, the intended semantics of multimedia documents is closely related to the layout of the presentation. Take, for example, the snapshot of the multimedia presentation depicted in Fig. 4.2. The presentation is

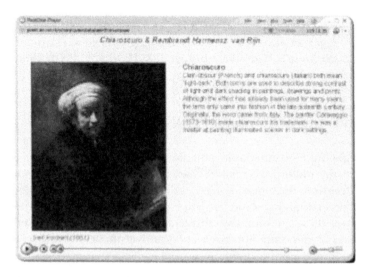

FIG. 4.2.   Example SMIL presentation, generated by Cuypers for display on a large screen. (Image courtesy Rijksmuseum, Amsterdam.)

intended to inform the user about the painting technique *chiaroscuro* (the use of strong contrast between light and dark), in particular about its use in the works of the Dutch 17th-century master Rembrandt van Rijn. While looking at this presentation, every human reader will assume that the text label "Self Portrait (1661)" below the image of the painting is directly related to the image, and not, or only indirectly, related to the text on the right. Most readers will even assume that the label refers to the painting's title and the year of creation. Note, however, that these (correct) assumptions are based purely on the layout of the media items: The image and label themselves do not refer to one another. The fact that there exists a strong semantic relation between the label and the image is conveyed by the layout, through the close proximity of the two items. The roles of the title and year of creation are conveyed using domain-specific conventions (e.g., in both museums and art books, titles are often positioned near the bottom of the painting, followed by the year of creation between parentheses).

The multimedia presentation in Fig. 4.2 was automatically generated by our Cuypers engine. The current version has, however, no explicit knowledge about the semantics of paintings, their titles and years of creation, or the layout conventions used to present these semantics. This, and other important information, remains implicit, hidden in the transformation rules. Producing the layout of the presentation in Fig. 4.2 still required the work of a human designer who selected an appropriate combination of border distances, padding distances, alignment styles, and other style properties and incorporated them into the transformation rules. The results of the selection of these individual, low-level style properties are represented explicitly. All knowledge about the reasons why these properties were chosen, and why they convey the intended semantics remains implicit. This has two undesirable consequences:

- Transformation rules mix two types of style properties: those that purely determine the aesthetics of the presentation, and those that are crucial for conveying the intended semantic relations among the constituent media items. The former are conventionally considered to be *style*, that is, those aspects of the presentation that represent the personal taste of the author and that can be changed without altering the semantics of the presentation. For example, the Helvetica font used in Fig. 4.2 can be changed to a similar font without changing the message that is conveyed. The latter type, however, are better considered as an intrinsic property of the content, that is, they implicitly encode important semantic information in the way implicit semantic relations are encoded in text, as discussed earlier. For example, the spatial proximity and vertical alignment of the painting's image and textual label are primarily intended to express the close semantic relation between the two items. That this alignment may also have aesthetic qualities is an important, but secondary, issue. The absence of a distinction between these two types of style properties makes it difficult to design and maintain transformation sheets or to manipulate them automatically.

• Because the transformation rules are merely a syntactic mapping from one syntax to another, they are brittle and applicable only in a very limited context. Subtle changes in the content or its structure may result in presentations that no longer convey the intended semantics. For other similar applications, all transformation rules will probably need to be rewritten from scratch, even when they are largely based on the same, implicit design knowledge.

In order to solve these problems, the following research questions need to be addressed:

1. To what extent can we make the intended semantics of a presentation explicit?

2. To what extent can we make the required design knowledge explicit?

3. Can we develop a system that deploys these explicit semantics and design knowledge to make appropriate design decisions automatically? That is, can we build a system that does not force a human designer to specify, for every new application, all the procedural transformation code and style sheets from scratch, thereby duplicating implicit design knowledge over and over again?

To get a better overview of the issues involved, we briefly recapitulate the most important characteristics of the current approach to document processing.

The Document-Engineering Perspective

The key concept in current document engineering is the notion of separation of content from style information. The underlying principle is that the essence of the message—the intended semantics of the presentation—is contained in the (XML-structured) text and remains unchanged when style parameters, such as screen width or font size, are varied. This principle allows the creation of an infrastructure where the file containing the content, the XML file, can be created and maintained separately from a style file, such as a CSS style sheet. The advantages discussed in the introduction are well known within the Web community.

A presentation, however, involves more than applying an appropriate style to the selected content. A third, and essential, ingredient is the structure of the presentation. The simple separation of content and style as described earlier suffices only when the presentation structure is similar to the content structure in the underlying XML. If this is not the case, then a syntactical transformation step, one enabled by XSLT, is needed to convert the content structure to the desired presentation structure. For example, the lexical order in a source XML document might need to be transformed to the order that is most appropriate in the text flow of the target HTML presentation.

The document-engineering process of creating Web presentations can thus be summarized in three steps:

1. Select or create the content (typically structured using XML).
2. Define a mapping from content to the presentation structure that defines, among other things, the most appropriate order (e.g., by using XSLT).
3. (Optionally) refine this presentation structure by applying preferred style parameters (e.g., by using CSS).

Essential in this approach is the assumption that the three steps can be carried out independently. Content can be entered into a database by a content provider. This content can then be extracted from the database in the desired order by a server-side script written by a Web site programmer. Finally, the preferred style parameters can be determined by a graphic designer's or end user's style sheet. For many database-driven Web sites, this assumption holds. The same applies to knowledge-driven or model-driven sites (cf., e.g., Jin, Decker, & Wiederhold, 2001). Furthermore, the current Web infrastructure, with its large number of XML-related tools, is well equipped to support this process.

However, as seen in the example, there are a number of other types of document processing, and other types of content, where this assumption does not hold. In many applications, there are strong dependencies between the three steps. Ignoring these dependencies is an oversimplification that may produce not only "ugly" presentations, but also presentations that no longer convey the intended semantics. In this respect, it is interesting to note that the document-engineering design perspective differs radically from that of the field of graphic design.

Document engineering assumes that the authoring process can be broken down into a sequence of subprocesses that are able to operate independently to generate the end result. The graphic design perspective assumes a content provider with a message to be communicated to a target audience, both of which the designer has to understand exactly before creating the appropriate mix of graphics and text to effectively communicate the content provider's message. We claim that both perspectives are valid and need to be understood before the advantages of semantic-driven document engineering can be appreciated. The lessons document engineers can learn from studying graphic design literature can be grouped in two categories. Graphic designers are more aware of the internal dependencies with a given design, and of the dependencies on forces external to a design. The dependencies in both categories require explicit semantic modeling, as discussed later.

Internal Design Dependencies

As exemplified by the Cuypers presentation about Rembrandt in Fig. 4.2, the assumption that content and layout are independent does not hold for most multimedia presentations. This section discusses the dependencies among presentation structure, style, and content in more detail. As illustrated in Fig. 4.3, the selection and design of content, presentation structure, and style are all essential ingredients for an effective multimedia presentation, and decisions made in any of the three can influence the other two. We give examples of how each ingredient influences the other two.

Presentation Structure Depends on Content (Arrow 1). The particular selection of content items can be used to determine the presentation structure of the items. For example, suppose that, for our Rembrandt presentation, a number of paintings have been selected. The paintings fall into three categories: landscapes, portraits, and still lifes. For printed graphics, Williams (1994) advocated the use of spatial layout to express grouping relationships in the underlying content. Our multimedia presentation structure could re-

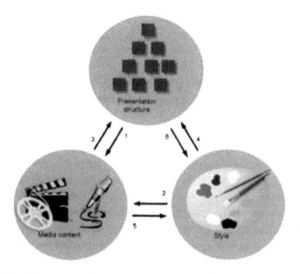

FIG. 4.3.   Dependencies between content, presentation structure, and style.

flect these categories using temporal grouping, by first displaying all items in a single category before displaying the items from another category. Both for multimedia and for printed material, however, the design decision to reflect the categorization of the input in the layout of the presentation can only be made by a designer who is aware of the semantic grouping relations of the input.

Style Depends on Content (Arrow 2). The content can also influence the overall style of the presentation. For example, suppose the selected images in our Rembrandt presentation share a number of color characteristics. This could lead to the choice of particular colors for the background and main text colors of the presentation. Other aspects, such as image texture, could, for example, also influence the selection of appropriate font typefaces. Content may also influence the choice of style through, for example, using a grayed version of an important image as a background for the rest of the presentation. Selection of such an image can only be done based on knowledge about the semantics of the image and its role in the overall semantics of the presentation.

Content Depends on Presentation Structure (Arrow 3). In the document-engineering perspective, presentation structure is always derived from the original content structure. Here, form follows function: The structure of the rendered presentation is determined entirely from the underlying content. In practice, however, when a Web site is created, the intended presentation structure, with the appropriate spatial layout and navigation structure among sections, is often determined before the document information is filled in. Then later, when the informative content is created or selected, it is often adjusted to fit into the style of the site. Thus, to a degree, function may end up following form, when it is necessary to adapt content to fit the presentation and the aesthetics of its design.

In our Rembrandt example, suppose our database query for chiaroscuro paintings by Rembrandt returned two portraits, two landscapes, and only one still life. Just to restore the symmetry in the presentation structure (that is, to get a balanced rhythm in the presentation), we could select another still life by Rembrandt from the database, even if it is not a very good example of the use of chiaroscuro. If we were using another layout, we may even decide not to include the still-life painting at all, for similar reasons.

Style Depends on Presentation Structure (Arrow 4). The style can also depend on the presentation structure. For example, if the presentation structure uses spatial alignment for conveying grouping relationships in the content, then the designer needs to choose a particular alignment style (e.g., left, centered, or right). In Fig. 4.2, for example, the title is centered above

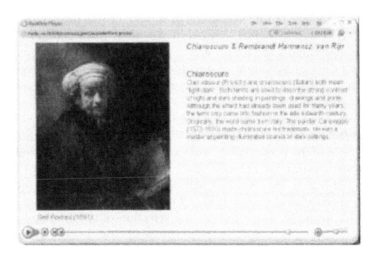

FIG. 4.4.   SMIL presentation, adapted to the smaller height of the user's display. (Image courtesy Rijksmuseum, Amsterdam.)

the text to convey the grouping relation, in this case that the title applies to both the example image and the explanatory text. Note that the same presentation structure could have been conveyed using a longer title aligned left with the image of the painting. However, a title that is left-aligned with the subtitle of the text, as depicted in Fig. 4.4, is less desirable, because it has the potential to create confusion about the roles of the title and the subtitle. Selecting the appropriate styles thus requires explicit design knowledge about the presentation structure.

Content Depends on Style (Arrow 5).   In the document-engineering perspective, style is often perceived as the "add-on" after the "important" decisions have been made. The "more fundamental" choice of content may, however, also depend on the style. For example, in order to preserve the visual unity in a presentation, relevant images may be selected for presentation only if their color histograms or clarity of images fit in with the style of the presentation as a whole (Oldach, 1995). For Web sites aiming for a strong visual effect (e.g., for branding purposes), the look and feel of the site is typically designed first. The content is selected, manipulated, or created to fit in with the chosen style. Obviously, selecting or disregarding content on the basis of stylistic properties is potentially dangerous and can only be done when taking into account the semantics of both the content and the overall presentation.

Presentation Structure Depends on Style (Arrow 6).   Similarly, an established style may prescribe certain limits on the spatial grid and pacing of the presentation. Ideal groupings and orderings of selected content may have to be put aside for reasonable alternatives that fit in with consistent use of margin widths and item alignments throughout the presentation. Similar effects and tensions are possible for temporal layout. A rhythmic presentation gives a certain desired effect, but may clash with specific durations needed to express the message at different points in the presentation. Modification of individual style parameters may have unintended results on the presentation structure. Conflicts can only be dealt with when such dependencies are made explicit.

In addition to the mutual dependencies between each of the three aspects, local presentation structure or style can depend on more global presentation structure or style. This can be used to provide continuity and consistency throughout the presentation.

In summary, in the graphic design perspective of creating a presentation, aspects of content, presentation structure, and style depend on each other in ways that are generally ignored in the document-engineering perspective. This is not to say that document-engineering tools are not useful, but rather that the extra dependencies that make the task of good design so complex, require more complex solutions. Because automated presentation generation requires finding solutions within this design space, the three aspects of content, presentation structure, and style need to be expressed and manipulated explicitly.

In this section, we limit the discussion to the dependencies that are internal to the process of designing a Web presentation. The presentation, however, also needs to fulfill external requirements of, for example, the user and content provider. In the next section, we discuss these external forces and how they influence the content, presentation structure, and style trade-offs that need to be made during the design process.

External Forces on the Design Process

The external forces that influence the design originate directly from the different interests of the parties involved. To determine the requirements of an automated system, we use the following motivating example, based on a typical scenario with three main parties: a content provider who wishes to effectively communicate a message to a user, aided by a skilled designer.

Examples of forces that originate from the content provider include the mission of the content provider's organization (e.g., making profit by selling books online), the limited availability of resources (e.g., the amount of time and money the organization is willing to spend on the design, the amount of disk space or bandwidth that is available at the server), and the content provider's preferences (e.g., the use of company colors in the Web forms).

Examples of forces that originate from the user include the user's needs (e.g., the desire to buy a book), the limitations imposed by the user's delivery context (e.g., the user could be driving a car, have a low bandwidth connection, have physical disabilities, or have strict time constraints), and the user's personal preferences (e.g., the user could prefer visual to textual information, dislike fast cuts in video material, prefer soft colors to primary colors).

Given a good understanding of the type of forces that play a role, it is the task of the designer to come up with a design that best matches the needs of the content provider and the user. In addition to the forces originating from the content provider and the user, there are additional forces originating from the designer, whose resources are also limited and who might also have personal preferences. Many of these forces could give rise to conflicts and may require the designer to make balanced trade-offs. For example, the designer might decide not to use the soft colors of the organization's company logo for users that need to fill in Web forms while working in bad lighting conditions.

Modeling Design Dependencies Explicitly

The role of an intelligent automatic presentation-generation mechanism is very similar to that of the human designer. Automatic presentation also has to deal with forces originating from content provider and user, as well as with forces originating from the generation process itself (e.g., limited computing resources, or personal preferences of the developer of the generation system). For example, in Fig. 4.2, the preferred design centers the title across the width of the screen. In Fig. 4.4, however, the client's platform display is shorter and the images are not to be scaled, a condition imposed by the copyright holder to preserve image quality. This forced our Cuypers system to search for an acceptable layout-design alternative within the given device and content-provider constraints. We do not claim that we can build an automated system that could make such decisions as well as a professional designer. Interactive multimedia applications, however, often need to make design decisions at run time, without the chance to consult a human designer. In such situations, intelligent presentation-generation systems such as Cuypers could make acceptable design decisions when dealing with these types of trade-offs. These decisions would be based on explicit knowledge about the design-space dependencies and external constraints, combined with an adequate search strategy. These characteristics require that document transformation be more than the application of a simple syntax mapping from source to destination format. Rather, it requires heuristic reasoning to find an optimal solution to balance the forces involved, taking into account the effect of each design decision explicitly.

The requirements for document transformation following from the discussions in the two previous sections can be stated as follows:

- Explicit representation of the semantics of the presentation; explicit representation of the knowledge reflecting the internal design dependencies among the semantics of content, presentation structure, and style; and external influences of the delivery context specifying the user's resources, preferences, and needs, as well as the content provider's server context.

- A transformation method that can make an informed choice in the internal design space by taking the aforementioned semantics and knowledge into account, while balancing the external trade-offs. Note that this transformation method cannot be based on simple syntax mappings.

CONCLUSIONS AND FUTURE WORK

In this chapter, we first explained the differences between text and multimedia document transformations, and how these are currently incorporated in our Cuypers system. In addition, we discussed the limitations of syntax-driven approaches by explaining the differences between the document-engineering and graphics design perspectives. This discussion was used to derive the requirements for semantic-driven document engineering.

In our current work, we are exploring the extent to which we can improve both document-transformation engines and intelligent presentation-generation systems to meet these requirements. Simply stated, the first requirement boils down to making explicit the various types of knowledge that remain implicit in current document-transformation approaches. To encode this knowledge explicitly, we are looking at new technologies that are being developed in the context of the Semantic Web. This will allow us not only to use commonly available tools, but also to reuse knowledge published by third parties and publish our own knowledge bases for reuse in other contexts.

Although the Semantic Web is still in its infancy at the time of this writing, languages and tools that address some of the problems mentioned in this chapter already exist. For example, metadata languages such as RDF (W3C, 1999) allow Web content to be annotated, making its (domain-dependent) semantics explicit. The vocabularies that represent the concepts used by these annotations, and the basic semantic relations among these concepts, can be defined by using schema languages such as RDF Schema (W3C, 2002a). Even richer semantic relations can be expressed by ontology languages such as OWL (W3C, 2002b) and DAML+OIL (Van Harmelen, Patel-Schneider, & Horrocks, 2001) that have been built on top of RDF Schema. The resource constraints of a user's access device can be specified using the RDF-based CC/PP (W3C, 2001a) specification, which has its roots in the mobile telecommunications industry. Even before the

Web was invented, several professional communities built thesauri and ontologies to provide a basis for their metadata requirements (e.g., for the domain of our example, the *Art and Architecture Thesaurus* [Getty Research Institute, 2000] could be used). It is expected that many of these resources will become available on the Semantic Web (cf., e.g., the RDF version of WordNet, Melnik & Decker, 2001).

When it comes to encoding the explicit knowledge we need for a next-generation intelligent presentation-generation system, we believe that the Semantic Web will provide us with standardized building blocks, especially when it comes to metadata, domain modeling, and device profiling. On the other hand, work on user modeling, modeling of discourse and narratives, and explicit graphic design knowledge still seems insufficiently mature to be standardized and applied "off the shelf" in presentation-generation systems such as Cuypers. In particular, the encoding and deployment of this type of knowledge will require further experimentation, and we believe that the semantic-driven version of our Cuypers engine, which we are currently building, will provide a good test bed for such experiments.

As members of the World Wide Web Consortium, we are also looking into how the results of these experiments could feed back into the next-generation Web specifications. We firmly believe that the current gap between the syntax- and XML-based document-engineering languages versus the RDF-based languages of the Semantic Web needs to be closed: Document presentation is simply too difficult to be done without semantics, and semantics are too important to be incorrectly presented.

ACKNOWLEDGMENTS

The research reported in this chapter has been funded by the Dutch NWO NASH and ToKeN2000 projects. Examples are taken from a ToKeN2000 demonstrator, and all media content has been kindly provided by the Rijksmuseum in Amsterdam. Part of the material presented here is based on fruitful discussions with Lloyd Rutledge and Joost Geurts.

REFERENCES

Berners-Lee, T., Hendler, J., & Lassila, O. (2001, May). The Semantic Web. *Scientific American* [Online], *XX.* Available: http://www.sciam.com/2001/0501issue/0501berners-lee.html

Bos, B., Lie, H. W., Lilley, C., & Jacobs, I. (1998). *Cascading style sheets, level 2 CSS2 specification. W3C recommendation* [Online]. Available: http://www.w3.org/TR/REC-CSS2

Bray, T., Paoli, J., & Sperberg-McQueen, C. M. (1998). *Extensible markup language (XML) 1.0 specification. W3C recommendation* [Online]. Available: http://www.w3.org/TR/REC-xml

Clark, J. (1999). *XSL transformations (XSLT) Version 1.0. W3C recommendation* [Online]. Available: http://www.w3.org/TR/xslt

Getty Research Institute. (2000). *Art and architecture thesaurus Version 2.0* [Online]. Available: http://www.getty.edu/research/tools/vocabulary/aat/

Geurts, J. (2002). *Constraints for multimedia presentation generation* [Online]. Unpublished master's thesis, University of Amsterdam. Available: http://www.cwi.nl/~media/publications/thesis_joost.pdf

Geurts, J., Van Ossenbruggen, J., & Hardman, L. (2001). Application-specific constraints for multimedia presentation generation. In *Proceedings of the international Conference on Multimedia Modeling 2001 (MMM01)* [Online]. Available: http://www.cwi.nl/~media/publications/mmm01.pdf

Jin, Y., Decker, S., & Wiederhold, G. (2001). OntoWebber: Model-driven ontology-based website management. In *Semantic Web Working Symposium (SWWS)* [Online]. Available: http://www.semanticweb.org/SWWS/program/full/paper55.pdf

Knuth, D. E. (1986). *TeX: The program*. Reading, MA: Addison-Wesley.

Little, S., Geurts, J., & Hunter, J. (2002). Dynamic generation of intelligent multimedia presentations through semantic inferencing. In *6th European Conference on Research and Advanced Technology for Digital Libraries* [Online]. Available: http://www.cwi.nl/~media/publications/ecdl2002.pdf

Mann, W. C., Matthiesen, C. M. I. M., & Thompson, S. A. (1989). *Rhetorical structure theory and text analysis* (Tech. Rep. No. ISI/RR-89-242). Information Sciences Institute, University of Southern California.

Martinez, O. R. (2002). *Design dependencies within the automatic generation of hypermedia presentations* (CWI Tech. Rep. No. INS-R0205) [Online]. Available: http://ftp.cwi.nl/CWIreports/INS//INS-R0205.pdf

Melnik, S., & Decker, S. (2001). *Wordnet RDF representation* [Online]. Available: http://www.semanticweb.org/library/

Oldach, M. (1995). *Creativity for graphic designers*. Cincinnati, OH: North Light Books.

Rutledge, L., Alberink, M., Brussee, R., Pokraev, S., Van Dieten, W., & Veenstra, M. (2003). Finding the story: Broader applicability of semantics and discourse for hypermedia generation. In *Proceedings of the 14th ACM Conference on Hypertext and Hypermedia* (pp. 67–76). Nottingham: ACM Press.

Van Harmelen, F., Patel-Schneider, P. F., & Horrocks, I. (2001). *Reference description of the DAML+OIL (March 2001) ontology markup language* [Online]. Available: http://www.daml.org/2001/03/reference.html

Van Ossenbruggen, J. (2001). *Processing structured hypermedia: A matter of style* [Online]. Doctoral dissertation, Vrije Universiteit, Amsterdam. Available: http://www.cwi.nl/~jrvosse/thesis/

Van Ossenbruggen, J., Geurts, J., Cornelissen, F., Rutledge, L., & Hardman, L. (2001). Towards second and third generation web-based multimedia. In *The Tenth International World Wide Web Conference IW3C2* [Online]. Available: http://www10.org/cdrom/papers/423/

Van Ossenbruggen, J., Geurts, J., Hardman, L., & Rutledge, L. (2003). Towards a formatting vocabulary for time-based hypermedia. In *The Twelfth International World Wide Web Conference IW3C2* [Online]. Available: http://www2003.org/cdrom/papers/refereed/p383/p383ossenbruggen.html

W3C. (1999). *Resource description framework (RDF) model and syntax specification* [Online]. Available: http://www.w3.org/TR/REC-rdf-syntax

W3C. (2000). *XHTML 1.0: The extensible hypertext markup language: A reformulation of HTML 4.0 in XML 1.0* [Online]. Available: http://www.w3.org/TR/xhtml1

W3C. (2001a). *Composite capability/preference profiles (CC/PP): Structure and vocabularies* [Online]. Available: http://www.w3.org/TR/2001/WD-CCPP-struct-vocab-20010315/

W3C. (2001b). *Device independence principles* [Online]. Available: http://www.w3.org/TR/2001/WD-di-princ–20010918/

W3C. (2002a). *RDF vocabulary description language 1.0: RDF schema* [Online]. Available: http://www.w3.org/TR/rdf-schema/

W3C. (2002b). *Web ontology language (OWL) reference version 1.0* [Online]. Available: http://www.w3.org/TR/owl-ref

Williams, R. (1994). *The non-designer's design book*. Peachpit Press.

Chapter 5

Model-Based Development of Educational ICT

Jan Herman Verpoorten
Utrecht University

Developing educational ICT (software also tagged as e-learning, computer-based training, courseware, interactive learning, [intelligent] computer-aided instruction, distance learning, Web-based learning, and more; see Institute of Electrical and Electronics Engineers [IEEE], 2002) that delivers education to learners is complex. This complexity has two main causes. First, educational ICT applications are a special category of professional software. Most software applications support users in performing a particular task. Educational ICT has a different focus, because the effect of the task is not on the outside world, but rather settles inside the user. E-learning applications are deployed for learning or learning support, so the effect is on the knowledge or cognitive skills of the user. Second, educational ICT contains a lot of data (educational content), often of a multimedia nature. Creating this data is time intensive and requires a high level of domain knowledge. But this is not the only complexity, which I discuss next.

Concerning educational content, a difference must be made between non- or low-interactive content, such as electronic book pages, and high-interactive learning data. Simple editors can create the first category. For instance, the online instructions found in many "electronic learning environments" are created with special (HTML) editors. Creating such documents does not differ much from creating documents with text processors. However, these editors are not capable of creating high-interactive instruction or more advanced test items. In such a case, so-called authoring systems or normal programming languages are needed. At the moment, high-interactive educational software is mainly developed this way. However, this mostly has the effect that content and application logic end up physically entwined, blocked from any access except by their developers. Originally, authoring systems were meant to be used by teachers in developing their own educational software. In reality, these tools turned out to be too complex for them, and are presently mainly deployed by professional developers. These people tend to protect the integrity of their software by locking it. Even if a regular teacher were afforded the desired access, he or she would have to deal with the inside complexities. Any way you look at it, regular teachers are excluded from the development of educational software.

Is this a bad thing? In my opinion, it is, because some type of teacher involvement might be a key factor for success in the long term. Developing applications is one thing, but keeping them relevant is another. This applies to a great extent to updating the content, which frequently needs to be done in education. Experience and research (e.g., Blom, 1997) have shown that, for this aspect, teacher involvement may be crucial for success in the daily situation. Content often has to be updated, for instance, to adapt it to special needs, for actualization, or to freshen up exercises and tests. If a teacher cannot perform this task, then the usability of the software is at risk.

Although computers are ubiquitous in our society, many still consider the use of educational software as an act of educational innovation. Several reasons for this can be summed up (see Rosenberg, 2001, for a discussion). One of them is the problem with keeping programs relevant and up to date. In the higher education domain, where I worked for several years, this was obvious from the beginning. At that time (the late 1980s) computer-aided instruction was deployed for innovative purposes. These teachers not only updated the content, but also gained new ideas and insight from the deployment itself. Software had to be changed frequently, both its application logic and content, for this reason. Blom (1997) confirmed these experiences with research focused on higher education, and underlined the importance of teacher involvement in the development process. Of course, this might be different in other educational settings (for instance, teachers in primary schools have little time to do this). Also, courses in Latin may turn out to be more stable than, for instance, contemporary music. But the updating conundrum remains to a certain extent a problem for all education.

My own experiences as a project leader of a few learning-with-ICT pilots directed me in research for a software-development methodology that enabled teachers to play a role. This research was conducted at the Utrecht University in an independent center. Concurrent with the development, the center also gave courses to practitioners of other institutions and companies on the development of educational ICT, using the research results. Hence, the research outcomes were used extensively in practice, leading to successive improvements. The results stabilized after a few years (Verpoorten, 1995). One of the outcomes is that content creation and application development must be rigidly separated, thus enabling content editing for teachers. For application development, an engineering methodology effective for educational applications has been developed. This methodology relies on a concept known in computer science as "application framework." Editing the framework itself is not open for teachers, although some may be able to master it. This framework differs greatly from tools like authoring systems. To make this difference clear, I give an overview of the ways in which educational ICT was and is developed, and I position my research in this field.

Authoring tools in general are computer programs, designed to be simple to use when building an application. Probably the first tool for creating computer-assisted learning applications was TIP (Translator for Interactive Programs), developed around 1960 for the IBM 650 mainframe computer, shortly after one of the very first computer-assisted learning programs was developed at the IBM Research Center in 1958 (Rath, Anderson, & Brainerd, 1959). The big breakthrough of computer-assisted learning, however, had to wait for the introduction of small personal computers (at that time called "microcomputers") in the mid-1970s. In the beginning, many such computers were delivered together with the (IEEE-standardized!) PILOT (Programmed Inquiry, Learning Or Teaching) authoring language, originally created by Starkweather (1977). This language was based on the BASIC programming language. Although PILOT was widely used for creating computer-assisted learning programs, new graphical capabilities of the microcomputer overtook this text-based authoring tool and gave birth to integrated program editors (application structure, text, graphics): the so-called authoring systems. These systems often used a graphical presentation, which promised to be much more user-friendly than bare languages such as PILOT. Therefore, the interest was great. An overwhelming number of articles devoted to authoring systems can be found in the 1980s and early 1990s. Relatively soon after, many authoring systems came into being. For instance, Locatis and Carr (1985) found 79 of them. This number has continually increased since then.

Already at an early stage, authoring systems began to be criticized. Developing turned out to be far too complex for technically unskilled teachers and it also took (and still takes) much time (see also Merrill, 1997, for a discussion on this topic). Merrill (1985) regretted the loss of flexibility (compared to programming languages) and doubted effective authoring for the target group, technically unskilled authors. Later, he published an alternative: instructional transaction theory (Merrill, 1991), describing, among others, "transaction shells," containing "instructional transactions" in specific authoring environments. Bork (1984) criticized authoring systems because of their inadequate coding practice and miserable implementation of software-engineering principles. Indeed, thus far, everyone's attention was fully dedicated to the creation and use of tools, at the cost of attention to a proper development methodology and engineering principles.

During the same period as the aforementioned developments, intensive research for both methodologies and accompanying techniques and tools found a place in computer science, for the purpose of developing information systems. Although some researchers studied ways to deploy the outcomes in the actual practice of the development of educational ICT (e.g., Van der Mast, 1995), the majority of educational ICT developers remained unaffected by this research, nor did it change the way authoring systems function. The same is true for many more topics from software-engineering research. One such topic is the "application framework" approach for application development, from which my own research benefited. Application frameworks are skeletons that define the basic design of an application (I explore this further in later sections). The very first frameworks were developed to support highly technical development issues, such as the graphical user interface of Apple's MacApp and Next's NextStep computers in the 1980s. At this moment, application frameworks are common practice in software engineering, although they are not easy to develop.

My own experiences with authoring systems led me to find a different way of development, and the framework presented in this chapter gradually evolved from the late 1980s. Its development is very similar to the general pattern for framework development, researched by Roberts and Johnson (1997). The first stable version was discussed in my dissertation (Verpoorten, 1995). Only very recently, other e-learning projects discovered the advantages of this way of developing applications. One example is the OpenACS Web application framework (Calvo, Sabino, & Ellis, 2003), which integrates a Web server, mail, news, and collaboration services. Another example is uPortal (http://mis105.mis.udel.edu/ja-sig/uportal/), a framework for producing a campus-wide portal for (and developed by) institutions of higher education. In the last few years, a massive effort has been made to produce standards in e-learning. For instance, recently the LOM (Learning Object Metadata) standard was established (IEEE, 2002). These projects concentrate on interoperability of programs (e.g., a test program with the storage system) and on content management and differ considerably from my own research, which focuses on the development of e-learning applications and the possible role of teachers in such development.

In the next section, I discuss the way teachers are enabled to create lesson content, using my framework approach. In the following section, the conceptual construction of the (application framework-) engineering methodology is presented. Although this is a technical topic by nature, I omit technical details and restrict the discussion to conceptual issues; see Verpoorten (2002) for a technical explanation. In the final section, some experiences and conclusions are summarized.

THE TEACHER'S ROLE

Teachers developing their own educational software is not a new idea. It received a lot of attention in the late 1980s and early 1990s. The aforementioned authoring systems, in particular, promised rapid and easy end-user computing. All authoring systems share a common approach: They are a type of visual programming tool with embedded content editors (text, graphics, animation, etc.). The entire program logic must be created by dragging, dropping, and editing symbols for loops, conditions, presentations, learner responses, and so on. One thing was already made clear by the first computer-based learning pilot projects in the mid-1980s, in my faculty: For teacher-authors, having to deal with all sorts of inner software details does not work.

It took a few development phases until research yielded a more suitable development methodology. The first attempt was based on the belief that using authoring systems could be made easier by constructing building blocks for ready-to-use exercises. These blocks were to be assembled by the author into a larger building block, resembling a program template (drill and practice, self-test, test, branched instruction, skinner machine, etc.). This worked better, but not well enough. Only the development process was speeded up, but all other disadvantages for teacher-authors remained. In the second attempt, educational content was separated from the building blocks. The content was now stored in database records. For the application logic, again, a particular program template was chosen. Editing this again had to be done with the authoring system, but was now reduced to only a few aspects such as screen settings (layout, colors, etc.), the lesson title, and a welcome screen. The main effort, editing the content, was performed by teachers in a special editor. Unfortunately, the many possible exercise variants were an obstacle to an effective (generic) solution. Moreover, editing the records, although an improvement compared to the authoring system, turned out to be impractical: Different exercises were represented by different edit screens and a lack of overview existed because exercises could only be shown one by one. Although this working method was again better, it was still not good enough. These experiences demonstrated the need for a better solution enabling teachers to play a role in the development process.

The Final Working Model for Content Authors

The third and final approach improved on all the previous disadvantages and was used extensively, both in my own faculty and in departments of other universities and vocational training schools. Users were not just the pioneers of the early days, but included people with varying backgrounds and professional affiliations. In the previous two phases of the research it became clear that most time had to be spent creating or updating lesson content. So, I decided to focus first on this aspect. The different existing program templates were merged into one program in such a way that a great variety of target applications could be achieved. This approach resulted in the application framework, discussed in the next section. From now on, using a suitable working model, teachers could be considered as possible authors of their own educational content.

The working model for content creation is founded on two strict principles. The first principle is that it should fit in with the mental model of the educational author, that is, it should introduce as few new concepts as possible. Early on in the research, the majority of the teachers knew the computer only as a text-editing machine. They were quickly confused by, and so unwilling to learn, other computer applications. As our editing task is important, but not frequently performed, the interface focus should be on ease of learning (Mayhew, 1992). Because users already knew text editing, a text-editor solution was chosen for content creation. The second principle of the working model is to hide as many program structures as possible, especially flow. The majority of educational authors have not learned (or find it difficult) to deal with if-then-else structures, which programmers typically use for exercises. Both flow-chart notations and grammatical if-then-else expressions have been shown to be counterintuitive and error prone. Although authors from a more technical domain tend to learn such a notation easily, others, like the majority of regular teachers, do not. Hiding such structures is done by using a text format in which they are implicit. Authors only use an associative style, relating conditions and expressions, and that has turned out to work just fine.

In practice, an author performs two simple steps:

1. Editing a file with an arbitrary text processor, using a particular editing format.

2. Executing a parser generator. This program checks the format of the content and, if correct, creates a format readable by the application framework. Technically speaking, the content is converted to a different file format, dependent on the information in a template. (In the recent framework version an XML template is created; in the earlier version, this information was edited inside the framework.)

This two-step approach is chosen for two reasons: to let authors work with a familiar tool, and to remove syntactical errors as early as possible, because run-time testing is very time consuming.

The editing format is extremely simple. The author uses headings (tags) above content pieces. One is completely free to choose a particular head-

```
.vraag [question]
Identifica el error en el siguiente pasaje y corrígelo:
'Como la dejes en Hoog Catharijne, con candado o sin él,
después de uno o dos dias, está robada tu bici.'
.selectie [error]
está#robada
.vraagdeel [activated when student fails to identify the
intended error]
está robada tu bici          .
.feedback
En holandés se dice 'is gestolen', pero and español se usa
una forma personal activa, con un complemento indirecto y
otro directo. El complemento directo viene al final. ¿Cómo
se expresa el agente cuando es anónimo?
.verbeter [the expected correction]
te#han#robado#la#bici
.keuzes [multiple choice]
Te han robado la bici.
Te robaron tu bici.
Te ha sido robala la bici.
Tu bicicleta te han robada.
.exit [The corrected sentence]
Como la dejes and HoogCatharijne, con candado o sin él,
después de uno o dos días, te han robado la bici.
```

FIG. 5.1.   Example of a user format for an item.

ing's text for optimal (human) recognition (of course, this is defined in the conversion template). The parser detects interaction types and exercise structures (flow). An example would be a single item in a Spanish–Dutch lesson (Slagter, 2000)[1]: see Fig. 5.1.

In Fig. 5.1, some lines start with a dot in the first position followed by a word (other solutions are possible), so-called tags. A tag denotes particular data, to be presented on the screen or used by the program, for example, in case of response checking. In the figure, the learner is first confronted with a text (.vraag) containing an error. First the error must be selected (.selectie). If selection fails, a clue is presented (.feedback). If selection fails again, the screen zooms into the particular part of the text (.vraagdeel). Next, the error must be corrected (conform .verbeter). If correction fails, a multiple-choice help question is presented (.keuzes). Correct or incorrect, the exercise is concluded with the same presentation (.exit). (The "#" characters inside control fields mean that the program accepts multiple spaces or an end of line.)

A single text file may contain several different exercise types. The layout of each type is not fixed: The author may both skip and add fields as de-

---

[1]Because the framework was used in The Netherlands only, practice examples in English do not exist.

sired. If, for example, the author needs feedbacks on specific responses, it suffices to add associated fields like .selectie1 and .feedback1. The framework will execute the "program flow" if such a condition is valid.

In this way, the content for several applications has been developed, and used in a variety of domains and at various instructional levels. Application types range from laboratory programs for educational research (De Graaff, 1997; Slagter, 2000) to computer-based training and testing (Slagter). Applications developed in the faculty of arts: Spanish language learning (nine programs in two to four versions by five different authors), English language learning (one), German language learning and testing (one program, three versions), Medieval Dutch language learning (one), Medieval French language learning (one), music theory learning and drilling (one program, several authors; see Fig. 5.2), self-assessment for a computer training course (one program, several versions). In my own educational practice, it was successfully deployed for testing approximately 1,000 students a year (Verpoorten, 1994) in a computer training course. It was also used by approximately 100 students for application prototyping in a course on computer-aided language learning. Outside the faculty of arts it was used for drilling and self-assessment of Latin (accompanying the book *Via Nova Urbs* by Derix, Assendelft, Gessel, Schaafsma, & Surber, 1997), learning and self-assessment of Hebrew, testing in several courses of civil engineering (technical university), and vocational learning and testing in a few insurance companies, a pharmaceutical company, a trade union, and a police academy.

Figure 5.2 is a simple multiple-choice question, part of a music theory lesson (in Dutch). The learner is asked for the name of the interval, printed in musical notation and played as an audio fragment. The list box contains all possible intervals. The audio fragment is pre-recorded, but the musical notation is generated from a code. For this exercise, the author edits the following line, containing three tags, now starting with a ## instead of the dot in Fig. 5.1:

##1:v5 ##2:<P>Dit interval is een verminderde kwint ##3:&G, [1F#4,1C5].

The third tag (##3:) contains the code for the musical notation, the first tag is used for response checking, and the second tag contains text used for feedback. In general, the only obstacle for authors proved to be the syntax of response patterns,[2] especially in more complex cases. For the rest, the majority, scarcely possessing any computer skills, turned out to be able to produce large amounts of content in a relatively short time.

---

[2]A response pattern is a representative part of a response, used for checking. In Fig. 5.1, it is the part to be found in the entire answer.

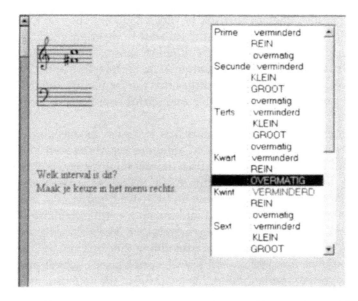

FIG. 5.2. Screen shot (detail) of a music theory application (in Dutch).

THE APPLICATION FRAMEWORK

Editing educational content in one simple way in spite of many differences in the generated content, like different types of interaction (selection, multiple choice, etc.), varying complexity of the exercise (help questions and presentations in case of particular responses) and differences between exercises of the same type (e.g., the number and types of help questions and presentations) requires a flexible "receiving mechanism." Partly this is solved by the parser converting the author's file. The remaining complexities are embedded in the program, running the exercises on the screen. Preferably, such a mechanism will be developed once, instead of each time for each new application. In other words, we want a generic piece of software. How can this be achieved? In analyzing educational software, equal processes can be discovered. These processes are candidates for generic software pieces. If such components are developed in such a way that they are connectable to each other (i.e., able to work together), some type of organized program library (components plus architecture) comes in sight. Of course, such a library must be able to construct the several types of programs needed (adventure game, self-assessment, test, drill and practice, tutorial, etc.). Such a library, also called an *application framework*, was developed.

In general, an application framework can be described as the software implementation of a reusable design. A framework can reduce development cost largely because both design and software can be reused over and over. The advantage of this will be clear, but only the combination of a not-too-complex structure and the capacity to meet the requirements in a broad application variety achieve effective reuse. Thus, an effective application framework is the combination of an architecture and a library, consisting of ready-to-use functionalities that are frequently needed in the application domain and are flexible enough to construct the many possible varieties.

The first application framework was just such a collection of software modules. A consistent number of modules was developed and was connected to the previously used authoring system. This system functioned as the glue between the components. Again, using the authoring system may sound surprising, but the purpose of this hybrid setup was to enable access to the design both to advanced authors and technically more skilled programmers. This way two access points existed: The authoring system could be used by advanced authors for assembling the components toward a particular application, and several so-called interfaces enabled programmers to access the software modules. The majority of the applications mentioned in the previous section are created in this way. The construction of this framework is extensively discussed in Verpoorten (1995). As expected, only a minority of teachers could handle the software, mainly due to the unsuitability of authoring systems for nonexperienced and nonskilled users, but also because of the learning curve for the framework design. Therefore, whereas authors created content, a technician constructed the application program with the help of the framework and using the authoring system as a kind of framework editor. Construction could be speeded up by editing a sort of generic application template, a ready-to-use typical framework implementation (see Table 5.1).

A few years ago, I decided to develop a new version of this framework with an improved technical structure and a number of additions, called ClassMate (Verpoorten, 2002). In ClassMate, one does not use an authoring system. The roles of the authors remained the same as in the previous situation. However, at the lesson-creation level (see Table 5.1), using the authoring system was replaced by editing a specification file (formatted in XML).

The prototype of this framework version was used for the development of two Web-enabled courses (in Hebrew and music theory). The differences between the old and new versions are mostly of a technical nature and therefore are not discussed further here. Instead, I present the conceptual structure, which is the same for both versions.

What is the scope of the framework? E-learning in general is about using computers in education, but in reality it can mean several things. A passive definition is "the electronic delivery of a learning or instruction content" and a more active definition is "a learning process created by combining digital

TABLE 5.1
Comparison of the Roles of Authors,
Using the Application Framework

	Activity of the Author		Type of Expertise Needed		
Goal	*Old Version*	*New Version (ClassMate)*	*Technical?*	*E-Learning?*	*Subject Matter?*
Content creation	Using text editor (teacher)	Same	No	Some to no	Yes
Lesson creation	Editing template with authoring system (technician)	Editing XML file with text editor (skilled author or technician)	Both versions: Knowledge of framework design Old version: Mastering authoring system	Yes	Some to no
Adding functionality	Using programming language (skilled technician)		Yes	Some to no	No

content with support and services." At present, many stress the importance of collaboration in the learning process (e.g., enabled by groupware services). The framework matches more closely the second definition, although the emphasis is on the teaching rather than the learning process: The framework has been developed with a scope for teaching and testing, directed to an individual student. Such a student performs a *session*, in the framework's parlance. The properties of a session determine whether this is a test, an adaptive test, an adventure game, a tutorial, or something else. To express this variation in a consistent way for application development, the notion *session* has been modeled. Perhaps others would prefer the term *lesson*. Unfortunately, the vocabularies of learning and education technology contain a great number of terms, still far from standardized. Thus, the exact meaning and granularity of many terms is imprecise. To avoid this, I have chosen the term *session*. In a session, the learner is busy with the educational content and it depends on the properties of this content, whether these are particular tasks, more passive instructions, or a combination of both. Tasks also can vary considerably. To catch this type of variation, educational content, just like a session, also has been modeled in a particular way. Both performed modelings, session, and educational content are discussed next.

Session Modeling in the Framework

As mentioned before, a session keeps a learner busy during a particular length of time. From the learner's perspective, it is a series of pieces of lesson content or tasks, offered or chosen one after the other. Such pieces are called *items* in the framework's modeling. The learner finishes the items, then task items are (mostly) graded and, if all can be graded, a single grade results. That is what I consider to be the scope of a ClassMate session: a coherent number of items, mostly resulting in a single final grade. For example, a drill-and-practice program presents a number of exercises (items) to the learner, keeping a record of how well the learner performs.

Teachers arrange the items in *topics*. From their perspective, educational topics are taught or tested. The term *topic*, however, is a bit vague. In a history lesson, for example, one might see the topic "ancient North Africa." This topic can be broken into several smaller topics, for instance, periods like Phoenician settlements, Greek Cyrenaica, and Carthaginian domination. Topics have little uniform granularity: They can be large or small, and can be of any nature. Therefore, in the modeling, a topic is used as a content label for a bundle of items; items fulfill the educational task. To indicate the subject matter, items are to be arranged in topics.

In a session, three matters are essential: the topic structure, the session course, and the control of either element by the program, the learner, or both. A session may cover several topics at the same time, for instance, all of the ancient North African periods. Control is an important aspect, present at various levels in a design. For instance, a designer of a session about ancient North Africa might define the topic Phoenician settlements as mandatory and the others as optional. Thus, selection of the first topic is program controlled whereas the others are learner controlled. The designer might also consider that the mandatory topic at least should contain a particular number of mandatory items, which may be extended by any number of optionally chosen items. This consideration affects the session course in both program- and learner-controlled ways. In the modeling, such control is an aspect of the topic structure.

Topic Structure. In the modeling, each topic has several properties, like a caption (e.g., Greek Cyrenaica), a weight relative to other topics, a control type (program or learner), an enumeration of the items coupled to it, and a few others. Take for instance a test on the topic ancient North Africa. All three subtopics will be tested, so the topic selection is made by the test designer instead of the learner (program control). Will all three subtopics have the same size or the same importance? Possibly not and, if not, the test designer can choose more items concerning one topic and fewer concerning another. In the session modeling, this is expressed as the (relative) weight of a topic. The same holds more or less for the session level: It also has a caption, possibly a minimum and maximum weight, a default number of items, possibly a minimum or maximum number, a control type for this number, and other attributes. The session's weight definitions are used to control topic selection (no less than . . . and no more than . . .), and only, of course, if the type of control (learner, program) allows it. The function of the topic's weight is to enable automatic division of the total number of items over the active topics. Depending on its weight, a number of items are assigned to a topic (see Fig. 5.3). These properties can be controlled during a session's course, so they might change depending on the learner's progress (a program-controlled aspect of the session course). In Fig. 5.3, the numbers indicate each topic's weight. If 40 items are assigned to the entire test, then the left and right topic will consist of 10 items, leaving 20 items for the middle topic. The advantage of this assignment method is that at any time, for example, during the test, a re-division of the total items can be forced by changing one topic's weight. The same happens if the total number of items is changed.

Coupling of items to topics is done by assigning *stores* to topics, where stores contain the items. A store is just a bundle of items, like a directory on a computer's file system. The reason for this in-between step (as said before, items are arranged in topics) is to further refine the content profile: Stores also have weights (defining the number of items that will be selected from the store) and in this way a designer can make a difference between items coupled to a topic, for instance, easy and more difficult ones. Coupling a store does not mean that all items in it will be presented. A store may contain any number of items, from which all or only a few may be presented during the session. This is controlled by its weight and further defined by the selection mechanism: Items may be picked out randomly, as arranged in the store. Defining the selection mechanism, which is specified for each store, is part of the topic definition (see Fig. 5.4).

In Fig. 5.4, selection of one item implies selection of all items in the store with the AND node type attribute (interdependent items). Because the shuffler type has a linear value, these items will be presented as located in the store. However, only one item will (can) be selected from the store in the middle (nodeType = XOR).

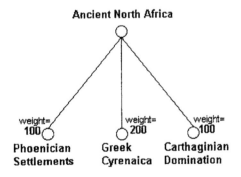

FIG. 5.3. A test about "Ancient North Africa," consisting of three topics.

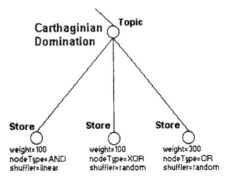

FIG. 5.4.   A topic consisting of three stores.

The selection of topics and items can be further influenced by particular settings. For instance, items and topics can be attached, so that selection of one results in getting others. The reverse can also be true: Selecting a particular item or topic now locks the attached ones for selection during the rest of the session (see the nodeType attribute in Fig. 5.4). An example applied to topics is the constrained selection of either the topic Microsoft Word or StarOffice in a text-editing skills test.

Session Course.   The course of a session is very comparable to the way single items will succeed one another. In the previous section, only the selection of topics and items was discussed. One aspect of the session course is to determine when such a selection occurs. Session course is modeled as a run strategy containing a number of properties, of which the item selector is the most prominent. An item selector can present an item list for letting the learner choose one item (learner control), can select each next item itself (under program control), or can combine both control mechanisms. The item selector couples one of the empty task spaces (x items to do, the number of items assigned to the entire session) in the session with a particular store (and thus one item from it). Item selectors are framework components that can display quite different behavior. For instance, reselection may be locked after a specified number of times, selection may follow the topic arrangement or not, item results may be shown in an overview or not, and so on. The choice of item selector that is on duty is a property of a run strategy.

Other properties of a run strategy are the possible restrictions on sessions over several days, and which of the (specified) services are available for the learner. For instance, a test designer might want to lock the online dictionary or help system, but if the test is finalized and the learner can inspect the answers (again a run strategy's property), this constraint can be cancelled again. To enable a learner to inspect his or her results after the session has ended, the framework has a locked mode (a run strategy property in which interactions can be viewed but not altered).

As explained before, in the application framework, the modeling issues are accommodated in different software modules. For instance, the session structure is defined in a topic structure (tree) that belongs to a core component, always running at the start of a session. Item selectors are individual components, from which one is selected. In the early framework implementation, the authoring system functioned as the glue between the components and was used as a framework editor. In the recently developed version, a specification (XML file) has taken over this role. The technical differences between these versions are huge. However, there is no conceptual difference between the two implementations.

Content Modeling in the Framework

As explained earlier, educational content is equivalent to the term item. An item is the smallest independent content unit. For those familiar with the terminology used in computer-based training systems: An item must not be confused with Skinner's frame, Crowder's unit, and so on. These terms express a particular content granularity. In contrast, an item is not meant to express content granularity. It is just a single piece of content of any possible size. A session may contain a large amount of items, or only a few.

So, item is a modeling issue. If an item only presents some educational content, then it is noninteractive. Interactive items not only present, but also receive responses from the learner. All interactive items share the common characteristics of showing a presentation, receiving a learner's response, and probably showing a reaction on this response. This system reaction, in turn, exhibits the same entire sequence: The reaction can consist of a noninteractive version of an interactive item (e.g., a feedback text or a help question). This sequence can be repeated a number of times, or interrupted if a particular result has been achieved. Following this sequence, an item is a bundling of presentations, interactions, and response patterns, causing the sequences. Viewed from the content's perspective, different presentations, interactions, and response patterns must be defined. This is the author's role: He or she must create a presentation, define an interaction type (e.g., multiple choice), create a list of possible responses, and define which item must be shown if a particular response is received by the system. Of course, to obtain a usable interface, much more must be carried out. For instance, presentations and interactions must be visually bundled somehow and rendered on the screen. Fortunately, rendering on the screen and interpreting the response patterns into sequences is done by the framework: The author is kept away from such aspects. His or her role is restricted to solely "filling" the presentations, defining the interaction type(s), and creating the response patterns.

This approach requires a modeling of different presentations and interactions. In the modeling of the framework, presentations are considered as "primitive data" views of text, images, and so on (in the latest version, this has been extended a bit). Interactions are very much the same as controls or widgets used in common applications, although in education they may differ considerably from these.

Modeling Interaction. Interaction is an important aspect of the framework modeling, because it is an essential hallmark of education. Several innovation projects have shown that teachers tend to concentrate on question types and structures when developing new lesson designs, often at the cost of the total session design (which is also at a greater distance from their current practice). Unfortunately, human–computer interaction has weak points compared to human–human or human–paper interaction. Human–computer interaction also offers possibilities not possible in other types of interaction. That is why it is a pitfall to ignore the computer's possibilities and to restrict oneself to interaction that reflects or echoes current classroom practices. A design challenge lies in establishing interaction types that are effective in human–computer interaction, specifically for educational software. There are many such interaction types. To avoid the nightmare of an endless collection of interactions, a suitable model should be able to limit interaction variants to a conceptually finite collection.

The modeling carried out represents such a collection. Any interaction is considered to have three aspects: the kind of data it works on (data type and data structure), the kind of action a learner performs (action type), and possible implementation variants, dependent on the kind of data and the action type. Only two action types are defined: selecting and editing (something). For instance, editing can be applied to text, but also to a mathematical formula. A formula editor differs considerably from a text editor: It uses a restricted character set and a strict syntax, and calculating the formula must result in a number. A text editor can have several implementation variants, for instance, as a *text field* (one-line entry of characters only), a *text area* (several lines of characters only), and a *text processor* (characters plus markup). Such editors can be given behavior impossible in current classroom practices. Think, for example, of an exercise for text entry that refuses incorrectly typed characters, or replaces wrong characters by correct ones, instantaneously correcting or supporting the learner (again, an implementation variant).

The same principle works for the selecting (something) action type. The most common interaction is the multiple-choice question, which is a selection (action type) of a text option (data type) in a list (data structure). In

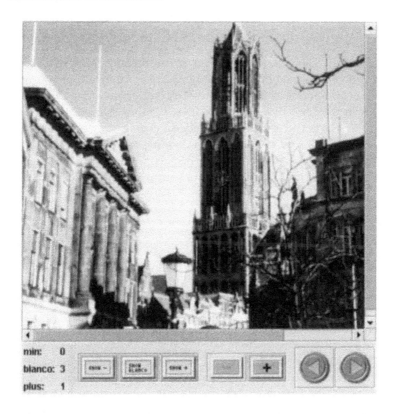

FIG. 5.5. Screen shot (fragment) of a multiple-choice question, implemented as a browse interaction.

the paper version used in the classroom, the text options at most can be replaced or extended by images. In a computer, much more is possible. In a particular implementation of this interaction type, the options are presented one by one, instead of all together (reducing guessing the right answer). Options can be numerous, and can consist of any (mixed) data type (see Fig. 5.5). In Fig. 5.5 the text presentation of the question itself is not shown, only the browse widget is. One of the options is shown, it contains a scrollable image of the city hall and the medieval "Dom" tower in Utrecht, The Netherlands. Anything can be placed in an option: text, images, Web pages, and so on, even editors are possible. The panel below the option contains buttons for browsing (arrows), marking (– and +), and skipping marked and/or unmarked options while browsing.

Interactions can also be combined into more hybrid ones. For instance, the browse interaction in Fig. 5.5 can have options that are editors instead of presentations. The same is true for the so-called combo-box widget, a list box whose text options can be both selected and edited. In both cases the learner performs a multistep action: First, the learner selects an option and next, it is edited.

The framework contains a number of interactions. Most can be configured in some way and exhibit behavior specific to education. For instance, browsing the options of the multiple-choice question of Fig. 5.5 can be set to linear or to a choice of random modes. Another example is the selection of text parts in a text-selection interaction: These selections can be set to multiple selections or to possibly overlapping selections, a feature sometimes necessary in language learning. Because of space limitations, I restrict myself to this general overview and the supplied examples.

CONCLUSIONS

In the early days of computer-based instruction, regular teachers tried to develop educational software for individual use, using so-called authoring systems, a process that turned out to be too complex and time consuming. At the moment, such pioneers are a small minority, more likely to shrink than to grow. However, the need for a particular role in the development process for all regular teachers was not only obvious from the very beginning, but has remained and is also confirmed by independent research: Teachers should have a role (at least) in content creation (see the introduction section) for reasons of adaptation and actualization. Therefore, research for a suitable development methodology was started. It resulted in an application framework and a working model for content authoring. The achieved framework is capable of delivering a broad variety of instruction types (see the section on the teacher's role). In the past 15 years, dozens of computer-based lesson and testing programs have been developed this way. The working model for content creation that accompanies the framework was explained. It was proved (De Graaff, 1997; Slagter, 2000; Verpoorten, 1995) that this working model is a good fit with the capabilities and perception of teachers. In this way, highly interactive digital content can be delivered to its end users. In spite of the complexity of this type of content, closely connected to its interactivity, the established working model is simple and straightforward, but relies heavily on the application framework on "the other side." The main points of the conceptual modeling of this framework were discussed earlier. Although some technically skilled teachers were able to handle this framework for development, most are not. It is not very likely that this will (or should) change in the future. The point of creating the working model is that it does not need to.

The final result of the application framework is the enablement of very rapid application development. Working prototypes can be delivered in hours. In practice, the application framework inspires teachers to use many interaction designs, because it showcases the many possibilities. Perhaps the most important achievement is that regular teachers have control over the educational content. The separation of the content from the application framework and the established working model eliminate the need for teachers to deal with technicalities, so that they can keep the software fresh and useful in their own daily practice.

REFERENCES

Blom, J. J. C. (1997). *Use-oriented courseware development for agricultural education: An ecological approach.* Unpublished doctoral dissertation, Landbouwuniversiteit, Wageningen, The Netherlands.

Bork, A. (1984). Production systems for computer based learning. In D. F. Walker & R. D. Hess (Eds.), *Instructional software, principles and perspectives for design and use* (pp. 52–56). Belmont, CA: Wadsworth.

Calvo, R. A., Sabino, J., & Ellis, R. (2003). *The OpenACS e-learning infrastructure, and case studies* [Online]. Available: http://www.weg.ee.usyd.edu.au

De Graaff, R. (1997). *Differential effects of explicit instruction on second language acquisition.* Doctoral dissertation. The Hague, The Netherlands: Holland Academic Graphics.

Derix, H. A., Assendelft, M. M. van, Gessel, H. L. van, Schaafsma, A., & Surber, J. C. (1997). *Via Nova Urbs.* Amsterdam, The Netherlands: Meulenhof Educatief.

IEEE Learning Technology Standards Committee. (2002). *Standard for information technology—Education and training systems—Learning objects and metadata* [Online]. Available: http://ltsc.ieee.org/doc/wg12

Locatis, C. N., & Carr, V. H. (1985). Selecting authoring systems. *Journal of Computer Based Instruction, 12*(2), 28–33.

Mayhew, D. J. (1992). *Principles and guidelines in software user interface design.* Englewood Cliffs, NJ: Prentice-Hall.

Merrill, M. D. (1985). Where is the authoring in authoring systems? *Journal of Computer-Based Instruction, 12*(4), 90–96.

Merrill, M. D. (1997). Learning-oriented instructional development tools. *Performance Improvement, 36*(3), 51–55.

Merrill, M. D., Li, Z., & Jones, M. K. (1991). Instructional transaction theory: An introduction. *Educational Technology, 31*(6), 7–12.

Rath, G. J., Anderson, N. S., & Brainerd, R. C. (1959). The IBM research center teaching machine project. In E. Galanter (Ed.), *Automatic teaching: The state of the art* (pp. 117–130). New York: Wiley.

Roberts, D., & Johnson, R. (1997). Evolving frameworks: A pattern language for developing object-oriented frameworks. In R. C. Martin, D. Riehle, & F. Buschmann (Eds.), *Pattern languages of program design 3* (pp. 471–486). New York: Addison-Wesley.

Rosenberg, M. J. (2001). *E-learning.* New York: McGraw-Hill.

Slagter, P. J. (2000). *Learning by instruction.* Unpublished doctoral dissertation, Utrecht University, Utrecht, The Netherlands.

Starkweather, J. A. (1977, April). Guide to 8080 PILOT, version 1.1. *Dr. Dobb's Journal,* 17–19.

Van der Mast, C. A. P. G. (1995). *Developing educational software: Integrating disciplines and media.* Unpublished doctoral dissertation, Delft University of Technology, Delft, The Netherlands.

Verpoorten, J. H. (1994). Informatietechnologie voor studenten letteren [Information technology for undergraduates in arts and humanities]. In M. J. A. Mirande (Ed.), *De*

Kwaliteiten van Computerondersteund Onderwijs (pp. 318–331). Bussum, The Netherlands: Coutinho.

Verpoorten, J. H. (1995). *A model based approach to courseware development.* Doctoral dissertation. Utrecht, The Netherlands: ECCO Expertise Centrum voor Computerondersteund Onderwijs.

Verpoorten, J. H. (2002). An application framework for e-learning. In A. Zemliak & N. E. Mastorakis (Eds.), *Advances in information science and soft computing* (pp. 36–40). Athens, Greece: WSEAS Press.

Chapter 6

Engineering the Affective Appraisal of 3-D Models of Buildings

Joske Houtkamp
Utrecht University

In the last decades of the 20th century, research in information visualization and virtual reality made substantial progress, and results of these efforts have gradually been incorporated in the daily practice of professionals in science and engineering. Since the emergence of affordable, powerful personal computers, images and graphics have become essential elements in many computer applications for communication, education, and entertainment that are used on a daily basis by people at home as well. Many computer applications for professional or personal use contain 3-D models of buildings and cities that represent real or imaginary environments, often called *virtual environments*. The models may either serve as a setting for simulation and training, or may themselves represent the main purpose of the program and enable the user to explore a historical building or environment, or compare the different designs made by architects for a new community building. These 3-D models of buildings and larger environments have become indispensable elements in computer games, and in applications with educational, military, and many other purposes. Research in development of these models has concentrated on technical and cognitive issues such as depth perception or distance estimation, often driven by the intent to make the models look "photo realistic" and to make navigation as easy as possible.

This chapter investigates another aspect of the design and use of 3-D models and explores the question of whether a 3-D model of a building on a desktop system can evoke subjective opinions in a user similar to those evoked by the building in reality. In other words: Can the affective qualities of a building's exterior or interior, for instance, impressive, engaging, gloomy, or frightening, be transferred to a computer model? How are the affective qualities changed by the fact that the viewer looks at a model on a flat computer screen, and is it possible to engineer a model to achieve the desired effect?

After a short introduction to 3-D models, I explain the subject of affective appraisal of buildings. Affective appraisals are judgments concerning the capacity of the appraised objects, in this case, buildings, to alter mood, expressed in terms such as *pleasant, repulsive,* or *attractive* (Russell & Snodgrass, 1987).

The central part of the text (the sections "Design of a Model and Loss of Information," "Display on a Monitor," and "Perception of the Model") elaborates on a basic framework used to identify the essential differences between viewing a building in reality and viewing a 3-D model of that building. These differences are the result of manipulations that are performed on the information in the process of creating a model, and of the display of the model on a computer monitor. The display of a 3-D model on a monitor affects the cognitive perception of the model considerably because of factors such as the restricted field of view and the means of navigation. I discuss evidence that, to bring about a desired affective effect on the user, modelers may use cues of different kinds, like manipulations of the shape or rendering of the model, and stimuli that trigger preexisting mental representations.

This chapter is an attempt to analyze the topic of affective appraisal of 3-D models of buildings, using literature on environmental and cognitive psychology, computer science, and cinematography. It suggests a method for measurement of appraisal that can be used as a starting point for experimental research. Furthermore, it contains practical suggestions that may be of interest to designers and developers of 3-D models, but that can also increase the general user's appreciation of the complicated technical and cognitive issues involved in (re)creating a building or an environment on a desktop computer.

3-D MODELS

"Experiencing" a 3-D Model

Advertisements for games and multimedia applications often suggest that viewing a 3-D model of a building can be compared to visiting a building in reality. For example:

Imagine for a moment, that you are flying through the air. You open your eyes and find yourself within an enormous eight-hundred year-old gothic cathedral, a monument to man's ingenuity and perseverance. . . . You find yourself soaring up to touch a cold arched ceiling, basking in the warm multi-colored sunlight pouring down on you from magnificent forty-foot stained-glass windows. You pause for a few moments to re-focus your eyes and you slowly descend to the cool, dark marble tile floor. . . . Meanwhile, hundreds of other ethereal glows race past you—exploring, communicating, experiencing one of the most intense real-time simulations ever created. Now imagine all of this running on your home PC! (Digitalo Studios, 1999)

The citation from the Web site of this Digitalo project, the 3-D reconstruction of the Notre Dame cathedral in Paris, claims that the impressiveness of the cathedral can be experienced through this medium, presumably by the special effects of lighting and illusion of speed. The application offers only visual display of a building on a desktop monitor, sound, and the means of navigating the environment, but the citation particularly refers to the sensation of 3-D vision, of temperature, touch, and movement.

Considering the differences between real buildings and 3-D models, it seems impossible that moving through a small model, viewed on a 15-inch or 17-inch display, can compare to the experience of walking through a huge building like a cathedral. The question of whether and how the affective qualities of a building's exterior or interior can be transferred to a computer model has not received much attention until recently. Most research has concentrated on the feeling of presence produced by virtual environments and on getting the more obvious, quantifiable objective elements of the models right, like real-time manipulation, textures, illumination, and shadows. The general opinion seems to be that making the models more realistic will create corresponding effects on the user and that this photo-realistic approach will create the best results for all purposes. But even if we are confronted with a high-quality rendered model, we still view this model on a flat, 2-D screen, in a confined field of view, and have to move through or around it using a mouse and keyboard.

Research on the affective qualities of 3-D representations of buildings or urban environments was carried out by Bishop and Rohrmann (2003), Rohrmann and Bishop (2002), Mahdjoubi (2001), Roupé, Sunesson, Wernemyr, Westerdahl, and Allwood (2001), Skog and Söderlund (1999), and de Kort, IJsselsteijn, Kooijman, and Schuurmans (2003). The experiments confirmed the assumption that participants would be confident of their ability to evaluate the affective qualities of a building or environment represented as a 3-D model on a desktop monitor. They did not reveal clearly, however, whether the appraisal is similar to the appraisal of the building or environment in reality, and it is also unclear which aspects of the representation and display influence the appraisal.

The issue of affective appraisal is an important one for many current and future applications and requires explicit attention in research:

> Affective quality is the bottom line of an accounting of the many features in a place, and is, we believe, a guide for much of your subsequent relationship to that place—what to do there, how well it is done, how soon to leave, whether or not to return. Afterward, you often remember little more about a place than its affective quality. (Russell & Snodgrass, 1987, p. 246)

Manipulation of the Model

The hypothesis made here is that many of the important characteristics of the interior and exterior of a building that contribute to the affective appraisal are not easily or completely transferred to a computer model shown on a desktop monitor. Furthermore, it is necessary to, first, carefully select the essential elements in a building for modeling that add to a certain affective quality, and, second, perform manipulation of these elements and their representation to create the effect experienced in reality.

If it is possible to identify cues in a model that contribute to a certain appraisal, this will help the designer of a model to decide whether to manipulate and overemphasize these cues, depending on the task the model is created for. If, to mention a simple example, the use of shadows makes a room appear larger and thus more impressive, the designer must realize that this effect may be used, but that, at the same time, the spatial information offered by the model is less accurate.

Examples of 3-D Models

In this chapter, I use the term *3-D models* to designate geometric, rendered models of buildings, displayed on the monitor of a desktop computer, and navigable with a mouse and keyboard. There are many varieties of 3-D models of buildings, which may have different purposes. The quality of the geometric model itself, of its rendering (textures and lighting), the interface for navigation, and the options for interactivity vary widely. Usually, the question of whether the affective qualities of the modeled building are important for the purpose of the application is not asked, or at least, not explicitly. I describe two very different examples to illustrate this point.

Theatron. The first example is the model of the theater of Dionysos in Athens (Fig. 6.1). It is one of the 3-D models of historic theaters in the Theatron program (2002), developed for the purpose of teaching theater

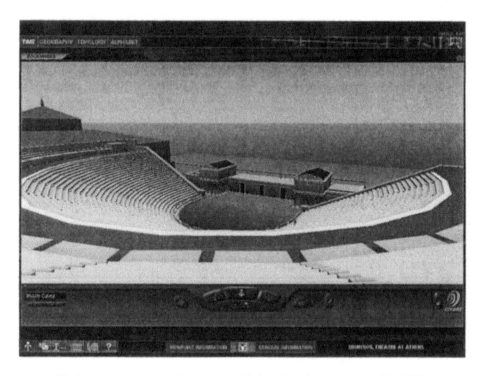

FIG. 6.1.   A screen shot of the Dionysos Theatre from *Theatron*. Copyright © 2002 by Theatron Consortium. Reprinted with permission.

and its history in an academic environment. Most of the ancient theaters in Europe have fallen into ruins or have been remodeled substantially. It is difficult to create a correct mental image and atmosphere of a theater of a certain period using ground plans, cross-sections, reconstructive drawings, and so on, especially if one has to add actors, décor, lighting, and so forth to create a complete impression of a performance. The reconstructions in the Theatron program help students to create a mental image of a theatrical performance. They offer the means for gaining a spatial understanding of the buildings, and facilitate navigating the model to examine sightlines and the areas visitors and actors would have occupied before and during the performance. Only the most important features of the constructions have been incorporated in the model, resulting in a high level of abstraction. The rendering is simple mainly because of technical requirements, such as the hardware available to students at universities. To create an affective appraisal, users of the program must complete their mental image by studying more detailed drawings of reconstructions and photographs of the remains. The model is viewed in a Web browser plug-in like CosmoPlayer. The user has to learn to use CosmoPlayer's navigation panel, which, also after some time, requires attention but offers some useful options like the choice between flying or walking, thus staying at about 1.80 m above ground level, and a series of viewpoints.

Myst. The second example is not a 3-D model at all, strictly speaking. Figure 6.2 shows a screen shot of Sirrus' bedroom in Channelwood Age, from the game Myst (Cyan Worlds Inc., 1993). The graphics are rendered using 3-D models, but all images are static and players cannot move freely to any location they can see in the virtual environment. Players use the mouse to point in a direction and every mouse click makes a full step in that direction. When pointing at an object the cursor takes the shape of a hand, and players can manipulate a doorknob to open a door or a switch to turn on a light, or cause more surprising effects.

In Myst, the player explores virtual worlds and closely examines buildings and environments to find clues for problems and riddles that have to be solved. The mysterious atmosphere created by the story is sustained by the sound effects and music as well as the content of the environment and the visual effects. The sound fragments form the background to the environment (e.g., waves and seagulls when near the water) or provide feedback when the player manipulates an object. These also add atmosphere

FIG. 6.2.   A screen shot of Sirrus' bedroom in Channelwood Age, from the game *Myst.* Available: http://sirrus.cyan.com/Online/Myst/GameShots. Copyright © 1993 by Cyan Worlds, Inc. Reprinted with permission.

because they give a very vivid impression of the material manipulated and the environment, like solid wood or heavy metal, and echoes when in a building constructed of stone. The developers have given careful attention to illumination and to detail, such as furniture and decoration, which creates a very realistic effect. Photographs of wood and stone were applied as texture maps, wrapped to 3-D models.

The previous two examples show the importance of choices made in the modeling process. The model of the theater of Dionysos offers real-time navigation so users may understand the spatial characteristics of the building, but at the cost of the detailed rendering that is necessary to properly represent the affective qualities of the building. The purpose of the models in Myst is to create a setting and a mood for the game itself and to invite the player to examine interesting elements of the building for clues. The rendering of the rooms has been performed with close attention to detail and illumination, which obviously provokes an affective appraisal in the viewer, but may obscure other information such as the spatial characteristics of the building.

AFFECTIVE APPRAISAL OF BUILDINGS

Affective Appraisal and Emotions

A person enters a building to perform a specific task, or to explore the building by moving around and looking at the construction itself and its contents. How does a person form a judgment of the building, and how does emotion relate to this judgment? Russell and Snodgrass (1987) distinguished long-term emotional dispositions from short-term states, which are most important in the context of this chapter. They mentioned three types of short-term states: affective appraisal, mood, and emotional episode, and stated:

> By affective appraisal we mean an aspect of how someone interprets other persons, places, events, or things. It is a judgment of something as pleasant, attractive, valuable, likable, preferable, repulsive, and so on. By mood we mean the core emotion-tinged feelings of a person's subjective state at any given moment. . . . By our definition, a conscious person is always in some mood, and mood per se is not directed toward any particular object. . . . By emotional episode we mean an emotional reaction to something, with the reaction typically involving coordinated and distinctive physiological, behavioral, and mental changes. (Russell & Snodgrass, p. 247)

My concern in this chapter is to explore whether affective appraisals of a 3-D model, which can be given without emotional involvement, are similar or can be made similar to the appraisal of the building in reality. A logical step is to ask whether in both situations these appraisals are accompanied by, or result in, emotional episodes or moods, or aesthetic response, as described by Nasar (1994). Although this is an interesting issue and may be related to the concept of presence, it is not explored further here. When I do refer to mood or emotion, this is generally because in the literature on this subject the distinction is not made, but the example or evidence is nevertheless valuable.

Physical Features That Influence the Affective Quality of a Building

Nasar (1994) distinguished two kinds of building features that are relevant for the aesthetic quality of buildings. The first category, formal attributes, relates to the structure of forms for their own sake and includes shape, proportion, rhythm, scale, complexity, color, illumination, shadowing, order, hierarchy, spatial relations, incongruity, ambiguity, surprise, and novelty. The second category comprises content variables that relate to physical features, but that also reflect the individual's internal representation of the building and meanings associated with that representation and building. Designers of 3-D models must be aware of the importance of certain physical characteristics that, alone or together, contain clues for the interpretation of the content of forms, a style, a type of building, or its function.

Mental representations of buildings play an important role in the affective appraisal of buildings. When individuals visit a place, they have a goal or a plan, and have expectations about the place in relation to this plan, and about certain characteristics for the particular function of a place (Russell & Snodgrass, 1987). Mental representations may include prototypic models of what a certain type of building, such as a church, should look like (Purcell, 1986). They may be based on earlier visits to the building or be formed by visits to other buildings, films, literature, and so on. Because individuals have different experiences, their mental representations are not identical, although they may be similar. Individual differences may also be explained by the concept of adaptation level, meaning that each individual has an optimum level of preference for a certain affective quality (Bell, Greene, Fisher, & Baum, 2001). The issue of realism and mental representations is discussed later.

Measuring Affective Appraisal

To measure and compare the affective appraisal of buildings and 3-D models in experimental research, I propose a multidimensional scale, such as the so-called SMB Scale (Semantic Environmental Scale or, in Swedish, *Semantisk Miljö Beskrivning*) developed by Küller (1977). Küller distinguished eight dimensions or factors to describe the experience of persons in a man-made environment, namely, complexity, unity, enclosedness, potency, social status, affection, originality, and pleasantness. Enclosure (openness, spaciousness, mystery), complexity (diversity, visual richness, ornamentation, information rate), and order (unity, clarity) were also mentioned by Nasar (1994) as formal variables that have emerged as prominent in humans' experience with their physical surroundings.

Simpler models exist that have proven their use in experiments (e.g., Bell et al., 2001; Russell & Lanius, 1984). They contain the terms most commonly used in appraising emotional reactions to an environment (e.g., *calm, dreary, forceful, pleasing,* etc.) and show a circular ordering, in a space defined by two underlying dimensions of qualities, a horizontal axis that ranges from unpleasant to pleasant, and a vertical axis from not arousing to arousing. However, we need a tool that is more fine-grained and uses more dimensions, because eventually we want to be able to relate these dimensions to the properties of a building, or to the formal and content variables mentioned earlier, as Küller tried to do (1977, 1991).[1] If these relations are more clear, we may understand in which way the consequences of the modeling process and the display on a monitor influence the appraisal of the modeled building.

The dimensions are structured and further described in Table 6.1. Although some of the described properties refer to the affective appraisal of interior rooms, they apply to the appraisal of the exterior of buildings as well.

The Relationship Between Physical Features and Affective Appraisal

Features of buildings, or formal attributes, that apparently are important elements for the dimensions of the SMB Scale are color, contrast, shape, and dimensions of the room or building and of the elements it contains, such as furniture; textures; the amount of elements, details, and decoration; illumination and light sources; the (number of) people present; and auditory

---

[1]The SMB Scale was used by Roupé et al. (2001) to measure the experiences of participants in virtual room environments.

TABLE 6.1
Dimensions of the SMB Scale and the Properties
of a Building or Room That Influence the Dimensions

Dimension	Description	Related Properties
Complexity	The degree of variation or, more specifically, intensity, contrast, and abundance	The experience of complexity is related to the number of components in the room and to the placement and intensity of the components, such as color strength and contrast. Furniture, light sources, patterns, auditive components, and the number of people present all influence the complexity.
Unity	How well all the various parts of the environment fit together into a coherent and functional whole	The experience of harmony, described in the factor unity, rests mainly on Gestalt principles of perceptual organization like similarity, proximity, continuation, and closure. These apply to the elements of the room itself (walls, surfaces) and to the furniture, decorations, and so on in the room, and concern shape as well as color. When the number of different colors or the intensity of the colors increase, the degree of unity decreases.
Enclosedness	A sense of spatial enclosure and demarcation	The sense of enclosure is determined by shape and size of a room, and the experience of a focal point. Light colors, a certain amount of well-suited furnishing, and diffused lighting decrease the impression of enclosure. Besides these visual characteristics, Küller (1977) mentioned auditive characteristics such as echo duration.
Potency	An expression of power in the environment and its various parts	Size, mass, coarse materials, rough surfaces, and dark colors contribute to the impression of potency.
Social status	An evaluation of the built environment in socio-economic terms, but also in terms of maintenance	Choice of materials and color scheme influence this dimension.
Affection	The quality of recognition, giving rise to a sense of familiarity, often related to the age of the environment	Related to combinations of elements or to characteristics of the viewer
Originality	The unusual and surprising in the environment	Related to combinations of elements or to characteristics of the viewer
Pleasantness	The environmental quality of being pleasant, beautiful, and secure	Spatial dimensions, color, the number of people, and (loud) noise may influence the impression of pleasantness.

characteristics. Customary practice in the creation and display of 3-D models of buildings, such as the omission of sound and other sensory channels, the absence of people, and the considerable reduction of details and furnishings depicted, inevitably influence the affective qualities of a building. If we take a closer look at the examples from Theatron (2002) and Myst described earlier, we can illustrate this effect. An observer will probably give a much lower score on the dimensions of complexity and potency to the model of the theater of Dionysos than to the building in reality, if it still existed in this condition. The relevant attributes are absent or simplified, for example, the number of components (architectural and other details, decoration, but also people) is very limited, the color scheme is subdued, there are no textures that give the impression of solid and durable materials. A more detailed rendering of the model would improve this, but the effect of, for instance, the display on a monitor on the perception of dimensions, and the absence of sound, would still cause a discrepancy with the appraisal of the real building.

The rendering of the scene in Myst (Cyan Worlds, 1993) is very detailed. The dimension of enclosedness is transferred to the model through the dark colors of the ceiling, the protruding ornamental edges that accentuate the heaviness of the ceiling, the dark walls and furniture, and the shadows cast by the lamps. Also, the view is partly blocked by a piece of furniture, indicating a limited space in which to move around. An observer is able to judge the dimension of social status using the abundance of details, the number and quality of the light sources, subtle color variations, and the textures that create a realistic impression of the rich materials used. The lack of details in the model of the Dionysos theater has a negative effect on the appraisal of the dimensions mentioned before, although it offers sufficient means for spatial understanding of the construction and for navigating the model to examine sightlines. It might even be conjectured that a full rendering of the model would distract the eye and conceal the main elements in the construction.

In the following sections, I examine the way in which the process of creating and displaying a 3-D model may alter the representation of the physical features of a building and thus the affective appraisal on the SMB Scale. Some suggestions for manipulations to correct or engineer the effects are discussed. I identify three phases of transformation. The first phase, which results in a rendered 3-D computer model, is mainly characterized by the loss of information. In the second phase, the effects of the characteristics of the desktop system for the display of the rendered model become apparent. The viewer's perception of the displayed model constitutes the third phase. In this phase, personal characteristics of the observer modify the incoming perceptive stimuli, resulting in a mental representation on which the viewer establishes his or her affective appraisal. The framework in Fig. 6.3 is used as a tentative inventory of relevant factors for each phase.

real building		
phase 1 selection		
restriction of the medium	loss of aural,haptic and other information	cross-modal enhancement or illusion may occur if aural and haptic information is absent; sound provides information on formal variables (dimensions, materials etc) and on content variables (use of room); haptic and olfactory information from the observer's environment may interfere with affective appraisal of model
	absence of body and point of view	3d p POV provides more information about dimensions and relative position
	absence of other persons	absence and presence of people influence formal variables (for instance complexity) and content variables (the use of the room, associated memories)
	unnatural boundaries, absence of environment	contrasts of model with the surrounding buildings or landscape influences perception of the model
demanded by goal	visual realism	the degree of visual realism or fidelity required depends on the function of the model; selection of elements and rendering must be deliberate choice in development process
	functionality	manipulation of objects may provide information on materials
choice of modeller	point of view	
	boundaries of the VE	
	level of abstraction, details	
	presence of other people	
	textures	
	illumination	light sources in the model influence colours and spatial dimensions, important for many dimensions of SMB-scale
	freedom of movement, velocity	3D model allows observer unusual and unrealistic standpoints and speed
	narrative	the *sequence* of the experiences of the observer is important for the affective appraisal of the model
complete (computer) model		
phase 2 moderations by characteristics desktop system		
	location of the system	sound, illumination, temperature at location of the desktop system may influence the experience of the observer
	means of navigation	
	field of view	restricted field of view has an impact on orientation and the effort to perceive the spatial dimensions
	perception of distance	accurate modeling of depth cues is very important for several dimensions of SMB-scale
	effect of display on colour and detail	colour and detail are distorted and may have unintended effect on affective appraisal
model on desktop monitor		
phase 3 user's perception		
	expectations related to purpose or task, earlier experience and existing mental models	
	mood at time of use	
	experience	
user's mental representation and affective appraisal		

FIG. 6.3.   The phases in the process of creating and representing a 3-D model, and their effects on the affective qualities. Explanations can be found in corresponding paragraphs.

DESIGN OF A MODEL AND LOSS OF INFORMATION

The creation of a 3-D model may be considered a phase of selection of elements that will and can be modeled, and thus loss of information. There are different reasons for the loss of information. In the first place, the medium compels the designer to cope with several restrictions such as the absence of a body. Second, the purpose of the application will (or should) determine decisions of the developer concerning, for instance, the level of detail. Topics on which decisions are made often intuitively, for aesthetic reasons or without obvious cause, form a third category. Some of the topics, such as the boundaries of the environment, can be assigned to several categories, but they are discussed at the point where they are most relevant. The purpose of the following discussion is to assess how the decisions and restrictions influence the affective qualities of the model, and how the effects may be compensated.

Restrictions of the Medium

The Loss of Multimodal Information. Until now, I have concentrated on the visual information a viewer can obtain from a 3-D model, and have neglected the other information a visitor to a real building, who is generally a multimodal being, gains from a visit. Current technology cannot provide realistic information to all senses in real time, and advances have been made mainly in visual and auditory display technology. Consequently, attention has been focused on the two sensory modalities of vision and hearing.

Phenomena called *cross-modal enhancement* and *cross-modal illusion* may explain why viewers of a model often do not miss sound or other modalities, and why designers do not worry about them. Experiments by Storms and Zyda (2000) showed the occurrence of auditory-visual cross-modal perceptions, which means that auditory displays influenced the quality perception of visual displays, and vice versa, although the subjects were not consciously aware of those intersensory effects. Biocca, Kim, and Choi (2001) concluded from experiments with (immersive) virtual environments that the mind attempts to integrate incomplete sensory cues to form a complete spatial mental model of the virtual environment. These phenomena may explain why we are able to give an affective appraisal of a building even if we only have very limited information: Unconsciously, our minds fill in the gaps to create a more complete mental representation, adding illusions of other modalities, and we evaluate the affective qualities of the mental representation.

Sound. Ambient or background sounds, which can be musical or more or less realistic, are used to set the mood of an experience in films and computer games. Examples of ambient sounds are the soundtracks of waves and seagulls in Myst, mentioned earlier.

Sounds provide information about the environment, such as the size of rooms, materials used, the presence and location of other people (even if they are outside the field of view), the origin of the sound, and one's own location in the environment. Sounds also may be used as sensory substitution events, like the "clunk" sound when a user collides with an object in a virtual environment.

Little is known of the influence of the presence or absence of sound on our affective appraisal of a building, but in providing information about spatial dimensions and materials used, they evidently play a role in Küller's (1977) parameters of complexity, enclosedness, and potency. Küller also mentioned that people associate long echoes with types of buildings like churches and indoor swimming pools. These associations, and associations triggered by ambient sounds, may influence our perception of the affective qualities of a place.

Environmental sound, or, more specifically, noise, can influence our mood and interpretation of events. The addition of sound of good quality enhances the user's experience and may also influence the user's opinion of the environment or building in general (Rohrmann & Bishop, 2002), and thus have an effect on other dimensions of the SMB Scale.

Sound displays for desktop systems usually involve small speakers. This complicates the presentation of sound because of possible noise pollution and the acoustics of the room in which the system is located. Headphones are more suitable to convey 3-D spatialized sounds, which provide the user with information on the direction and distance of the origin of the sound (Sherman & Craig, 2003).

In short, sound may be used by designers of 3-D models to supply information that is for some reason difficult to convey visually, such as characteristics of a material like weight and absorbent quality, the dimensions of very large or high rooms, the presence of other people that are out of direct sight, or associations on the function of a building. Experimental research is needed to reveal more about the effect of these important cues on the observer.

Other Sensory Channels.   3-D models on desktop systems generally do not include other sensory displays such as haptic (touch), vestibular (balance), olfactory (smell), or taste. Again, very little is known about how much these senses contribute to our affective appraisal of the environment. I mention just a few examples to demonstrate the importance of these channels. In reality, we are aware of the texture and weight of materials we touch, we perceive the temperature and humidity of the air, we notice wind or a draft, and we are aware of smells that may alarm us (fire) or remind us of a pleasant place. Bell et al. (2001) discussed comfort and discomfort as a result of high or low temperatures and wind, and their effect on affective feelings and social behavior. Further research is required to link these kinds of information to the dimensions of the SMB Scale, described earlier. Of course,

I can mention familiar assumptions, such as that the feeling of enclosed-ness will probably be greater if the temperature is high, and the pleasant-ness of a room will be less if one feels a strong cold draft. Ambient factors in computer labs such as temperature and smell must be taken into account when designing experiments to compare the appraisal of 3-D models with buildings in reality.

Absence of Body and Point of View. In many applications containing 3-D models, the user has a first-person point of view (POV) on the environ-ment. The advantage of the first-person POV is purported to be a greater involvement with the environment and the game play (Clarke-Willson, 1997). On the other hand, the absence of the body as a reference for scale and position in a first-person POV on a desktop computer makes it more difficult for users to estimate dimensions and locate their position in a com-plex building. And, although most people get used to it quickly, movement is distorted; in fact, users do not move at all—the world moves around them.

In a third-person POV, often used in computer games, the position of the camera is related to the *avatar* (digital representation of a person) so that the person is visible, often from some distance behind. The implemen-tation of a third-person POV is more complex, because there may be posi-tions of the avatar in which the software has difficulties producing a full view: Imagine the avatar leaning with her back to a wall (Rouse, 1999). The advantages are that the field of view is wide and resembles the peripheral view we experience in daily life; this makes it easier to locate the position of the avatar in the building or room, and see how the avatar moves in relation to other objects.

Absence of Other Persons. The absence of other people in many 3-D mod-els has without doubt an important effect on the affective appraisal of the building. When we consider people as visual and auditory elements in the room, they influence affective qualities like complexity, unity, and en-closedness, and they serve as a reference for the perception of dimensions. The sounds they produce provide information about dimensions and mate-rials used. On a behavioral level, they provide clues for the function of the building and the way to behave (e.g., move reverently and whisper), and may influence social status, potency, and pleasantness. The presence of other persons may influence the affective appraisal through the feeling of copresence.

Unnatural Boundaries and Absence of Environment. Just as the setting or environment of a building in reality may influence the affective qualities of the building, so may the absence of an environment, or a very abstract depiction of the environment, influence the affective qualities of the 3-D model. Contrasts in size, color, style, and so on of buildings adjacent to the modeled building may affect the appraisal of the building. Designers also have to cope with the fact that their virtual environments have boundaries. Cinematographic conventions like the display of doors, to suggest the existence of off-stage space to the audience and thus maintain the user's illusion of interacting in a larger virtual space than the space that is displayed on the monitor, may be used to compensate for this problem (Marsh & Wright, 2000). Another issue for designers is that users may try to explore the surroundings of the buildings represented and find an empty space. Tactics to avoid this are widely used in games and include gradually decreasing the level of detail, and offering more interesting perceptual opportunities in or near the areas that are modeled in detail (Fencott, 2001).

In the example of the theater of Dionysos, the view from the seats on the stage is influenced by the fact that the landscape is not modeled. It denies the user the possibility of considering the impact it may have had on the visitor when first entering the theater, and of judging the effect of the view as a background for the performance. (In the subsection "Narrative" the problem of boundaries of the environment is discussed further.)

Requirements Related to the Goal of the Model

Visual Realism. As noted before, 3-D models of buildings can vary widely in their appearance and can offer different kinds of functionality. It is often assumed that high-quality 3-D models that resemble the real building or environment as much as possible provide a better learning or training experience. However, many authors now support the idea that photo realism is not always the best solution, nor is it even necessary to make a virtual environment effective. Scaife and Rogers (1996), for instance, pointed out that a virtual environment should include those aspects that are necessary for performing the appropriate activity for a given task at a given time, that some aspects should be omitted, and that additional information that is not visible in the real world, but might facilitate learning, might be represented. To make these choices, the function of the virtual environment should be defined as precisely as possible, but in many computer applications 3-D models seem to fulfill several goals. For example, for the purpose of the reconstructions of theaters in the Theatron (2002) program, one of the designer's tasks is to create the correct impression of shape and size of the structure and facilitate navigation so that the user can experience the stage view from different seats. An implicit purpose, however, is to convey the affective qualities of the building, also necessary for the mental image of the theatrical performance. A similar problem is found in the more common genre of the architectural walk-through, where the clients want to gain an impression of the aesthetic effect of the design.

As noted before, photo realism is not necessarily the best solution if the models are used for learning or training experience, but is it the best answer if the goal of a 3-D model is primarily to evoke affective appraisals similar to those of the building in reality? Or does the photo-realistic rendering, including many details and complex illuminations, create distractions and cause an annoying delay in viewing the model? Several authors (Davide & Walker, 2003; Mahdjoubi, 2001; Slater, Steed, & Chrysanthou, 2002) pointed out that the illusion of realism for the observer of a representation of a virtual environment is not necessarily the result of a very close visual, for instance, geometrical, similarity to the real world, and an increased level of detail, but the result of the representation of relevant properties of reality, essential elements that have been selected depending on the purpose of the representation. This simplistic approach may help to explain the realistic effect of 3-D models that consist of only very basic shapes and few details: A few simple lines, planes, and shadows trigger a preexisting mental image of a (3-D) building, room, or corridor. As a consequence, the approach suggests that the designer select cues that capture the "essence" of rooms, buildings, and spaces. In Fig. 6.4, the process is shown in a schema. The observer looks at a representation of a building on a desktop monitor, which triggers internal representations of other buildings that in some way resem-

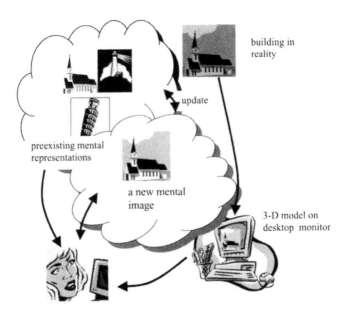

FIG. 6.4.   Creation of a mental image, based on the 3-D model and preexisting mental representations.

ble the representation. A new mental image is created that contains, or is associated with, much more information than the current representation. The observer may even experience emotions that are associated with the preexisting mental representation. This view helps to explain why we feel able to give an affective appraisal of a picture of a building and describe affective qualities of the building, instead of affective qualities of the representation.

This confidence does not necessarily mean that our appraisal of the 3-D model is identical to the appraisal of the building in reality; it might evolve when an observer feels that the representation contains a sufficient quantity of information to meet his or her demands or expectations. The information in 3-D models is generally more abundant than that in drawings, photographs, or other static representations. By moving around, viewers can obtain more effective depth cues and in general more information on spatial dimensions, illumination, position of elements, and so on.

It may be concluded that a high degree of realism in 3-D models on desktop computers is not always necessary, but depends on the specific task. Obtaining an affective appraisal of a room requires a different set of information from cognitive tasks such as estimating the size of a room. The designer has to have a good sense of the essential elements of a building or environment to create the best possible representation for the goal of the model, as well as creativity, to trigger the mental representation of the intended viewer and the desired appraisal. By deserting the realistic approach, the designer may choose to leave out unnecessary and distorting details, and to include and emphasize details that attract the viewer's attention.

Functionality. The functionality offered in a 3-D model of a building is often limited to moving around, exploring the building and its surroundings. Fortunately, a visitor to an unfamiliar building in reality often does not do much more than wander, look around, and open and close doors. But even here the experience is different from reality due to the loss of haptic feedback: Manipulating objects produces information on the materials used. In computer games, the player can usually manipulate all kinds of objects that are part of the environment. This adds to the involvement of a player and creates a sense of reality, but what impact it has on the affective appraisal of the building is, again, difficult to say and requires further study.

Choices Made in the Modeling Process

Even within the restrictions of the software, hardware, and purpose of the model, developers have numerous choices in designing a 3-D model of a building. Important choices made by the modeler concern, for example, textures, representing materials, and decoration that are relevant for several dimensions of the SMB Scale. One of the most obvious differences between the examples of the theater of Dionysos and the scene from Myst are the textures and the information they contain for the observer. Other options concern the presence of other people, the level of abstraction and amount of details included, ways to handle the environment of the 3-D model, and the choice of POV. These were discussed earlier, as consequences of the restrictions of the medium.

Illumination. The simulation of lighting is "the major and central conceptual and practical problem of computer graphics" (Slater et al., 2002, p. 73). The complexity of illumination and shadows is such that real-time rendering demands a great deal of computing power. I do not explain the technical problems and techniques developed to create realistic effects, but only mention possible effects of choices of illumination in a 3-D model on the affective appraisal of a building. First of all, the location, type, and intensity of the light sources, or the absence of light, may influence the colors of a room and the perception of spatial dimensions. Colors and spatial dimensions are important for many of the affective qualities mentioned by Küller (1977). He also mentioned other effects of lighting: The impression of enclosure increases as lightness in a room decreases, but more diffused lighting makes the degree of enclosure lower than if the light is concentrated on one point in the room; by the use of light or dark colors on walls the impression of the shape of the room can be altered as well; and the use of many strong lights increases the complexity of a room. The time of day and season and the weather, as noticeable in a clear-blue or threatening sky, not only influence perception of the colors in the building, but also affect the atmosphere of a model, comparable to the effects in films. Cinematographic techniques of lighting are especially effective for establishing a desired atmosphere, and for attracting attention to relevant areas and creating depth in an image (Giannetti, 2002).

Freedom of Movement and Control Over Velocity. Freedom of movement and control over velocity are often mentioned as the main advantages of 3-D models compared to static representations, because navigating a model helps the user to gain an overview and understanding of the spatial construction.

A factor that is difficult to assess without further research is the effect of speed of moving in or around the model. Judgment of complexity is different when we move at walking speed and can detect small-scale details, or when we "fly" or "jump" at high speed to another location in a 3-D model and only notice large-scale elements (Nasar, 1994). When users leave the "walking mode" of moving through the model to fly or jump, they also lose the point of reference of viewing the environment at a height of about 1.80 m and at walking speed, and consequently experience dimensions differently. The effects of velocity and viewpoint can be used by developers to manipulate the affective appraisal of the building. If the model contains few details, the speed of movement might be increased to keep the information rate at a level that still holds the attention of the viewer, thus maintaining the appraisal of the dimension complexity. The simulation of moving very fast over or through a building may also add to the aesthetic pleasures of the model (Fencott, 2001) and may produce a sensation that makes the viewer of the model forget about elements in the model that are of lesser quality. An example can be found in the game Myst, where the speed of navigation is slowed down when the player explores underground chambers to create suspense and tension.

Narrative.   When we visit a building in reality we create our own narrative, a sequence of views, actions, experiences, and affective appraisals of the locations visited. The similarities and contrasts between locations affect our perception of the different locations, and of the building as a whole, and can create surprise and contribute to Küller's (1977) dimension of originality. Users of a 3-D model can place themselves in any position from which to observe the building or a room, and can fly or jump quickly to other positions to compare elements of a building that are located at some distance from each other. This influences the affective appraisal of a building to an extent that is difficult to determine. In some cases, it might be better to offer the user a guided tour that simulates the passage of the visitor to and through the building and recreates the contrasts the visitor experiences from one moment to the next.

The developer of a model or environment can also allow the user freedom as in reality, but may organize the content of the environment in such a way that a user is invited to proceed or persuaded to stop and look around, or choose a different direction, and thus influence the creation of the narrative. Fencott (2001) and Isdale, Fencott, Heim, and Daly (2002) described a Perceptual Opportunities model of the content of virtual environments that helps the developer to arrange the elements of a virtual environment into a perceptual map. The Perceptual Opportunities model consists of syntactic categories that can be seen as attributes of any object that can be placed in a virtual environment. An example of perceptual opportunities is a category called *surprises*, which can draw the attention of the user from one point to another. A reward may follow, such as an interesting view or some kind of interactivity. In this way a preferred route may be designed, and attention may be drawn to important features of the building, thus manipulating the series of experiences of the user and the affective appraisals of the building. In the example of the theater of Dionysos, the first view of the theater might be the entrance for ordinary people, followed by a slow climb up to the upper cavea or level of seats, and a sudden view down on the theater and the surrounding landscape. After some time, when the thrill of this impressive scene has worn off, the attention of the visitor might be drawn to some people on the lower seats or on stage, which is an invitation to explore the orchestra and inspect the buildings. The effects created by the contrasts may be enhanced by illumination, camera angle or lenses, avatars in certain positions, and architectural details.

In this section, the loss of information as a result of the process of design and modeling was discussed. I now turn to the next step in Fig. 6.3 and investigate the effects that the display of a 3-D model on a desktop monitor may have on the user's perception of the model.

DISPLAY ON A MONITOR

The display of a 3-D model on a monitor and the means of moving around or through a model generally offered by a desktop system (a keyboard and mouse) have an important effect on our perception of the represented building, which undoubtedly influences our affective appraisal. As far as visual information is concerned, we may mention the generally small size of a desktop monitor, the distance between viewer and the monitor, the restricted field of view, the issue of depth perception on a flat screen, perception of spatial dimensions, the resolution of the images, and the colors that are influenced by the characteristics of the display. Visual perception of images on a desktop monitor and means of moving using a keyboard and mouse obviously have an effect on orientation and finding one's way. These topics received attention in research in recent years because of reported problems of the feeling of getting lost in a 3-D model and virtual environments in general (Darken & Peterson, 2002), which negatively influences the affective appraisal of a building (Evans & Gärling, 1991).

Several factors of the direct environment of the displayed model may influence our perception and appraisal of the representation of the building as well, such as the ambient illumination, the visual characteristics of the monitor itself and its direct surroundings, the ambient sounds, and the presence of other people.

Field of View

The extent of our visual field without movement of eyes or head is approximately 160° horizontally and 120° vertically (May & Badcock, 2002). Movement of the eyes and the head add substantially to the horizontal and vertical distances. The view a desktop display offers is much more restricted. Although the quality of our perception diminishes near the edges of our visual field, at any moment we view a larger area of our environment than that of a monitor, and the periphery may interfere with our perception of the virtual environment.

To explore an environment on a desktop monitor requires actions with a mouse or keyboard and an effort to complete a mental model of the environment. This characteristic of a desktop system and the chosen geometric field of view generated in the display seem to have the greatest effect on our perception of spatial dimensions and on our awareness of the position in the room or environment. Neale (1996) concluded from experiments that 60° is the optimum geometric field of view for perspective displays to perceive the basic characteristics of space accurately. The designer of a model can select a wider geometric field of view to allow more of the environment to be displayed and to improve spatial orientation, but this may lead to distortions in perceived distances, angles, and shapes (Neale, 1997; Waller, 1999). Another way to improve spatial orientation is the use of symbolic enhancements in the environment such as visual-momentum techniques (e.g., landmarks) used in film to provide continuity between scenes. Or, a solution may be found in using a third-person POV, which produces the effect of a wider field of view on the virtual environment. Distortions of the model or variations in the field of view can be used on purpose, to compensate for the effect of a chosen geometric field of view, or to strengthen or diminish a certain feeling such as enclosedness.

Perception of Distance

Although we generally use the term *3-D models*, we actually view computer models on a monitor as perspectival representations on a 2-D viewing plane (Whyte, 2002). The perception of depth is one of the most important factors for estimating spatial dimensions and thus is a major condition for Küller's (1977) dimensions of potency, enclosedness, and social status. It contributes to other dimensions as well; it is easy to imagine that the display on a monitor can have unwanted effects on complexity, for instance, when a large room contains many different elements such as furniture and decorations, but they all seem to clutter on a single plane as a consequence of a diminished perception of depth.

Depth cues in reality generally provide redundant, and sometimes conflicting, information and it is important to be aware of the relative weight when designing a 3-D model. Sherman and Craig (2003) described four varieties of depth cues people use in a real environment, two of which are applicable to viewing desktop monitors, namely, monoscopic depth cues and motion depth cues. Monoscopic depth cues include interposition (most important), shading, size, linear perspective, surface-texture gradient, height in the visual field, atmospheric effects, and brightness. Motion depth cues come from the parallax created by the changing relative position between the eyes and the object being observed, and have a very strong effect. (For a more complete description, refer to the literature on this subject, e.g., May & Badcock, 2002; Sherman & Craig.)

Evidence from experiments by Waller (1999) and Witmer and Kline (1998) is not conclusive on the question of whether distances in virtual environments can be accurately estimated. Important factors that emerge from their studies are feedback, which helps participants to correct their estimations in a following session, a sufficiently wide geometric field of view, varying between 50° and 80°, and the ability to move in the environment. By moving around, observers can view objects from different angles and relative positions, and estimate distances traversed using the time that passes. A final factor is the availability of some sort of reference for scale, necessary because an observer of a 3-D model in first-person POV cannot use his or her body for comparison. Familiar references for scale in daily life are other people, doors, windows, furniture, and trees. If in a virtual environment the dimensions of these elements are unusual, the observer may be confused (de Kort et al., 2003). In an evaluation of an alpha version of the Theatron program by a group of students of the Department Computer & Letteren, Utrecht University (2000), participants who were not familiar with the type of building in reality generally used doors and entrances as a reference and underestimated the dimensions of these elements and, accordingly, of the whole construction.

Characteristics of the Display and Their Effect on Color and Detail

Technical characteristics of the hardware used as well as environmental factors influence the display of a 3-D model on a monitor. Although spatial resolution, color, and motion can be displayed adequately owing to technological advances, resolution of the display used, viewing distance, color settings, and ambient light influence the perception of detail and the colors of the model. Color and color contrast are important factors in the affective appraisal of the environment and are relevant for most of the dimensions of the SMB Scale. There is little recent empirical research directed specifically at the effectiveness of manipulations of environmental color, let alone at the effects of color in virtual environments. Bell et al. (2001, p. 387) mentioned results from studies in environmental psychology indicating that perception of spaciousness, or conversely, crowding, may be influenced by color. Lighter rooms were seen as more open and spacious. Perhaps in the use of contrast and color, cinematographic knowledge can contribute to compensating for lost impact and to engineering the desired effects on the viewer of a 3-D model, as mentioned earlier.

PERCEPTION OF THE MODEL

The survey of factors that influence the affective appraisal discussed in previous sections primarily contains features of the modeled building and its representation on a monitor. The effects of these factors are, of course, related to the personal characteristics of the observer, such as expectations of a place and preexisting mental representations, as well as to prior mood, which modifies the perception of a place (Russell & Snodgrass, 1987). They influence the creation of a mental image, which, according to the present theory, is the real subject of the affective appraisal (Fig. 6.4).

Experience with the medium may also be an important factor (Sherman & Craig, 2003). Just as people needed to get used to cinematographic conventions, users have to learn to interpret the information a 3-D model contains and get acquainted with the techniques for moving around or through a building.

CONCLUSIONS AND FUTURE RESEARCH

Although it is reasonable to assume that affective qualities of a building can be transferred to a computer model, it is not possible to say in general which of the dimensions of the SMB Scale suffer most by the loss of information and the display on a desktop monitor. This depends on the characteristics of the building, such as physical properties, style, and function, and the characteristics of its representation, the 3-D model. It is highly probable that the dimensions in which sizes and distances play an important role (especially enclosedness, potency, and pleasantness) are affected most, especially if measures for reference are absent. Moreover, the dimensions in which the presence of many components is important will be influenced, because components such as people, decorations, and furniture are often omitted from the model or represented unconvincingly. Many aspects mentioned here require further investigation.

Although talented designers have succeeded in creating very effective models, mainly through experience and trial and error, a more systematic approach is required to gain precise control over this aspect of 3-D models of buildings. In the process of design, designers should determine if one of the requirements is to offer the information for affective appraisal. If so, an analysis of the real building to assess its affective qualities, for instance, by using the SMB Scale, should be carried out. The analysis should attempt to reveal the characteristics of the building that are linked to the affective dimensions because they provide evidence for the architectural style and its function. Extra attention must be paid to the visual and, if possible, auditory modeling of these characteristics, in compensation for the loss of information in the process of modeling and the display. Cues that may trigger preexisting mental representations in the intended audience and thus induce the desired effect can be included. Important cues and techniques are, among others, addition of sounds, lighting effects, a third-person POV, and velocity when moving through or around the model. Experiments with controlled manipulation of selected elements and cues will provide data that can be used to engineer the desired effects in the observer.

Once our understanding of cues and manipulations has increased, it may be possible to study other aspects of the models and their effect on the affective appraisal, such as the fact that an observer has freedom of movement and control over velocity. The succession of viewpoints a visitor observes in the real building, and the series of contrasts experienced as a result, may be simulated to achieve a desired effect. To design such a narrative or sequence of experiences, the Perceptual Opportunities model of the content of the virtual environment containing the 3-D model can be used to arrange the elements into a perceptual map (Fencott, 2001; Isdale et al., 2002). At this stage, a question left unanswered, of whether the emotional reactions that may accompany affective appraisal are similar to the reactions when visiting a building in reality, might be addressed. It is hoped that such a systematic approach will prove effective in the design of the aesthetic effects of a 3-D model that at present is based largely on experience, trial and error, and intuition.

REFERENCES

Bell, P. A., Greene, T. C., Fisher, J. D., & Baum, A. (2001). *Environmental psychology* (5th ed.). Fort Worth, TX: Harcourt College.

Biocca, F., Kim, J., & Choi, Y. (2001). Visual touch in virtual environments: An exploratory study of presence, multimodal interfaces, and cross-modal sensory illusions. *Presence: Teleoperators and Virtual Environments, 10,* 247–266.

Bishop, I., & Rohrmann, B. (2003). Subjective response to simulated and real environments: A comparison. *Landscape and Urban Planning, 65,* 261–277.

Clarke-Willson, S. (1997). Applying game design to virtual environments. In C. Dodsworth, Jr. (Ed.), *Digital illusion* (pp. 229–239). New York: Addison-Wesley.

Cyan Worlds Inc. (1993). Myst.

Darken, R. P., & Peterson, B. (2002). Spatial orientation, wayfinding, and representation. In K. M. Stanney (Ed.), *Handbook of virtual environments. Design, implementation, and applications* (pp. 493–518). Mahwah, NJ: Lawrence Erlbaum Associates.

Davide, F., & Walker, R. (2003). Engineering presence: An experimental strategy. In G. Riva, F. Davide, & W. A. IJsselsteijn (Eds.), *Being there: Concepts, effects and measurements of user presence in synthetic environments* (pp. 41–57). Amsterdam: IOS Press.

de Kort, Y. A. W., IJsselsteijn, W. A., Kooijman, J., & Schuurmans, Y. (2003). Virtual laboratories: Comparability of real and virtual environments for environmental psychology. *Presence, Teleoperators and Virtual Environments, 12*(4), 360–373.

Department Computer & Letteren, Utrecht University. (2000). *Evaluation of Theatron software: Final report.*

Digitalo Studios, Inc. (1999). *VRND: A real-time virtual reconstruction.* Retrieved March 17, 2004, from http://www.vrndproject.com/vrndfr.htm

Evans, G. W., & Gärling, T. (1991). Environment, cognition and action: The need for integration. In T. Gärling & G. W. Evans (Eds.), *Environment, cognition and action. An integrated approach* (pp. 3–13). New York: Oxford University Press.

Fencott, C. (2001). Virtual storytelling as narrative potential: Towards an ecology of narrative. In O. Balet, G. Subsol, & P. Torguet (Eds.), *Proceedings of the International Conference of Virtual Reality, 2001, Virtual storytelling: Using virtual reality technologies for storytelling* (pp. 90–99). Heidelberg, Germany: Springer.

Giannetti, L. (2002). *Understanding movies* (9th ed.). Upper Saddle River, NJ: Prentice-Hall.

Isdale, J., Fencott, C., Heim, M., & Daly, L. (2002). Content design for virtual environments. In K. M. Stanney (Ed.), *Handbook of virtual environments* (pp. 519–532). Mahwah, NJ: Lawrence Erlbaum Associates.

Küller, R. (1977). Psycho-physiological conditions in theater construction. In J. F. Arnott, J. Chariau, & H. Huessmann (Eds.), *Theater space. An examination of the interaction between space, technology, performance and society* (pp. 158–180). Munich, Germany: Prestel.

Küller, R. (1991). Environmental assessment from a neuropsychological perspective. In T. Gärling & G. W. Evans (Eds.), *Environment, cognition, and action. An integrated approach* (pp. 110–147). New York: Oxford University Press.

Mahdjoubi, L. M. (2001). *An investigation of computer-generated architectural representations on design decision-tasks* [Online]. Doctoral dissertation, University of Newcastle upon Tyne, England. Available: http://pers-www.wlv.ac.uk/~me1970/phdprint/

Marsh, T., & Wright, P. (2000). Using cinematography conventions to inform guidelines for the design and evaluation of virtual off-screen space. In *Proceedings of AAAI 2000 Spring Symposium on 'Smart Graphics'* (pp. 123–127). Stanford, CA: AAAI Press.

May, J. G., & Badcock, D. R. (2002). Vision and virtual environments. In K. M. Stanney (Ed.), *Handbook of virtual environments* (pp. 29–63). Mahwah, NJ: Lawrence Erlbaum Associates.

Nasar, J. L. (1994). Urban design aesthetics: The evaluative qualities of building exteriors. *Environment and Behavior, 26,* 377–401.

Neale, D. C. (1996). Spatial perception in desktop virtual environments. In *Proceedings of the Human Factors and Ergonomics Society 40th annual meeting* (pp. 1117–1121). Santa Monica, CA: Human Factors and Ergonomics Society.

Neale, D. C. (1997). Factors influencing spatial awareness and orientation in desktop virtual environments. In *Proceedings of the Human Factors and Ergonomics Society 41st annual meeting* (pp. 1278–1282). Albuquerque, NM: Human Factors and Ergonomics Society.

Purcell, A. T. (1986). Environmental perception and affect: "A schema discrepancy model." *Environment and Behavior, 18,* 3–30.

Rohrmann, B., & Bishop, I. (2002). Subjective responses to computer simulations of urban environments. *Journal of Environmental Psychology, 22,* 319–331.

Roupé, M., Sunesson, K., Wernemyr, C., Westerdahl, B., & Allwood, C. M. (2001). Perceived meaning in virtual reality architectural models. In O. Tullberg, N. Dawood, & M. Connell (Eds.), *Applied virtual reality in engineering and construction* (ss. 117–127). *Proceedings of the conference AVR II and CONVR 2001 Conference on Applied Virtual Reality in Engineering & Construction Applications of Virtual Reality: Current Initiatives and Future Challenges.* University of Teesside och Chalmers University of Technology, Göteborg, Sweden.

Rouse, R. (1999). What's your perspective? *ACM SIGGRAPH Computer Graphics, 33*(3), 9–12.

Russell, J. A., & Lanius, U. F. (1984). Adaptation level and the affective appraisal of environments. *Journal of Environmental Psychology, 4,* 119–135.

Russell, J. A., & Snodgrass, J. (1987). Emotion and the environment. In D. Stokols & I. Altman (Eds.), *Handbook of environmental psychology* (pp. 245–280). New York: Wiley.

Scaife, M., & Rogers, Y. (1996). External cognition: How do graphical representations work? *International Journal of Human–Computer Studies, 45,* 185–213.

Sherman, W. R., & Craig, A. B. (2003). *Understanding virtual reality. Interface, application, and design.* San Francisco: Morgan Kaufmann.

Skog, D., & Söderlund, M. (1999). Virtual information representation. In *Proceedings of the 22nd Information Systems Research Seminar in Scandinavia (IRIS 22)* [Online]. Available: http://iris22.it.jyu.fi/iris22/pub/Skog_vir.pdf

Slater, M., Steed, A., & Chrysanthou, Y. (2002). *Computer graphics and virtual environments. From realism to real-time.* Harlow, England: Pearson Education.

Storms, R. L., & Zyda, M. J. (2000). Interactions in perceived quality of auditory-visual displays. *Presence: Teleoperators and Virtual Environments, 9,* 557–580.

Theatron Consortium. (2002). *Theatron. Theatre History in Europe: Architectural and Textual Resource Online.* Retrieved March 10, 2004, from http://www.theatron.org

Waller, D. (1999). Factors affecting the perception of interobject distances in virtual environments. *Presence: Teleoperators and Virtual Environments, 8,* 657–670.

Whyte, J. (2002). *Virtual reality and the built environment.* Oxford, England: Architectural Press.

Witmer, B. G., & Kline, P. B. (1998). Judging perceived and traversed distance in virtual environments. *Presence: Teleoperators and Virtual Environments, 7,* 144–167.

Part II

USING DIGITAL INFORMATION

Chapter 7

How the Format of Information Determines Our Processing: An IPP/CIP Perspective

H. J. M. (Tabachneck) Schijf
Utrecht University

Increasingly, we are confronted with having to process multimodal formats of information. In the past half-century, technology has pushed the development of hi-tech information presentation much faster than theory on processing such information could progress. This is not likely to change. As I argue, information processing psychology (IPP) and its successor, complex information processing (CIP), remain an excellent choice for spending scarce research monies, because they accomplish methodologically rigorous, reliable research on this subject that will lead to solid theory with predictive possibilities. Findings on the importance of external memory (in brief, human-recorded information) and its formats for processing information illustrate this.

Digital information is different in many ways from earlier printed formats. For instance, digital media offer many more ways of presenting information (*representational formats*) and offer an explosively larger quantity of information. The format of the external information turns out to have a profound influence on information processing. IPP's earlier findings about the human system, for example, about mechanisms (e.g., using heuristics) and limitations (e.g., of working memory), still hold, but the many internal structures and processes shaped by a task's external information are continually altering, adapting to new types of input. In spite of this, IPP/CIP, which emerged more than a half-century ago, can still help to shed light on how humans process multimedia information. In the context of explaining human behavior on a modern, multimedia task, this chapter discusses how such research is continuing to contribute to our knowledge. The discussion addresses behavior as processing and integrating information from various media, comparing behavior in various representations and forming mental models of the information, as well as behavior that is reactive to and interactive with the external information available for the task. As research shows, the format of the information available on an interface has a profound influence not only on supplying facts (declarative information), but also on supplying process steps (procedural information), as well as on formation and choice of strategies (metacognitive information).

First, I set out a contemporary hypermedia task and give examples of research in which the issues outlined earlier were addressed. A brief sketch of the theoretical principles and methodology then familiarize the reader with IPP's ways of thinking. The chapter ends with a brief summary and conclusion.

INSIGHTS ON PROCESSING A MULTIMEDIA TASK

In this section, I examine some insights into human information processing of behavior in multimedia tasks gained via IPP/CIP research. To situate the discussion and in order to give examples of particular behavior, I first construct a description of behavior on a multimedia task I happened to be working on while writing this chapter.

Information Processing on a Random Multimedia Task

Constructing a presentation slide in Microsoft PowerPoint is a task probably familiar to most of the readers of this book. My simple, run-of-the-mill PowerPoint slide consists of verbal text, a picture, and some interactive elements. I am about halfway finished constructing a lecture on the working of perceptual systems. My goals are to construct a new slide and to generate lecture notes to go with the information. To situate you a little, Fig. 7.1 shows the resulting slide (its truthfulness is not the point here), which consists of a discussion of the olfactory system.

In a real CIP study, I would have computer recorded my interaction with the computer and recorded on video my behavior, while generating a concurrent verbal report. In this simulation, I constructed the slide and wrote down what I was going to do just before executing it. For brevity, I have left out my errors and changes.

The Table of Events

Please take a quick look at the table in Fig. 7.2. This simple-sounding task actually has a lot of complexity and no clearly defined goals—the goals resemble more closely a set of constraints that could have been satisfied in

▶ **Olfactory System**

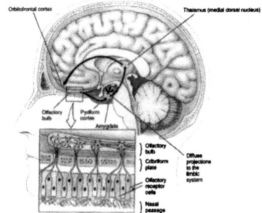

- Similar to all perception systems in:
  - receives outside info
  - converts it to electrical signal → cortical area
  - many receptor cells to one nerve cell
- Dissimilar in:
  - receives molecular content info
  - nerve cells are cortical cells
  - cortical cells renew

FIG. 7.1.   The olfactory system slide; arrows are not shown. From "Smell and the Olfactory System" by Lydia Kubiuk. Reprinted with permission. Source: www.sfn.com (Society for Neuroscience, brain briefings section). Permission obtained for use from the artist, Lydia Kibiuk.

any number of ways. Hence, this is a typical multimedia design task. Whether this time-sequential table of events is complete does not really matter. What matters is the *Gestalt* of the table, the way the types of processes alternate. Note that, also for brevity, the level of detail is not the same everywhere; for instance, in line 32, "Compare likely candidates" could be unpacked into a whole table itself, whereas line 5, "click 'insert' " is a single, very specific act.

The codes in the right-hand column indicate the likely most-used modality of this process. "A" stands for auditory, mostly verbal, "V" for visual; and "M" for motoric. Dual letters indicate mixed processes. In the five leftmost columns, the events have been categorized as to their likely main source of information.

The table in Fig. 7.2 only covers entering the slide's title and finding and inserting an appropriate visual. The task was continued by constructing a set of arrows that can be made visible one by one to point out relevant parts of the picture while explaining the workings of the olfactory system. Next, the text was constructed and typed in, and finally, the lecture notes were constructed and typed in.

Note that the events in Fig. 7.2 have been divided into episodes with triple lines; an episode starts with the setting or recall of a goal and stops when that goal has been satisfied (more about this later). Were I to construct a

INT	INT→EM	INT&EM	EM→INT	to-M	THE TABLE OF EVENTS	
	■				1. Remember: Last slide is finished. and thus, a new slide needs to be inserted.	A
■					2. Make goal: Insert new slide.	V
■					3. Search for and find main menu bar.	V
		■			4. Scan main menu for useful term and recognize "insert".	VA
				■	5. Click "insert".	M
		■			6. Scan insert menu for useful term and recognize "new slide".	VA
				■	7. Click "new slide".	M
		■			8. Scan Autolayout menu and recognize needed Autolayout (text and picture).	VA
	■				9. Recognize that menu items need to be clicked to be activated.	V
				■	10. Click needed Autolayout (mixed visual-verbal) Clip Art and Text.	M
		■			11. Survey slide: Title bar empty.	V
		■			12. Recognize that empty title bar requires filling with topic	VA
■					13. Make goal to fill title bar with topic.	A
	■				14. Retrieve topic of new slide from layout previously written down: olfactory system.	A
				■	15. Type in "olfactory system" in title bar PowerPoint slide.	M
		■			16. Survey slide: Clip Art square empty.	V
		■			17. Recognize that empty Clip Art square requires filling with appropriate visual.	V
■					18. Make goal to search for visual.	A
	■				19. Recall: You have been successful using Google for finding visuals before.	A
■					20. Search for and find icon for web engine on desktop computer (here, Netscape).	V
				■	21. Click on icon (this brings up search engine (here, Google.) on the home page).	M
	■				22. Recall: There is an item in Google that will bring up visuals, named "images".	A
		■			23. Search for and find "images" above search window.	VA
				■	24. Click "images".	M
■					25. Retrieve subtopic from WM.	A
			■		26. Type in the subtopic, "olfactory system" as search keyword in the search window.	M
			■		27. Scan search window for what to do next and recognize "search".	VA
				■	28. Click "search".	M
		■			29. Survey the resulting mini-images for a usable visual.	V
		■			30. Recognize that menu items need to be clicked to be activated.	V
				■	31. Click on and view likely candidate.	M
		■			32. Compare likely candidates (details here omitted).	VA
		■			33. Decide on best image for purpose: schematic image of the olfactory system.	VA
■					34. Recall: You first have to save the visual to your computer before you can use it.	A
■					35. Make goal to save picture to own computer.	A
	■				36. Recall: Right-clicking an image will provide a menu with items.	MA
				■	37. Right-click on image.	M
		■			38. Survey menu for usable terms and recognize "save image as".	VA
				■	39. Click on "save image as".	M
■					40. Retrieve from WM the local name of image: olfactory system.	A
				■	41. Type in "olfactory system" in box provided.	M
		■			42. Recognize your way through local file structure, remember where you need to go.	A
			■		43. Click on correct folder until destination has been clicked on.	M
			■		44. Search box for next thing to do; find "save" in box.	VA
				■	45. Click "save".	M
		■			46. Survey slide: Clip Art square empty.	V
		■			47. Recognize that empty Clip Art square requires filling with appropriate visual.	V
■					48. Make goal to insert visual into the empty square.	A
			■		49. Read instruction to "double-click" on Clip Art box.	V

FIG. 7.2. *(Continued)*.

INT	INT→EM	INT&EM	EM→INT	toEM	THE TABLE OF EVENTS	
				■	50. Double-click on Clip Art box.	M
			■		51. Survey menu that comes up for usable terms and recognize "import clips".	VA
				■	52. Click on "import clips".	M
		■			53. Recognize your way through local file structure to image on own computer, remember where you need to go.	A
				■	54. Click on appropriate folder/file name until file has been reached.	M
			■		55. Read description of empty textbox "description of this clip".	A
				■	56. Type "olfactory system" into "description of this clip".	M
			■		57. Scan box for useful terms for next action and recognize "ok" button.	VA
				■	58. Click "ok" and Click "ok" (result: image appears on slide).	M
			■		59. Notice that image is too small for available space.	V
■					60. Recall: To do anything with an image you need to click on it.	MV
				■	61. Click on image.	M
			■		62. Notice small "grabbing" squares on corners of image.	V
			■		63. Recognize these are for changing size of image.	V
				■	64. Click down on corner; drag diagonally down until space is filled. Click up.	MV
			■		65. Survey slide: Remember that visual will need explaining in college.	VA
	■				66. Make goal to construct notes to go with the visual.	A
			■		67. Make subgoal: Construct arrows on the visual to point at the part under discussion.	VA
■					68. Gather info: Search notes for info on olfactory systems (details omitted).	A
			■		69. Find info ass. with topic: search verbal and visual memory on olfactory system.	VA
				■	70. Note down usable info on parts and path on notes page in PowerPoint.	A

Due to lack of space, the table has been truncated here.

LEGEND:
Circling arrows on both sides of a set of grayed rows combined with centered text indicate iterative behavior.
Bold-edged rows: goals.
Triple bold line: divides one episode from the next.
INT: within the internal representation; processes mostly within the brain.
INT→EM: mostly top down processes: search driven by working memory (WM) (e.g., by a mental model) and attention, to match what is in the external memory (EM) to what is in WM.
EM&INT: processes driven equally bottom up by the EM and top down by WM contents.
EM→INT: mostly bottom up recognition processes: matching of information perceived from the EM to information in long-term memory (LTM) or WM.
toEM: to external memory, direct interaction processes providing instructions to the computer.
Codes in right-hand column: A=mostly auditory (verbal); V=mostly visual; M=mostly motoric.

FIG. 7.2. The table of events.

problem-behavior graph of this task execution, then (as there were no errors) the conclusion of each episode would bring me further to the right, toward the final goal. Most subgoals that have a reach of only one or two rows have been left out for brevity.

Five categories of where information to run the process is likely to come from have been distinguished and are distributed throughout the table. The first is INT, from within the internal representation, mostly within the brain. The second is INT→EM, from WM (mental model) and attention, attempting a WM→EM match (top down). In these first two categories, internal information has the most influence. The third is INT&EM, processes driven equally bottom up from EM and top down by WM contents, mainly goal-driven and mental-model-driven search. The fourth category is EM→INT, mostly bottom-up recognition processes: an EM→LTM/WM match. Three of the episodes begin with these processes, looking for something to trigger the next goal. The fifth category is toEM, external memory, direct interaction processes providing information to the EM device, such as writing, keystrokes, and mouse clicks.

The Role of EM in Tasks Using Digital Multimedia Information

Now that an example multimedia task has been set out, I provide some insight into information processing in multimedia tasks, particularly with respect to the role the EM plays therein, using descriptions of a few IPP/CIP experiments and the previous task description as illustrations. However, first I address a few preliminaries: definitions and methodological issues.

Preliminaries

Definition—Representation. By *representation*, or rather, a *representational format*, I mean: "a *format* for recording, storing and presenting information together with a set of *operators* for modifying the information" (Tabachneck [-Schijf] & Simon, 1996, p. 29). For example, in arithmetic the format consists of data (numbers) and precise ways to order them on paper; operators would be adding, subtracting, multiplying, and so on. Both components are needed, and often a representation also includes constraints on operators (also called *rules*). Information can be translated from one representational format to another, though this is usually an effortful business. For instance, numerical data can be presented in a table, as a graph, or in sets of equations. Note that there can be internal as well as external representational formats. It is the latter, and their influence on the former, that are of interest here.

Definition—External Memory (EM). Newell and Simon (1972) proposed that there are three aspects of the task environment that should be kept distinct. There is the environment itself (the external representation), the internal representation of the environment as used by the subject (also called the *mental model*), and the theorist's objective description of that environment, called the *problem space* (this term is currently also used to denote that part of memory a person uses to execute a particular task). A special part of the external representation is EM, which consists of information recorded elsewhere than in our own brain but, potentially, available for processing:

on external materials, such as rocks, books, and computers, in artifacts, but also in other people's memories. It is the format of the EM, and its accessibility, that the digital revolution has changed so much. Think of hypertext, interactive multimodality, and the use of search terms for indexing and finding information. Generating and characterizing old and new representational formats, and finding out how people process such formats and combinations of formats, is essential in examining task execution in complex, multimodal formats.

Methodology: Comparing Behavior in Multiple Representations. The format of EM has a strong influence on how we process information. Hence, an important question in multimedia processing research is which advantages and disadvantages different representations have for carrying out particular tasks. Therefore, one wants to be able to compare the relative merits of different representational formats. A CIP methodology does this by constructing the information in the different representations to be informationally equivalent (i.e., all the information available in one representation is available in the other). Having eliminated differences in informational content, the differences in behavior can be assigned to computational differences of the two representations: the differences in types and amounts of processing that need to be done to do the same task in both. However, that is only a valid assumption if people are indeed using the representation offered to them externally, internally as well. This is one of the issues examined in Tabachneck(-Schijf) (1992). In this study, effects of visual, verbal, mathematical, and recognition-based thinking processes on problem solving were investigated in different data formats (tabular, algebraic, and graphical), which were informationally equivalent. The task is a common learning task taken from an introductory college economics class. It was concluded that the subjects were all internally processing the same representations that they were exposed to externally. This is an especially strong finding, because the subjects were all quite familiar with the different representations, and all possessed the capacity to translate between them, especially because the problems were very simple. Yet, this did not happen.

Offloading WM: Externalizing Information Can Help

How could I pick up many of the goals in the table in Fig. 7.2? How was I able to find the menu items and much other visual information I needed to progress with my task? The answer is in the EM→INT rows: because the information I needed was available right on the interface. It was externalized. On the other hand, other episodes start with goals that I had to pull from my memory (INT rows). That information was not externalized on the interface; I had to internalize it, taking up valuable WM space, and perhaps necessitating long-term memory (LTM) recording.

Zhang and Norman (1994) and Zhang (1997), looking for better descriptions of representational formats, searched for sources of difficulty in problems other than those found in problem space differences:

> The basic finding is that different representations of a problem can have dramatic impact on problem difficulty even if the formal structures are the same. One characteristic of these problems is that they all require the processing of both internal and external information. However, most of these studies either exclusively focused on internal representations, or, when taking external representations into account, failed to separate them from internal representations. (Zhang & Norman, p. 89)

Framed as "distributed processing," Zhang and Norman pulled processing to be done apart into requiring internal (INT, INT→EM) and external (EM→INT) representation involvement. Comparing informationally equivalent representations, a significant source of difficulty turned out to be WM capacity (five subsources were identified), as already predicted by Simon and colleagues a decade earlier (e.g., Simon, Kotovsky, & Hayes, 1989). Zhang and Norman's research shows that, the more a person can offload WM by using externalized information, the easier solving a problem becomes. Multimedia offers many different opportunities not only for externalizing static information, but also for externalizing organization of information, search help, and dynamic processes in many perceptual modes. However, externalizing information's biggest advantage, not having to learn it, comes at a cost: It indeed is not learned, making one dependent on the availability of the information to continue the task. It can make task performance brittle (e.g., Mayes, Draper, McGregor, & Oatley, 1988; Van Nimwegen, Van Oostendorp, Tabachneck(-Schijf), & Van Vugt, 2003).

Larkin and Simon (1987) also found externalization of information to be one of the most important advantages of certain pictorial over certain verbal information. The authors examined problem solving in two informationally equivalent representations, a sentential one and a diagrammatic one. For instance, one problem concerned figuring out how a pulley arrangement works. The diagrammatic representation showed an arrangement of three pulleys, two weights, and four ropes. The sentential representation consisted of a rather long list noting the parts and relations between them. The pros of the diagrammatic representation were: The information could be much more efficiently searched because it was ordered by location, and the needed information for an operator to apply was explicitly available (i.e., externalized), unlike in the sentential representation, where one first had to construct a mental model looking much like the diagrammatic representation, a WM-clogging action. The pictorial EM provided a static mental model on which the processing could take place.

An interesting modeling architecture developed especially for examining WM issues, initially in reading but now also in other tasks such as spatial reasoning and mental modeling, making it suitable for multimedia tasks, is CAPS (cf., e.g., Hegarty, 2000; Just & Carpenter, 1992). CAPS is in its fourth version now, 4CAPS, and includes explanations of data obtained through MRI studies (e.g., Just, Carpenter, & Varma, 1999).

External Memory Can Store Information, But Also Drive Processing

The table in Fig. 7.2 shows that my processing is very interactive with the EM: the digital multimedia information provided by the computer, as well as some nondigital information. I use available information, cause changes to the EM (toEM), and react to the newly emerging information by recognizing elements (EM→INT) that may start new processes. An episode is often started by an EM→INT process, meaning that external information drives the startup of this series of associated events, including formation of the goals. In summary, I could not have done this task without information from EM, and that holds for the great majority of tasks.

EM Information Is Important for a Great Many Tasks. Larkin (1989) coined the term *display-based problem solving* for the process outlined earlier, but terms like *interactive, reactive,* and *recognition driven* refer to something similar. Larkin observed people in everyday tasks like making coffee in a variety of coffeepots and under various circumstances. Some coffeepots were entirely transparent so that the state of all their parts could be viewed (i.e., externalized), some were entirely opaque so that the state of their parts had to be known (i.e., internalized), and some were a combination of the two. People tried to make coffee with or without interruptions with these various types of coffee machines, with, as you can imagine, various levels of success. As a hypothesis, a computer model named DiBS (display-based solver) was constructed. DiBS uses external objects as the major component of its data structure. The EM itself offers the cues to move the problem solving along. Looking at an object and recognizing its features triggers productions that take another process step. DiBS uses means-end analysis to solve impasses and remove blockages. DiBS predicted that the more features of the state were visible, the more error-proof and interruption-proof the problem solving would be—and this prediction was correct.

Besides the fact that the EM provided data elements here, I want to emphasize that the EM also pushed problem solving ahead by supplying goals, and served as an indicator of where one was in the process. Still, it is important to realize that learning is required to be able to "recognize" what the display state is "signaling." A reservoir looks empty only because you know it can be filled. Problem solving often is a continuous see-recognize-act cycle, interrupted and completed by internal processing where needed, and supplemented by internal knowledge.

In digital multimedia information processing, the role played by the EM in processing is becoming more and more important as the possibilities to express and externalize information increase. For many tasks, this can potentially lighten processing loads considerably.

EM information is not only important for relative novices; it also turns out to be crucial for expert behavior. CaMeRa (Tabachneck[-Schijf], Leonardo, & Simon, 1997) emulates the behavior of an economics expert who was asked to explain economics principles to a novice student. The model explicates the nature of his expertise, which was very much dependent on EM to explain such principles, drawing a graph while supplying verbal explanations. Interaction with and reactivity to the EM, as well as frequent interweaving of multimodal component processing, is thus inherent in the architecture of CaMeRa. The model is based on separate and different but interactive visual and verbal representations, and employs both a parallel network to be able to be truly reactive to external (emerging) elements, and a rule-based architecture to supply verbal reasoning and occasionally patch holes in the recognition-based visual reasoning.

Summarizing, being able to use many recognition elements in reasoning lowers computational loads. In addition, storing information in LTM so it can be recognized requires much less time than encoding it so it can be actively remembered (Anderson, 2000; Simon, 1979). Much of our memory consists of material usable for recognition only. Not only can declarative information be cued, but procedural information can similarly be recognized. When external information cues the order of steps, one does not have to learn many plans either, saving both WM capacity and LTM-encoding costs (O'Hara & Payne, 1998, 1999), the cost naturally being another source of task-performance brittleness.

If EM Lacks Information, Fall Back on LTM-Supplied Mental Models

***Definition of* Mental Model.**   Having a mental model of a task means, at some level, having an idea of how the task is to be done. Mental models are concrete rather than abstract; they are constructed as needed in WM from information available internally and externally. Most mental models are only partially correct and incomplete: They are probably only as correct and complete as we need them to be to reasonably, reliably execute the task at hand. Even mostly incorrect models can still support correct task execution, as long as the incorrectness is never challenged in the task (Bruer, 1994; Tabachneck[-Schijf], 1992). I can have a completely incorrect model of car mechanics and still use it to successfully drive the car. The mental model would certainly be challenged if I tried to fix the car.

Mental models of multimedia tasks are by definition multimodal, and more likely dynamic and "runnable" than static. A mental model can be run in its entirety or in parts, as it is needed to perform the task. The latter is much more likely, because both constructing and running mental models hogs WM capacity. Mental models are most suited to providing qualitative inferences. Because mental models are based on a build-up of experiential knowledge, along with external information, they are strictly individual and the parts to be run are most likely task specific.

Note the INT, INT→EM, and INT&EM rows in Fig. 7.2 and what comes after and before them. Often, things I recall push the processing along, and I recall and recognize things as I get information from the interface. Clearly, I have a mental model running as needed in the background, filling in missing information from the EM. Reciprocally, the information in the EM fills in the mental-model gaps. My mental model is not perfect or complete: For instance, I recall that it is possible to perform some task, but have to search the interface for ways to perform it.

Effects of Constructing and Running Multimodal Mental Models. Running complex mental models requires much WM capacity (e.g., Hegarty, 2000), hence use and capacities of working memory arise as significant factors in this research. Current theories (e.g., Baddeley, 1986; Kosslyn, 1980, 1994) hold that information that is in different perceptual modes (visual, auditory, olfactory, etc.) is processed by different components of WM, though a "central executive" part is involved in all, coordinating the efforts of the specialized components. Thus, one should be able to process more information in multimodal mental models at the same time than in a single-mode mental model. Research generally holds this to be true only for very simple information. For complex information, there is the extra overhead of trying to integrate the two modes (e.g., Tabachneck[-Schijf] et al., 1997; Tardieu & Gyselinck, 2003; and many others).

Summarizing, there are (at least) two main effects of building up multimodal mental models. First, constructing a new mental model while integrating information in multiple modes takes extra effort; however, it has been shown that elaboration of this type can result in the bonus of better memory and more flexible problem solving. Second, building up a mental model with the aid of EM takes less effort than doing so without. Hegarty and Just (1993) and Hegarty (2000) found just this on a multimedia task combining text and visuals. Students of various ages were shown rope-and-pulley systems of varying complexity, and were asked to predict what happens elsewhere in the system if a handle is turned or a rope is pulled (testing kinetics comprehension). Later, they were asked questions about the configuration of the system. To compute the outcome, the students mentally moved the system. Hegarty and Just compared comprehension outcomes if subjects were given only a diagram, only a text, or a combination of the two. Results were that presentation mode did not matter for configuration questions, but that the combination facilitated comprehension. Moreover, presentation mode had a strong influence on reading time. Subjects took four times as long to read the text as they did to view the diagram. The combination's time was exactly between these two times. Studying eye-movement protocols along with videotape data and concurrent verbal protocols, Hegarty and Just concluded that the extra time to study the text alone was a result of trying to build up a mental model of the diagram—without that, kinetics questions could not be answered. The buildup exceeded WM limits, therefore necessitating time-costly updating using the EM.

Modeling Multimedia Mental Modeling. Hegarty (2000) described an effective implementation of her theory using the 3CAPS production system architecture, which is especially suited to modeling WM-capacity effects. On a different theoretical tack, Payne (1988) advocated extending the problem-space construct to build up and run mental models, using a dual space: a goal space, modeling "all the meaningful objects and possible states of the task domain," and a device space, modeling "all meaningful objects and states of the device" (p. 81). In addition, the user must construct a semantic mapping between the two spaces. Unfortunately, Payne did not implement his ideas in a computer model, but only theoretically discussed them.

Summarizing, mental models form an effective addition to EM information and are almost always dependent on that information. However, three problems result from building mental models. First, the more complex the task, the more complex the mental model, and the more WM capacity is needed to construct and run it. This, of course, interacts with expertise: the less expertise, the worse the problem. Second, the more modes the information is in, the more linking of information is needed to integrate it. This is especially true if there is different information in those different modes. Finally, these two add up: The more there is of both, the more likely that performance will break down, and the more likely that good EM design will aid performance.

The Role of EM in Metacognitive Processing

Process step ordering, strategizing, and monitoring the task execution are all examples of metacognitive abilities, long recognized to be an important factor in successful learning and problem solving (e.g., Bruer, 1994).

These tasks are called "metacognitive" because they appear to run one level higher than the problem-solving processes themselves. One would thus think that these processes are mainly run with internal information. However, choosing strategies appears to be at least partly EM dependent, and many other metacognitive skills may be as well.

In the multimedia task's table in Fig. 7.2, some EM→INT processes are shown as instantiations of strategies. For instance, if we are looking for a particular operation that we know the program can carry out, it is a good idea to scan the menus (e.g., line 4) and, if a window pops up, we should probably scan its contents (e.g., line 27). Monitoring is going on in the background, evidenced, for instance, by the fact that I realized at some point (line 67) that coordinating the visual with the lecture a bit more dynamically would be a nice thing. Actually, I ran a mental model "using the slide in a lecture" and "saw" the lack—certainly EM dependent—I could never have managed that feat without the slide as WM support. Furthermore, there is a definite ordering in the task's process steps: First I do the visual, then the text, and then the animation of both, suggesting planning. But this order was partly determined by the EM, for example, the choice of slide type was internally determined, but "first the visual" is an EM-driven, culturally determined "natural," because the visual was on the left-hand side and, in the West, people read from left to right. Next I present some examples from CIP literature on the role of EM in metacognitive processing.

Strategizing and EM Involvement.   Forming, picking, and using a strategy often appears to be driven by the way in which a problem is presented (e.g., Lemaire & Siegler, 1995; Tabachneck[-Schijf], Koedinger, & Nathan, 1995). A *strategy* is a way to attack a problem. Strategies run from very general (e.g., weak methods like means-end analysis) to very specific (e.g., add all the numbers in the rightmost column first when adding a set of numbers in a decimal representation). It stands to reason that, the more specific a strategy is, the more dependent it is on EM. For instance, regarding multimedia a problem will trigger different strategies if it is presented in a verbal than in an algebraic format (Tabachneck[-Schijf] et al., 1995); if it is presented in a graphical format one uses different strategies than if it is presented in tables (Tabachneck[-Schijf], 1992).

Extra WM Capacity for Expert Behavior, Shaped by External Information

Puzzling were findings that some people could remember over 100 four-digit numbers in minutes, or 10 or more three-course restaurant orders at a time without writing anything down, or, for that matter, could handle the complexity of chess or medical diagnosis in real time. In fact, how can anyone process language so quickly? Any of these tasks alone should quickly overrun our limited WM, not to mention combinations thereof that occur in multimedia information processing. It is now theorized that people, in the course of becoming experts on such tasks, cope with such demands by building special LTM memory structures (Chase & Ericsson, 1981; Staszewski, 1987). These were later dubbed "long-term working memory" (LT-WM; Ericsson & Kintsch, 1995). LT-WM consists of specialized retrieval structures that can be imagined as empty sets of hierarchically arranged slots. LT-WM is like WM in that these slots can be accessed, filled, and used for retrieval at the same speed as WM. It is unlike WM because its structures take considerable time to build up, its capacity can be built up to a greater degree than WM, and, importantly, it is more specific: The LT-WM structures only work for the one type of information they were built for. It is hypothesized that information is slotted using a discrimination network where a few categorical decisions put it in the "correct" slot (Chase & Ericsson). Perhaps no other types of information will fit because the network is very specific. Importantly, Ericsson and Kintsch hypothesized that there is nothing really special about LT-WM structures; in fact, they are ubiquitous, that is, all language-competent people have formed such structures for processing language. If Ericsson and Kintsch are right, while executing a multimedia task, we use such LT-WM structures at least for interacting with language, both written and spoken, and probably for standard computer interactions.

Offloading WM: Constructing New EM Formats

Constructing a new representational format is even more difficult than describing a representational format, because we have to figure out not only the description of the old format, but also why it apparently does not work very well. To do that, we have to find exactly what all the elements of the problem space are, and which tasks need to be accomplished using that format. Cheng and his colleagues have set out to find new diagrammatic representations for tasks that humans historically have had many problems with, such as carrying out computations regarding energy conservation, electricity, and probability (e.g., Cheng, 2002; Cheng, Cupit, & Shadbolt, 2001; Cheng, Lowe, & Scaife, 2001; Cheng & Simon, 1992). The representations resulting from their new systematic approach are called *law-encoding diagrams* (LEDs). These diagrams are designed to externalize precisely that information needed to carry out the needed computations, and thus to further understanding. In the process, many descriptive variables have been discovered as well.

IPP/CIP AND MULTIMEDIA INFORMATION: A GOOD COMBINATION

IPP is an old theory-building methodology: It was developed in the late 1950s as a reaction both to the omissions of behaviorism and to the emergence of a new technology: the computer (Newell & Simon, 1972). Although IPP's first goal was to find human information-processing limiting factors, its practitioners quickly realized that looking for ways that humans adapted to cope with these limits, and still reasonably efficiently and effectively process information, would also be profitable. Gradually, however, it became clear that even these two sets of factors together could not produce programs that would do significant problem solving, such as playing chess (Feigenbaum, 1989). IPP/CIP had by then begun to concentrate on characterizing the influence of the environment on how information can be processed, in particular on how presentation of information influences its processing. It evolved into complex information processing (CIP), to reflect its adaptation to more complex tasks and, in relation to that, its shift to studying the task environment in at least as much detail as it studied the human system (Klahr & Kotovsky, 1989). It is this shift in attention to effects of external information that makes it still applicable today, in combination with its sound methodology.

IPP was built on three ideas: the decomposability of the human system, the characterization of thought as computation, and the computer as symbol manipulator, just like the human. The human system was cast as a hierarchical, complex, decomposable combination of simple parts that are each easy to define. The system is "nearly" decomposable, because there is information exchanged between the parts, which means they are not completely independent (Simon, 1981). Newell and Simon (1972) characterized thought as computation with elementary elements, allowing comparison with computations carried out by a computer. According to Simon (1981): "A man, viewed as a behaving system, is quite simple. The apparent complexity of his behavior over time is largely a reflection of the complexity of the environment in which he finds himself" (p. 65). The crux of this hypothesis is that it is the environment that is complex, not the human. Thus, complexity in behavior arises from a nearly decomposable system consisting of relatively simple parts dealing with or reacting to a complex environment.

Hence, the first goal of IPP was to determine those simple human parts: the mechanisms and limitations causing particular task-performance behavior. (Space limitations prohibit a full discussion of all the findings generated by the early IPP research; for summaries of earlier findings, see Klahr & Kotovsky, 1989; Newell, 1990; Newell & Simon, 1972; Simon, 1979, 1989.) Of course, when examining and explaining human behavior, we must take into account the pros and cons of such general mechanisms as working memory, long-term memory and their limitations; general coping factors, such as the use of heuristic methods and heuristic search strategies for problem solving; the use of "chunking" to abstract and organize information into meaningful units; and the tendency to keep subject areas apart so that different types of knowledge do not interfere with each other.

Almost as a side effect of their search for simple human parts, Newell and Simon (1972) also wanted to precisely describe the task environment: As variability in behavior is caused partly by demands of the task environment and partly by the sources of variation in the human system, the better one can describe the former, and factor them out as a source of the variation in human behavior, the better one can describe the latter. This turned out to be a very beneficial side effect.

To accomplish their goals, IPP theorists coined four theoretical methods (Newell & Simon, 1972): for recording traces of internal processes, for cleanly defining the task environment, for encoding the behavior within the task environment, and for constructing the theory for the behavior. Following are brief discussions of these four theoretical constructs that, with extensions, are still suited today for theory building on the processing of multimedia information.

Recording Fine-Grained Traces of Internal Processes

IPP needed fine-grained data that provided insight into internal processes. For this, the method of obtaining data by recording concurrent verbal reports was developed (for details, see Ericsson & Simon, 1993). In short, the subject is trained to report information that passes through working memory while doing the task. Concurrent verbal reports is still a good method, but to examine information processing of multimedia information, additional data-gathering methodology will need to be developed. Verbal reports are impoverished as to visual-spatial and motoric process cues, because such processing does not leave many verbal traces. In CIP, other data-gathering methods are used in addition to concurrent verbal reports, such as video recording, collecting eye-movement protocols, recording all motoric interactions with the computer, and retrospective reporting. Concurrent verbal protocols can also be supplemented by other knowledge-elicitation techniques (see, e.g., Burton, Shadbolt, Hedgecoch, & Rugg, 1988; Olson & Biolsi, 1991).

Defining the Task Environment

Newell and Simon (1972) wanted to describe the task environment in an objective, abstract manner that could be applied to any problem-solving sit-

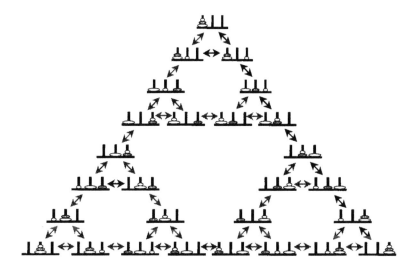

FIG. 7.3.   The problem space for the three-disk Tower of Hanoi. The top node is the initial state, the rightmost lower corner the goal. All rules and constraints have been instantiated: The nodes represent all possible legal states and the edges represent all possible legal moves. The most efficient path is indicated by the black arrows.

uation. Problem spaces (PSs) resulted; these are directed graphs[1] that consist of (a) a set of elements representing knowledge states (the nodes), (b) a set of operators, processes that can produce a new knowledge state (the edges), (c) an initial state of knowledge (top node), (d) a problem, stated as a goal to be reached by application of operators to states, and (e) the total knowledge available to the problem solver when he or she is in a given knowledge state, including heuristic problem-solving processes and search strategies (Newell & Simon, 1972, p. 810). Figure 7.3 shows the first four elements of the PS for a three-disk Tower of Hanoi (ToH) puzzle; the fifth is individual.

The most efficient solution to the ToH problem corresponds to the shortest path through the PS from start to goal. Both deviations from this path and the length of time spent on each step give cues to psychological mechanisms and limitations. In addition, the size of the PS, the branching factor, and the depth of the space are good predictors of the difficulty of a problem, though by far not the only ones, as PSs abstract away from the problem's representational format.

In theory, a PS can be constructed for any task. However, PSs become more complex as the number of nodes and edges increase (compare PSs

---

[1]A graph (mathematical) is a collection of points (nodes) and lines (edges). In a directed graph, all edges are one way.

for the three-disk ToH and for chess, which is finite but extremely large), but it is even more problematic when a goal cannot be clearly defined, as in many design tasks including design of multimedia information. Then, PSs become intractable. Still, as was seen in Fig. 7.2, one can define a goal as a number of constraints to satisfy, and then, after ordering them, satisfy the constraints one by one; one can also define data formats, operators, and rules.

Encode the Behavior Within the Task Environment

To relate a behavioral trace to the task's PS, problem-behavior graphs (PBGs) were invented. These show subjects' step-by-step progress toward the goal, using symbol structures, expressing time horizontally and progress toward the goal vertically. Because PBGs only represent one subject's behavior, and thus only one path through the PS at a time, they can be constructed for all types of problem solving (Newell & Simon, 1972), including highly complex and intractable PSs such as those for digital multimedia information tasks. The PBG for my PowerPoint slide design would not be very interesting: Going down as time progressed, progress is continually to the right, toward the goal. Had I included all my errors, it would have been much more interesting. The behavior, going down, would still have steadily progressed rightward toward the goal, but now interleaved with many steps back, to the left.

Constructing a Theory Format to Describe the Behavior

Computer modeling was chosen as the theory format. For this, Newell and Simon (1972) first invented list languages, and later settled on production systems. The recorded information processing within the task environment (complete with flawed behavior) was accounted for by constructing a program (the theory) that included more mechanisms and limits of the human processing system as research discovered them. Computer modeling demands very precise and operational definitions, and allows little hand waving; in addition, in the production-system format, such theory is relatively easy to construct and to understand. It is suited to model behavior with multimedia content: Computer programs are very expressive, capable of modeling a large range of multimodal behavior (e.g., Hegarty, 2000; Larkin, 1989). Extensions using other modeling environments such as neural networks also have a place in CIP, especially to model perceptual reactivity to the environment. The addition of a small parallel distributed processing network to the rule-based program in CaMeRa is an example (Tabachneck[-Schijf] et al., 1997). However, neural networks and other such mathematical, statistical modeling should be kept understandable for humans. Explanations that cannot be understood are of questionable value.

CONCLUSION

The ant's path is to the beach as our processing path is to the multifaceted formats of information.

On IPP/CIP and Multimedia Information Processing

CIP, in my opinion, still offers many features that make research on digital, multimedia information processing worthwhile even though it is rather time consuming, especially when its methodology is extended to other data-gathering and theorizing methods. Looking at human information processing of multimedia information with CIPs thorough methodology, and constructing computer programs to explain the behavior and predict behavior on other tasks, is bound to steadily and reliably increase our knowledge. As CIP studies are quite detailed, many more results ensue than with simple studies, giving high-quality information on the entire information-processing experience, and warranting the time spent on them.

On the Findings for Information Processing in Multimedia Representations

All the previous findings appear to point to a single theme: Representations are better—that is, computations in those representations are easier—as more of the work of the processing is offloaded from working memory to other constructs (external memory and long-term working memory) and as costly encoding into LTM at the level of active remembering is avoided. EM, coupled with recognition-level LTM information, offers the most important source of relief:

1. EM can be used as extended memory for static information by recording any type of information on it that we can express, either temporarily or permanently.

2. EM can be used to aid processes:

- By providing goals and pushing processing by triggering recognition, thus activating needed elements to keep a process going, obviating much of the need to encode goals and process steps in LTM and relieving use of WM.

- By serving as a placeholder, because, often, the EM's state can provide feedback as to where one was in the process. This is important because, when a task is suddenly interrupted, placeholder information is often not recorded in WM.
- By serving as a summary of a whole process.

3. EM can provide cues for forming a representation-specific strategy and for choosing a specific strategy.

Recording information on the EM, and carrying out tasks using EM is thus often very advantageous, but there are always costs as well:

1. EM information must have counterparts in LTM to be useful, such as a link to semantics to recognize it, and steps that are missing in EM in a process. For some tasks, those semantics are trivial, but for others, such as for more abstract representations like mathematical languages, graphs, or schemata, they take considerable time to acquire. Here is where re-representing information so that learning semantics can be minimized, such as in the research of Cheng and colleagues (Cheng, 2002; Cheng, Cupit, & Shadbolt, 2001; Cheng, Lowe, & Scaife, 2001; Cheng & Simon, 1992), really pays off, and where considering encoding in a different format could possibly be a big gain.

2. The most important cost of recording information in EM is that we are dependent on its continued existence to be able to use it. As this dependence becomes greater (and who does not depend on the contents of their computer and the World Wide Web?) task performance will become more brittle (Van Nimwegen et al., 2003).

In conclusion, the format of the external information is extremely important to the ease and speed of multimedia task execution. Indeed, like the ant's path is for a large part determined by the shape of the sand on the beach, so is our processing path for a large part determined by the shape of the information. Already in the small task I set out, this is obvious. I think the most pressing needs in multimedia information processing are: (a) to try to find out which representations, alone or in combination, are the most suited to encoding information with which we are going to carry out tasks, (b) to do this for declarative and procedural information as well as information to aid shaping metacognitive knowledge, and (c) to do more research on how one can most efficiently create EM recordings that aid task execution in these three categories. These are large, complex tasks, but I feel there is an excellent possibility that the different formats that multimodal, digital information offer can be exploited to a much greater extent. I feel that the rigor and systematic approach of extended CIP methodology have a lot to offer in unraveling the complexities.

REFERENCES

Anderson, J. R. (2000). *Cognitive psychology and its implications* (5th ed.). New York: Worth.

Baddeley, A. D. (1986). *Working memory.* Oxford, England: Clarendon Press.

Bruer, J. T. (1994). *Schools for thought: A science of learning in the classroom.* Cambridge, MA: MIT Press.

Burton, A. M., Shadbolt, N. R., Hedgecoch, A. P., & Rugg, G. (1988). A form evaluation of knowledge elicitation techniques for expert systems: Domain 1. In D. S. Moralee (Ed.), *Research and development in expert systems IV* (pp. 136–145). Cambridge, England: Cambridge University Press.

Chase, W. G., & Ericsson, K. A. (1981). Skilled memory. In J. R. Anderson (Ed.), *Cognitive skills and their acquisition* (pp. 141–190). Hillsdale, NJ: Lawrence Erlbaum Associates.

Cheng, P. C. H. (2002). Electrifying diagrams for learning: Principles for complex representational systems. *Cognitive Science, 6,* 685–736.

Cheng, P. C. H., Cupit, J., & Shadbolt, N. R. (2001). Supporting diagrammatic knowledge acquisition: An ontological analysis of Cartesian graphs. *International Journal of Human Computer Studies, 54,* 457–494.

Cheng, P. C. H., Lowe, R. K., & Scaife, M. (2001). Cognitive science approaches to understanding diagrammatic representations. *A.I. Review, 15,* 79–94.

Cheng, P. C. H., & Simon, H. A. (1992). The right representation for discovery: Finding the conservation of momentum. In D. Sleeman & P. Edwards (Eds.), *Machine learning: Proceedings of the 9th International Conference (ML92)* (pp. 62–71). San Mateo, CA: Morgan Kaufmann.

Ericsson, K. A., & Kintsch, W. (1995). Long-term working memory. *Psychological Review, 102,* 211–245.

Ericsson, K. A., & Simon, H. A. (1993). *Protocol analysis: Verbal reports as data* (2nd ed.). Cambridge, MA: MIT Press.

Feigenbaum, E. A. (1989). What hath Simon wrought? In D. Klahr & K. Kotovsky (Eds.), *Complex information processing: The impact of Herbert A. Simon* (pp. 165–182). Hillsdale, NJ: Lawrence Erlbaum Associates.

Hegarty, M. (2000). Capacity limits in diagrammatic reasoning. In M. Anderson, P. C. H. Cheng, & V. Haarslev (Eds.), *Theory and application of diagrams: Proceedings to the First International Conference, Diagrams 2000.* Edinburgh, United Kingdom. London: Springer.

Hegarty, M., & Just, M. A. (1993). Constructing mental models of machines from text and diagrams. *Journal of Memory and Language, 32,* 717–742.

Just, M. A., & Carpenter, P. A. (1992). A capacity theory of comprehension: Individual differences in working memory. *Psychological Review, 99,* 122–149.

Just, M. A., Carpenter, P. A., & Varma, S. (1999). Computational modeling of high-level cognition and brain function. *Human-Brain-Mapping, 8,* 128–136.

Klahr, D., & Kotovsky, K. (Eds.). (1989). *Complex information processing: The impact of Herbert A. Simon.* Hillsdale, NJ: Lawrence Erlbaum Associates.

Kosslyn, S. M. (1980). *Image and mind.* Cambridge, MA: Harvard University Press.

Kosslyn, S. M. (1994). *Image and brain: The resolution of the imagery debate.* Cambridge, MA: MIT Press.

Larkin, J. H. (1989). Display-based problem solving. In D. Klahr & K. Kotovsky (Eds.), *Complex information processing: The impact of Herbert A. Simon* (pp. 319–344). Hillsdale, NJ: Lawrence Erlbaum Associates.

144   (TABACHNECK) SCHIJF

Larkin, J. H., & Simon, H. A. (1987). Why a diagram is (sometimes) worth 10.000 words. *Cognitive Science, 11*, 65–100.

Lemaire, P., & Siegler, R. S. (1995). Four aspects of strategic change: Contributions to children's learning of multiplication. *Journal of Experimental Psychology: General, 124*, 83–97.

Mayes, J. T., Draper, S. W., McGregor, A. M., & Oatley, K. (1988). Information flow in a user interface: The effect of experience and context on the recall of MacWrite screens. In D. M. Jones & R. Winder (Eds.), *People and computers IV* (pp. 275–289). Cambridge, England: Cambridge University Press.

Microsoft PowerPoint™. (2000). Version 9.0.2716. Copyright © 1987–1999 Microsoft Corporation: Mountain View, CA.

Newell, A. (1990). *Unified theories of cognition.* Cambridge, MA: Harvard University Press.

Newell, A., & Simon, H. A. (1972). *Human problem solving.* Englewood Cliffs, NJ: Prentice-Hall.

O'Hara, K., & Payne, S. J. (1998). The effects of operator implementation cost on planfulness of problem solving and learning. *Cognitive Psychology, 35*, 34–70.

O'Hara, K., & Payne, S. J. (1999). Planning and the user interface: Effects of lockout time and error recovery cost. *International Journal of Human–Computer Studies, 50*, 41–49.

Olson, J. R., & Biolsi, K. J. (1991). Techniques for representing expert knowledge. In K. A. Ericsson & J. Smith (Eds.), *Toward a general theory of expertise: Prospects and limits* (pp. 240–285). New York: Cambridge University Press.

Payne, S. J. (1988). Methods and mental models in theories of cognitive skill. In J. Self (Ed.), *Artificial intelligence and human learning: Intelligent computer-aided instruction* (pp. 69–87). London: Chapman & Hall.

Simon, H. A. (1979). *Models of thought.* New Haven, CT: Yale University Press.

Simon, H. A. (1981). *The sciences of the artificial* (2nd ed.). Cambridge, MA: MIT Press.

Simon, H. A. (1989). *Models of thought: Vol. 2.* New Haven, CT: Yale University Press.

Simon, H. A., Kotovsky, K., & Hayes, J. R. (1989). Why are some problems hard? Evidence from the Tower of Hanoi. In H. A. Simon (Ed.), *Models of thought* (Vol. 2, pp. 289–321). New Haven, CT: Yale University Press.

Staszewski, J. J. (1987). *The psychological reality of retrieval structures: An investigation of expert knowledge.* Unpublished doctoral dissertation, Cornell University, Ithaca, NY.

Tabachneck(-Schijf), H. J. M. (1992). *Computational differences in mental representations: Effects of mode of data presentation on reasoning and understanding.* Unpublished doctoral dissertation, Carnegie Mellon University, Pittsburgh, PA.

Tabachneck(-Schijf), H. J. M., Koedinger, K. R., & Nathan, M. J. (1995). A cognitive analysis of the task demands of early algebra. In J. D. Moore & J. F. Lehman (Eds.), *Proceedings of the 17th annual Conference of the Cognitive Science Society* (pp. 397–402). Hillsdale, NJ: Lawrence Erlbaum Associates.

Tabachneck(-Schijf), H. J. M, Leonardo, A. M., & Simon, H. A. (1997). CaMeRa: A computational model of multiple representations. *Cognitive Science, 21*, 305–350.

Tabachneck(-Schijf), H. J. M., & Simon, H. A. (1996). Alternative representations of instructional material. In D. Peterson (Ed.), *Forms of representation: An interdisciplinary theme in cognitive science* (pp. 28–46). London: Intellect Books.

Tardieu, H., & Gyselinck, V. (2003). Working memory constraints in the integration and comprehension of information in a multimedia context. In H. Van Oostendorp (Ed.), *Cognition in a digital world* (pp. 3–24). Mahwah, NJ: Lawrence Erlbaum Associates.

Van Nimwegen, C., Van Oostendorp, H., Tabachneck(-Schijf), H. J. M., & Van Vugt, H. C. (2003). *Externalization vs. internalization: The influence of externalization on problem solving performance.* Manuscript in preparation.

Zhang, J. (1997). The nature of external representations in problem solving. *Cognitive Science, 21*, 179–217.

Zhang, J., & Norman, D. A. (1994). Representations in distributed cognitive tasks. *Cognitive Science, 18*, 87–122.

Chapter 8

Supporting Collective Information Processing in a Web-Based Environment

Herre van Oostendorp
Utrecht University

Nina Holzel
Utrecht University

This chapter describes a study on collective problem solving and decision reaching in a computer-supported collaborative work (CSCW) environment. More specifically, the research described is concerned with the influence of adding chat boxes and making explicit the roles of participants with icons while collectively processing information needed to solve presented tasks.

Collective information processing (CIP) involves the degree to which information, ideas, or cognitive processes are shared among the group members and how this sharing of information affects both individual- and group-level outcomes (Hinsz, Tindale, & Vollrath, 1997; Propp, 1999). CIP consists of a few stages. The first, searching for information, involves acquiring information via communication in order to make decisions and to construct a larger fund of common knowledge. The second is storing and having available in an easy accessible manner information in a common workspace. The third is weighing and using information, that is, evaluating the importance of information for the common problem and deciding in which way this information has to be used in decision making (Hinsz et al.; Propp). To work together successfully, individuals must perceive, encode, store, and retrieve information in a parallel manner. That is, they must hold a shared mental model (Langan-Fox, Wirth, Code, Langfield-Smith, & Wirth, 2001). Communication is needed to share and fine tune this knowledge construction.

The possibility of users communicating with each other is very important for building a shared mental model of the task, the interface, and other users. The effective and efficient solving of a common task or problem depends on this communication (Stroomer & Van Oostendorp, 2003).

Most research on CSCW is limited in that it focuses on global effects and pays little attention to specific effects under certain conditions, such as the role of interface features and task characteristics. The main purpose of the present chapter is to gather more in-depth knowledge about these specific effects. We believe that the collective information-processing framework, briefly described earlier, can play a useful heuristic role.

The interface in a CSCW environment may support the communication processes in order to progress toward building a shared mental model. Adding a chat box and making participants' roles explicit could considerably improve this support. The chat-box facility allows each participant the possibility to easily and directly check the intentions of the other participants. The aforementioned search and weigh processes can be supported by this facility. Chat systems support synchronous communication, which facilitates rapid turn taking in discussions (Ter Hofte, 1998). This synchronous characteristic enables retention of the context of specific information, which could reduce problems in asynchronous contexts. It provides participants with the opportunity to check immediately what the other means.

In addition, icons could indicate what each message conveys. Making group members "visible" can enhance "group awareness," that is, the mental model of users themselves and other group members. Erickson et al. (1999) found that people prefer to know who else is present in a shared space, and they use this awareness to guide their work. In an asynchronous bulletin-board system, icons could contribute to a rapid and easy recognition of the author of a certain message. In this way, the previously mentioned processes like storing, retrieving, and weighing can be supported.

The influence of these features is investigated by using two experimental tasks. One of the tasks is less structured than the other and we expect a particularly positive effect from adding a chat box and indicating roles on communication and performance for the less structured task, because in this case communication could profit more from the offered support. The two tasks that had to be solved in the present study were an intellective problem-solving task and a decision-reaching task, and these tasks need two slightly different communication and thinking processes. Problem solving is a process in which a gap is perceived and resolved between a present situation and a desired goal, with the path to the goal blocked by known or unknown obstacles. In a problem-solving task, as we see it here, there is only one correct answer. In contrast, decision reaching is a selection process where one or more possible solutions is chosen to reach a desired goal. For this type of task, more answers are possible and the participants have to negotiate to come to a solution (McGrath & Hollingshead, 1993). The steps in both processes are similar and their names are sometimes used interchangeably (Huit, 1992). Winograd and Flores (1986) summarized the key elements of problem solving: A problem is characterized in terms of a task environment in which there are different potential states of affairs, actions available to the participant to change the state, and goals from which rational actions can be derived. The participant has an internal representation of the task environment and searches for courses of action that will lead to a desired goal. Finally, the participant makes a choice among those courses of action.

Problem solving is finding a way to solve a problem in an area determined by the internal representation of the task environment. Decision reaching, however, is not discovering the "right" answer, but rather coming to a group consensus (Propp, 1999). The decision-making process is almost the same as the problem-solving process, with the difference that participants do not make a choice among courses of action, but rather negotiate to come to a consensus. In the present study, for both tasks, communication between the group members is necessary to come to a final solution. For the decision-reaching task, members need to negotiate with each other and exchange information. The problem-solving task primarily requires communication to exchange information, because, particularly, in the less structured, decision-reaching task it is important to know who says what (role identification can be facilitated by means of icons) and, especially there, to be able to check whatever was intended to be said (by means of a chat box) could be helpful. Consequently, we expect a positive effect of the experimental interface on the decision-reaching task.

METHOD

Participants and Design

Sixty participants (students), arranged in groups of three, performed a low- and a high-structured task in a Web-based environment. Half of the participants worked in an experimental condition in which the aforementioned interface (with chat boxes and role indication) was used, and the other half in a control condition in which an interface without those features was used. The order of tasks was counterbalanced over participants.

Tasks

The tasks were conceived in such a way that the (three) participants possessed different information and they needed to put it together in order to solve the problem or make the decision. Two types of tasks were used.

The first was a high-structured task, the so-called "train" task. This problem-solving task had only one good solution. The participants were asked to plan a train route to a specific destination with a given amount of money to be spent and a specified duration of travel. Thus, the two restrictions were time and money. There were three information sources distributed to the three participants in a group. Information about prices was given to the ticket seller, about hours to the conductor, and about stations and stops to the station chief. The problem could be solved only if the information exchange between these three roles was adequate. The best solution from an individual perspective was not the best solution for the group (e.g., the fastest connection—the best from a conductor's perspective—was not the cheapest solution; on the contrary, it was rather expensive).

The second was a low-structured task, the so-called "park" task. In this decision-reaching task, several good solutions were possible, which the participants had to negotiate. The task of the participants was to design a recreation park. It had only one objective restriction: the available space. Next to that, there were also more subjective concerns and requirements that did not directly fit with each other and required negotiations. In comparison with the train task, the criteria were less explicit. There were again three roles: municipality, interest group, and landscaper, with their own interests and demands; the municipality wants a park for the whole city, requiring the park to be easily accessible from the highway, the interest group needs the park to be safe for children (thus not near the highway), and the landscaper wants an appropriate grouping and size of elements such as lakes or waterfalls (a map with images of park elements was given in advance).

Scoring

All proposed solutions were scored on a scale from 0 to 5. A score of 0 was given for a solution that did not correspond to the instruction; the maximum score of 5 was given for solutions with a compromise character that took into account objective requirements (like prices, time, etc.), considering also subjective interests and requirements (like accessibility from the highway). Solutions that partially corresponded with an ideal solution (e.g., when not all the criteria were met) received scores between 0 and 5, based on a detailed scoring prescription depending on the quality of the solution. The interrater reliability was high ($r_\kappa = .91$).

Interface

In the control condition, participants could communicate with each other only by an asynchronous bulletin-board system. There, messages could be placed, preceded or not by a short verbal label, in a hierarchical tree structure similar to the one in Microsoft Explorer (see Fig. 8.1).

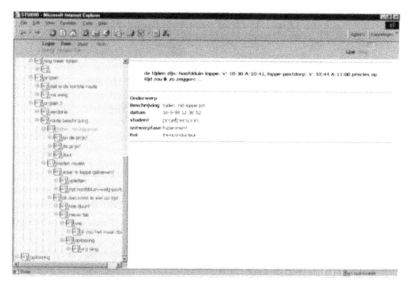

FIG. 8.1.   The interface of the control condition.

In the experimental condition, icons were associated with messages to indicate roles (added to the left of the interface) and two chat boxes were added, one for each participant (see Fig. 8.2). The chat was performed by typing messages in the chat windows.

In Fig. 8.3 the icons used in the experimental condition are presented in more detail. For the park task, three roles were used: somebody from the

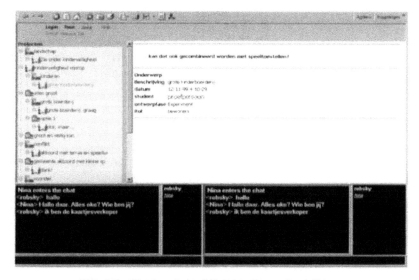

FIG. 8.2.   The interface of the experimental condition.

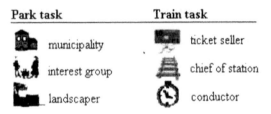

Park task		Train task	
	municipality		ticket seller
	interest group		chief of station
	landscaper		conductor

FIG. 8.3.   The icons used in the "park" and "train" tasks.

municipality, somebody from an interest group, and a landscaper. For the train task, there was a ticket seller, a station chief, and a conductor.

The asynchronous part of the system, the bulletin board, was implemented using generally available Web and database technology. The system was running on a Microsoft personal Web server on a generic personal computer, with Microsoft Windows installed. The backend database was a Windows port of MySQL. This database was used to track and store the messages posted to the board. Active Server Pages was used as the interface between the database and the Web server. When a user wanted to read a certain page on the bulletin board and clicked on the link, the user's Web browser was sending a request to the Web server. This request was accepted and read by the Web server, parsed into a database query, and passed to the database server. The database server retrieved the requested data and sent it back to the Web server. The retrieved data was constructed into a Web page using Active Server Pages technology, and sent back to the user's Web browser.

For the second part of the system, the synchronous chat system, we used ICQ. This is a freely available chat system for the internet. There are several chat systems available, like IRC Clients, Yahoo Buddy List, AOL Messenger, and Microsoft Chat. All of these systems are very similar in use and options. ICQ was chosen because it has a nice option to store and replay chats. It is also possible to export and import chats.

Communication Analysis

The communication between participants (the chat as well as the bulletin-board messages) was analyzed based on the method proposed by Erkens (1997). The communicative functions of utterances were encoded and registered. The following communicative functions were distinguished:

- Attending: implicitly or explicitly asking for attention.
- Informative: providing or storing information.
- Reasoning: giving reasons or drawing conclusions.

- Eliciting: checking of or asking for information.
- Responsive: confirming, accepting, or denying information.

In Erkens's method, more subcategories were distinguished, but we limit ourselves to these five main categories. The value of this method was shown in Erkens and in Erkens, Andriessen, and Peters (2003). On the basis of a literature review (Stroomer & Van Oostendorp, 2003), we chose this method of analysis because it appeared to be reliable, sensitive, and valid. *Sensitive* means here that the method was sensitive enough to detect effects of experimental manipulations (i.e., variations implemented by the researcher). With regard to the validity, Erkens et al. showed that some of the communication categories significantly correlated with performance of group members. This is important because it reveals the relative importance of different communication processes (see also Stroomer & Van Oostendorp). For instance, checking of information (an aspect of eliciting) appeared in Erkens et al. to be an important predictor of performance, and to be more important than other intermediating processes indicated by the other categories. In the present study we also examine whether the presence of the chat possibility and icons have an influence on the different communication characteristics. Board messages and chats were scored based on the occurrences of these five types of dialogue actions (in terms of frequencies).

Procedure

The participants first received a practice task to get acquainted with the system. They were asked not to speak with each other during the experiment and were separated by walls so they could not see each other. By selection, it was ensured that participants at least knew how to use Microsoft Windows (1998). The order of tasks was changed between participants. For each experimental task, the participants received a maximum of 30 minutes. After completing these tasks, participants received a questionnaire to measure the usability aspects of the system. The total duration of a session was approximately 1.5 hours.

RESULTS

Communication

More communication actions were registered in the experimental condition than in the control condition, $F(5,54) = 3.51$, $p < .01$, as a result of the extra utterances in the chat box. On average, 24 communicative actions (in the experimental condition) versus 15 actions (in the control condition) in total per person were counted. In the experimental condition, there were more eliciting, informative, and responsive remarks. Because of comparability between conditions, it is better to base our analyses on the relative contribution of the types of communicative actions in the total of produced communicative actions. When relative frequencies were considered, the results showed that there were significant differences between conditions with regard to attending and eliciting. In Table 8.1, the average percentage of dialogue actions per category for each condition is presented. These means are based on individual scores because here—as opposed to the (group) scores on the tasks—communication contributions for all persons are available.

A two-by-two analysis of variance (with task and condition as factors) showed a significant effect of condition, $F(1,58) = 15.6$, $p < .001$, with regard to the relative frequency of attending remarks. The other effects were not significant ($p > .05$). Participants need fewer attending interventions in the experimental condition, and this effect is somewhat stronger for the park task than for the train task; the interaction effect was $F(1,58) = 2.31$, $p = .13$. With regard to eliciting remarks, there was a main effect of condition, $F(1,58) = 3.93$, $p < .06$. In the experimental condition, on average, more checks were performed than in the control condition. The effects on the other three types of (relative) dialogue actions were not significant.

TABLE 8.1
Mean Percentage Dialogue Actions

	Control Condition		Experimental Condition		
	Mean	SD	Mean	SD	Significance
Train task					
Attending	12.2	(12.1)	6.3	(9.0)	*
Informative	29.0	(13.6)	30.6	(11.1)	
Reasoning	10.9	(8.8)	10.3	(7.7)	
Eliciting	27.6	(13.0)	29.6	(11.8)	*
Responsive	20.4	(11.9)	23.1	(12.3)	
Park task					
Attending	17.9	(14.7)	6.2	(8.4)	*
Informative	31.1	(14.6)	26.7	(14.8)	
Reasoning	9.8	(11.4)	10.5	(9.0)	
Eliciting	22.5	(13.6)	32.8	(11.8)	*
Responsive	18.6	(13.0)	23.7	(13.3)	

*Denotes a significant difference ($p < .05$) between conditions.

Task Performance

The number of correct solutions and the quality of solutions were higher on average in the experimental condition, especially for the highly structured train task (Fig. 8.4). An analysis of variance (with task and condition as factors) showed a significant effect of condition, $F(1,18) = 4.58$, $p < .05$, and, more importantly, the interaction effect was also significant, $F(1,18) = 7.23$, $p < .05$. Moreover, the performance in the park task was on average higher than in the train task, $F(1,18) = 13.79$, $p < .01$.

CONCLUSION AND DISCUSSION

The experimental manipulation improved communication and performance, especially in the train task. Results of the usability evaluation questionnaire additionally showed that communication was improved (or would improve) by adding chat boxes and role-indication icons. The more effective communication (less attending needed, relatively more elicitation, and [absolutely] more informative and responsive remarks) indicates that the participants in the experimental condition were, to a larger extent, confident that messages addressed to another person would indeed reach their destination. Moreover, they check information more often. In this way, a contribution could have been made in the form of better encoding of the information needed for solving collective problems. These outcomes support the hypothesis that the construction and availability of an accurate, shared mental model is very important for the effective solving of a common problem in a group (Hinsz et al., 1997; Levine & Moreland, 1999; Propp, 1999). Knowing who says what and being able to check whatever was intended to be said are important conditions for that. Supporting these with icons or chat boxes could be helpful.

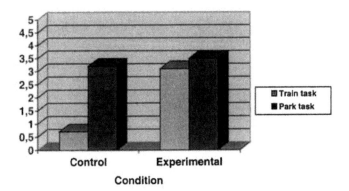

FIG. 8.4. Task performance (average score).

Regarding the type of task, the expectation was that the experimental manipulation would have a greater impact on the park task than on the train task because the former is a decision-reaching task and therefore would benefit to a greater extent from enrichment of the interface. Indeed, the communication improved in the experimental condition more for the park task, but on the other hand the performance improved more for the intellective, problem-solving train task. The latter finding is contrary to the "task-media fit" theory of McGrath and Hollingshead (1993), but can probably be explained by the difficulty of the tasks. Carey and Kacmar (1997) found an effect of task complexity: Simple tasks can be accomplished successfully, but complex tasks result in larger error. As task complexity increases, more information processing is required. The intellective problem-solving train task was indeed more complex than the decision-reaching park task. Participants got a lot of information from different information sources, depending on the various roles (the train tracks, the timetable, or the prices). They had to look up and exchange certain information to solve the problem. For the park task, the information needed to come to a solution was minimal. It is possible that the intellective problem-solving train-task group improved more in terms of performance than the decision-reaching park-task group because a greater amount of information needed to be processed. Enrichment of the interface in the experimental condition improved aspects of information processing, that is, certain steps in the problem-solving process, such as the encoding and retrieval of information, could have been effectively supported.

Whether the improvement in performance and communication is due to the role-identification icons, the chat boxes, or both is not yet clear. The design of the experiment does not allow a decision on this issue. For research-strategic reasons, we did choose a strong experimental manipulation in order to maximize the chance of detecting a significant effect. Follow-up research is necessary to make an unambiguous judgment about the effect of the two separate aspects of the experimental manipulation on collective information processing and mental-model building.

The outcomes of the present study show that changes in interface features and task characteristics result in differences in group communication processes and task outcomes (at least for small groups). The collective information-processing view appeared to be a useful framework for understanding the effects, because it takes information as a central departure point.

REFERENCES

Carey, J. M., & Kacmar, C. J. (1997). The impact of communication mode and task complexity on small group performance and member satisfaction. *Computers in Human Behavior, 13*, 23–49.

Erickson, T., Smith, D. N., Kellogg, W. A., Laff, M., Richarda, J. T., & Bradner, E. (1999). Socially translucent systems: Social proxies, persistent conversation, and the design of "babble." In *Proceedings of the ACM Conference on Human Factors in Computing Systems (CHI '99)* (pp. 72–79). New York: ACM Press.

Erkens, G. (1997). *Cooperatief probleemoplossen met computers in het onderwijs* [Cooperative problem solving with computers in education]. Unpublished doctoral dissertation, Utrecht University, Utrecht, The Netherlands.

Erkens, G., Andriessen, J., & Peters, N. (2003). Interaction and performance in computer supported collaborative tasks. In H. van Oostendorp (Ed.), *Cognition in a digital world* (pp. 225–251). Mahwah, NJ: Lawrence Erlbaum Associates.

Hinsz, V., Tindale, R. S., & Vollrath, D. A. (1997). The emerging conceptualization of groups as information processors. *Psychological Bulletin, 121*, 43–64.

Huit, W. (1992). Problem solving and decision making: Consideration of individual differences using the Myers-Briggs Type Indicator. *Journal of Psychological Type, 24*, 33–44.

Langan-Fox, J., Wirth, A., Code, S., Langfield-Smith, K., & Wirth, A. (2001). Analyzing shared and team mental models. *International Journal of Industrial Ergonomics, 28*, 99–112.

Levine, J. M., & Moreland, R. L. (1999). Knowledge transmission in work groups: Helping newcomers to succeed. In L. L. Thompson, J. M. Levine, & D. M. Messick (Eds.), *Shared cognition in organizations: The management of knowledge* (pp. 267–296). Mahwah, NJ: Lawrence Erlbaum Associates.

McGrath, J. E., & Hollingshead, A. B. (1993). Putting the "group" back in group support systems: Some theoretical issues about dynamic processes in groups with technological enhancements. In L. M. Jessup & J. S. Valacich (Eds.), *Group support systems: New perspectives* (pp. 78–96). New York: Macmillan.

Propp, K. M. (1999). Collective information processing in groups. In L. R. Frey (Ed.), *The handbook of group communication theory and research* (pp. 225–250). Thousand Oaks, CA: Sage.

Stroomer, S., & Van Oostendorp, H. (2003). Analyzing communication in team tasks. In H. van Oostendorp (Ed.), *Cognition in a digital world* (pp. 175–204). Mahwah, NJ: Lawrence Erlbaum Associates.

Ter Hofte, G. H. (1998). *Working apart together: Foundations for component groupware*. Unpublished doctoral dissertation, Telematics Institute, Enschede, The Netherlands.

Winograd, T. A., & Flores, F. (1986). *Understanding computers and cognition: A new foundation for design*. New York: Addison-Wesley.

Chapter 9

Adaptive Learning Systems: Toward More Intelligent Analyses of Student Responses

Peter W. Foltz
New Mexico State University

Adrienne Y. Lee
New Mexico State University

A critical issue for using information systems is the need for assessing what people have learned and for using that information to provide substantive additional instruction. The creation of electronic training material is relatively easy; however, creating systems that truly adapt to an individual student is more difficult. For example, textbooks can be scanned to create electronic textbooks for students to read, but these electronic textbooks may be no better than the paper version if they do not assess what the student knows or present only material the student needs.

Electronic documents could be converted into a learning system by assuming that the sequencing of the documents as described by the author is accurate. If the electronic document happens to be a textbook, then the author has probably provided questions for students to answer; otherwise, questions would have to be generated. Questions test a user's understanding and, without assessment, a learning system cannot be adaptive or intelligent. The minimum requirement for an adaptive system is that it be able to adapt to a learner's needs through providing aids and hints when a user requests them; however, an intelligent, adaptive learning system should be able to detect a user's knowledge level and adapt the training material to the needs of the user. For example, if a student is asked what he or she knows about heart disease, we would like to be able to quickly zero in on what level of knowledge the student has, what knowledge the student already has, what knowledge is missing, and what misconceptions are present. Although human tutors are able to do this quite well (e.g., Bloom, 1984), it is a task for computers to interpret the student's response, map it onto the appropriate knowledge for the domain, and determine the next appropriate thing to say to the student in order to maximize learning.

Computers have been used to train and assess individuals, and the information gained through developing these systems has improved both theories of learning (e.g., Anderson, Corbett, Koedinger, & Pelletier, 1995) and computer-based training systems. However, previous computer-based training systems were limited to recording the actions of students to infer their abilities or to using multiple-choice questions, entering numbers, or entering words from a limited vocabulary for assessing students' knowledge representations (Polson & Richardson, 1988; Sleeman & Brown, 1982; Wenger, 1987; see also Edelson, 1996; Graesser, 1985). Current advances in technology (particularly in computational linguistics) have allowed for assessing students' knowledge based on analyzing essay answers to open-ended questions (e.g., Foltz, 1996; Landauer, Foltz, & Laham, 1998).

Essays can more accurately capture a student's current knowledge representation because they require the creation of the answer by the student rather than just a choice of answers provided by an instructor. As a student's knowledge representation changes, so too should their essay responses change, including more knowledge and improving in quality. Providing accurate information about the state of a student's changing knowledge representation can be used to provide individualized instruction (scaffolding) and specific feedback. Because writing essays requires more recall and organization of information than other means of question answering (such as multiple-choice or fill-in-the blank questions with limited vocabulary choices), it also can induce a richer knowledge representation in a student and improve writing abilities. Thus, in order to develop an adaptive learning system, one must incorporate assessments beyond simple multiple-choice questions.

This chapter ties together research on adaptive learning systems with research on automated assessment of essays. An adaptive system can only be as good as the assessments it makes. In turn, accurate assessment of learning can only succeed when it is tied to a system that can then modify the content in a way that maximizes learning. Furthermore, the chapter summarizes previous research on adaptive learning systems and then describes new efforts to create even more intelligent analyses of student responses that can be incorporated into the adaptive learning systems. Although it covers a range of methods and theories, the chapter focuses on applying a model called Latent Semantic Analysis to the automated analysis of student responses and its potential for adaptive learning systems.

THEORETICALLY BASED ADAPTIVE LEARNING SYSTEMS

Originally, learning systems that could adapt to students were called *computer-aided instruction* (CAI). These systems often took the format of drill and practice or simple tutorial (for a review, see Kearsley, 1993). When a knowledge module was added to the system, it became known as *intelligent CAI* (or ICAI) or *intelligent tutoring system* (ITS)[1] (cf. Polson & Richardson, 1988; Sleeman & Brown, 1982; Wenger, 1987). Four different types of knowledge modules are possible; these include a model of the student (an ideal student and the current student user) and a model of an expert (domain expert and teaching module). For an ITS, the student's interaction with the computer is monitored and compared against either an ideal student or expert, and the pedagogy of the system is determined by the knowledge included in the teaching module. Some systems have been developed from an expert-systems perspective, where first an expert system is developed and then a teaching interface is added, for example, Neomycin and Guidon (Clancey, 1987; Clancey & Letsinger, 1981). Unfortunately, most of these systems, although functional and able to teach how-to knowledge, are not based on a learning theory.

The most extensively tested ITSs were developed (and tested) by John Anderson and colleagues (Anderson et al., 1995). These systems are unique because they are based on a learning theory derived from a unified theory of human cognition. Advances in learning theories help us to develop better instructional systems and advances in technology allow us to study human learning through instruction (cf. Anderson et al.). Some critical principles derived from Anderson's (1990, 1996) theory are: to develop a production system model of the student's representation, to provide immediate feedback, to represent the goal structure for the student, and to provide initial shared problem solving between ITS and student that decreases as the student becomes more proficient (Anderson et al.). The primary means of determining both what a student should learn and whether a student has learned is captured in the use of production-system modeling. Production-system rules specify what actions need to be taken for particular goals. For example, if you are driving a car and you see a red stoplight, then you step on the brakes. The goal is driving the car (without an accident) and the action is stepping on the brakes. In student learning, two production rules in algebra learning could be:

---

[1]Adaptive tutoring systems are referred to as "ITS" throughout the chapter.

IF the goal is to solve the problem $(x + 3 = 6)$, THEN set the subgoal to isolate the variable (x).

IF the subgoal is to isolate the variable (x), THEN subtract 3 from both sides.

As a student solves a problem, the ITS is creating a production system model of what the student is doing and this production system serves as a representation of what the student's current knowledge state is. The student production model can be compared with an expert production-system model that contains knowledge about how to solve the problem. This comparison is called *model tracing* and can be used to determine not only which pieces of knowledge are missing (e.g., production rules that exist in the expert model but not in the student model), but also which problems to present to the student (Corbett, McLaughlin, & Scarpinatto, 2000). Using this model tracing methodology, the tutors have been found to be effective for training programming and topics in mathematics at various levels of education.

Unlike Anderson's systems (Anderson et al., 1995), where problems are well defined, some early systems based upon the Socratic method[2] were developed (as summarized in Sleeman & Brown, 1982); however, these systems were not extensively tested or developed. Although recent research has moved in focus from simple training problems to complex ones, the test questions must still use clear-cut student responses in order to perform accurate knowledge assessment (Paradice, 1992). Ideally, some combination of examining complex, conceptual topics and the use of open-ended (Socratic-style) questions would produce the best assessment of a student's current knowledge level. Thus, the type of question may be important in the assessment of complex skills.

ASSESSING A STUDENT'S KNOWLEDGE THROUGH QUESTIONS

Although some instructional systems may merely present material without assessment, typically adaptive learning systems (ICAI or ITS systems) present text (and sometimes illustrations or tables) to students and then students are asked to answer questions, solve problems, or write essays. Questions can be posed before the learner starts to study the material, during

---

[2]The Socratic method in its purest form is a way to teach where the instructor directs only questions to the student. Through careful question selection, the instructor can lead the student to the correct knowledge without directly giving the student any information.

the learning of the material (reflection questions), and after the material has been studied completely. Through pretest assessment, an ITS can present only the material that the student needs to learn and present it at the appropriate level for the student. In the same way, through posttest assessment, an ITS can determine that the student has not yet fully learned the material and the student's responses could be used to determine which sections the student needed to relearn.

Reflection questions placed throughout the training material can provide poorer students with a greater opportunity to learn from that material (Lee & Hutchison, 1998; see also Chi, Bassok, Lewis, Reimann, & Glaser, 1988; Klahr & Dunbar, 1988; Nickerson, Perkins, & Smith, 1985; Palinscar & Brown, 1984). Furthermore, depending on how the questions are answered, an ITS can adjust the level of the material to fit the student. This is known as *scaffolding* (Vygotsky, 1962; see also Bodrova & Leong, 1996; Carroll & McKendree, 1987). The basic idea is that students need an ITS to help them overcome the difference between their current knowledge state and their potential skill level (Driscoll, 1994). Questions therefore serve the purpose of determining what knowledge a student has acquired and what knowledge is missing.

Unlike learning how to solve algebra problems, questions derived from text may require a range of responses, from multiple-choice answers to long essay responses. The difficulty for an ITS is in assessing the many different possible types of student answers to written responses that are not multiple-choice answers, and mapping those answers onto knowledge representations. Although recent research has begun to focus on complex questions, most of the earlier work involved questions that required only very simple answers and not deep responses (e.g., Graesser, 1985). Multiple-choice questions or other constrained methods also do not provide a rich representation of students' learning from the text or examples that they have read. For example, students could choose the correct answer because they were lucky or because they used trial and error to find the correct answer.

In the past, computers have had difficulty understanding natural language and tests had to be in the form of multiple-choice questions or problems requiring discrete responses (e.g., selecting from a field of choices, clicking plus and minus keys to increase or decrease numbers, entering digits or letters, etc.). In studying tutorial dialogues, it becomes clear that the give and take of conversation does not always translate well into multiple-choice questions or responses. Furthermore, asking students questions that require a deeper level of reasoning may produce better learning outcomes (Graesser & Person, 1994; Graesser, Person, & Huber, 1992; Person, Graesser, Magliano, & Kreuz, 1994). Therefore, the integration of open-ended questions into an ITS as a form of reflection question would allow for greater understanding of what a student has really learned.

SCAFFOLDING

The concepts related to feedback used in an adaptive tutoring system are similar to the idea of scaffolding. Scaffolding has meant defining the sequence of the material (information to be learned and problems to solve) with the idea that each student starts with a different set of abilities and the material should be within the extent of their abilities (Vygotsky, 1962; see also Moll, 1990; Tharpe & Gallimore, 1988; Van der Veer, 1991). Because answers to questions give only a snapshot view of the initial state of a student's knowledge representations, students who answer the same question in the same way may nevertheless have different levels of abilities that would create differential learning of the material (zone of proximal development, Vygotsky, 1986). Thus, an ITS can create a context in which students can learn with the aid of an "expert" and within their ability level.

Scaffolding provides additional aid to learners and reduces that aid as students become more knowledgeable (for an example system, see Carroll & McKendree, 1987). This aid should allow students to build connections between their previous knowledge and the new knowledge. Then, gradually, the additional help is removed as the learner becomes more familiar with the material. For elementary-school children, scaffolding has been effective both when teachers act as aids and when two students act as aids for each other (Palinscar & Brown, 1984; for a review, see Nelson, Watson, Ching, & Barrow, 1996). However, use of scaffolding for teaching complex topic areas or skills has not been extensively explored. In addition, the difficulty often comes in determining when a student needs the extra help and supplying it only at those times (Bliss, Askew, & MacRae, 1996). Systematic research analyzing a gradual increase in the difficulty level versus computer-adjusted presentation has not been performed in the area of computer training in complex skills.

To solve this problem, an ITS can present essay questions throughout the tutorial. The answers to initial questions could determine the initial difficulty level of instruction and which topics need to be covered (e.g., Wolfe et al., 1998). Assessment reflection questions throughout the material could be used to identify when more practice is needed and when the level of difficulty of the material can be increased. This ability to adjust the level of difficulty of the presented material can allow an ITS to adjust to students with varied abilities and background knowledge.

EFFECTIVENESS OF EVALUATING STUDENTS' RESPONSES

Some research has been performed to address whether adaptive training systems are more beneficial than other strategies. Software that analyzes student errors and adapts instruction has been found to be better than learner-controlled instruction, in which a student has to ask for help, or nonadaptive instruction, in which the feedback does not adjust to the learner; however, some researchers have found that software that evaluates students is not accurate enough in the evaluation of students' knowledge to create adequate adaptive instructional software (cf. Park & Tennyson, 1980; Ross, 1984; Tennyson, Tennyson, & Rothen, 1980; for contradictory evidence, see Hativa & Lesgold, 1991).

On the other hand, as mentioned earlier, ITSs developed by Anderson and colleagues have been successful to a certain extent because the computer can maintain an idealized student model and compare the students' actions to that ideal student model (Anderson et al., 1995) Generally, though, production systems are easily designed for problem solving activities such as geometry or LISP programming, which evaluate based on multiple-choice questions or limited programming vocabulary.[3] Less effort has been devoted to the problem of developing models of students' knowledge derived from writing open-ended essays. An alternative solution, described later, is to use Latent Semantic Analysis (LSA) to provide a space of possible models based on an expert or other students' previous essays (Foltz, 1996; Foltz, Laham, & Landauer, 1999; Landauer & Dumais, 1997). These model essays represent the appropriate knowledge of the topic and any student's progress can be determined by comparing his or her essay to this pool of essays of known quality. This approach has the further advantage that digital information can be more quickly converted into an ITS through training to generate a knowledge representation based on the essays.

In addition, in contrast to Anderson and colleagues (1995), Eberts' (1997) summary of the use of individual difference measures for adaptive instruction found few successes. He speculated that the lack of success in using individual difference characteristics to tailor computer-aided instructional systems is due to inadequate gathering of individual difference information. Thus, some controversy exists over whether a computer can accurately assess students for adaptive instruction and whether adaptive

---

[3]Anderson et al.'s (1995) tutors have not focused as much on dialogue understanding, although they have used the study of human tutor dialogues to improve the interactions between the computer tutors and humans (for an analysis of dialogue-based systems, see Cook, 2002). However, this observation can be gleaned merely from an examination of the literature (Anderson et al.).

instruction is beneficial. The benefits of individualized instruction suggest that additional research is needed to determine whether students learn more from adaptive instruction and what the difference in that learning might be. Thus, new techniques that focus on evaluating open-ended questions, combined with production systems for maintaining student models and deciding appropriate feedback, may produce the most accurate models of student knowledge (cf. Graesser, Wiemer-Hastings, Wiemer-Hastings, Harter, et al., 2000).

It should be noted that, in the field of adaptive learning systems, there has been a considerable amount of research on tutorial dialogue (cf. Rose & Freedman, 2000). This research investigated a range of issues in how to include natural-language dialogue in intelligent tutoring systems. These issues include much of the student modeling issues described earlier in order to accurately gauge the learner's knowledge. However, in order to have an appropriate system to give natural language feedback, the research has also covered such issues as the architectures for communication and dialogue management, techniques for processing natural language input, and processing the pragmatic aspects of tutorial dialogues. Because this chapter focuses on the adaptive portion of tutoring systems, it does not cover the aspects of processing and providing the intelligent dialogue needed for such systems. Nevertheless, the adaptive modeling techniques described in this chapter can be integrated with natural language dialogue systems.

TECHNIQUES FOR EVALUATING OPEN-ENDED QUESTIONS USING LSA

Open-ended questions pose their own problems. With open-ended questions, the ITS must check students' answers and provide feedback, based on an analysis of natural language input. Although some researchers have tried to address this problem, their systems have limited the types of responses that students could provide (Edelson, 1996). In addition, the systems usually took a long time to respond, represented a limited amount of knowledge, or graded entirely on grammar (Edelson; Page, 1994). In order to address these problems, LSA can be employed to analyze students' typed responses to open-ended questions presented by the ITS (e.g., Foltz, 1996; Foltz et al., 1999; Landauer & Dumais, 1997).

OVERVIEW OF LSA

LSA is a computational technique that can provide measures of the quality of a student's knowledge representation based on analyses of a corpus of textual information on a domain and a student's essay. This approach permits assessment to be done entirely based on essays.

LSA is both a computational model of knowledge representations and a method for determining the semantic similarity between pieces of textual information. LSA generates a high-dimensional semantic representation of a body of knowledge based on a statistical analysis of textual information of the domain. LSA assumes that there is some underlying, or latent, structure in the pattern of word usage across texts. Based on an analysis of the occurrences of words in contexts, a representation can be formed in which words that are used in similar contexts will be more semantically related. To perform the analysis, a corpus of text is first represented as a matrix in which the columns stand for passages (usually paragraphs or sentences), and rows stand for unique word types found in the text. The cell entries represent the frequency with which a given word appears in a given context, transformed to provide a measure of the information value of that word. A singular value decomposition (SVD), which is a variant of factor analysis, is performed on this matrix. (For a review of SVD, see Golub & Van Loan, 1996.) This decomposes the matrix into three matrices, one representing loading of k dimensions or factors for words, one representing loading of k dimensions or factors for passages, and the third a set of k singular values. By retaining typically 300 to 500 of the largest singular values, setting the smallest singular values to 0, and remultiplying the matrices, we derive a least squares approximation of the original matrix. This matrix approximates the original matrix while ignoring smaller differences that will primarily be due to idiosyncrasies of word usage in the texts.

Based on this analysis, words can be represented as vectors in this high-dimensional semantic space. Words that tend to be used in semantically similar contexts tend to have highly similar vectors, even if they seldom co-occur in the same context. This permits a characterization of the degree of semantic similarity between words. Larger text units, such as paragraphs and whole essays, can similarly be represented as averages of the vectors of the words that they contain. The similarity of meaning between two text passages can be measured by determining the cosine or correlation between the two vectors representing their words. This measurement of similarity characterizes the amount of shared meaning between the passages. Because the similarity is performed in the reduced dimensional semantic space, the measurement captures more than just direct word overlap, in that it also captures the degree of semantic relatedness of terms used in the passages. Thus, two sentences, such as *The surgeon operated on the patient* and *The doctor wielded his scalpel*, which use different, but semantically related, words, tend to have a large cosine, given the appropriate training space. This would indicate that the two sentences have highly similar content.

Evaluations of LSA have shown that it can be used to derive representations that are similar to humans' representations from text and be used as a basis for analyzing the quality of content in student essays. Foltz and Wells

(1999) used LSA to analyze an introductory psychology textbook in order to predict similarities among common psychology terms (e.g., *ebbinghaus, decay, Hippocampus*). They then had students at different levels of knowledge rate the relatedness of the same terms. A semantic space was then derived by computing the SVD on the entire text of the textbook that the students had read, and the semantic distances between the different terms were computed. Results showed that LSA's semantic representation was more similar to that of a domain expert than to that of a novice, and that students' representations changed to be more similar to LSA's representation after exposure to additional texts and training. This method also proved successful for modeling term relationships for synonyms and for student knowledge of domains. For example, based on an LSA analysis of *Grolier's Academic American Encyclopedia*, Landauer and Dumais (1997) found that LSA could perform at the same level as the average non-English college student for the multiple-choice synonym portion of the TOEFL[4] test. Based on an LSA analysis of an introductory psychology textbook, LSA was able to perform at the 47th percentile when taking an introductory psychology multiple-choice test. These studies indicate overall that the representation generated by LSA can serve as a general model of the knowledge of domain-based analyses of texts from that domain. This model can be further be used for analyzing students' knowledge based on their essays.

ADAPTIVE LEARNING WITH LSA

LSA has been applied to the analysis of student essays for (a) providing a measure of the overall quality of an essay, (b) providing indications of which specific subtopics are discussed in an essay, and (c) measuring the student's knowledge level for determining which text a student should read. In all of these cases, LSA is performing assessment at a conceptual level because it determines the degree to which the conceptual information expressed in an essay matches the conceptual information in some model texts. By comparing student essays to pregraded or model essays, or to passages from the original texts, LSA can predict the overall quality of an essay (Foltz, 1996; Foltz et al., 1999; Landauer et al., 1998). For example, a grade can be assigned to an essay based on a weighted grade from the pregraded essays to which it is most similar. This weighting is based on the degree of similarity of the essay to each pregraded essay. So, an essay that is conceptu-

---

[4]The Educational Testing Service administers a test of English as a foreign language to students who wish to pursue an education in a college in the United States. This test provides a measure of proficiency that can be used by colleges to determine whether a student will succeed.

ally similar to other essays that received a grade between 70 and 75 tends to also be assigned a grade in that range. For this approach, LSA has been shown to be as accurate in assigning grades as teachers, graduate teaching assistants, and professional graders of testing organizations in over 30,000 essay exams across more than 50 topics. This approach has been applied to both factual-type essays (e.g., history, biology) and more open-ended or creative-style essays (e.g., "Describe a role model in your life"). LSA has proven to be equally successful in both cases. Even though creative writing is assumed to involve a much wider range of responses, there is still a limited vocabulary and style that is expressed in creative essays and can be successfully modeled by LSA.

Individual subtopics found within a student's essay can also be analyzed by comparing each sentence of an essay against a list of important sentences, representing subtopics a student should discuss for any particular topic. These important sentences are typically determined by having domain experts provide sentences describing the subtopics. By measuring which components are missing from an essay, the ITS can determine which subtopics need additional training and can automatically point the student to the appropriate places in the text in which to find the information (Foltz, 1996; Foltz, Gilliam, & Kendall, 2000).

Finally, by comparing a student's essay to a set of sample texts written at different levels of complexity on the same topic, LSA can match the appropriate level of text to the student's level of knowledge on the topic (Wolfe et al., 1998). In this way, LSA can first predict the appropriate level of text that a student should read in order to gain the optimal amount of information, then it can provide scaffolding for students. Once a student has read the text and answered essay-based questions on the text, LSA can provide an overall measure of the quality of a student's answer, as well as a categorization of which specific pieces of semantic knowledge appear to be missing from the essay. This permits the applications to provide feedback to students about information that is not present in their essays, or to provide additional training on those subtopics.

INTEGRATING LSA INTO AN ITS

A critical aspect of learning is reading comprehension. Although many ITSs have focused on training in technical domains such as physics and math in which there are fairly set answers and orders of training information, the ability of an ITS to train in reading comprehension can cover a wide range of domains. In this section, we outline several applications that have been developed using LSA to illustrate the approach of integrating LSA into an ITS. LSA can be used in any application in which knowledge assessment is done through open-ended questions. In addition, LSA can be used to analyze tutorial dialogues, as well as dialogues among participants in learning environments, in order to gauge their skills.

Learning for Knowledge Acquisition

In order to study learning through writing, a tutoring system for three topics in cognitive psychology was developed. One version of the tutor included an LSA grader that provided students with feedback about what was missing from their essay answers; the other tutor without the grader provided encouragement. All students were asked to rewrite each tutor essay question twice. For a Fall 2000 cognitive psychology course, half the students used the LSA tutor and half did not. The tutors were Web based so that students could complete them before the exams to fit their own schedule and pace. For one topic, target questions were used on each in-class exam that related directly to the tutors and had been used in previous years when the instructor taught the course. (The same textbook and instructor were used for the classes; however, differences between years, such as quality of students enrolled or instructor health could not be controlled.) Results indicated that students who used a tutor outperformed previous classes who did not have access to any type of computer tutor, and that the LSA feedback was better than general feedback (Lee, Foltz, Biron, & Gilliam, 2000).

Training Summarization Skills

Summary Street (Kintsch et al., 2000) is an ITS that uses LSA for judging students' written summaries of texts. Students read a story, write a summary, and receive feedback that indicates which sections they have adequately or inadequately covered. After students submitted their summaries, they saw bars representing how well they had covered a number of subtopics. By revising and improving their summaries, they could extend the length of the bars until they exceeded a threshold, indicating that a subtopic was covered (see Fig. 9.1 for an illustration of the interface). Kintsch et al. (2000) found that students who received feedback from Summary Street, compared to those who just wrote on word processors, produced better summaries and had better performance on later writing tasks without using the automated feedback. Thus, the ITS could teach better skills of reading comprehension through judging the quality of the students' writing of summaries and providing feedback.

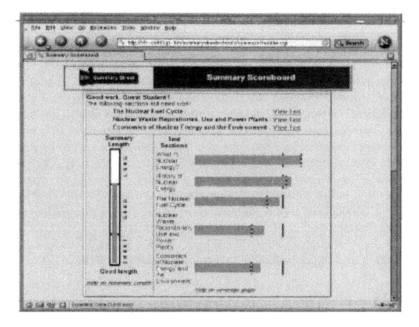

FIG. 9.1.   Student feedback from Summary Street, showing scoring of components of knowledge.

Analyzing Dialogue

While LSA can be applied to scoring essays and summaries, it can also be used for measuring the content of dialogues between a computer-based tutor and a human, or between two humans. In one application, soldiers using an LSA-enhanced threaded-discussion system had to write responses to what they would do in particular scenarios. By analyzing the discussion, the system permitted users to find points that were being made by other users that were similar to their own. The results showed that users of the system produced better responses to the scenario, as rated by military experts, than those who did not. In a second study analyzing dialogues, LSA was used to measure the quality of information conveyed by team members jointly flying an unmanned air vehicle (Kiekel, Cooke, Foltz, Gorman, & Martin, 2002). LSA's measures of information quality were then compared against objective measures of the teams' performance (a combined score including the number of errors made during the flight, amount of fuel used, number of successful reconnaissance photos taken, etc.). LSA correlated strongly with this performance measure, $r = .75$, indicating that it can be used to rate the quality of dialogue of teams and predict their performance. Further research is needed to investigate how these automated analyses can be incorporated into providing tutorial feedback to teams in near real time.

In another application called Autotutor (Graesser, Wiemer-Hastings, Wiemer-Hastings, Kreuz, et al., 2000; Graesser, Wiemer-Hastings, Wiemer-Hastings, Harter, et al., 2000), LSA was used as a component of a fully automated tutor to evaluate the quality of the students' contribution in the dialogue. Graesser and colleagues found that LSA was able to evaluate students' answers to the automated tutor at a level equivalent to an intermediate expert in the field. Autotutor also illustrated how LSA can be incorporated as a component into a larger scale ITS. Although LSA is used to evaluate the semantic content of the dialogues, its results are combined with the input of a number of other modules, including a speech-act classifier, a curriculum script, dialogue-move rules, and an animated talking head. Taken together, this approach can be used to provide an effective tutoring system that can adapt to students' knowledge while interacting with students in a manner similar to a tutor-student interaction.

WHAT IS REQUIRED TO INTEGRATE LSA INTO AN ITS?

The typical stages involved in integrating LSA into an ITS are: (a) developing a domain-relevant semantic space, (b) collecting examples of student responses and incorporating those responses into a scoring model, and (c) embedding the scoring and feedback system into an existing ITS. Although the final step requires some computer technical knowledge, the critical aspect is still to make that integration in such a way that the assessment and feedback are pedagogically effective. The full details of the integration of LSA into an ITS are beyond the scope of this chapter, but are discussed in Foltz et al. (1999), Kintsch et al. (2000), and demonstrations can be found at http://knowledge-technologies.com.

Although the development of the semantic space requires a moderately powerful computer, depending on the amount of text to be analyzed, modern desktop computers are now at a level such that they are able to generate a semantic space for a set of textbooks in a matter of a few hours rather than days. Once this space is created, though, the actual scoring of an essay takes only a second or two. Thus, feedback can be delivered almost instantaneously. Indeed, the scoring model can reside on a separate server from the training system and can be sent essays to score over the internet. This provides the distinct advantage that the architecture of the ITS can be different from that of the LSA scoring, and there need only be agreement on the protocol for transferring essays and feedback between the two systems. For demonstrations and additional information about the technology, see http://knowledge-technologies.com and http://lsa.colorado.edu.

CONVERTING DIGITAL MEDIA TO AN ITS

One critical issue for developing ITSs is the conversion of digital media into an ITS. In the past, most ITSs developed were the result of much laborious hand coding. For example, production-system-based ITSs still require developers to generate the underlying production rules and to tie them to the feedback that is given to the learner. Information retrieval and computational linguistic techniques hold the promise of automating some of the conversion process, however. With LSA, a knowledge base on a topic can be automatically derived through the analysis of textbooks or training manuals relevant to the topic within a matter of minutes. In contrast, production-system and ontology-based approaches can take weeks or months to develop a knowledge base. Once such a knowledge base is developed, concept-based search on the material can further permit better linking of appropriate material that may be found across sections or across texts. Through monitoring learners' progress, the system can then automatically suggest relevant information from digital sources that would be appropriate for them to learn at the time. It can therefore adapt to a user's knowledge level and tasks.

Creation of ITSs will still never be fully automatic. Some amount development, monitoring, testing, and verification will always need to be done by hand even if a computer is able to structure the information. Some amount of the skill of effective teaching is implicit and it is difficult to extract the information from watching or interviewing teachers, or to extract it from published sources. These implicit skills can affect the decisions on how to organize the information for particular students, how to effectively motivate the students, and how to be able to accurately judge when a student does not know the information. New technology that can detect emotions, facial expressions, and eye movements may hold the promise of producing additional improvements in judging a student's performance. Nevertheless, although the technologies provide additional automation and individualization, it is still critical that people trained in pedagogy be involved in the development and structuring of the training materials. Thus, fully automatic development of ITSs is not yet at a viable level.

APPLYING TOOLS FOR ADAPTIVE LEARNING

No technique, approach, or tool serves to completely model a domain, the knowledge needed to comprehend a topic within that domain, the language used by a tutor, and the procedures that must be learned. Nevertheless, modeling techniques can sufficiently approximate aspects of human tutoring so that alone, or in combination with other techniques, they can be used as an effective ITS.

For example, production systems excel at diagnosing procedural errors and modeling what the student is doing. They can monitor the progress of a student, determine which types of misconceptions a student might have, and suggest the appropriate feedback. LSA does not have the level of refinement of production-system models for procedural knowledge. It excels at permitting rapid development of declarative (and potentially procedural) knowledge bases, diagnosing misconceptions and gaps in knowledge through analyzing open-ended responses, detecting a student's knowledge level, and providing appropriate feedback. Thus, each approach can be applied on its own for specific needs in tutoring. In addition, the two can be combined to provide a more complete adaptive training system.

CONCLUSIONS

As technology permits greater access to training material in digital form, the ability to use that material in effective ways for learning will be critical. Although the mere presentation of training material can be useful, it does not permit the active learning found in classroom situations. The ability to turn digital information into something that can interact more like a teacher, peer, coach, or guide can lead to much more effective training systems. The critical aspect of doing this, though, is the ability to interpret student responses appropriately.

With the advent of new technologies, training can become more individualized. The technologies can result in ITSs that are more sensitive to an individual's level of expertise, can diagnose gaps in knowledge, and can automatically determine the appropriate type of training material needed to remediate the individual. Thus, tools and techniques for the integration of digital training material into adaptive learning systems can result in the development of both improved and novel ways of helping students learn.

With greater amounts of information available in electronic form, it becomes critical to present that information in a pedagogically effective manner. Although tutoring systems have been researched and developed for a number of years, it is only recently that they are able to effectively adapt to a learner's needs. The next step is to permit easier integration of electronic texts with these adaptive systems. With the advent of improved theories of learning, new techniques for assessment of learners' knowledge, automatic structuring of instructional information, and better ways of providing directed feedback to the learner, the development of new adaptive training systems from electronic material holds great promise.

REFERENCES

Anderson, J. R., Corbett, A. T., Koedinger, K. R., & Pelletier, R. (1995). Cognitive tutors: Lessons learned. *The Journal of the Learning Sciences, 4*, 167–207.

Bliss, J., Askew, M., & MacRae, S. (1996). Effective teaching and learning: Scaffolding revisited. *Oxford Review of Education, 33*, 37–61.

Bloom, B. (1984). The 2 sigma problem: The search for methods of instruction as effective as one-to-one tutoring. *Educational Researcher, 13*(6), 4–16.

Bodrova, E., & Leong, D. J. (1996). *Tools of the mind: The Vygotskian approach to early childhood education.* Englewood Cliffs, NJ: Prentice-Hall.

Carroll, J. M., & McKendree, J. (1987). Interface design issues for advice-giving expert systems. *Communications of the ACM, 30*, 14–31.

Chi, M. T. H., Bassok, M., Lewis, M. W., Reimann, P., & Glaser, R. (1988). Self-explanations: How students study ad use examples in learning to solve problems. *Cognitive Science, 13*, 145–182.

Clancey, W. J. (1987). *Knowledge-based tutoring: The GUIDON Program.* Cambridge, MA: MIT Press.

Clancey, W. J., & Letsinger, R. (1981). NEOMYCIN: Reconfiguring a rule-based expert system for application to teaching. In A. Drinan (Ed.), *Proceedings of the Seventh international Joint Conference on Artificial Intelligence* (pp. 829–836). Los Altos, CA: Kaufmann.

Cook, J. (2002). The role of dialogue in computer-based learning and observing learning: An evolutionary approach to theory. *Journal of Interactive Media in Education, 5.* [www-jime.open.ac.uk]

Corbett, A. T., McLaughlin, M., & Scarpinatto, K. C. (2000). Modeling student knowledge: Cognitive tutors in high school and college. *User Modeling and User-Adapted Interaction, 10*, 81–108.

Driscoll, M. P. (1994). *Psychology of learning for instruction.* Boston, MA: Allyn and Bacon.

Eberts, R. E. (1997). Computer-based instruction. In M. Helander, T. K. Landauer, & P. Prabhu (Eds.), *Handbook of human–computer interaction* (2nd ed., pp. 825–847). North-Holland Elsevier Science.

Edelson, D. C. (1996). Learning from cases and questions: The Socratic case-based teaching architecture. *The Journal of the Learning Sciences, 5*, 357–410.

Foltz, P. W. (1996). Latent semantic analysis for text-based research. *Behavior Research Methods, Instruments and Computers, 28*, 197–202.

Foltz, P. W., Gilliam, S., & Kendall, S. (2000). Supporting content-based feedback in online writing evaluation with LSA. *Interactive Learning Environments, 8*, 111–129.

Foltz, P. W., Laham, D., & Landauer, T. K. (1999). The intelligent essay assessor: Applications to educational technology. *Interactive Multimedia Education Journal of Computer Enhanced Learning, 1.* [imej.wfu.edu/articles/1999/2/04/index.asp]

Foltz, P. W., & Wells, A. D. (1999). Automatically deriving readers' knowledge structures from texts. *Behavior Research Methods, Instruments & Computers, 31*, 208–214.

Golub, G. H., & Van Loan, C. F. (1996). *Matrix computations* (3rd ed.). Baltimore: Johns Hopkins University Press.

Graesser, A. C. (1985). An introduction to the study of questioning. In A. C. Graesser & J. B. Black (Eds.), *The psychology of questions* (pp. 1–14). Hillsdale, NJ: Lawrence Erlbaum Associates.

Graesser, A. C., & Person, N. K. (1994). Question asking during tutoring. *American Educational Research Journal, 31*, 104–137.

Graesser, A. C., Person, N. K., & Huber, J. (1992). Mechanisms that generate questions. In T. Lauer, E. Peacock, & A. C. Graesser (Eds.), *Questions and information systems* (pp. 149–172). Hillsdale, NJ: Lawrence Erlbaum Associates.

Graesser, A. C., Wiemer-Hastings, K., Wiemer-Hastings, P., Kreuz, R. J., & Tutoring Research Group. (2000). AutoTutor: A simulation of a human tutor. *Journal of Cognitive Systems Research, 1,* 35–51.

Graesser, A. C., Wiemer-Hastings, P., Wiemer-Hastings, K., Harter, D., Person, N. K., & the Tutoring Research Group. (2000). Using latent semantic analysis to evaluate the contributions of students in AutoTutor. *Interactive Learning Environments, 8,* 129–148.

Hativa, N., & Lesgold, A. (1991). The computer tutor: Competition in individualized CAI. *Instructional Science, 21,* 365–400.

Kearsley, G. (1993). *Computer-based training: A guide to selection and implementation.* Reading, MA: Addison-Wesley.

Kiekel, P. A., Cooke, N. J., Foltz, P. W., Gorman, J., & Martin, M. (2002). Some promising results of communication-based automatic measures of team cognition. In *Proceedings of the Human Factors and Ergonomics Society 46th annual meeting* (pp. 298–302). Santa Monica, CA: Human Factors and Ergonomics Society.

Kintsch, E., Steinhart, D., Stahl, G., Matthews, C., Lamb, R., & LSA Research Group. (2000). Developing summarization skills through the use of LSA-based feedback. *Interactive Learning Environments, 8,* 87–109.

Klahr, D., & Dunbar, K. (1988). Dual space search during scientific reasoning. *Cognitive Science, 12,* 1–55.

Landauer, T. K., & Dumais, S. T. (1997). A solution to Plato's problem: The latent semantic analysis theory of the acquisition, induction, and representation of knowledge. *Psychological Review, 104,* 211–240.

Landauer, T. K., Foltz, P. W., & Laham, D. (1998). An introduction to latent semantic analysis. *Discourse Processes, 25,* 259–284.

Lee, A. Y., Foltz, P. W., Biron, H., & Gilliam, S. (2000, November). *Effects of LSA-based feedback on learning form writing.* Poster session presented at the annual meeting of the Psychonomics Society, Orlando, FL.

Lee, A. Y., & Hutchison, L. (1998). Improving learning from examples with reflection questions. *Journal of Experimental Psychology: Applied, 4*(3), 187–210.

Moll, L. C. (1990). *Vygotsky and education: Instructional implications and applications of sociohistorical psychology.* Cambridge, England: Cambridge University Press.

Nelson, C. S., Watson, J. A., Ching, J. K., & Barrow, P. I. (1996). The effect of teacher scaffolding and student comprehension monitoring on a multimedia/interactive videodisk science lesson for second graders. *Journal of Educational Multimedia and Hypermedia, 5,* 317–348.

Nickerson, R., Perkins, D. N., & Smith, E. (1985). *The teaching of thinking.* Hillsdale, NJ: Lawrence Erlbaum Associates.

Page, E. (1994). Computer grading of student process, using modern concepts and software. *Journal of Experimental Education, 62,* 127–144.

Palinscar, A. S., & Brown, A. L. (1984). Reciprocal teaching of comprehension-fostering and comprehension-monitoring activities. *Cognition and Instruction, 1,* 117–175.

Paradice, D. B. (1992). A question theoretic analysis of problem formulation: Implications for computer-based support. In T. W. Lauer, E. Peacock, & A. C. Graesser (Eds.), *Questions and information systems* (pp. 287–303). Hillsdale, NJ: Lawrence Erlbaum Associates.

Park, O., & Tennyson, R. D. (1980). Adaptive design strategies for selecting number and presentation order of examples in coordinate concept acquisition. *Journal of Educational Psychology, 72,* 362–370.

Person, N. K., Graesser, A. C., Magliano, J. P., & Kreuz, R. J. (1994). Inferring what the student knows in one-to-one tutoring: The role of student questions and answers. *Learning and Individual Differences, 6,* 205–229.

Polson, M. C., & Richardson, J. J. (1988). *Foundations of intelligent tutoring systems*. Hillsdale, NJ: Lawrence Erlbaum Associates.

Rose, C. P., & Freedman, R. (2000). *Building dialogue systems for tutorial applications* (Tech Rep. No. FS-00-01). Menlo Park, CA: AAAI Press.

Ross, B. H. (1984). Remindings and their effects in learning a cognitive skill. *Cognitive Psychology, 16*, 371–416.

Sleeman, D., & Brown, J. S. (1982). *Intelligent tutoring systems*. New York: Academic Press.

Tennyson, C. L., Tennyson, R. D., & Rothen, W. (1980). Content structure and management strategy as design variables in concept acquisition. *Journal of Educational Psychology, 72*, 491–505.

Tharpe, R. G., & Gallimore, R. (1988). *Rousing minds to life*. Cambridge, England: Cambridge University Press.

Van der Veer, R. (1991). *Understanding Vygotsky: A quest for synthesis*. Oxford, England: Blackwell.

Vygotsky, L. S. (1962). *Thought and language* (Eugenia Hanfmann and Gertrude Vakar, Trans.). Cambridge, MA: MIT Press.

Vygotsky, L. S. (1986). *Thought and language* (Alex Kozulin, Trans.). Cambridge, MA: MIT Press.

Wenger, E. (1987). *Artificial intelligence and tutoring systems*. Los Altos, CA: Kauffman.

Wolfe, M. B., Schreiner, M. E., Rehder, B., Laham, D., Foltz, P. W., Kintsch, W., & Landauer, T. K. (1998). Learning from text: Matching readers and texts by latent semantic analysis. *Discourse Processes, 25*, 309–336.

Chapter 10

Knowledge-Based Systems: Acquiring, Modeling, and Representing Human Expertise for Information Systems

Cilia Witteman
Radboud University

Nicole Krol
Radboud University

In the 1960s, expert systems were proposed as the solution to the scarcity of human expertise. Experts were expensive or hard to find, and technology seemed ready to replace them. The only task for knowledge engineers was to acquire expert problem-solving rules, which could then readily be implemented as production rules in an expert system. Advantages were also expected in the quality of the conclusions: Computer systems did not get tired or bored, would not be distracted by irrelevant details, and would always perform consistently and correctly.

The view of expertise at that time was of a general ability to consistently perform above the average. The first-generation theories of expertise did not give much attention to domain-specific knowledge; experts were superior general problem solvers (Ericsson & Smith, 1991). Newell and Simon (1972) launched their ambitious general problem solver (GPS) with the claim that it provided a general-purpose program that could simulate all human problem-solving methods. However, the GPS turned out to be inapplicable to real problems without the addition of domain-specific data. These and similar disappointing results with this general approach led to a shift, in second-generation theories of expertise, toward domain specificity (Ericsson & Smith). Experts were found not to be able to transfer their problem-solving skills to domains other than that of their expertise, and problem-solving rules could not be formulated in isolation of domain-specific facts. The task of knowledge engineers now became one involving the acquisition and elicitation of the experts' knowledge—both facts and rules.

To date, knowledge engineers do not develop simulation models of human cognition. Simulation is the aim of artificial intelligence (AI) researchers who strive either to design computer systems with "real," that is, human, intelligence ("strong" AI) and who aim to actually emulate the expert in an expert system, or to test theories of human intelligence against an implemented computational model ("weak" AI). Knowledge engineers have more modest aims. On the other hand, their goals are more ambitious than simply to store facts in a database that may be queried. Their goal with knowledge systems is to provide users with expert knowledge, in the form of advice or arguments in favor of or against certain conclusions, without taking away the users' responsibility for accepting or not accepting the advice or drawing the conclusion. The system may be used as a knowledgeable sparring partner or as a critical audience for the user's argumentations. It may also be helpful in combining different pieces of knowledge in a mathematically or logically correct way. It also supports the generation of new knowledge from elements of knowledge about the domain of application stored in its knowledge base, complemented with inference rules that allow well-founded conclusions to be drawn from this knowledge, given data provided by the user for a specific case.

It has become generally accepted practice to separate domain facts and problem-solving rules, which are encoded in different modules. This has distinct advantages: Problem-solving rules may apply not to all domains but to a category of problems, and be reused in different systems that model a problem of the same category (e.g., fault diagnosis of machines, cars, computer systems). The database or knowledge base with the domain-specific facts may easily be updated without having to rewrite all of the code. The task of knowledge engineers may be divided into the acquisition of facts for the database and the elicitation of problem-solving strategies for the rule base. These two subtasks require different knowledge-acquisition techniques, as will be described later.

Because expert systems are meant to advise people as an expert would, they need another module: the interface with the user. This interface needs special attention, as it needs to take into account users' expectations and mental models of the system's operation. Designing the interface is not generally the task of the knowledge engineer, but of a human–computer interaction specialist.

The term *expert system* has slowly been replaced by *knowledge-based system* or simply *knowledge system*. This reflects the more modest aims of system designers to date: to develop an intelligent adviser that will support users in their decision-making processes, without pretending that the system contains the only indubitably true answers. Users need to retain their own responsibility for their decisions. More fundamentally, the infallible nature of expertise has become doubtful. Research into expertise has revealed that, on closer inspection, many experts do not perform as well as expected (Garb, 1989; Shanteau, 1992). A large body of research in the "heuristics and biases" tradition (Tversky & Kahneman, 1974) has shown that people's cognitive makeup precludes their faultless decision making in many cases, and experts are not exempt from this phenomenon (see, e.g., Wright & Bolger, 1992). The most well-documented findings include the (unconscious) application of the availability heuristic: What is easily available to one's memory is judged to happen more often than it does in reality. It should be noted that people cannot be faulted for using such cognitive shortcuts; they enable them to respond effectively and efficiently in demanding situations, and the possible detrimental side effects are taken for granted. However, this insight warns knowledge engineers against simply emulating experts' behavior (Carroll, 1987). It appears far more useful to indeed use experts, but as examples and inspiration only, and not to copy their reasoning strategies in a system. Experts are fruitfully consulted to gather insight into their domain, their selection of relevant variables, and their actual practice. But the validity of their selections and the correctness of their reasoning and decision making should certainly be checked, to avoid implementing systems that are as biased and uncalibrated as most experts are found to be.

The task of the knowledge engineer may then be divided into three steps. First, he or she performs descriptive studies of experts in action. This results in a *performance model*, that is, a model of how the experts perform their task(s). Subsequently, this expert performance model is compared to normatively correct models, usually based on logic or probability theory. Finally, the discrepancies between the two models are identified, and choices are made for the design of a system that will yield better results than experts do, but does not deviate from experts' reasoning so much that it becomes incomprehensible to them. These annotated choices may be viewed as a prescription that users are well advised to follow if they wish to draw well-founded conclusions. Such a prescription constitutes the blueprint of the knowledge-based system.

It is no easy task to develop knowledge-based systems, as will become clear from the description that follows. They are not meant to replace human experts, but to offer support in reasoning or decision-making tasks that surpass human capacities. Domains in which they are traditionally proposed are medical diagnosis and planning. Applications we have been, and respectively still are, working on are the selection of treatment for depressed patients (SelectCare, described in Witteman & Kunst, 1999; Witteman, 2003), the classification of childhood psychopathology (Machine-AidedDiagnosis [MAD], described in Krol, De Bruyn, Van Aarle, & Van den Bercken, 2001), and the decision about therapies for patients with esophageal cancer (Van der Gaag, Renooij, Witteman, Aleman, & Taal, 1999,

2002). These systems are designed to be used by health care professionals, not by patients. They contain a knowledge base, which is used, in combination with user input, to propose the most suitable treatment or classification for a patient. With these applications we will illustrate the process of acquiring, modeling, and representing expertise in the next paragraphs.

This chapter does not address issues such as the influence of knowledge-based systems on the organization for which they are developed, or the personal fears and hopes of professionals whose knowledge is captured in a system. The perspective taken is that of the builders of the systems: the knowledge engineers. The order in which experience has shown that they most sensibly perform their various subtasks is elucidated, and the subtasks themselves are explicated and illustrated. The examples clarify some pitfalls in the different subtasks, and possible solutions are offered. The chapter concludes with a summary and a discussion of how such a methodological approach may improve the chances of success of the knowledge engineers' task.

DEVELOPING KNOWLEDGE-BASED SYSTEMS

When it has been decided that a knowledge-based system is to be developed for a certain problem, the knowledge engineer starts the cyclical process of design and development. The subprocesses, sometimes performed consecutively and sometimes iteratively or in parallel, are task analysis, knowledge acquisition, modeling and representing knowledge, implementation, and testing.

Task Analysis

A task analysis answers, at a descriptive level, the question of what is involved in solving the problem for which the system is to be developed. In performing a task analysis, the knowledge engineer studies textbooks, performs literature searches, and interviews professionals (Carroll, 2000; Jonassen, Tessmer, & Hannum, 1999). What type of information is needed, where can it be found, and how do professionals typically solve the problem? Do they make forward or backward inferences (Anderson, 2000; Van Bemmel & Musen, 1997)? The difference between forward and backward reasoning, or forward and backward "chaining," as it is called in AI handbooks (e.g., Cawsey, 1998; Winston, 1992), is one of direction. Forward reasoning is data driven. One starts with the data and checks whether there are any rules that may be used with these data to make inferences. If so, these rules are executed. The conclusions from these inferences are added to the data set, and then other rules may be triggered if the latter rules depend on the new data that have just been concluded. Backward reasoning is goal driven. One starts with the goal or conclusion and then attempts to find one or more rules that yield this conclusion, and whether these can be used, in light of data known about the case. While one is trying to establish the truth value of a conclusion, other rules and even more data about the case may need to be evaluated recursively, until either the conclusion is proven to be false or until no more rules are found to be applicable. When there are few data, when one does not know the possible conclusion(s) yet, or when one wants to draw as many conclusions as possible from the data, it is better to reason forward. But when there are many data about the case at hand, forward reasoning could lead to too many conclusions. Then, and when one has a preliminary conclusion and wants to know whether this conclusion is true, backward reasoning is more efficient. Reasoning forward is problematic when one knows less about the domain and has fewer constraints on the search for valid conclusions. Novices therefore typically reason backward, whereas experts reason toward a conclusion (Ayton, 1992).

The results of a task analysis are represented in, for example, a flow diagram. Typically, two related but distinct diagrams result, one that captures habitual performance by professionals and one that describes optimal performance. If, for example, a professional states that he or she generates one decision option at a time and stops processing when he or she finds that option satisfactory on important dimensions, that may not be the process as it should be implemented in the system. The system should perform correctly, in this case, by generating all possible options and comparing them to each other. Setting up the task analysis thus requires more than talking to professionals; it also involves determining the optimal strategy to solve that particular problem.

Often, the type of problem for which a knowledge-based system is to be developed does not have an easy-to-reach, straightforward optimal or correct solution, otherwise no support would be needed by professionals who solve that type of problem. That means that the knowledge engineer may have to be content with criteria that an optimal solution has to meet instead of a full-proof algorithm. One way to find out what these criteria are is to ask domain experts questions such as "How should this problem be solved?," "How would you instruct novices to solve the problem?," and "How do you recognize a good solution?".

While developing SelectCare, we asked experienced psychotherapists which decision procedures they thought should be taught to psychotherapists in training (Witteman & Kunst, 1997). They were in agreement that their reasoning should be logical. By this, they meant that different hypothetical treatment options should be considered on the basis of information about the client and her or his complaint. Then each of these options should be weighted, by making an inventory of its pros and cons, referring to the information gathered, and annotating each piece of information as a reason for or against that option. Finally, the option with the best foundation in justifying arguments and the fewest counterarguments should be chosen. This prescriptive model, which was proposed by the clinicians themselves, strikingly resembles models or diagrams derived from decision theory, in particular, the empirical (or diagnostic) cycle of generating and testing hypotheses.

Comparing the two models, the one representing habitual performance and the other optimal performance of the same task, reveals discrepancies between actual and ideal processes, which may be taken into account in the further development of the system. Notably, the discrepancies point out where human professionals could benefit from support because they perform suboptimally, and they inform the human–computer interaction specialists in their design of the interface, which should take users' habitual ways of approaching the problem into account. The task analysis thus yields the blueprint for the eventual system: what information is needed and how that information should be integrated and combined to solve the problem at hand.

In developing MAD, a somewhat different approach was followed. Instead of consulting clinical diagnosticians, we first analyzed knowledge from textbooks and review articles to obtain the best way to diagnose a childhood problem (Krol et al., 2001). We found that, in order to obtain the most adequate diagnosis in an individual case, different classification systems or procedures should be used simultaneously. So the application we were developing needed to contain information from different classification systems used in childhood psychopathology, and to integrate and combine these different systems.

Knowledge Acquisition

Knowledge acquisition is the process of acquiring the necessary information from experts and other sources, and detailing the problem-solving rules. To elicit knowledge from experts, different methods are available, ranging from elaborate methods, such as think-aloud protocols, open and closed interviews, card sorting, and repertory grid methods, to easier methods such as written questionnaires and computerized acquisition tools (see, e.g., Cooke, 1994; Evans, 1988; Leddo & Cohen, 1989; Schreiber et al., 2000). To utilize the information stored in large databases, techniques such as data mining may be used, or other statistical analyses may be performed to capture regularities. Of course, the "old-fashioned" literature studies will help: What do textbooks say about inference methods or about causal relations between domain variables?

Different elicitation methods are suitable for different queries. If the knowledge engineer is interested in the problem solver's cognitive processes, thinking aloud is often the best method. While developing Select-Care, we applied the think-aloud method to psychotherapists' treatment-selection processes (Witteman & Kunst, 1997), with the aim of deriving a descriptive model: How do therapists, unaided, perform this selection task? Eleven more or less experienced clinical psychologists participated individually. They were first given a brief training in thinking aloud. Then they were given a paper description of a (fictitious) Mr. Johnson, who had been diagnosed as suffering from major depression, and instructed to imagine that Mr. Johnson had come to them for treatment. The precise question we put to them was: "Tell us which intervention method or methods you would use to start therapy with Mr. Johnson and how you come to that decision." They were asked to think aloud all the time while solving this task, and told that they could take as long as they needed. We tape recorded their verbalizations, typed up these tapes verbatim, and consequently had a hard-copy protocol for each subject. Then followed the very time-consuming process of segmenting the protocols in independent thoughts (sentences or closely associated groups of sentences), developing encoding categories for these segments, and assigning each segment one of these codes (see also Ericsson & Simon, 1993; Van Someren, Barnard, & Sandberg, 1994).

Developing encoding categories was done, as it should be, before scrutinizing the protocols, because the categories are a translation of expectations one has, on theoretical grounds, about the thought processes under study into sets of verbalizations that would express these thoughts. For example, we expected therapists to first formulate a hypothetical plan, which could be expressed as: "I think a psychodynamic approach, let's see. . . ." As may be expected, subjects used other expressions than were foreseen in the encoding categories, and some of their verbalizations were difficult to score. Our endeavor followed the usual procedure, therefore, of iteratively designing, testing, and refining. Eventually, two independent judges were given the coding categories and the segmented protocols, and asked to assign each segment one of the codes. Then we drew up 11 matrices, one for each therapist, with segment numbers on the x axis and category of thought (i.e., diagnosis, treatment option, consideration) on the y axis (for full details, see Witteman & Kunst, 1997).

We finally aggregated these 11 matrices. We had not been interested in individual differences, but in common patterns, in how therapists in general perform the treatment-selection task. We found that most subjects first gave an interpretation of Mr. Johnson's complaint and then immediately suggested a form of treatment, for which they, selectively, found confirming information. They did not seriously consider alternatives, but were generally satisfied with their first option. This order of decision steps does not conform to normative standards, but is in line with practical and efficient considerations. Ideally, one lists alternatives and weighs them against all available information, in fact, one takes shortcuts through this search space by relying on one's expertise and checking that one is justified. This conclusion constituted very important information for the design of our decision support system; it looked as if therapists would benefit from support in checking lists of alternatives and lots of information. In short, although applying the think-aloud method was indeed very time consuming, it was still very much worth our while because it gave us information about therapists' decision making in practice from which we certainly profited in the further design of our system.

Besides being time consuming, the think-aloud method is also not without perils, for example, it may disrupt the usual process or at least slow it down. But it is, to date, the only method to directly tap thought processes. Other elicitation techniques are available to acquire different aspects of expertise. For declarative knowledge, the engineer may, for example, use interviews, laddering, concept sorting, or repertory grids (see, e.g., Schreiber et al., 2000). If the knowledge engineer's interest is in categorizing domain variables, card sorting may be the best method. Professionals are presented with cards (on cardboard or a computer screen) on which domain variable names are written, and are asked to group them into plausible categories, to name these, and to specify the relations of these categories to each other. This method is easy on the experts, and yields a road map of the domain variables, which may subsequently be encoded in the database.

The system to support oncologists' decisions about the treatment of patients with esophageal cancer is implemented as a probabilistic network. A probabilistic network is a mathematical model for reasoning with domain knowledge (Pearl, 1988). It contains a set of statistical variables that represent important decision ingredients, for example, "metastases of the lungs." Associated with each variable are conditional probabilities that describe the influence of values of that variable on other variables, for example, the probability that a patient has metastases of the lungs when a CT scan of the lungs is positive. We needed 4,000 probabilities for the network. These were not to be found in the literature and therefore had to be acquired from experts. No straightforward, easy-to-use method was available to efficiently acquire such a large amount of estimates; we therefore devised our own (Renooij & Witteman, 1999; Witteman & Renooij, 2003).

Our point of departure was the acknowledgment that people often feel uncomfortable expressing their beliefs numerically: They seem to prefer words. On the other hand, probability, or uncertainty, assessment scales almost always ask judges for numbers. We performed a series of four experiments in which we first made an inventory of probability expressions people normally use, then their order from impossible to certain, then their distances, and finally their numerical equivalents (Renooij & Witteman, 1999). The result was a scale with seven anchors, with verbal expressions on one side and numerical expressions on the other side. Although the experts had become quite desperate about the probability judgment task before, when standard elicitation methods such as lotteries had been used (Renooij, 2001), they were now able to efficiently assess many probabilities in one session. They felt quite comfortable with the scale, indicating that they approached it through the verbal side when they felt quite uncertain, and through the numerical side when they were sure of their assessments. They appreciated the opportunity to use either format, depending on their own preference.

Knowledge acquisition is quite time consuming. Knowledge engineers need to familiarize themselves with the domain, to identify seminal textbooks, and to find experts who have the time and are willing to spend that time dissolving their knowledge. Usually, knowledge acquisition is done in iterative cycles: an acquisition session, analysis of the results, identifying aspects that need further inspection, and so on. Indeed, the acquisition of knowledge for MAD has been an iterative process. It started with the conversion of the classification systems developed by Vermande, Weusten, Coppen, and Kracht (2002), who had consulted three experts and had asked them to translate the symptoms of one system into the other system. This conversion was implemented in a program, and next validated in a clinical trial. The content of the program was judged by nine experienced clinicians, who rated the levels of similarity for 241 symptom pairs. Adjustments in the content of the program were made on the basis of the outcome of these expert ratings.

Knowledge acquisition has been called the "bottleneck" in the development of knowledge-based systems: The hardware is willing, but the knowledge slow in coming to specification. However, in a feasibly restricted problem domain, the knowledge engineer may eventually map out the relevant variables and combination rules.

Modeling and Representation

Acquired knowledge needs to be modeled and represented in a notation that may be encoded in a computer program. Which representation is most suitable depends, obviously, on the characteristics of the knowledge (Markman, 1999; Sowa, 2000). Are there static facts only, are there default rules, are the relations between facts of a causal nature only? Initially, knowledge-based systems were encoded as a production system: facts plus if-then rules. Given some facts, applicable rules "produce" a result: R is-a bird plus IF x is-a bird THEN x can fly produces R can fly. Production rules are a powerful formalism, in which many domain problems may be encoded. But when the data are more plausibly represented hierarchically, frames may be used. They specify a class of facts and incorporate slots that describe typical attributes of that class. Birds typically fly, and when a robin has been identified as a bird, one may infer that it flies. Frames are more flexible than simple lists of facts: Slots may contain default values that may be overridden in special situations. A penguin, for example, is a bird, but cannot fly.

In SelectCare, the knowledge elements that are used, in combination with user input, to propose a suitable treatment plan to a psychotherapist for his or her depressed patient, are represented in a frame structure (Witteman & Kunst, 1999). We used frames, because we wanted to efficiently represent all decision elements as they could be used to justify any of a set of possible decisions (i.e., types of treatment). In a frame structure, each element is represented in the title slot of a frame, with other slots of that frame containing positively or negatively justifying links to the different types of treatment. Advantages of such a representation, compared to a production system, are, first, that each element needs to be represented only once and still have different roles in the decision process, and, second, that elements and links may simply and locally be added or removed.

With production systems, frames, and other logical representations that are not elaborated here, the inference rules are generally represented separately from the knowledge base. Some extra rules are then added to control the order in which inferences are made. In a production system, for example, a metarule may specify the order in which data are fitted to the rules. Such a metarule may specify that the rule that is most explicit, that is, has the most IF parts, will fire first; and whether data are matched to the rules in a forward-chaining (to the IF part) or backward-chaining (to the THEN part) direction. In a frame system, rules may specify the direction of inheritance of slot values and the way in which new facts are added.

Another increasingly popular representation is that of the aforementioned probabilistic network, also known as a Bayesian or causal network, which is used in the esophagus system (Van der Gaag et al., 2002). The network consists of a graphical structure, with variables and the probabilistic relationships between them. Each variable represents a diagnostic or prognostic factor that is relevant for establishing the stage of a patient's cancer or for predicting the outcome of treatment. The probabilistic influences between the variables are represented by directed links; the strengths of these influences are indicated by conditional probabilities. To give an example: The variables "X-ray of the lungs" and "metastases into the lungs" have a relationship through a directed link, which represents the fact that the absence or presence of lung metastases directly influences the outcome of an X-ray (Sent, Van der Gaag, & Witteman, 2001). The strength of this relationship is captured in four conditional probabilities: the probability that the X-ray is positive when there are metastases, that the X-ray is positive when there are no metastases, that the X-ray is negative when there are metastases, and that the X-ray is negative when there are no metastases, or $p(t+|m+)$, $p(p+|m-)$, $p(t-|m+)$, and $p(t-|m-)$.

The network for esophageal cancer currently includes over 70 statistical variables and more than 4,000 conditional probabilities. Consulting such a network is quite flexible and fast: Any probability of interest of a variable can easily be computed. The stage of a patient's cancer, for example, can be established by entering his or her symptoms and test results into the network, and computing the effect of these observations on the probability of the variable that models the cancer's stage. A drawback of these and other networks, apart from the time-consuming work needed for constructing them, is that facts and inference rules are modeled in one representation, which means that it is quite costly to repair them if some facts or rules are later found to be superfluous, missing, or faulty.

The representation of the syndrome definitions of mental disorders for the automated comparison of two classification systems was more complicated than it seemed at first. This was due to the differences in, and the complexity of, syndrome definitions in psychopathology (Vermande et al., 2002). For most disorders, the definition requires that only an optional and minimal subset of symptoms be present. Any subset consisting of a minimal number of symptoms would thus be sufficient (at least n out of x symptoms). Production rules were judged inconvenient representations of such a definition because any possible combination of n or more symptoms had to be considered and would thus have to be explicitly written out in a production rule. Some disorder definitions require one or more symptoms to always be present, in addition to an optional and minimal subset of symptoms. For example, the definition of a major depressive episode in the *Diagnostic and Statistical Manual of Mental Disorders* (American Psychiatric Association, 1994) states that at least five out of nine symptoms should be present and that one of these symptoms is depressed mood or loss of interest or pleasure. Furthermore, sometimes the absence of certain symptoms or even the absence of other disorders is required. For example, the definition of a major depressive episode requires that symptoms do not meet criteria for a mixed episode. According to Vermande et al., none of the established representation schemes appeared to be adequate to represent these sometimes complex syndrome definitions of mental disorders. Therefore, they developed their own representation scheme, the RLIST (requirement list). The RLIST offers a compact representation of psychopathological syndromes that can be used in computer programs (Vermande et al.). For example, the RLIST [[95,3,[[22,23]1],[[16,94],1],6,86,7,8,90],5] reads as follows: At least five of the following items (symptoms) must be present: 95, 3, 1 of 22 or 23, 1 of 16 or 94, 6, 86, 7, 8, and 90. In MAD, this representation scheme, the RLIST, was also used (Krol et al., 2001).

Representations other than frames and rule-based or Bayesian models may sometimes be more suitable, such as neural networks or genetic algorithms (see, e.g., Haykin, 1994; Mitchell, 1996; Pham & Karaboga, 2000; Principe, Euliano, & Lefebvre, 2000). Both are used mainly for purposes of machine learning. They are said to be "subsymbolic" representations: They do not represent symbols, but very simple and highly interconnected elements. These elements in themselves mean nothing, but only become meaningful through their weighted connections to each other. On their own, neural networks or genetic algorithms are not suitable for incorporation into a knowledge-based system, because the knowledge is hidden and distributed in the model. Some input pattern is matched by hidden procedures to some output pattern, but what goes on inside is not very informative to someone who wishes to know the best course of action. Indeed, neural networks are very suitable for such cognitively speaking low-level tasks as the recognition of signatures, but not for more abstract problem solving. Sometimes subsymbolic systems are coupled with a symbolic system in a hybrid system, recognizing that the intelligence of human beings does not derive from one system by itself either.

Implementation

When the data and rules have been represented adequately, the system may finally be implemented. The choice of a programming environment is constrained by the representation: A probability network is usually implemented in LISP, for example. But most programming environments can handle different representations, and the choice more often than not depends on the preferences and capacities of the programmer.

Testing

The final step is testing the system. Does it do what it was designed to do, and does it do so adequately? This may be tested empirically, with different methods. Users may be observed while they are working with the system, their actions on the keyboard may be logged, they may be asked to think aloud while they are at work, they may be interviewed, or they may be asked to participate in a usability test (cf., e.g., Preece, Rogers, & Sharp, 2001).

EVALUATING SELECTCARE

With SelectCare, we conducted both a usability test, to test whether it was easy and pleasant to use, and an experiment, to find out whether psychotherapists could and would use it (Witteman, 2003; Witteman & Kunst, 1999).

Usability Test

The usability test was designed as a task plus questionnaire. The task was similar to the task for which SelectCare was designed, that is, to describe a patient and propose a treatment method. Because usability of the interface or the "outside" of the system was the major issue, the acceptability of the "inside" being tested in the later experiment, the task was shortened by supplying the subjects with a brief list of symptoms and factors that described a fictitious patient. In the execution of this task, the subjects had to use all SelectCare's functions.

The questionnaire was based on an existing questionnaire, Quis (Preece et al., 1994; Shneiderman, 1992). Quis has been designed as an instrument to determine the usability of an interface. It was slightly modified, leaving out irrelevant questions and clarifying the wording of some questions. The questions addressed the following usability criteria: general reaction, screen layout, terminology and system information, and learnability. They were to be answered on rating scales. Some questions were added that specifically addressed SelectCare's interface, on the points of generalizability (of knowledge of other programs to the use of SelectCare), ease of use (of the scales to mark the presence of items), and attractiveness. These extra questions were answered "yes" or "no."

The subjects for the usability test were 16 students of Utrecht University, with equal numbers of men and women. All but one subject were experienced computer users. Eight subjects were advanced psychology students who had completed a course in clinical diagnostics, and the other eight students were from various disciplines. Because the answers of the advanced psychology students differed only slightly, and in both directions, from those of the other students, all answers were analyzed together. The results are presented in Table 10.1.

The subjects were altogether quite uniform and approving in their judgments. Although SelectCare forces subjects to first describe the patient and check all contraindications before being allowed to get advice, the flexibility was judged to be sufficient. We therefore concluded that SelectCare is quite usable.

Experiment

In the experiment, we tested whether SelectCare led to a better decision process, and we asked the subjects whether the decision elements and the argumentation were acceptable. Because, in this domain, a better decision process cannot be identified by its output, we chose three other criteria: a more comprehensive description of the patient, more time taken to perform the task, and satisfaction with the resulting decision.

TABLE 10.1
Usability Results

Usability Criterion	Endpoints of 1–10 Rating Scale	Mean Ratings (n = 16)
General reaction	terrible-great	7.5 (1.2)
	frustrating-satisfying	7.1 (1.4)
	boring-stimulating	6.8 (1.6)
	difficult-easy	8.2 (1.4)
	rigid-flexible	6.2 (1.8)
	Total	7.2 (1.6)
Screen layout		
Characters	unreadable-readable	9.1 (1.5)
Layout helpful?	not at all-very	8.3 (1.4)
Order of screens	confusing-clear	8.3 (1.3)
	Total	8.6 (1.4)
Terminology/System information		
Use of terms	inconsistent-consistent	8.3 (1.0)
Terms appropriate to task?	no-yes	8.1 (0.9)
Messages on screen	inconsistent-consistent	8.1 (0.9)
	confusing-clear	8.0 (1.0)
	Total	8.1 (0.9)
Learnability		
Learning to use	difficult-easy	8.6 (1.2)
Trial and error	discouraged-encouraged	6.8 (1.4)
Task could be performed as expected?	never-always	7.8 (1.5)
Help messages	confusing-clear	7.5 (1.1)
	Total	7.7 (1.4)
Generalizability (menus/windows correspond to other applications?)	Yes	14 (88%)
Ease of use (easy to mark presence of items?)		11 (69%)
Attractiveness (attractive program?)		16 (100%)

The task to be performed was to study the case description of a patient who had been diagnosed as suffering from depression and to propose a treatment method for this patient. We had two conditions: a paper condition and a system condition. In the paper condition, subjects were asked to write down in their own words their considerations for their proposal; in the system condition, subjects described the patient's disorder by selecting elements they judged to apply.

After having performed the task in the system condition, subjects were handed a short list of questions about their satisfaction with the system, in particular, with the terminology used, the categorization of the elements, the completeness of the lists of elements and decision options, the order in which the steps had to be executed (descriptions, assessments, contraindications, conclusions), and the treatment proposed by the system. All these questions were answered by marking one of seven points on a line, with completely satisfactory at the one extreme and completely unsatisfactory at the other extreme.

A final question asked which of a short list of adjectives applied to their experience with SelectCare: useful, irritating, boring, or stimulating. We expected a significantly more comprehensive description of the patient in the system condition, because subjects did not have to think of possibly relevant descriptions themselves, but were offered lists to choose from. Subjects would consequently also need more time to perform the task. Because of their more thorough considerations, we expected subjects to be more satisfied with the resulting decision.

Two groups of subjects participated: 11 advanced clinical-psychology students and 9 practicing clinical psychologists. Of the students, 10 were female and 1 was male. Their ages ranged from 20 to 25 years. All of them had followed diagnostics classes. We used a within-subjects design with the student subjects, who performed the same task twice: first on paper and then with the system, for two different paper patients. Of the psychotherapists, four were female and five were male. Their ages ranged between 39 and 55, with an average of 45.6 ($SD = 5.9$). They had had 9 years of experience on the average ($SD = 7.4$). The psychotherapists only performed the task in the system condition. Their numbers of descriptions and proposals were compared to those of a larger group of therapists who had proposed and justified their treatment option for the same case description on paper, for an earlier study (Witteman & Koele, 1999).

We found that the students, who had performed the task twice in one session, gave a significantly more comprehensive description of the patient in the system condition, with a mean of 18 descriptions selected in the program versus 6.4 written down (two-tailed paired t test = 6.541, $p = .0001$). They also spent significantly more time on the task with the system, with a mean of 34 minutes versus 23 minutes when performing the task on paper (two-tailed paired t test = 2.559, $p < .05$). The subjects were also more satisfied with their decision after having used the system, but not significantly ($p = .22$), with 7 of the 11 equally satisfied in both conditions.

The students' answers to the questions about their satisfaction with the system were mostly favorable, with an average of, on the seven-point scale, a 5.5 for the terminology, a 4.8 for the categorization of elements, a 4.5 for completeness, and a 5.6 for order. The advice given was rated 3.6, just slightly above the midpoint. Comments on this point mainly concerned a lack of precision (only the main treatment methods were used) and doubt about the weight factors of different decision elements for some decisions.

We found that the therapists selected a mean of 23.8 descriptions ($SD = 10.6$). The number of descriptions given by colleagues in their own words on paper in an earlier questionnaire for the same patient was 2.8. The difference between system and paper conditions is quite remarkable, and much more significant than with the student subjects.

The psychotherapists' answers to the questions about their satisfaction with the system were, overall, more favorable than those of the students, with an average on a seven-point scale of 5.2 for terminology, 5.3 for categorization, 4.9 for completeness, 6 for order, and 4.6 for the advice given by the system.

The adjectives selected by the nine psychotherapists to describe their experience with SelectCare were: pleasant ($n = 7$), useful ($n = 6$), stimulating ($n = 4$), easy ($n = 4$), comfortable ($n = 3$), difficult ($n = 2$), and tiring ($n = 2$). Nobody chose useless, boring, or irritating. "User friendly" was added by one subject. Another subject wrote that SelectCare forces a closer look at the patient and diagnosis.

EVALUATING MAD

The MAD program was tested in actual clinical practice. In order to ascertain how clinicians work with the program, MAD was installed on the computer(s) in eight clinical settings: a council for child protection, four different semiresidential treatment institutions for children with emotional and behavioral problems, one mental health service for youth, a private pedagogical advice agency, and a clinic for child psychiatry. Given our interest in how the clinicians actually worked with MAD, we did not give them specific instructions. We only asked that they work with the program for 3 months.

To detect any deficiencies in the interface of the program, we asked the participants to fill out a problem registration form during their first 10 sessions with the program. We asked the participants to write down what they did with the program, the sorts of problems they encountered using the program, whether they were able to solve the problems themselves, and whether they made use of the help file or not. After about 6 weeks, we interviewed the participants in their office. They were asked eight open questions: four referring to the content of the program and four referring to the use of the program during clinical practice (Would you continue to use the MAD program in the future?; If yes, what sort of task would the program have; If no, why not?; What are the drawbacks of MAD and what are the benefits?). At the end of the 3-month period, we sent a final evaluation form to all of the participants for completion. We asked them the same open-ended questions as in the interview, and we asked them to rate the content and the user friendliness of MAD on a 10-point scale. This form was filled in anonymously.

Nine participants from four different settings filled in the problem registration forms; a total of 45 forms were returned. In one setting (a residential treatment institute), the program was installed but hardly ever used. In the other three settings, the participants worked with the program but did not fill out a problem registration form. All settings were visited during the study and eight clinicians were interviewed. Nine participants from six different settings returned the final evaluation form. The participants from the other two settings did not return the form due to lack of time. All participants who took part in this study had more than 2 years of experience.

Interface and Content

On 8 of the 45 problem registration forms, problems using the program were reported. The problems mainly involved unfamiliarity with the Microsoft Windows operating system (e.g., how to delete files or change filenames). Other problems related to printing and understanding the use of certain symbols in a result window. The average judgment of the user friendliness of the program along the 10-point scale was 7.1 (SD = 1.5, range 4–9, n = 8). The content of MAD was judged 7.25 (SD = 1.6, range 5–9, n = 8).

Use and Application

The program was used by the participants mainly to structure their problem descriptions, screen for possible disorders, and generate questions for further diagnostic assessment. Seven of the eight participants indicated that they would like to use the MAD program in the future. One participant did not answer this question. On the final evaluation form, participants described the function or task of MAD as follows: (a) to screen for symptoms of psychopathology, (b) to make the problem description more concrete, (c) to guide diagnostic decision making, (d) to generate hypotheses, and (e) to make an inventory and check the diagnostic data and grouping of symptoms. As disadvantages of the program, participants reported: (a) the limited specificity of the translation component, (b) lack of report clarity, (c) lack of weighting for the information included, and (d) the danger of getting lost in the exhaustive detail of the program. The following benefits were mentioned: (a) MAD is extensive, careful, and systematic; (b) MAD provides a logically consistent relation between problem descriptions and classifications; (c) MAD provides a useful link between the classification systems and makes the *DSM-IV* (1994) criteria available online; (d) MAD guides the thought process during problem description and hypothesis formulation and also helps generate alternative classifications or hypotheses.

USE OF KNOWLEDGE-BASED SYSTEMS

An often referred-to example of an expert system is MYCIN (Shortliffe, 1976), one of the first systems to be developed, in the 1970s, for the diagnosis of infectious blood diseases. In fact, MYCIN was never actually used in practice. This was not because of any weakness in its performance—in tests it outperformed members of the Stanford medical school. It was mainly because of ethical and legal issues related to the use of computers in medicine: If it gives the wrong diagnosis, who do you sue? Other classical examples, such as Dendral, Teiresias, and Guidon are now considered completed work because their goals have been met, and research attention has moved on to new areas (Russell & Norvig, 1995).

As mentioned in the introduction, developers have not been able to fulfill the promise of those days of a rosy future for expert systems. The more research that has gone into such projects, the more it has become clear that we simply do not know enough about human expertise to simulate human experts in machines. Some of the strong points of human experts, such as their use of intuition or a gut feeling about a suitable solution, do not, as yet, lend themselves to computational modeling.

As for intelligent systems with more modest pretensions, knowledge systems, the irony is that, when they are successful, their "intelligence" becomes invisible. Their performance seems trivial once we understand it. Yet they are quite valuable in making expert knowledge more widely available, and there are many knowledge-based systems in operation, as a search query on the internet will quickly reveal. To give some examples: Most banks have intelligent software to advise clients about their mortgage, architects use 3-D simulations and virtual-reality technology when they create new buildings, air traffic control is supported by decision-support systems, health care is provided online, sentencing in magistrates' courts is assisted by computers, and physicians are supported in their diagnostic task by a range of dedicated decision software programs.

The irony then is that, as with most AI research, as soon as a program has been implemented that performs well in a knowledge-rich domain, it is regarded as just a set of facts and rules. When a knowledge engineer has been successful in his or her task, the outcome is taken for granted.

A closer scrutiny of the different and often difficult subtasks the knowledge engineer has to perform in order to be successful shows that a positive outcome is not always to be expected. To develop these intelligent or knowledge-based systems, often not explicitly referred to as such, the subtasks of task analysis, knowledge acquisition, modeling and representing knowledge, implementation, and testing need to be performed. If this process is structured along the lines presented in this chapter, and if in their design knowledge engineers reckon with the users' mental models of the task, the chances of success are greater than if knowledge engineers do not think before they begin.

The activities related to the design of human–computer interfaces (HCI) are not highlighted here, but are of course of great importance. Develop a very valuable and useful system that users cannot easily access, and it will not be used. However, HCI is a specialism in its own right, and deserves its own chapter.

REFERENCES

American Psychiatric Association. (1994). *Diagnostic and statistical manual of the mental disorders* (4th ed.). Washington, DC: Author.

Anderson, J. R. (2000). *Cognitive psychology and its implications* (5th ed.). New York: Worth.

Ayton, P. (1992). On the competence and incompetence of experts. In G. Wright & F. Bolger (Eds.), *Expertise and decision support* (pp. 77–105). New York: Plenum Press.

Buchanan, B. G., Sutherland, G. L., & Feigenbaum, E. A. (1969). Heuristic DENDRAL, a program for generating explanatory hypotheses in organic chemistry. In B. Meltzer, D. Michie, & M. Swann (Eds.), *Machine intelligence 4* (pp. 209–254). Edinburgh, Scotland: Edinburgh University Press.

Carroll, B. (1987). Expert systems for clinical diagnosis: Are they worth the effort? *Behavioral Science, 32,* 274–292.

Carroll, J. M. (2000). *Making use of scenario-based design of human–computer interaction.* Cambridge, MA: MIT Press.

Cawsey, A. (1998). *The essence of artificial intelligence.* London: Prentice-Hall.

Cooke, N. J. (1994). Varieties of knowledge elicitation techniques. *International Journal of Human–Computer Studies, 41,* 801–849.

Ericsson, K. A., & Simon, H. A. (1993). *Protocol analysis: Verbal reports as data.* Cambridge, MA: MIT Press.

Ericsson, K. A., & Smith, J. (1991). *Toward a general theory of expertise: Prospects and limits.* Cambridge, England: Cambridge University Press.

Evans, J. St. B. T. (1988). The knowledge elicitation problem: A psychological perspective. *Behaviour and Information Technology, 7*(2), 111–130.

Garb, H. W. (1989). Clinical judgement, clinical training and professional experience. *Psychological Bulletin, 105,* 387–396.

Haykin, S. S. (1994). *Neural networks: A comprehensive foundation.* Upper Saddle River, NJ: Prentice-Hall.

Jonassen, D. H., Tessmer, M., & Hannum, W. H. (1999). *Task analysis methods for instructional design.* Mahwah, NJ: Lawrence Erlbaum Associates.

Krol, N. P. C. M., Wouters, G. P. J. G., & De Bruyn, E. E. J. (1998). Machine-aided diagnosis 2.0 (computer software). Nijmegen, the Netherlands: Auteurs.

Krol, N. P. C. M., De Bruyn, E. E. J., Van Aarle, E. J. M., & Van den Bercken, J. H. L. (2001). Computerized screening for DSM classifications using CBCL/YSR extended checklists: A clinical try-out. *Computers in Human Behavior, 17,* 315–337.

Leddo, J. M., & Cohen, M. S. (1989). Cognitive structure analysis: A tool for eliciting the structure and content of expert knowledge. *Proceedings of the Annual AI Systems in Government Conference, X,* 275–280.

Markman, A. B. (1999). *Knowledge representation.* Mahwah, NJ: Lawrence Erlbaum Associates.

Mitchell, M. (1996). *An introduction to genetic algorithms.* Cambridge, MA: MIT Press.

Newell, A., & Simon, H. A. (1972). *Human problem solving.* Englewood Cliffs, NJ: Prentice-Hall.

Pearl, J. (1988). *Probabilistic reasoning in intelligent systems: Networks of plausible inference.* Palo Alto, CA: Kaufmann.

Pham, D., & Karaboga, D. (2000). *Intelligent optimisation techniques: Genetic algorithms, tabu search, simulated annealing and neural networks.* Heidelberg, Germany: Springer.

Preece, J., Rogers, Y., & Sharp, H. (2001). *Interaction design.* New York: Wiley.

Preece, J., Rogers, Y., Sharp, H., Benyon, D., Holland, S., & Carey, T. (1994). *Human–computer interaction.* Reading, MA: Addison-Wesley.

Principe, J., Euliano, N., & Lefebvre, W. C. (2000). *Neural and adaptive systems: Fundamentals through simulations.* New York: Wiley.

Renooij, S. (2001). Probability elicitation for belief networks: Issues to consider. *Knowledge Engineering Review, 16,* 255–269.

Renooij, S., & Witteman, C. L. M. (1999). Talking probabilities: Communicating probabilistic information with words and numbers. *International Journal of Approximate Reasoning, 22,* 169–194.

Russell, S. J., & Norvig, P. (1995). *Artificial intelligence: A modern approach.* Upper Saddle River, NJ: Prentice-Hall.

Schreiber, G., Akkermans, H., Anjewierden, A., De Hoog, R., Shadbolt, N. R., Van de Velde, W., & Wielinga, B. (2000). *Knowledge engineering and management: The CommonKADS methodology.* Cambridge, MA: MIT Press.

Sent, D., Van der Gaag, L. C., & Witteman, C. L. M. (2001). *Modeling test characteristics in probabilistic networks.* Poster session presented at the Proceedings of the 13th Dutch-Belgian Artificial Intelligence Conference, 433–440.

Shanteau, J. (1992). The psychology of experts: An alternative view. In G. Wright & F. Bolger (Eds.), *Expertise and decision support* (pp. 11–23). New York: Plenum Press.

Shneiderman, B. (1992). *Designing the user interface: Strategies for effective human–computer interaction.* Reading, MA: Addison-Wesley.

Shortliffe, E. H. (1976). *Computer-based medical consultations.* New York: Elsevier Press.

Sowa, J. F. (2000). *Knowledge representation: Logical, philosophical, and computational foundations.* Pacific Grove, CA: Brooks/Cole.

Tversky, A., & Kahneman, D. (1974). Judgment under uncertainty: Heuristics and biases. *Science, 185,* 1124–1131.

Van Bemmel, J. A., & Musen, M. A. (Eds.). (1997). *Handbook of medical informatics.* New York: Springer.

Van der Gaag, L. C., Renooij, S., Witteman, C. L. M., Aleman, B. M. P., & Taal, B. G. (1999). How to elicit many probabilities. In K. B. Laskey & H. Prade (Eds.), *Uncertainty in artificial intelligence* (pp. 647–654). San Francisco: Kaufmann.

Van der Gaag, L. C., Renooij, S., Witteman, C. L. M., Aleman, B. M. P., & Taal, B. G. (2002). Probabilities for a probabilistic network: A case-study in esophageal cancer. *Artificial Intelligence in Medicine, 25*(2), 123–148.

Van Someren, M. W., Barnard, Y. F., & Sandberg, J. A. C. (1994). *The think aloud method: A practical guide to modelling cognitive processes.* London: Academic Press.

Vermande, M. M., Weusten, M. C. M., Coppen, P. A. J. M., & Kracht, D. (2002). RLIST: A representation scheme for the automated comparison of psychopathological scales and syndromes. *Computers in Human Behavior, 18,* 353–367.

Winston, P. H. (1992). *Artificial intelligence.* Reading, MA: Addison-Wesley.

Witteman, C. L. M. (2003). Psychotherapy treatment decisions supported by SelectCare. In F. J. Maarse, A. E. Akkerman, A. N. Brand, & L. J. M. Mulder (Eds.), *Clinical assessment, computerized methods and instrumentation* (pp. 144–154). Lisse: Swets & Zeitlinger.

Witteman, C. L. M., & Koele, P. (1999). Explaining treatment decisions. *Psychotherapy Research, 9,* 100–114.

Witteman, C. L. M., & Kunst, H. (1997). Planning the treatment of a depressed patient. *Clinical Psychology and Psychotherapy, 4*(3), 157–171.

Witteman, C. L. M., & Kunst, H. (1999). SelectCare: In aid of psychotherapists' treatment decisions. *Computers in Human Behavior, 15*, 143–159.

Witteman, C. L. M., & Renooij, S. (2003). Evaluation of a verbal-numerical probability scale. *International Journal of Approximate Reasoning, 33*, 117–131.

Wright, G., & Bolger, F. (Eds.). (1992). *Expertise and decision support.* New York: Plenum Press.

Chapter 11

Collaborative Voices: Online Collaboration in Learning How to Write

Eleonore ten Thij
Utrecht University

How do I know what I think until I see what I say?

—E. M. Forster

There is no question that in academic education you must be able to write well. As an academic, a considerable part of your life is spent writing and, if successful, publishing your work. As a student, developing your research skills is connected to writing, and you are judged on the basis of what you have written. As a student in the Netherlands, as in other European countries, you probably have to learn written composition by an instructional method that can best be described as "learning by doing" (Couzijn, 1995; EATW, 2001). You work on an assignment and, when you are finished, your teacher will judge it and write some comments in the margins. Such a method does not provide for process instruction, the feedback you get, if you get any, is often not well structured, and you almost certainly do not get that feedback when you need it most. As a result, you have little opportunity to evaluate and correct yourself (Couzijn, 1995).

As teachers, we tend to assume that students know how to write when they enter a university. In doing so, we seem to consider writing a skill that can be isolated from knowledge construction or from genre. At the time students have to write a thesis, they find themselves in a situation in which they are supposed to know what in fact they have yet to learn: how to write an academic text.

In ConCourse, an international multidisciplinary project, we developed an online expert center to provide students of European modern languages with better educational resources to help them learn how to write

(De Vries, Ten Thij, & Cromwijk, 2001). Our expert center was designed to integrate written composition into the learning (and teaching) of a specific discipline. It provided students (and teachers) with an opportunity to exchange and discuss information and documentation on various subjects, writing tasks, tools, and best practices, and allowed them to publish their texts in an easy way. Based on a social constructionist perspective on learning (Lave & Wenger, 1991; Säljö, 1999; Vygotsky, 1978), our main focus in developing the expert center was to support students collaborating on more or less realistic writing assignments while being given adequate feedback instruction.

Pilot studies indicate that feedback instruction needs improvement, and that student motivation to write realistic text genres and publish them on the internet was not sustained as long as we had hoped. Moreover, although the expert center was intended to reinforce students' learning from each other more independently, teachers reported that guiding, amplifying, and monitoring feedback was quite laborious (Jauregi, Nieuwenhuisen, & De Graaff, 2003; Van den Berk, 2003). We suggest improvements by stressing orientation on subject and genre, and organizing it as an audience of students commenting on other students' texts to further learning from text and interaction models; and by explicit instruction with respect to genre characteristics and role taking. We assume that improving prewriting feedback as intended requires a more salient representation of texts and interaction models. In order to assess the effects of instruction and support, we need greater insight into the way students learn from peer feedback. Therefore, we propose a method of analysis, based on discourse theory, that relates qualities of successful interaction to text qualities.

In this chapter, I first elaborate on the design and use of the online expert center and propose needed improvements. Then I focus on a method to assess the effect they might have on the texts students write. Research on peer collaboration in writing and learning shows that collaboration can benefit learning, but is less informative on how collaboration relates to improvements in students' texts (Chan, 2001; Hillocks, 1986; Mercer & Wegerif, 1999). A better understanding of how the process of collaboration relates to the products that result from it provides us with a better monitor on how effective instruction and support have been. I conclude with an outline of possible experiments to test my assumptions regarding the proposed adjustments, and of the anticipated results.

SETTING UP THE ONLINE EXPERT CENTER

As is the case with most skills, learning to write well requires a lot of practice and scrutinized evaluation of both product and process. The first requisite for good writing education is a curriculum that allows for frequent and consistent attention to writing. In order to gain consistency and continuity, the language-skill curriculum has been set up as a type of writing studio with a series of workshops related to the subjects taught in the literature and linguistics modules.

Writing is a complex cognitive process (Alamargot & Chanquoy, 2001; Erkens, Andriessen, & Peters, 2003; Kellogg, 1994). Didactical strategies such as structuring the writing process itself or drilling subskills may not be very helpful. Apart from the problem of how to isolate subskills, such as organizing, from a specific text in a meaningful way, mastering an independent subskill does not necessarily amount to using it well in the complex act of a real writing task (Alamargot & Chanquoy; Flower & Hayes, 1980; Hayes & Nash, 1996). For that reason, I favor an approach that integrates learning how to write into the various disciplines of the curriculum.

The nature of the writing assignments in these workshops has been based on a growing body of research on authentic and situated learning that emphasizes the importance of solving authentic problems in authentic contexts. Engaging in authentic activities can facilitate transfer of learning to new problem-solving situations (Williams, 1999). I interpret this research as a directive for writing tasks that involve realistic genres: Students should practice writing assignments that are at least functionally related to genres current in professional (academic) life. In ordinary life, texts are situated in a discourse community that has some genuine interest in them. Presumably, students writing in front of a real audience that is responding to their texts more closely resembles a discourse community than writing only for a teacher, and theoretically this may improve their motivation to write and discuss texts.

The instruction method supported in the online expert center is one of collaboration on inquiry and feedback. This choice was motivated by Hillocks' (1986) meta-analysis of experimental writing research, which showed that students benefit most from an environmental (i.e., interactive) instruction method in which objectives and goals are specific and operationally clear, writing principles are taught not only by illustrating them but also by engaging students in their use, and there are high levels of peer interaction (in small-group discussions). As a focus of instruction inquiry, text scales and sentence combining seemed to be most effective. For an overview of Hillocks' report see Rijlaarsdam, Van den Bergh, and Couzijn (1996).

As well as supporting collaboration in a direct way, it was hoped that the expert center would allow students to learn from observing the interaction of other students, given that the research of Couzijn and Rijlaarsdam (1996), Braaksma (2003), and Braaksma, Rijlaarsdam, and Van den Bergh (in press) showed some promising results here. It was felt that a digital environment would be specifically appropriate for implementing such a strategy, because of its potentialities to store and retrieve online interaction.

In order to meet these didactical requirements, the online expert center should provide for a knowledge base, consisting of resources such as classified (and rated) text models, documents on various subjects (because the workshops are not confined to a single course), and assets of classified linguistic constructions. It should also support student-centered collaboration. Accordingly, ConCourse was set up as an object-oriented groupware tool.

There are three kinds of spaces in ConCourse: the personal space, the group space, and the public space. In the personal view or work space, students can find hyperlinks to the group spaces of which they are members, to the public space, and to all the new information they have access rights to, be it a file, a URL, a message, or a discussion. A group space consists of a collaborative work space, in which all the relevant information of a specific workshop is stored, and of selected communication tools: Members of a workshop can down- and upload files, send a message to other members, read, start, or contribute to a bulletin board, or chat. All documents and comments can be labeled, archived, and searched for further study. A teacher can define and manage a workshop with the help of some simple procedures. In defining a workshop, a teacher can retrieve and copy files (bulletin boards and chats included) from the database and thus reuse information in a simple way. Finally, because the workshops are aimed at realistic genres, students have to write essays, scientific articles, reviews, and so on for an online journal, and lexicographical entries, bibliographies, and the like for an online museum. Even though the internet makes publishing journals comparatively easy, converting text documents into refined publishable HTML documents can be rather time consuming without the appropriate level of programming literacy. As a response to this dilemma, ConCourse allows for automatic publishing of texts, after assessment, in an online journal or in an online museum. The online journals and museums can be accessed from the public space, and from ConCourse's home page (http://www.concourse.nl; see Figs. 11.1, 11.2, and 11.3). (For more detailed information, see De Vries, Ten Thij, & Cromwijk, 2001.)

During a year-long period, ConCourse was tested and used in several pilot studies. I reflect on selected aspects of those findings in the next section. The findings are based on spontaneous reports and on questionnaires (see Jauregi, Nieuwenhuijsen, & De Graaff, 2003; Van den Berk, 2003).

REFLECTING ON EXPERIENCES

Students appreciated the library function and the opportunity to work on their assignments at their chosen time and place. They valued giving and receiving feedback on each others' texts, but valued the feedback of their

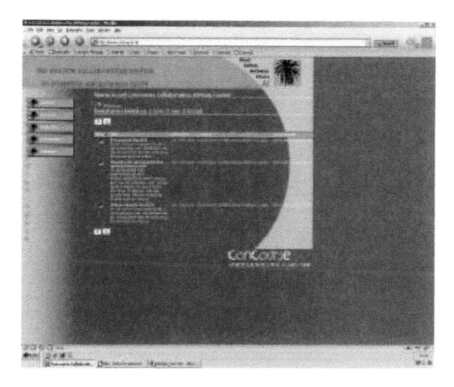

FIG. 11.1.   ConCourse homepage.

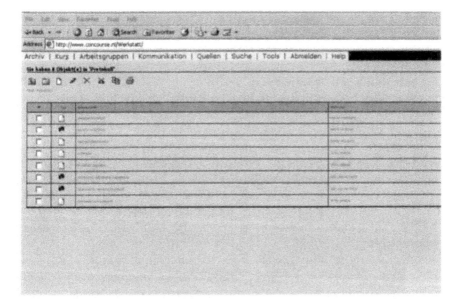

FIG. 11.2.   ConCourse, group space.

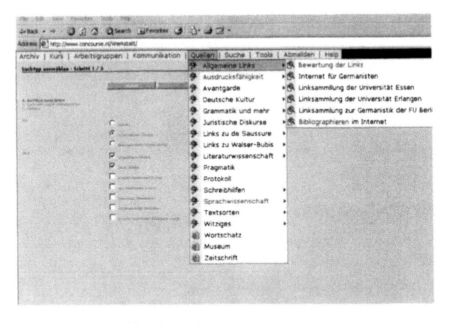

FIG. 11.3.   ConCourse, search and resources.

teachers even more. They thought peer feedback was more effective on lower level issues of writing, such as spelling, grammar, or overall text structure, than on communicative or subject-related issues of writing. This is in line with a pilot study conducted on online peer feedback with the help of a bulletin board before ConCourse was completed. Students were asked to discuss text criteria and to rate text models accordingly. The criteria they came up with—like "good structure," "convincing argumentation," "grammatically correct sentences," or "correct spelling"—seem hardly effective in meeting text goals, or making the means to realize them operationally clear.

Teachers were convinced of the importance of peer feedback, but also felt that commenting on students' texts as well as monitoring the peer feedback was quite laborious. Students as well as teachers reported a lack of good resources to guide students' feedback. The opportunity to let students learn from observing the interaction of other students was largely ignored. Both students and teachers found the message system quite helpful, and the bulletin board was considered useful if serious discussions were required.

Contributing to online publications was exciting as long as it was new. However, because there was no actual audience responding to students' publications, this effect wore off quite quickly. Some students reported that they did not feel the online expert center was a real (discourse) community.

These experiences point to a need for improving feedback instruction and support. Collaboration may be more productive with explicit guidance to help in analyzing genre characteristics and role taking, especially in the orientation phase. Such guidance may give students a better understanding of the communicative purposes and rhetorical conventions of texts (Lewin & Fine, 1996; Rubin, 1996), and give them the opportunity to depend less on teacher comments. Knowledge of the text genre at hand at an operational level could lessen the cognitive load students experience in writing and could help them in reading, discussing, and scaling texts written by other students (Hillocks, 1986). A second strategy to help students improve their ability to comment on texts is to provide them with models of other students' comments. As stated earlier, Couzijn and Rijlaarsdam (1996) and Braaksma (2003) reported promising results experimenting with students by observing their reading and writing activities. However, in their studies, students observed other students' reading as part of postwriting feedback or they observed exercises in argumentative writing. Whether models of collaboration in the orientation phase (hereafter referred to as "prewriting feedback") on larger and more complex texts will help improve students' understanding of text genre is yet to be researched. I expect to foster this type of learning by stressing prewriting feedback in the online expert center.

It is also necessary to address the community aspect in the online environment: If we want to motivate students by offering an audience that responds to their texts, we have to organize one. Published texts may function as resources for inquiry or as text models in the prewriting phase of the workshops discussed here. Students may benefit from the texts of other students, and the authors may benefit from the comments on their texts when they have to write similar texts in another part of their curriculum.

Improving the support the expert center has to offer will partly depend on the organization of instruction and the resources therein. However, I expect that this also will require some adjustments in the design of the online expert center.

PROPOSING ADJUSTMENTS IN DESIGN AND USE OF THE EXPERT CENTER: RESEARCH QUESTIONS

Ellis, Gibbs, and Rein (1993) stated that "selecting a groupware system means identifying characteristics of common tasks and shared environments" (pp. 10–11). This statement does not acknowledge the eventuality that an online environment itself may further shape our actions. In the common-sense view, supported by some (early) research (see Walther, 1996), online communication is by definition less interpersonal, and less social, than face-to-face communication. However, there is a significant amount of research contradicting this view as well (Walther, 1996). Among the factors that influence the degree of interpersonal communication are the sociocognitive cues and the kind of communication tools an online environment provides (Walther, 1996). If the online environment affects the online collaboration, it may affect the outcome of this collaboration. Identifying characteristics of groupware systems that make collaboration more effective is also relevant in designing a specific groupware system supporting specific collaborative activities. Here I am interested in the saliency of representing types of collaboration in the interface, which I refer to as the "framing perspective."

In talking about the internet, we tend to use spatial metaphors. We speak of a "virtual museum" or a "digital marketplace." By using these metaphors, we tend to let our conceptions of these spaces guide our actions, much in the same way physical characteristics of spaces—the architecture, the furnishings, and conventions of use—shape our actions in actual physical spaces. There is a specific set of actions for a kitchen and another for a bedroom; we behave differently in a small-town shop versus a huge supermarket; procedures for attending church differ from those for attending school, and so on. How can we imagine evaluating our online actions within these conceptual spaces in the same way we assess our actions in a physical environment?

The interface of a groupware system represents a specific functionality, but can also represent a specific use of this functionality. The interface presents the user with choices being made regarding naming, structure, visual presentation, and procedures to follow, and a groupware system in use will very likely show the user earlier interactions as well. In this way, the interface induces specific expectations of how to frame interaction in the groupware system as a specific communicative practice. Course-management systems like Web CT or Blackboard, for instance, illustrate this by using the metaphor of an "electronic classroom." Some teachers use such a system as a syllabus or a reader, whereas others make use of the communication tools to facilitate classroom discussions. As such, these systems represent a specific, institutionalized, often teacher-led interaction. Once used, the groupware system's interface represents a specific communicative practice or, in terms of structuration theory, it represents a specific structuration of group actions (Scott Poole, 1999).

We now assume that new users of a groupware system somehow adapt the specific communicative practice that is represented by its interface. This representation functions as a context for the process of *grounding*, a joint activity in which participants build a *common ground*, a mutual understanding of their communicative acts (Clark & Brennan, 1991). The culturally defined and situated expectations in which grounding takes place we call *framing perspective*.

General groupware systems to support online groups can be compared along a scale with respect to the framing perspective of their interfaces. At one extreme, there is the group support system (GSS), at the other the community support system (CSS). A GSS typically supports a work group and a CSS an online community (cf. Mulder, Verwijs, & Swaak, 2002). I understand an online community to be a group of people who communicate with each other on the basis of mutual interest and a shared identity for a considerable period of time, on a (semi)public accessible Web site, with the help of discursive media. When prototypical examples of these two categories of groupware systems are compared (e.g., a GSS such as BSCW [see Fig. 11.4], Viadesk, or Groove with a CSS like www.slashdot.org, www.tappedin. org, or www.utne.com), we find several characteristics to discriminate between the framing perspectives of an online work group and an online community (see Table 11.1).

Resources are confined to a specific task in a GSS. As is seen later, for instance, with BSCW, access rights are typically granted to small groups, mostly activated by a systems administrator. As such, the collaborative space is strictly confined. Group members have a shared file system at their disposal or tools that support them in fulfilling specific tasks (or both). Goals

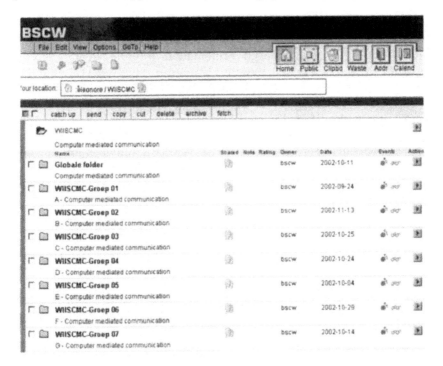

FIG. 11.4.   BSCW, a shared directory in a GSS.

TABLE 11.1
Framing Perspectives of a GSS and a CSS

	GSS (Framing Perspective = Task Group) Task Related	CSS (Framing Perspective = Online Community) Task Exceeding
Resources	On demand	At supply
	Work or study group	(Semi)public
Access	(+ tutor)	
	Task related	Related to identity-building
Tools		and social activities
Goal setting	Convergent goal setting	Divergent goal setting
Conceptual boundaries	Collaborative space(s) strictly confined by work group and task	Collaborative space(s) roughly confined by network and common interests
	Temporally bounded conversation	Ongoing conversation

and communication are devoted to completing tasks. Briefly, the basic ingredients for framing communicative practices a GSS has to offer all come down to getting a job done together.

A CSS, on the other hand, should enable its users to enhance and maintain social relationships. Task-related communication and casual conversation are more or less interwoven. Presentation of resources quite often is designed to draw new people into the community. They reflect common interests and can consist of files and (archived) discussions; they can connect (via hyperlinks) to other Web sites, online communities, or networks (as is the case with the journal-related communities www.utne.com and www.speakeasymagazine.org; see Fig. 11.5). Access is often granted to anyone who is interested (and who subscribes). A CSS is centered around talk. Tools help members, moderators, and community managers to regulate online behavior and to enhance social coherence. Online communities are communities by virtue of ongoing talk about shared interests. Spaces for discussion and social talk develop as subjects and social networks evolve. As a result, collaborative spaces have conceptually fuzzy boundaries and goal setting is divergent. Thus, a CSS offers participation in social networks focused on (a) specific type(s) of purpose(s) as a focus for framing communicative practices.

In the previous section it was suggested that feedback might be improved by organizing prewriting feedback as a community where students comment on other students' published texts. My first research question addresses the effect a groupware system's framing perspective may have here: Do differences in framing perspective between a GSS and a CSS affect online feedback and will these differences contribute to better writing? More

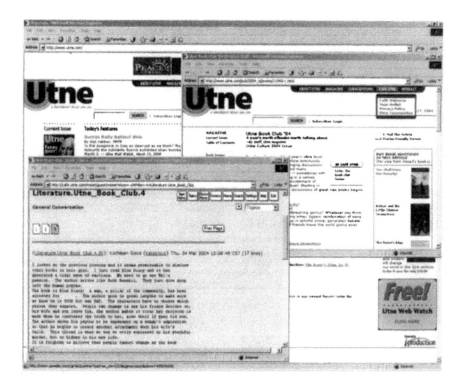

FIG. 11.5. Focus on discussing articles in a CSS.

specifically, I assess which framing perspective is more suitable to support either pre- or postwriting feedback.

It was stated before that my experiences with the current design of Con-Course led me to believe that feedback support had to be improved, especially with respect to prewriting feedback. I felt that prewriting feedback could be organized as an audience of student authors, responding to the texts of other student authors. To improve online support here, it may be necessary to make the commenting and scaling of texts more salient in the interface. I suggest that a CSS-like framing perspective will be more apt to do so. Postwriting feedback, on the other hand, may be best supported by a GSS-framing perspective, as it is now. I derive my arguments from the nature of the collaborative activities, the opportunities to learn from interaction models, and the sociability characteristics of both framing perspectives.

First, the collaborative activities in pre- and postwriting feedback differ considerably in my opinion. Prewriting feedback, as Hillocks (1986) suggested, consists of group discussion whose purpose is to gain operative knowledge of subject and genre. It is a "many-to-many" activity, directed toward orientation and inquiry, evidently somewhat divergent of character, by comparing and discussing different kinds of resources and text models. Understanding a text in its context, that is, the discourse community's use of a text, may help here. In the present case the discourse community takes the shape of students learning how to write about specific subjects in line with specific genres, and the texts they use for this are their colleagues' contributions to an online journal or museum. In my view, the main focus of a system supporting group discussions should not be a shared directory, but the comments of a responding audience integrated in the texts of the journal. The divergent character of this orienting phase requires easy and flexible access to different kinds of discussion with differing participants. Presentation and accessibility of resources should make its use more likely. These requirements are more likely to be met within the framing perspective of a CSS than that of a GSS.

Another argument for using a CSS to support prewriting feedback can be found in its greater accessibility of interaction models and thus the opportunities it offers to students to learn from previous discussions. This way of learning will very likely not survive if the expert center does not offer intrinsic motivation for group discussion, which it may have once it has a critical mass of exemplary discussions. This is especially true when students can communicate face to face as well, starting costs for using the online expert center for direct communication might be too high, or it might not be the proper medium (Flaherty, Pearce, & Rubin, 1998). Students may download the assignment, as well as the available resources. For discussing the assignment and task planning, they will probably stick to face-to-face communication, their standard e-mail program, or telephone (or, if they are more sophisticated addicts of computer mediated communication (CMC), to their standard chat application). But if attending online group discussions is rewarding enough, media preferences and starting costs may be irrelevant.

Finally, the characteristics of a CSS as a social space allow the stipulation that a CSS is better equipped for supporting prewriting feedback than a GSS. Research on collaborative interaction shows that, the more argumentative or exploratory the talk is, the more collaboration contributes to learning (Howe & Tolmie, 1999; Mercer & Wegerif, 1999; Van Boxtel, 2000). In-depth argumentative talk requires sound collaborative relationships. These relationships thrive on good social-psychological relations that get established in various levels of off-task interaction in addition to the on-task interaction. Informal communication also helps to establish sound collaborative relationships (Kreijns, Kirschner, & Jochems, 2002). The focus on identity and social relationships in a CSS may be of even greater importance when we keep in mind that the expert center will also have to host study groups consisting of members located in different countries, who are unlikely to know each other in advance. Although more intensive second-language use can be very helpful in learning how to write in a foreign language, there are some inhibiting factors to overcome as well. Intercultural differences might disturb communication, online collaboration without a shared external context might be hard to establish, and different time zones may cause organizational problems. I expect a CSS to afford better opportunities to represent the social and (inter)cultural contexts of communication and this may help to overcome some of the difficulties of intercultural communication and the lack of a shared external context.

Postwriting feedback, on the other hand, is directed toward revision, integrating and modeling knowledge in a specific text. This is also a one-on-one activity, and is more convergent and more limited in the use of resources: It consists of cooperation as a writer and a reviewer on a specific document. A GSS, with its prominent place for a shared directory and its secluded workspaces, may be more suitable here.

As stated before, part of improving the support the online expert center has to offer rests on the organization of the instruction. A relevant question here is whether the online environment itself, that is, the resources and interaction models, will allow for enough cues to induce relevant reasoning practices, or whether we have to provide students with explicit instruction as well. Therefore, my second research question concerns the support to provide students within the expert center: Will scripts containing explicit directions for role taking and genre characteristics lead to more effective feedback?

There is some debate about the shape directions for genre characteristics should take. Some researchers claim that providing students with formal genre characteristics alone is insufficient to help them improve their texts. It is not the formal characteristics that are difficult to grasp, but the communicative purposes and rhetorical conventions that lie underneath (Epstein, in press; Lewin & Fine, 1996; Rubin, 1996). We expect scripts, containing explicit instructions regarding genre characteristics in terms of communicative moves, to give students a better anchorage. They may help in discussing and comparing texts adequately and also provide for a problem-based approach to constructing subject knowledge. As such, they may lessen the cognitive load involved with writing.

Like Miller (1984), Swales (1990), and Bazerman (1988), I view genres as regularities in communicative acts as responses to recurring communicative situations. In professional life, writing is usually not an individual activity. Professionals write texts interacting with, among others, colleagues, expert advisors, editors, principals, and clients (Posner & Baecker, 1993). Next to the "common" reader, these people represent participant roles in specific genres. In providing directions for adopting roles, I hope to increase the opportunity for these perspectives to be represented in the interaction. Also, if collaborators take different roles, they may more easily surprise each other with complementary information. Complementary knowledge, skills, or resources make collaboration more desirable (Erkens, 1997).

In my opinion, measuring the effects of framing perspective and feedback scripts requires an analysis of patterns of interaction that relates the process of collaboration to its outcome. When we know which qualities of feedback make it effective, we can better assess which kind of groupware characteristics and instruction help to bring them about. In the next section, I take a preliminary view of how such an analysis might be performed.

ASSESSING THE EFFECTS: PATTERNS OF INTERACTION IN RELATION TO OUTCOME

Hillocks' (1986) findings tell us that discussion and feedback do help, but they do not inform us about the qualities of interaction making collaboration and feedback on writing tasks so effective. If we are to assess the effect different experimental conditions have on the process and outcome of collaboration, we first need to address how collaboration and writing processes are related.

Generally, it is assumed that knowledge is stored in schemata: structured anticipations about physical, social, cultural, and task environments. These schemata direct our exploration of the environment and are formed in interaction with it. In the present case, schemata representing discourse and content knowledge help the writer to explore the problems related to the writing task at hand (Kellogg, 1994). The principal question here is: How does collaboration help to achieve these schemata? As human beings, we do not just "process" information. Whoever has made a presentation, and taken the trouble to talk about it with the audience afterwards, may have had the experience of being confronted with a diversity of understandings. We construct knowledge actively and we do so with the help of others. Entering a new domain of knowledge also means entering a new social and cultural world, and mastering the rules that obtain there: What are the significant and valid concepts, how are they used, and what are the guiding reasoning principles, and so on. In order to acquire the relevant schemata that allow us to use concepts and reasoning principles adequately, we need to negotiate their meaning (see Van Boxtel, 2000, for a comprised overview of the constructivist, situational, and social-cultural perspective on learning). Krummheuer's (1992) outline of a discourse-theoretical-oriented learning theory shows us how this negotiation of meaning is brought about. In his analysis of classroom interaction on mathematics, he focused on the formats in which differences in interpretation regarding concepts and reasoning principles (framing differences) are solved, that constitute mathematical reasoning. The teacher proposed mathematical problems, whereupon the pupils presented her and each other with their differing interpretations of concepts and reasoning principles. Consecutively, they tried to agree on a mutually held interpretation that would enable the pupils to continue solving the mathematical problem. Learning is situated in the exchange and solving of differences of interpretation. Krummheuer's research was primarily focused on the interaction between teachers and primary-school children, where the teachers guided the interaction relying on their completed knowledge of the relevant reasoning schemata. Nevertheless, on some occasions, formats established themselves in the interaction of the pupils as well, according to Krummheuer.

This method of analysis may be useful to us, because it identifies successful and unsuccessful patterns of discourse in relation to learning (see also Chan, 2001). Analyzing talk data along categories of individual speech acts does not show us the development of valid meanings as a joint activity (Mercer & Wegerif, 1999). Analyzing episodes of speech acts as related to their function in finding a mutual frame of interpretation might be more helpful here. I propose a categorization of interaction episodes that is based on the formats of (not) solving framing differences, as described by Krummheuer (1992).[1] (See Tables 11.2 through 11.6.)

In the experiments I intend to conduct, I will focus on the development of genre characteristics in students' writing. I expect more successful interaction to show more formats labeled "coordinated" than less successful interaction; these formats will be related to more feasible genre characteristics in the texts students produce. I research this by analyzing which genre characteristics are addressed in the interaction, in which order they appear, and the formats in which they appear. I relate this analysis to ratings of the way these genre characteristics are realized in the drafts and final texts students produce. By situating the collaboration in different experimental conditions, I expect to gain insight into some of the qualities of feedback that make it effective, and in the way the online environment and method of instruction affect these qualities.

SETTING UP EXPERIMENTS

In the first experiment I intend to set up, I will test my assumptions regarding the effect of framing perspective on collaboration. I assume a CSS framing perspective is more apt to support prewriting feedback, because it enables an integrated representation of text and interaction models, available on re-

---

[1]Chan (2001) identified (un)successful discourse patterns in a comparable way. Her approach of identifying such patterns by identifying the moves that constitute them may be helpful in coding the intended patterns.

TABLE 11.2

Interaction Patterns for (Not) Solving Framing Differences: Coordinated

Format Label	Description
Coordinated	Discrepancies in interpretation are sought out actively. An adequate mutual understanding is constituted by adapting one of the interpretations that have been put forward, or by integrating various interpretations in a new interpretation.

Protocol example

H: I see some differences with the two of you. The most important to me is: is the argumentation clear, does it answer the problem statement in a scientific way, is some sensible conclusion reached.

J: Ok, I can see what you mean. Could we replace 'scientific argumentation' with 'is the argumentation supported by results and arguments from scientific research'? To me depth as regards content is also important. I didn't find that in 'Misconceptions' or 'Reading Methods'. If you don't consider substance, you could present an argumentation that fits all our criteria, but has nothing new to add.

E: Maybe you're right, but 'substance' is rather subjective, isn't it.

H: I think an argumentation that pretends depth as regards content but isn't supported by scientific research, doesn't realize its pretentions.

J: You've got a point there. Can we add as a criteria then 'provides new insight on the subject'? 'Misconceptions' describes previous research, but doesn't really add something.

TABLE 11.3

Interaction Patterns for (Not) Solving Framing Differences: Superficial

Format Label	Description
Superficial	Differences in interpretation are acknowledged, but rather compromised or rejected than sought out. A mutual understanding is reached, but it remains superficial or is inadequate.

Protocol example

B: J, I think your criterium 'clear cut content' means the same as my 'feasible problem statement'. I see we have a lot of criteria in common like 'title', 'structure', 'language'. I mentioned 'use of literature' as well. 'Content' and 'Presentation' I used as umbrella terms. Are we done with the criteria now, can we keep them as they are now?

J: I agree with you about 'content' and 'presentation'. I would like to add 'audience' there, since it's very important to know what's the intended audience. With regard to 'argumentation' I don't really understand the difference between 'build up' and 'structure'. Your 'use of literature' is very smart, I didn't think of it while it is very important. Shortly, I think our list of criteria is good now, and that we can stick to it.

C: Hi girls, I read B's criteria and J's repsonse. I agree with the two of you, I only would like to add 'no unnecessary information' to 'argumentation', since I saw a lot of it in one the articles. As far as I'm concerned we're done now.

TABLE 11.4
Interaction Patterns for (Not) Solving Framing Differences: Postponed

Format Label	Description
Postponed	A working consensus has been achieved, whereas solving differences of interpretation has been postponed.

Protocol example

K: I think our criteria are more or less the same, we just phrased them differently. The criterium 'intended audience' may be hard to apply, since we don't really know who they are. 'Plagiarism' is hard to apply as well, at least for me, since I'm not really an expert on these subjects.

D: As far as the intended audience is concerned, I think they should be our fellow students. They have to be able to understand the argumentation.

P: D might be right, it's not possible to write without an intended audience. On the other hand, I find it difficult to add it to our list of criteria, I don't consider it that important. 'Misconception' scores low, when you consider 'intended audience' as a criterium, but I still think it's better than the other articles.

K: Let's stick to the criteria we have now. We still have to decide upon scaling the articles: 'Misconceptions' and 'Self Guided Learning': Good; 'Good and Weak Readers' and 'Mathematics and Language Problems': Average; 'Enjoying Mathematics' and 'Methods': Less. Well, I have to go now, I'm leaving tonight.

D: Allright, this discussion is getting rather complicated anyhow, with all these replies and counter replies. We can apply the criteria in our own writing as each of us feels like, since we formulated them rather broadly.

TABLE 11.5
Interaction Patterns for (Not) Solving Framing Differences: Skipped

Format Label	Description
Skipped	A working consensus has been established without exchanging differences of interpretation.

Protocol example

G: I put both of your lists of criteria together and divided them into three categories, to clarify them to myself. I also added some details. I did rank the articles a bit differently. I think 'Self Guided Learning' was good, and 'Enjoying Mathematics' was less, the rest is in between. My ranking is now as follows: Self Guided Learning' and 'Misconceptions' are good, 'Methods' and 'Mathematics and Language Problems' are in between, 'Enjoying Mathematics' and 'Good and Bad Readers' are less. What do you think?

R: Or should we interchange the articles on mathematics? I think they are more or less the same. In both articles there's something wrong with the problem statement and the argumentation, but I don't know in which article this is more serious. I liked your list of criteria, I think we can keep it that way.

L: Yeah, you might be right, I find it hard to rank these articles as well, and we still have a lot of work to do.

G: Ok, shall I hand our stuff in then?

TABLE 11.6
Interaction Patterns for (Not) Solving
Framing Differences: Unbridgeable

Format Label	*Description*
Unbridgeable	As a result of differences of interpretation the (superficial) working consensus collapses, the interaction stagnates.

Protocol example

M: I think 'Misconceptions' is a rather weak article. The introduction is too brief, the problem statement too simple, and the argumention answers a different question. 'Good and Bad Readers' on the other hand, has a very powerful introduction. The problem statement seems to fill a gap in the current research. Most concepts are clearly described, and there are some interesting references.

A: I thought we agreed upon a list of criteria: Good structure, Clear problem statement, Good Readability, Relevant literature, References in line with APA? Therefore I think 'Misconceptions' is a good article. It has a well-ordered structure, and the abstract in the beginning guides the reader through the article. The problem statement is very clear, and the argumentation extensive. 'Good and Bad Readers' is reasonably structured as well, but the conclusion is not that articulated. The problem statement makes the rest of the article superfluous. There are too many tables, which does not contribute to reading it easily. References are not completely consistent with APA. I think it's a lesser essay than "Misconceptions."

M: I don't know. I think you can find the problem statement in 'Misconceptions' in a dictionary as well. And since the problem stated was simple, the answer is as well.

P: I think we should stick to our criteria.

M: I just don't agree with your ranking.

P: It's too late now to change the whole thing. Let's agree to disagree then?

quest. Accessibility in a CSS is flexible, thus allowing for a greater quantity and diversity of group discussions. Discussions are (semi)public, which could further commitment to contributing to discussions. Identity formation is explicitly supported, and a CSS more easily allows for socially oriented interaction support. This may be beneficial for accessing role-taking information and for the perceived sociability of the online environment (Kreijns, Kirschner, & Jochems, 2002; Van Oostendorp, chap. 8, this volume). Therefore, I expect more successful interaction patterns here and, as a result, better scores on first drafts on the related genre characteristics.

With respect to postwriting feedback, I expect more successful interaction patterns in the GSS. As a result, final texts may show more progress in proportion to first drafts on related genre characteristics. In nonexperimental conditions, I would expect students to be reluctant to expose their drafts to a larger audience and, as a consequence, to stop using the groupware system and collaborate face to face or via their standard e-mail program instead. In the CSS condition, students might hesitate to confront others with differing opinions, or work out their differences of interpretations sufficiently.

In the second experiment I intend to test my assumptions regarding the effect of explicit instruction on feedback. Half of the students in both the GSS and CSS environments will have an instruction script at their disposal, with explicit directions for scaling text models, based on genre analysis, and for reviewing drafts, based on role taking. The other half of the students in both environments will collaborate without these scripts. Explicit instruction may give students a better anchorage to observe and contribute to discussions in the online environment. Therefore, I anticipate more successful interaction patterns in prewriting feedback from students collaborating with the help of explicit instruction in a CSS, whereas postwriting collaboration with the help of explicit instruction may be more successful in a GSS. (However, the explicit instruction may lessen students' hesitation to discuss their drafts in front of a greater audience.) The scaling of text models may be best motivated in the CSS-with-explicit-instruction condition, and the drafts may show the best coverage of genre characteristics and role-related text qualities. Final texts may show the most improvement in proportion to first drafts in the GSS-with-explicit-instruction condition.

The dependent variables, interaction formats and text qualities, will be scored as described in the previous section, with a focus on genre characteristics, and on text aspects related to role taking. My categories of genre characteristics will be based on Lewin and Fine's (1996) analysis of the experimental research article in the social sciences, because this analysis is rather comprehensive, directed toward communicative acts, and, in my opinion, also suitable to direct a problem-based approach to the required knowledge construction.[2] (It is beyond the scope of this chapter to give a full account of their analysis, but see Lewin & Fine.) Role-taking directions will concern an editor and a reviewer role, translated into text aspects as reader friendliness, suitability with respect to the policy of the online journal (e.g., methodology), structure, coherence, and argumentation. I will also conduct some additional analysis of page views and the amount of social interaction to relate specific characteristics of the groupware systems to

---

[2]More specifically, I will analyze whether and how students discuss communicative moves and semantic participants, and whether they realize them in their texts. Examples of communicative moves in scientific research articles are "claiming relevance," "previewing," "stating the hypothesis," "report accomplishments," and "offer interpretation." Semantic participants are components of a move that make it recognizable as an instantiation of the same communicative purpose along different texts. Examples of semantic participants in, for instance, claiming relevance, are the phenomena being studied, the population affected by the phenomena, or the research. (In other words, in scientific articles claiming relevance is regularly realized by stating that the phenomena being studied are relevant for human behavior [of a specific group of people] or for furthering the research in the field at hand.)

the collaboration in the online environment. Subsequently, I will evaluate students' opinions and motivations concerning collaboration in the online environments with the help of questionnaires.

I have not yet discussed the analysis of the order in which genre characteristics and other text qualities are discussed in students' interaction. As I know of little previous research on this matter,[3] it is hard to make any motivated assumptions about productive strategies in terms of order when discussing text characteristics in relation to interaction formats. I will search for trends here and, if discovered, will elaborate on them in following research.

CONCLUSION

Reinforcing students' capabilities to learn from each other more independently is motivated primarily by a social-constructionist learning perspective. However, there is a practical incentive as well. Because (academic) teachers only have limited resources to engage in writing education, the more self-sufficient students are in learning how to write, the better their chances to learn it at all. Online support may be beneficial here, but developing appropriate support demands a careful approach in determining how online support affects collaboration. In this chapter, I suggested a first step toward such an approach: I presented a method to test my assumption that feedback can be improved by a CSS-framing perspective supporting prewriting feedback, organized as a community where students comment on other students' published texts, and by providing students with explicit instruction on genre characteristics and role taking.

Analysis of individual speech acts indicated that more explorative and argumentative talk is beneficial for learning (Howe & Tolmie, 1999; Mercer & Wegerif, 1999; Van Boxtel, 2000). We learn little from it, however, about how meaning is negotiated (which, in a social-constructionist perspective on learning, is crucial for learning), how it relates to mastering specific subjects, or how an online environment affects the negotiation of meaning. If we are able to relate the process of collaboration to the texts that result from it by analyzing interaction patterns in relation to specific text qualities, we will be better equipped to assess the kind of instruction that benefits collaboration in learning how to write, and the characteristics of an online environment that support specific instruction most effectively.

Further steps could involve researching additional instruction methods such as phasing strategies in peer feedback, peer assessment, composition

---

[3]But see Erkens, Andriessen, and Peters (2003), where they quoted Bereiter and Scardamalia (1987) and Galbraith and Rijlaarsdam (1999) about the absence of constraints for planning, organization, and dealing with an audience being beneficial for rough drafting.

of feedback groups, and related support such as structuring collaborative writing processes, assistance with finding suitable (rated) text and interaction models, and suitable collaboration partners.

ACKNOWLEDGMENTS

ConCourse was cofinanced by SURF, as a cooperative venture of Utrecht University, the University of Twente, Konict, Radboud University Nijmegen, the University of Bochum, and the University of Granada. One of the pilot studies was held in cooperation with Keio University, Japan. I would like to thank W. Herrlitz, H. Van den Bergh, L. Klein Gunnewieck, H. ten Thij, G. Koefoed, and H. van Oostendorp for (criticizing) ideas, feedback, and support, and J. Lynch for editing this text.

REFERENCES

Alamargot, D., & Chanquoy, L. (2001). *Through the models of writing*. Dordrecht, The Netherlands: Kluwer.

Bazerman, C. (1988). *Shaping written knowledge. The genre and activity of the experimental article in science*. Madison, WI: University of Wisconsin Press.

Bereiter, C., & Scardamalia, M. (1987). *The psychology of written composition*. Hillsdale, NJ: Lawrence Erlbaum Associates.

Braaksma, M. (2003). *Observational learning in argumentative writing*. Amsterdam: Amsterdam University Press.

Braaksma, M., Rijlaarsdam, G., & Van den Bergh, H. (in press). Orchestration of writing processes. Observational Learning and its effect on the orchestration of writing processes. *Cognition and Instruction*.

Chan, C. K. K. (2001). Peer collaboration and discourse patterns in learning from incompatible information. *Instructional Science, 29*, 443–479.

Clark, H., & Brennan, S. (1991). Grounding in communication. In L. B. Resnick, R. M. Levine, & S. D. Teasley (Eds.), *Perspectives on socially shared cognition* (pp. 127–149). Washington, DC: American Psychology Association.

Couzijn, M. (1995). *Observation of writing and reading activities. Effects on learning and transfer*. Dordrecht, The Netherlands: Dorfix.

Couzijn, M., & Rijlaarsdam, G. (1996). Learning to read and write argumentative text by observation. In G. Rijlaarsdam, H. Van den Bergh, & M. Couzijn (Eds.), *Effective teaching and learning of writing* (pp. 253–272). Amsterdam: Amsterdam University Press.

De Vries, S. A., Ten Thij, E., & Cromwijk, J. (2001). *Het gedetailleerd ontwerp van ConCourse. Een online expertisecentrum op het gebied van bedrijfsmatig en wetenschappelijk schrijven* [The detailed design of ConCourse. An online expert center for scientific and business writing]. Utrecht, The Netherlands: Utrecht University.

Ellis, C., Gibbs, S., & Rein, G. (1993). Groupware: Some issues and experiences. In R. Baecker (Ed.), *Groupware and computer-supported cooperative work. Assisting human-human collaboration* (pp. 9–28). San Francisco: Kaufmann.

Epstein, M. (in press). Genre as a frame for meaning construction. In G. Rijlaarsdam & H. Van den Bergh (Eds.), *Studies in the effective teaching of writing*. Amsterdam: Elsevier.

Erkens, G. (1997). *Coöperatief probleem oplossen met computers in het onderwijs. Het modelleren van coöperatieve dialogen voor de ontwikkeling van intelligente onderwijssystemen* [Cooperative problem solving with computers in education. Modeling of cooperative dialogues for the design of intelligent educational systems]. Utrecht, The Netherlands: Brouwer, Utrecht University.

Erkens, G., Andriessen, A., & Peters, N. (2003). Interaction and performance in computer-supported collaborative tasks. In H. van Oostendorp (Ed.), *Cognition in a digital world* (pp. 225–252). Mahwah, NJ: Lawrence Erlbaum Associates.

Flaherty, L., Pearce, K., & Rubin, R. (1998). Internet and face-to-face communication: Not functional alternatives. *Communication Quarterly, 46,* 250–268.

Flower, L., & Hayes, J. R. (1980). The dynamics of composing: Making plans and juggling constraints. In L. W. Gregg & E. Steinberg (Eds.), *Cognitive processes in writing* (pp. 31–49). Hillsdale, NJ: Lawrence Erlbaum Associates.

Galbraith, D., & Rijlaarsdam, G. (1999). Effective strategies for the teaching and learning of writing. *Learning and Instruction, 9,* 93–108.

Hayes, J. R., & Nash, J. G. (1996). On the nature of planning in writing. In C. M. Levy & S. E. Ransdell (Eds.), *The science of writing: Theories, methods, individual differences and applications* (pp. 29–55). Mahwah, NJ: Lawrence Erlbaum Associates.

Hillocks, G. (1986). *Research on written composition: New directions for teaching.* Urbana, IL: ERIC Clearinghouse on Reading and Communication Skills.

Howe, C., & Tolmie, A. (1999). Productive interaction in the context of computer-supported collaborative learning in science. In K. Littleton & P. Light (Eds.), *Learning with computers. Analysing productive interaction* (pp. 24–45). London: Routledge.

Jauregi, K., Nieuwenhuijsen, D., & De Graaff, R. (2003). A virtual writing environment for peer feedback in Spanish as a second language. In J. Piqué-Angordans, M. J. Esteve, & M. L. Gea Valor (Eds.), *Internet in language for specific purposes and foreign language teaching* (pp. 445–457). Universitat Jaume 1, Castelló, Spain.

Kellogg, R. (1994). *The psychology of writing.* New York: Oxford University Press.

Kreijns, K., Kirschner, P., & Jochems, W. (2002). The sociability of computer supported collaborative learning environments. *Educational Technology and Society* [Online], *5.* Available: http://ifets.fit.fraunhofer.de/periodical/vol_1_2002/kreijns.html

Krummheuer, G. (1992). *Lernen mit >>Format<< Elemente einer interactionistischen Lerntheorie. Diskutiert an Beispielen mathematischen Unterrichts* [Learning in formats. Elements of an interactionist learning theory]. Weinheim, Germany: Deutscher Studien.

Lave, J., & Wenger, E. (1991). *Situated learning: Legitimate peripheral participation.* Cambridge, England: Cambridge University Press.

Lewin, B., & Fine, J. (1996). The writing of research texts: Genre analysis and its applications. In G. Rijlaarsdam, H. Van den Bergh, & M. Couzijn (Eds.), *Current trends in writing research: Theories, models, and methodology in writing research* (pp. 423–444). Amsterdam: Amsterdam University Press.

Mercer, N., & Wegerif, R. (1999). Is "exploratory talk" productive talk? In K. Littleton & P. Light (Eds.), *Learning with computers. Analysing productive interaction* (pp. 79–101). London: Routledge.

Miller, C. R. (1984). Genre as social action. *Quarterly Journal of Speech, 70,* 51–167.

Mulder, I., Verwijs, C., & Swaak, J. (2002). A comparative study on task groups and communities. In D. Purdue & M. Stewart (Eds.), *Understanding collaboration. Faculty of the built environment* (pp. 37–44). Bristol: University of the West of England.

Posner, I., & Baecker, R. (1993). How do people write together? In R. Baecker (Ed.), *Groupware and computer-supported cooperative work. Assisting human-human collaboration* (pp. 239–250). San Francisco: Kaufmann.

Rijlaarsdam, G., Van den Bergh, H., & Couzijn, M. (Eds.). (1996). *Effective teaching and learning of writing. Current trends in research.* Amsterdam: Amsterdam University Press.

Rubin, B. (1996). The writing of research texts: Genre analysis and its applications. In G. Rijlaarsdam, H. Van den Bergh, & M. Couzijn (Eds.), *Effective teaching and learning of writing* (pp. 37–50). Amsterdam: Amsterdam University Press.

Säljö, R. (1999). Learning as the use of tools: A sociocultural perspective on the human-technology link. In K. Littleton & P. Light (Eds.), *Learning with computers. Analysing productive interaction* (pp. 144–161). London: Routledge.

Scott Poole, M. (1999). Group communication theory. In L. Frey, D. Gouran, & M. Scott Poole (Eds.), *The handbook of group communication theory and research* (pp. 37–70). Thousand Oaks, CA: Sage.

Swales, J. (1990). *Genre analysis: English in academic and research settings.* Cambridge, England: Cambridge University Press.

Van Boxtel, C. (2000). *Collaborative concept learning. Collaborative learning tasks, student interaction, and the learning of physics concepts.* Enschede, the Netherlands: Ipskamp.

Van den Berk, I. (2003). *Eindrapport ConCourse. Deelproject Duits* [Final report ConCourse: German language and culture project]. Unpublished manuscript. Utrecht University, Utrecht, The Netherlands.

Vygotsky, L. S. (1978). *Mind in society: The development of higher psychological processes.* Cambridge, MA: Harvard University Press.

Walther, J. (1996). Computer-mediated communication: Impersonal, interpersonal, and hyperpersonal interaction. *Communication Research, 23,* 3–43.

Williams, D. (1999). The effects of expert stories on sixth grade students' achievement and problem solving in hypermedia-supported authentic learning environments (HALE). In D. Williams, B. Collis, & R. Oliver (Eds.), *World Conference on Educational Multimedia, Hypermedia and Telecommunications 1999(1)* (pp. 112–118). Charlottesville, VA: Association for the Advancement of Computing in Education.

DEPLOYING DIGITAL INFORMATION

Chapter 12

Feedback in Human–Computer Interaction: Resolving Ontological Discrepancies

Robbert-Jan Beun
Rogier M. van Eijk
Utrecht University

It was only twenty years ago that interaction with computers was for the most part only possible through symbols that could be understood exclusively by expert users. Today we can hardly imagine that the interface once did not include the graphical apparatus of icons, buttons, pictures, and diagrams that we have become so accustomed to. But when we interact with computers, we also want them to react to our actions as a cooperative partner and to provide adequate feedback in case of communication flaws. In fact, we want them to be endowed with characteristics that closely mimic human conversation. Whereas the visual interactive qualities of interfaces have improved a lot, computers are still unable to generate the basic communication structures in a similarly powerful and cooperative way as we find in human–human communication. Today's commercially available systems hardly ever answer questions in a proper way, are unable to argue about particular information, and rarely provide relevant or even truthful feedback in case of communication or other errors.

The goal of this chapter is to discuss some of the theoretical principles that drive a conversation and to present a computational framework that enables us to generate elementary feedback sequences at the knowledge level of dialogue participants. One of the prerequisites for successful communication—both human–human and human–computer—is that the participants have a shared conceptualization of the meaning of the communication symbols. Here, we focus on the feedback process that regulates the repair of communication flaws caused by conceptual disparities between a computer system and its user when using particular terms in a communication language. For reasons to be explained later, we call these disparities *ontological discrepancies.*

In our approach, two agents—the user agent and the computer agent—play a dialogue game in which feedback is produced to transfer relevant information with respect to a particular agreement about the meaning of the words in the vocabulary. In line with Beun (2001), agents and their behavior are modeled, respectively, by mental states in terms of goals and various types of beliefs[1] and by the rules that generate feedback sequences and determine the change of the mental states as a result of the subsequent dialogue contributions. We distance ourselves from the idea that conversation can be modeled by a concatenation of speech acts (Searle, 1969) regulated by a set of sequencing rules or a grammar (see also Levinson, 1983, and Good, 1989).

Describing the properties and the dynamics of the mental states in relation to the various dialogue contributions is an essential part of this work. In order to develop such a framework, the following questions are addressed:

1. What type of mental states should be included to model the dialogue's basic structural properties? (See Taylor, Carletta, & Mellish, 1996.)
2. How do the various feedback contributions change the existing mental states? (See, e.g., Gazdar, 1981, and Bunt, 1989.)
3. How do these changes influence the generation of new contributions?

In what follows, we show some of the necessary ingredients for a corrective feedback process when a user and a computer system have different conceptualizations of a particular domain of discourse. We carefully describe which aspects of the situation have to be modeled to generate adequate conversational sequences and show how the information that the system holds about a domain and about the user influences the course of the dialogue between the system and its user. Based on a precise description of this type of information, the system is able to play the conversational game with the user. As a result, an interface designer may obtain rules with sufficient detail for adequate feedback, given the system's ability to model the various types of information about the domain and about the user.

---

[1]In this chapter, we are not concerned with the differences between *belief* and *knowledge* and the terms are used interchangeably.

COOPERATIVE FEEDBACK IN COMMUNICATION

The term *feedback* originates from the area of cybernetics and refers to the information that a system receives from its environment about the consequences of its behavior (Wiener, 1948). Feedback information is often used to regulate the behavior and guides, in the case of purposeful behavior, the actions toward a particular goal. The concept of feedback in cybernetics has had many successful applications in engineering and physics, because the performance of electronic and other physical systems can be modeled quite accurately. We know, within certain limits, how the output of a system (e.g., an electronic circuit) depends on the value of the input variables and we have accurate mathematical tools that predict the system's response to a change of the input variables as a result of feedback information.

In both human–human and human–system communication, feedback is used for a broad range of communicative responses at various levels and displays enormous diversity, varying from a simple nod or a beep that indicates the receipt of a message to a written comment that evaluates the quality of a scientific paper. However, for various reasons, we have no accurate mathematical theory for natural communicative behavior, and the application of cybernetic models to human communicative activities has only a limited scope of relevance (Spink & Saracevic, 1998).

When we look at feedback phenomena in conversations between humans, sequences in terms of speech acts appear to be rather chaotic and seem hardly subjected to any rules. Questions can be followed by answers, denials of the relevance of the question, rejections of the presuppositions of the question, statements of ignorance, and so on (see, e.g., Levinson, 1983). An example of general rules for cooperative contributions, and conversational feedback in particular, are the Gricean maxims for conversation, such as "tell the truth" (quality), "say enough, but not too much" (quantity), "be relevant" (relevance), and "use the appropriate form" (manner) (Grice, 1975). Clearly, not all people follow the four rules to the letter, but Grice's point is that, contrary to particular appearances in conversation, the principles are still adhered to at some deeper level. An example is given in the following dialogue (from Sacks, 1968, cited in Levinson, p. 292):

A: I have a fourteen-year-old son.
B: Well, that's all right.
A: And I also have a dog.
B: No, I am sorry.

At first sight, B's feedback looks unacceptable or even bizarre, and his contributions appear to be a blunt violation of the Gricean maxim of rele-

vance (Grice, 1975). However, once the circumstances are given—A is trying to hire a room from the landlord, B—the dialogue sounds perfectly normal. So it seems that we hardly have a criterion for the acceptability
of feedback information without contextual knowledge. In other words,
sequencing rules in conversation can never be captured in terms of speech-
act terms only, such as question-answer and assertion-denial, and our de-
termination of the correctness of a sequence of utterances is heavily influenced by the circumstances of the conversation. From this, we conclude
that modeling and generating acceptable feedback sequences involves at
least an explicit representation of the circumstances of the dialogue in
terms of shared background knowledge and intentions of the dialogue
participants.

In human–system interaction—where a system is represented by some
kind of electronic equipment, such as a computer or a video player—a diversity of heuristics for feedback is suggested. Nielsen (1993), for instance,
stated that a system should continuously inform the user about what it is doing and how it is interpreting the user's input. More detailed heuristics concern the different degrees of persistence in the interface, response times,
and corrective feedback in case of errors. Just as the Gricean (Grice, 1975)
maxims form guidelines for the acceptability of human conversational sequences, the heuristics offer an important and practical handle for a systematic evaluation of user interfaces. However, both types of rules are
underspecified in case an interface designer wants to realize the actual implementation. In other words, the rules have some explanatory power, but
no predictive power, and they do not provide the designer with sufficient
detail about the type, content, and form of the feedback that has to be generated in a particular situation.

In this chapter, we concentrate on feedback sequences that are compul-
sory at the knowledge level; we focus in particular on the generation of
those sequences that support the establishment of a common ontology between two dialogue participants. Before we explain the details of the generation mechanism, we first elaborate on the role of ontologies in communication.

COMMUNICATION ABOUT ONTOLOGICAL
DISCREPANCIES

In communication, a distinction is usually made between the conceptualization of a particular domain of discourse and the communication symbols
that refer to various aspects of the domain. In some respect, the communication symbols and, more specifically, a particular language in terms of a
lexicon and grammatical rules, can be considered as an interface between

the conceptualizations of the two dialogue partners. Whereas we have no direct access to the conceptualizations of humans, the conceptualizations of computer systems can be expressed in a so-called *ontology*, which is often defined in a formal language, such as a programming language or a formal logic. An ontology abstracts the essence of the domain of interest and helps to catalogue and distinguish various concepts such as types of objects in the domain, along with their properties and relationships.

In the domain of e-commerce, for instance, important concepts are those that relate to the issue of trust. Interactions between participants take place over the internet without any personal contact, so consumer trust in the internet vendor is an issue of major concern (Chen & Dhillon, 2003). But what exactly does it mean for a vendor to be trustworthy? Many aspects play a role; it is the purpose of an ontology to give structure to the domain and enable the cataloguing of internet vendors.

Figure 12.1 depicts an example of a simple ontology O_1 of trust, which organizes some of the relevant concepts in a tree-like structure. The concept *trust* constitutes the root of this ontology. It has three subordinate nodes: the concepts *competence, candor,* and *benevolence*. The ontology defines consumer trust as the conjunction of the vendor's competence, candor, and benevolence. The ontology can also be expressed in predicate logic:

$$\forall Y: (trustworthy(Y) \leftrightarrow (competent(Y) \wedge candid(Y) \wedge benevolent(Y)))$$

The predicate logic expresses that trustworthy internet vendors are those vendors that are competent, candid, and benevolent. The ontology enables the computer system to reason and to communicate about issues of trust. So, in principle, a user can now ask questions such as "Is this particular vendor trustworthy?" or "What does it mean to be trustworthy?" Note that ontologies, in general, can be complex structures. For instance, the concept *candor* may in turn constitute the root of a subtree with concepts like *honesty, consistency,* and *reliability* as its subordinate nodes; these subordinate nodes may each have other subtrees, and so on. Complex structured ontologies are beyond the scope of the current chapter, however. Here, we

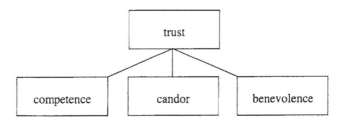

FIG. 12.1.   Ontology O_1 of *trust*.

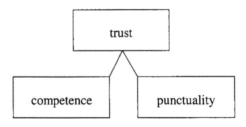

FIG. 12.2.   Ontology O_2 of *trust*.

only consider ontologies like O_1 that define a nonbasic concept in terms of one or more basic concepts.

Suppose we have another agent that holds a deviated ontology O_2 (see Fig. 12.2). In ontology O_2, consumer trust in internet vendors is defined as a conjunction of the vendors' competence and punctuality. Similar to ontology O_1, this ontology defines the concept *competence* as a subordinate node of *trust*, but unlike O_1 it contains *punctuality* as a subordinate instead of *candor* and *benevolence*. We refer to such disparities between O_1 and O_2 as *ontological discrepancies*.

It goes without saying that, in successful communication and in collaborative performance of tasks, agreement with respect to the ontology is crucial or, at least, the dialogue partners should be aware of existing discrepancies. In case of discrepancies, various troublesome situations may arise. For instance, one of the participants by mistake may assume that a particular concept is shared, whereas the other has no knowledge about it. Or worse, both dialogue partners initially have different conceptualizations, but the relevant discrepancy remains unnoticed. Ontology discrepancies may cause serious communication flaws and the generation of adequate utterances in order to repair these flaws is an essential part of modeling a proper feedback process.

In this chapter, we make some important simplifications. First, we assume that every word in the communication language with respect to the domain of discourse has one and only one corresponding concept in the ontology.[2] So, for instance, the word *trustworthy* in the vocabulary corresponds to the concept *trust* in the underpinning ontology. Second, we do not consider the problem of the detection of ontology discrepancies but only concentrate on the feedback process of avoiding or repairing the discrepancy. Third, we do not consider cases where the two partners use different words for the same conceptualization.

---

[2]This assumption allows the dialogue partners to hold different vocabularies, but does not allow words in the communication language to be ambiguous.

A corresponding concept and its substructure in the ontology of a word in the communication language is also called the *interpretation* or the *meaning* of that word. For instance, the word *trustworthy* has the interpretation of Fig. 12.1 in O_1 and Fig. 12.2 in O_2. Initially, three basic settings with respect to ontology discrepancies will be distinguished:

1. The ontology of both agents agrees with respect to a particular word, that is, there is no discrepancy and the interpretations of both agents are the same.
2. Both agents have different interpretations with respect to a particular word.
3. Only one agent has an interpretation of a particular word.

Note that the third assumption, together with the first, implies that the corresponding word is also absent from the other participant's vocabulary. Moreover, the first assumption helps us to avoid rather marginal cases where the participants use words that have no corresponding interpretation in both ontologies.

To make things a little more concrete, let us first consider a situation where a user U intends to purchase a particular item X, and where different internet vendors have the item in their catalogue. Assume vendor Y is the cheapest and the user uses a computer agent C who mediates the transaction. The user may start the dialogue as follows:

U: I want to purchase item X from vendor Y. Is Y a trustworthy vendor?

Now suppose that U and C have an agreement about the domain words *purchase, item, vendor,* and the references of X and Y, and that the computer agent understands the grammatical rules to interpret U's utterance. Depending on the situation, C has various possibilities to continue the dialogue:

1. C may simply respond to the question (e.g., "Yes, it is," "No, it is not," "I don't know").
2. C may answer the question and add extra information about the interpretation of the word *trustworthy* (e.g., "Yes, Y is competent, benevolent, and candid," "No, because Y is not competent").
3. C may give a tentative answer (e.g., "In case you mean by *trustworthy* that Y is . . . , yes, Y is trustworthy").
4. C may ask a counterquestion for the interpretation of the word *trustworthy* (e.g., "Do you mean that Y is . . . ?," "What do you mean by *trustworthy?*").

This may result in the following sample dialogues. In Dialogue 1, for instance, C explicitly states his[3] interpretation of the word *trustworthy* and, because the user does not deny the interpretation, it can be concluded that she agrees.

Dialogue 1

U: Is Y a trustworthy vendor?
C: Yes, Y is competent, candid, and benevolent.
U: OK, thanks.

In Dialogue 2, neither of the two participants accepts the other as an expert on the interpretation and neither contributes extra information that forces a decision. The dialogue ends in an infinite loop.

Dialogue 2

U: Is Y a trustworthy vendor?
C: Yes, Y is competent, candid, and benevolent.
U: Well, in my opinion a trustworthy vendor is competent and punctual.
C: In my opinion, a trustworthy vendor does not need to be punctual.
U: Well, it does.
C: No, it doesn't. . . .

Clearly, infinite dialogues have to be avoided and in the generation rules presented later we give preference to a strategy where C tentatively accepts the interpretation by U (see also Dialogue 3). This implies that C has to make at least a distinction between his own private beliefs and his beliefs about U's beliefs.

Dialogue 3

U: Is Y a trustworthy vendor?
C: Yes, Y is competent, candid, and benevolent.
U: Well, in my opinion a trustworthy vendor is competent and punctual.
C: In that case, no, Y is not trustworthy, because he is not punctual.
U: OK, thanks.

---

[3]Throughout this chapter, the computer agent will receive masculine pronominalization and the user will be feminine.

Note that we assume that the word *punctual* is also part of C's vocabulary and, therefore, underpinned in C's ontology. From the dialogue fragment we cannot conclude, however, that C also adopts the user's interpretation of the word *trustworthy* as his own interpretation.

C also has various strategies in the second turn. If, for instance, C has a private interpretation, but a shared one is doubted, he may simply ask for the meaning without manifesting his own interpretation.

Dialogue 4

U: Is Y a trustworthy vendor?
C: What do you mean by *trustworthy*?
U: A trustworthy vendor is a vendor that is competent and punctual.
C: In that case, he is trustworthy.
U: OK, thanks.

A problem in Dialogue 4 is that the dialogue suggests that C has no private interpretation. So, depending on C's tenacity, U may incorrectly come to believe that U's interpretation of the word is a shared belief. Not manifesting C's interpretation may in these cases be considered a violation of the Gricean maxim of quantity (Grice, 1975). A possible solution is given in Dialogue 5, where C immediately provides the extra information after U has manifested her interpretation of the word.

Dialogue 5

U: Is Y a trustworthy vendor?
C: What do *you* mean by *trustworthy*?
U: In my opinion, a trustworthy vendor is a vendor that is competent and punctual.
C: Well, I think that a trustworthy vendor is competent, benevolent, and candid.
U: I prefer my own interpretation.
C: In that case, he is trustworthy.

In Dialogue 5, C gives another cue by stressing the pronominal reference *you*, which already implicates that there may be other interpretations as well, in particular, C's interpretation. In the framework provided later, we avoid the extra turns and, in case of absence of a shared interpretation, C does not ask for one, but explicitly states his interpretation of the word (if he has a private one).

In conclusion, in order to be able to distinguish between the previous situations, the content of the computer agent's response depends not only on his beliefs about the domain of discourse, but also on his beliefs about the user's beliefs and their shared beliefs. In case the user indicates an interpretation that differs from the computer's concept of *trust*, it should be decided whose interpretation should prevail. In principle, this is a matter of expertise: The interpretation of an expert usually takes preference over that of a nonexpert. If neither of the participants is more an expert than the other, they could start an argument about the interpretation. In this chapter, however, we assume that the computer treats the user as an expert on the interpretation, and thus gives priority to her interpretation while answering the initial question. We adopt the strategy that the computer agent tentatively accepts the user's interpretation and drops it after the initial question has been answered.

THE FORMAL FRAMEWORK

In this section, we outline a computational framework for the generation of human–computer dialogues in which the computer provides feedback in case of ontological discrepancies. For reasons of legibility, we do not give a full formalization, but describe the various aspects of the framework in a semiformal way. In particular, instead of specifying the behavior rules in their most general form, we define them in terms of typical examples. The generalizations of the rules should be evident from these examples and are not further worked out in this chapter.

Ontologies are used to define the meaning of nonbasic predicates (like *trustworthy*) in terms of basic predicates (like *competent, candid,* and *benevolent*). It is assumed that both agents know the meanings of the basic predicates and that these predicates are part of the agents' shared beliefs, have the same interpretation for both agents, and, consequently, the meaning of basic predicates is never part of the discussion. Moreover, we assume that for basic predicates p the computer agent is able to decide whether $p(X)$ holds for each individual X. So, this implies that the computer agent is always able to give an answer to the initial question whenever a meaning of the nonbasic predicate is available. A basic predicate applied to some individual is called a "basic proposition" throughout.

In order to play the dialogue game, the user will be simulated by a so-called user agent that has an explicit representation of the user's domain conceptualization in terms of an ontology. An agent's mental state (both user and computer agents) consists of the following constructs:

1. Information about the domain of discourse (private beliefs).

2. Information about the beliefs of the other agent (beliefs about beliefs of the other).
3. Information about the shared beliefs of both agents (beliefs about shared beliefs).
4. A pending stack containing dialogue moves that have to be processed (the goals of the agents).

Note that an agent's mental state contains not only propositions, but also the underpinning ontologies.

We assume that both agents can reason about their beliefs by *modus ponens* and that the following dependencies exist between the mental states of an agent:

Rule R1

IF a proposition or a meaning is part of the belief about the shared belief of an agent

THEN it is also part of the agent's private belief

AND of its beliefs about the other agent.

It is important to note that the opposite of R1 does not hold.

Rule R2

IF the user agent believes that the computer agent believes some basic proposition to hold

THEN the user agent also itself believes this basic proposition to hold.

In fact, R2 establishes particular roles in the dialogue, because the computer agent is considered as an expert on basic propositions. A problem could be that the information state of the user agent becomes inconsistent. This has to be prevented by an update function, which is not discussed in this chapter.

THE DIALOGUE RULES

Dialogue contributions, or so-called "moves,"[4] are fully determined by the mental state of the agent who performs the move and the rules that are applicable to this state. We assume that the initial question by the user agent

---

[4]In line with a more Searlian tradition (Searle, 1969), we also call these moves "speech acts."

has been asked in the first turn of the dialogue. For reasons of legibility, we describe the rules in the order of the various turns. It should be stressed, however, that the applicability of the rules depends on the preconditions of a particular move and is not determined by the turn.

The Second Turn

After the user agent has asked the initial question, the computer agent has three possibilities to continue the dialogue:

- It believes that an interpretation is shared by its partner and so gives the answer (Generation Rule 1).
- It believes an interpretation, but does not believe that its partner shares it (Generation Rule 2).
- It does not know an interpretation (Generation Rule 3).

Generation Rule 1

IF the agent is processing $ask(trustworthy(X))$
AND it believes that the meaning $trust = competence \wedge candor \wedge benevolence$ is shared
THEN it responds with:

(a) $tell(trustworthy(X))$
     if it believes $trustworthy(X)$ to hold
(b) $deny(trustworthy(X))$
     if it believes $trustworthy(X)$ not to hold

Note that we do not consider the case where the computer agent does not know the answer, because we assume that it is always able to find an answer to the question as long as the proposition is built up from basic predicates and the interpretation is available.

Generation Rule 2

IF the agent is processing $ask(trustworthy(X))$
AND it does not know the other agent's meaning of $trust$
AND its own meaning is $trust = competence \wedge candor \wedge benevolence$
THEN it responds with:

(a) $tell(trustworthy(X) \mid trust = competence \wedge candor \wedge benevolence)$
     if it believes $trustworthy(X)$ to hold
(b) $deny(trustworthy(X) \mid trust = competence \wedge candor \wedge benevolence)$

if it believes *trustworthy(X)* not to hold

IF the agent is processing *ask(trustworthy(X))*
AND it believes the other agent's meaning of *trust = competence ∧ punctuality*
AND its own meaning is *trust = competence ∧ candor ∧ benevolence*
THEN it responds with:

(c) *tell(trustworthy(X) | trust = competence ∧ punctuality)*
if it believes both *competent(X)* and *punctual(X)* to hold
(d) *deny(trustworthy(X) | trust = competence ∧ punctuality)*
if it believes either *competent(X)* or *punctual(X)* (or both) not to hold

In Generation Rule 2, the computer agent knows a meaning of the predicate, but does not believe that his partner shares this meaning. As a result, a conditional answer (expressed by the symbol "I" in the move) is generated and extra information about the interpretation is added. Note that in Generation Rules 2c and 2d the user agent is considered to be the expert on the meaning of the nonbasic predicate and this meaning takes priority over the computer agent's beliefs (see also the fourth turn).

Generation Rule 3

IF the agent is processing *ask(trustworthy(X))*
AND it does not have its own meaning of *trust*
THEN it responds with *ask(trust)*

So, if the computer agent has no meaning, it manifests its ignorance by asking the user agent for the meaning. In natural language, this can be expressed by a *wh*-question (e.g., "What is the meaning of trust?").

The Third Turn

Just before the third turn, the response of the computer agent is on top of the stack of the user agent (see the update rules). Depending on this response and the mental state of the user agent, the user agent has three possible reactions:

• The computer agent's response may be accepted (Generation Rule 4).
• The response may be rejected and a meaning may be provided (Generation Rule 5).

- The user agent may indicate that he or she has a meaning available (Generation Rule 6).

Generation Rule 4

(a) IF the agent is processing *tell(trustworthy(X))*
     THEN it responds with *stop*
(b) IF the agent is processing *deny(trustworthy(X))*
     THEN it responds with *stop*
(c) IF the agent is processing *tell(trustworthy(X) | trust = competence ∧ punctuality)*
     AND it does not have a different meaning of *trust*
     THEN it responds with *stop*

In Generation Rule 4, the user agent accepts the statement by the computer agent and subsequently stops the dialogue.

Generation Rule 5

IF the agent is processing *tell(trustworthy(X) | trust = competence ∧ candor ∧ benevolence)*
AND its own meaning is *trust = competence ∧ punctuality*
THEN it responds with *tell(trust = competence ∧ punctuality)*

In this rule, the meaning *competence ∧ candor ∧ benevolence* of *trust* is rejected because the user agent has found a meaning that does not correspond to his or her own. In a rejection, the agent tells the grounds for his or her rejection, so that the computer agent has knowledge about the reason of the discrepancy.

Generation Rule 6

IF the agent is processing *ask(trust)*
AND its own meaning is *trust = competence ∧ punctuality*
THEN it responds with *tell(trust = competence ∧ punctuality)*

Generation Rule 6 expresses that, if a question has been asked by the computer agent about the meaning of the predicate, the user agent manifests his or her meaning if he or she has one. Note that we already excluded the situation where the user agent has no interpretation.

The Fourth Turn

Depending on its mental state, the computer agent may apply one of the previous rules, or a rule that stops the dialogue. If, for instance, the user agent has manifested a meaning and the computer agent has no meaning available, the meaning will be used by the computer agent to provide an answer to the initial question. This is expressed in Generation Rules 2c and 2d.

THE UPDATE OF MENTAL STATES

The update rules yield a new mental state depending on the old state and the move just performed. We are not concerned with the full details of the update mechanism and assume that the mental states will be updated in accordance with the principles expressed in Rules R1 and R2. In the postconditions we always represent the weakest conditions. If, for instance, the shared beliefs are represented in the postcondition, the private beliefs and beliefs about the other are automatically updated in accordance with Rule R1.

Update Rule 1

(a) The postcondition of the question *ask(trustworthy(X))* of the user agent is:
   the question is pushed on the stack of the computer agent
(b) The postcondition of the question *ask(trust)* of the user agent is:
   the question is pushed on the stack of the computer agent

These rules express that a question is pushed on top of the stack of the recipient and that the speech act has no further consequences for the mental state of the dialogue partners. Note that the main difference between (a) and (b) is that (a) concerns a question about propositions (yes-no questions) and (b) about the meaning of a term (*wh*-questions).

Update Rule 2

The postcondition of the response *tell(trustworthy(X))* of the computer agent is that the response is pushed on the stack of the user agent

AND the stack of the computer agent is popped

AND the user agent believes that *trustworthy(X)* is part of the shared beliefs

AND the computer agent believes that *trustworthy(X)* is part of the shared beliefs

Update Rule 2 expresses that a proposition is simply added to the shared beliefs of the dialogue participants and pushed on the stack of the partner. The rule for *deny(trustworthy(X))* is similar and omitted here.

Update Rule 3

The postcondition of the response *tell(trust = competence ∧ punctuality)* of the user agent is that the stack of the user agent is popped
AND the computer agent believes that the user agent believes *trust = competence ∧ punctuality*

Update Rule 3 states that, in case the statement contains an explanation of the meaning, it is added to the belief state of the partner about the other and the stack of the performer of the speech act is popped. Note that Update Rule 2 concerns the manifestation of a domain proposition and Update Rule 3 the manifestation of the interpretation of a nonbasic predicate.

Update Rule 4

The postcondition of the response *tell(trustworthy(X) | trust = competence ∧ candor ∧ benevolence)* of the computer agent is that this response is pushed on the stack of the user agent
AND the user agent believes that the computer agent believes *competent(X), candid(X),* and *benevolent(X)* to hold

The rule for *deny(trustworthy(X) | trust = competence ∧ candor ∧ benevolence)* is similar to Update Rule 4 and omitted here. Note that Update Rule 4 does not express that the computer agent's interpretation is accepted.

EXAMPLE

We conclude with an example of a dialogue between the computer agent C and the user U that is generated by the previous rules. The computer agent employs the ontology O_1, which defines the nonbasic concept *trust* as a conjunction of the basic concepts *competence, candor,* and *benevolence*; the user employs ontology O_2. Initially, C does not believe that the meaning of the ontology is a shared belief and also believes that the firm Asbelix is not very punctual. The user starts with a question:

U: Is Asbelix a trustworthy internet vendor?

This question is pushed onto the stack of the computer agent (Update Rule 1a). According to the computer agent's interpretation (based on O_1), the firm Asbelix is indeed trustworthy, but because the computer agent does not know that the meaning is shared, it responds with (Generation Rule 2a):

> C: Yes, because Asbelix is competent, candid, and benevolent.

This response is pushed on the stack of the user and the user now comes to believe that Asbelix is competent, candid, and benevolent (Update Rule 4 and Rule R2). The user agent, however, employs the ontology O_2, which defines *trust* to be the conjunction of the basic concepts *competence* and *punctuality*. It manifests this discrepancy by responding with (Generation Rule 5):

> U: In my opinion, trust amounts to competence and punctuality.

The stack of the user is popped and the computer agent now knows the user's interpretation of trust (Update Rule 3) and, because it believes that this particular vendor Asbelix is not punctual, it gives the following answer to the initial question (Generation Rule 2b):

> C: Well, if trust amounts to competence and punctuality then Asbelix is not a trustworthy internet vendor.

This response is pushed on the stack of the user agent and the user now knows that Asbelix is not punctual (Update Rule 4 and Rule R2). The user agent has received an acceptable answer to its question and ends the dialogue (Generation Rule 4c):

> U: OK, thank you.

Note that, if in the second turn, the computer agent had not manifested its interpretation of trust, the ontological discrepancy would have remained unnoticed, possibly leading the user agent to draw incorrect conclusions from the answer.

DISCUSSION

In the previous sections, we sketched a dialogue framework that enables a computer system to generate particular feedback sequences in interaction with a user of the system. The framework is comparable to approaches in dialogue game theory (Carlson, 1985) and consists mainly of two parts: a gameboard that contains information about a particular state of the game (i.e., the mental states of the participants) and the dialogue rules that control the behavior of the participants (generation rules) and that prescribe how the gameboard changes (update rules). The framework is based on an explicit modeling of mental states in terms of the beliefs of the dialogue participants and their goals. Parts of these mental states function as preconditions for the generation of feedback contributions. In this chapter, we applied the dialogue game to problems that may arise as a result of conceptual disparities about a particular domain of discourse between a user agent and a computer agent, and we showed how the framework enables the system to generate feedback either to resolve the disparity or to accept it and respond in an adequate manner.

How does this framework contribute to the interaction between a computer system and its user and what are the limitations of the framework? This question brings us back to the idea stated in the introduction, that a computer interface may also be considered as a cooperative agent. This was already suggested in Hutchins (1989), where a model for human–computer interaction was presented that distinguishes between two types of interaction: symbolic and physical. The essential difference between the two types of interaction is that actions of the first type (e.g., speech acts) need an interpreter who can bridge the gap between the symbols and their actual meaning and purpose, whereas actions of the second type (physical acts) are related in a more direct manner to human perception and action (see also Ahn, Beun, Borghuis, Bunt, & Van Overveld, 1995). Nowadays, interface designers focus mainly on the second type of interaction (remember the graphical apparatus for direct manipulation and observation mentioned in the introduction) and are rarely concerned with the rules for interaction and feedback that can be observed in natural human communication.

Viewing a computer interface as a cooperative dialogue partner has important consequences for the design of the interface, because the designer has to include the mechanisms that drive a natural human dialogue. In this chapter, we tried to show a small part of the machinery needed for modeling such a dialogue. In order to behave cooperatively, the agent has to be equipped with various mental constructs so that information about a particular domain of discourse (private beliefs) and about its dialogue partner (beliefs about beliefs) can be separated. Moreover, we distinguished between beliefs about the dialogue partner, or "beliefs about the partner's private beliefs" (e.g., the computer's belief about ontology O_2) and "beliefs about shared beliefs" (the propositions and interpretations that were already agreed on).

Including these types of mental constructs enables the computer agent to adapt its feedback in a number of ways. Information that is part of the shared beliefs can be considered as presupposed and should not be stated explicitly; this can be viewed in Generation Rule 1, where shared information is not discussed. Beliefs by the agent about private beliefs of the user influence feedback contributions in another way. In Generation Rule 2, extra information is added because the computer agent has no knowledge about the beliefs of the user (a and b) or because the agent believes that the user has a distinct belief (c and d). In fact, the distinction between the various beliefs enables a designer to give concrete form to the Gricean maxim of quantity (Grice, 1975) that we mentioned earlier, because shared beliefs give the designer a criterion to leave out particular information in the dialogue move and beliefs about the other's beliefs give a criterion to include particular information.

It can be verified that the dialogue rules discussed in this chapter yield 16 different dialogues in terms of speech-act sequences, such as *ask/ tell/ stop, ask/ deny/ stop, ask/ deny/ tell/ deny/ stop*, and *ask/ ask/ tell/ deny/ stop*, and that the exact type and order of speech acts depends on the initial state of the beliefs of the dialogue participants. (Note that *ask/ tell/ tell/ tell/ stop* is the sequence of speech acts in the example discussed in the previous section; the difference between the three *tell* moves can be found in the semantic content of the speech act.) In order to avoid infinite sequences of disagreement, we defined roles that the two dialogue partners play in the game: The computer is considered to be the expert on the propositions with respect to the domain of discourse and the user is considered to be the expert on the meaning of the vocabulary. In our "simple" version of the dialogue game, these roles are implicitly built into the dialogue rules, but in more refined versions of the framework, roles could be defined explicitly and included as an extra precondition in the generation rules. In even more sophisticated versions, it can be imagined that the roles can be learned by the computer agent or that they differ with respect to the type of predicates that are used to describe the properties of objects (see later discussion).

Evidently, the framework is still rudimentary and extensions can be developed along many different lines. One of these lines is, for instance, the use of more complex ontologies. Concepts in real life can be defined in an almost infinite number of different terms and subterms, with complex interrelationships and constraints, and with different degrees of certainty and relevance. Because the dialogue rules in this chapter are based on the structure of the ontology, adapting the rules to the metaproperties of the ontology (e.g., structure, complexity) seems inevitable. And, although effective, the distinction between basic and nonbasic predicates is too simple. In practice, it may also be useful to classify predicates as observable or nonobservable. Depending on the communicative situation (e.g., "Who can observe what?"), this may also have important implications for the role distinction between expert and nonexpert and for the dialogue rules.

Another simplification is the treatment of goals. Here we presented goals as a simple stack with the operations "push" and "pop." In these simple cases, it seems that neither a planning approach (see, e.g., Allen & Perrault, 1980), nor a speech-act grammar approach is needed (or wanted) to build coherent structures of conversation, and that feedback generation can be based on the immediately preceding conversational unit. Note that, in general, the consequences of the speech act *ask* is that goals are added to the stack of the receiver and that the speech act *tell* deletes goals from the stack of the sender. An important shortcoming of this approach is that, once the goals are deleted, the agents "forget" what has been discussed before, so a "rule designer" has to be careful in popping goals from the stack. An advantage is that the framework does not suffer from the same computational complexity as most planning approaches, where agents are able to reason not only about the discourse domain in the future, but also about their own and their partner's beliefs and intentions. We do not expect, however, that nested beliefs have to be modeled beyond the third level (A believes that B believes that A believes), because they simply seem to be unnecessary for modeling the basic properties of a cooperative dialogue (see also Taylor et al., 1996).

It seems that the general framework of a dialogue game, in terms of the defined mental states and the generation and update rules applicable to these states, is a powerful and fundamental framework for adequate feedback generation. The framework does not suffer from the problems found in speech-act grammars, such as a lack of situational dependency, or those found in planning approaches, such as computational complexity. In the long run, a planning approach is inevitable, but it remains to be seen which dialogue phenomena have to be modeled with a planning approach and which phenomena can be modeled without planning. It seems reasonable not to include complex methods as long as we can solve the same problems in a computationally more simple and, therefore, more attractive way.

ACKNOWLEDGMENT

The authors would like to thank the three anonymous reviewers who read an earlier draft of the chapter and suggested valuable improvements.

REFERENCES

Ahn, R. M. C., Beun, R. J., Borghuis, T., Bunt, H. C., & Van Overveld, C. W. A. M. (1995). The DenK-architecture: A fundamental approach to user-interfaces. *Artificial Intelligence Review, 8*, 431–445.

Allen, J. F., & Perrault, C. R. (1980). Analysing intention in utterances. *Artificial Intelligence, 15*, 143–178.

Beun, R. J. (2001). On the generation of coherent dialogue. *Pragmatics and Cognition, 9*, 37–68.

Bunt, H. C. (1989). Information dialogues as communicative action in relation to partner modelling and information processing. In M. M. Taylor, F. Néel, & D. G. Bouwhuis (Eds.), *The structure of multimodal dialogue* (pp. 47–73). Amsterdam: Elsevier Science.

Carlson, L. (1985). *Dialogue games. An approach to discourse analysis.* Dordrecht, The Netherlands: Reidel.

Chen, S. C., & Dhillon, G. S. (2003). Interpreting dimensions of consumer trust in e-commerce. *Information Technology and Management, 4*, 303–318.

Gazdar, G. (1981). Speech act assignment. In A. K. Joshi, B. L. Webber, & I. A. Sag (Eds.), *Elements of discourse understanding* (pp. 64–83). Cambridge, England: Cambridge University Press.

Good, D. A. (1989). The viability of conversational grammars. In M. M. Taylor, F. Néel, & D. G. Bouwhuis (Eds.), *The structure of multimodal dialogue* (pp. 135–144). Amsterdam: Elsevier Science.

Grice, H. P. (1975). Logic and conversation. In P. Cole & J. Morgan (Eds.), *Speech acts. Syntax and semantics* (Vol. 11, pp. 41–58). New York: Academic Press.

Hutchins, E. (1989). Metaphors for interface design. In M. M. Taylor, F. Néel, & D. G. Bouwhuis (Eds.), *The structure of multimodal dialogue* (pp. 11–28). Amsterdam: Elsevier Science.

Levinson, S. C. (1983). *Pragmatics.* Cambridge, England: Cambridge University Press.

Nielsen, J. (1993). *Usability engineering.* San Diego, CA: Kaufmann.

Searle, J. R. (1969). *Speech acts.* Cambridge, England: Cambridge University Press.

Spink, A., & Saracevic, T. (1998). Human–computer interaction in information retrieval: Nature and manifestation of feedback. *Interacting with Computers, 10*, 249–267.

Taylor, J. A., Carletta, J., & Mellish, C. (1996). Requirements for belief models in co-operative dialogue. *User Modelling and User-Adapted Interaction, 6*, 23–68.

Wiener, N. (1948). *Cybernetics or control and communication in the animal and the machine.* Cambridge, MA: MIT Press.

Chapter 13

Old and New Media: A Threshold Model of Technology Use

Lidwien van de Wijngaert
Utrecht University

"Fast," "easy," and "to get a correct answer to my question": These are the reasons that users mention when asked why they choose to use a specific medium when searching for information (Van de Wijngaert, 1999). Information and communication technology (ICT) and new means of communication, such as the internet, offer seemingly endless possibilities in the area of information retrieval, communication opportunities, and entertainment. Virtually anything can be built using ICT: Services range from online medical care, to ordering flowers using the internet, to sending pictures via mobile phones. However, not all of these possibilities have found their way to the mass (consumer) market. Some of the new possibilities are very successful (such as the Web, e-mail, and mobile telephony), whereas others are only used by a small number of people in a niche market (e.g., Videotex in garages for license plate registration), have been replaced by new and improved technologies (compact disc interactive by DVD), or even have disappeared (video disk).

The starting point of this chapter is the assumption that new technologies enable all kinds of applications and services. However, technology does not define which of the many services and applications are actually used. This depends on the users of technology, not on the technology itself. By starting from a user perspective, it is possible to see what traditional media or new ICTs are used in what context. *Use* refers to an individual's broad pattern of technology usage over time, whereas the actual choice of a medium refers to a specific decision of an individual to use a technology in a particular communication situation (Trevino, Webster, & Stein, 2000). My research focuses on how consumers make voluntary choices to use ICT in specific contexts; more specifically, I am interested in intensity of use.

   The objective of this chapter is to provide a framework that explains, from a user perspective, how consumers make choices between old and new technologies when they have to deal with a situation in which a need has emerged. This framework builds on the notion that there are needs, wants, and desires on the one hand and costs, thresholds, and barriers on the other. When a need outweighs a threshold, a specific medium or new technology is used.

A THRESHOLD MODEL OF MEDIA CHOICE

The choice to use a medium is the dependent variable in my approach: I try to explain under what conditions people choose to use a specific medium, by making a trade-off between needs on the one hand and barriers on the other, within a given context. The use of media depends first on its accessibility. Therefore, accessibility is central to this discussion. The degree to which the accessibility of a medium or an ICT matches user requirements explains the success or failure of the medium or technology. Based on an extensive literature research, McCreadie and Rice (1999) distinguished six types of accessibility: physical, economic, political, cognitive, affective, and social. Because the present perspective is that of the user, I look into the following types of accessibility in which the typology of McCreadie and Rice is embedded:

- Physical accessibility: This form of accessibility is related to the first three types of accessibility of McCreadie and Rice and has to do with the question of whether a medium is physically and financially accessible for someone with a specific question in a given situation. Does he or she have access to the right equipment (e.g., computer and modem) and does he or she have to subscribe to the application or service?
- Suitability: Here the important question is whether a medium is suitable to meet the user's needs. Does the medium provide a solution to a specific need?
- Affective accessibility: This form of accessibility is related to the last three types of accessibility of McCreadie and Rice and refers to the question of whether the medium has a place in a person's daily environment. Although users may have access to a medium, this does not mean that they have internalized use in their daily habits.

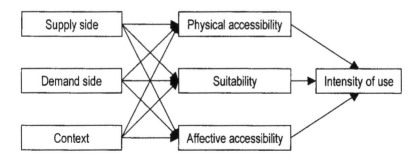

FIG. 13.1. Threshold model of technology use.

It is important to realize that all these forms of accessibility depend neither on technology (i.e., the infrastructure and service that is being offered), nor on consumer demand exclusively. According to Bouwman, Nouwens, Slootman, and Baaijens (1996), accessibility is influenced both by the possibilities consumers have for making an effort and by the extent to which suppliers manage to keep the effort required for users at a minimum. Furthermore, context plays an important role. Context is both the larger picture in which the potential user operates, and the specific situation, the particular set of circumstances from which a need for information arises, that play a role in the final decision to make use of a specific old or new medium (McCreadie & Rice, 1999). Context and situation include the computing, user, and physical context (Schilit, Adams, & Want, 1994), but social context and arrangements (Lievrouw & Livingstone, 2002) and time (Chen & Kotz, 2000) also have to be considered. In earlier research, it was shown that context plays a role if people have to make a choice between different old and new media (Bouwman & Van de Wijngaert, 2002).

To summarize, all forms of accessibility (physical accessibility, suitability, and affective accessibility) might be influenced by supply and demand factors and are, moreover, dependent on the context of use. The basic model, as discussed in this chapter, is presented in Fig. 13.1. In the next part of this chapter, I elaborate the model further. The present approach is illustrated by presenting an example. I conclude the chapter with a discussion and suggestions for further research.

Physical Accessibility

With regard to physical accessibility, the central question is to what degree users have direct access to technology. There are three factors that are of relevance. The first is technology itself: what equipment is needed in order to have the opportunity to use it. Does a user need a connection to the in-

ternet, and, if so, what subscriptions are necessary? Besides being dependent on the technology, physical accessibility also depends on the user. Is the
user willing to invest in the new technology, to adopt the new technologies,
or does he or she already have access to the proper equipment? Finally,
context is of importance. On a microlevel, this relates to the question of
where in a certain situation the equipment is physically located, if it is available or in use by somebody else, where it is located, and so on. However,
this is already based on the assumption that the user has adopted the technology in the first place. Thus, this assumption has to be addressed first.
When does a user choose to adopt a technology? Rogers (1983) offered an
excellent starting point to answer this question. He defined the diffusion of
innovations as "the process by which an innovation is communicated
through certain channels among the members of a social system" (p. 5). In
this definition, Rogers summarized a number of factors that can influence
the (rapid) adoption of an innovation by an individual. The first factor relates to the nature of the innovation. Innovations differ from each other in
several ways: relative advantage (the degree to which potential customers
perceive a new product as superior to existing substitutes), compatibility
(the degree to which potential customers feel a new product is consistent
with their present needs, values, and practices), complexity (the degree to
which a new product is difficult to understand or to use), triability (the degree to which a new product is capable of being tried on a limited basis),
and communicability (the degree to which the results of technology are visible and can be communicated to others). Second, Rogers mentioned both
personal and mass communication as means to create shared meaning of
and to change attitude toward the innovation. Third, Rogers mentioned
the time that is needed for potential users in order to make a decision on
whether to adopt the innovation. Furthermore, social influence is an important factor in the decision of individuals to adopt an innovation.

Therefore, adoption should also be discussed on a collective level. The
large-scale use of technologies can depend on the existence of a critical
mass. For many technologies, the expectations with regard to the presence
of other users is an important factor in the decision to adopt that new technology. If there are enough other users (to communicate with, for example), new users will follow. On the other hand, when there are not enough
other users, it is not interesting to adopt that new information and communication technology. *Critical mass* is defined in the literature as the point in
time when it becomes interesting to join in (Markus, 1990). The crucial
problem with creating a critical mass of users is that, as long as the critical
mass has not been reached yet, it is not interesting for an individual user to
start using the new technology. Therefore, costs for development of a new
medium have to be supported by a small group that is willing to invest a lot,
whereas the majority of people do little or nothing (Markus; Marwell & Oli-

TABLE 13.1
Supply, Demand, and Context Factors

	Supply-Side Factors	*Demand-Side Factors*	*Context Factors*
Physical accessibility	Characteristics of required equipment and subscription (e.g. compatibility, triability, etc.)	Individuals innovativeness and willingness to invest	Social influence Critical mass
Suitability	Characteristics of the technology (e.g. capabilities with regard to information, communication, entertainment and transactions)	Relation user needs and gratification pattern Task characteristics (e.g. uncertainty and equivocality) and perceived usefulness	Relation non-rational factors and degree of fit (e.g. social influence, social attraction, etc.)
Affective accessibility	User friendliness	Perceived ease of use (TAM) Habitual and ritual technology use	Domestication: the process of mutual shaping The way in which people learn to use new technologies

ver, 1993). These investors are not likely to be able to communicate with a number of users that might be interesting to them.

Summarizing (see Table 13.1), the concept of physical accessibility is much broader than the simple question of whether an individual has a computer and modem. Physical accessibility is also related to characteristics of required equipment, such as compatibility and triability. Furthermore, the individual's innovativeness and willingness to invest are important factors. The context in which communication takes place should also be taken into account (e.g., social influence and the emergence of a critical mass of other users). Physical accessibility can be a serious threshold for potential users and a limitation of alternatives consequently defines media choice and use. In many cases, users simply do not have a choice.

When users do have access to several media and new technologies, the question of which medium is most suitable becomes apparent. The next section deals with this subject, by first discussing the uses and gratification (U&G) theory and then media-choice theories.

Suitability: The Uses of Technology

Katz, Blumler, and Gurevitch (1974) stated that U&G is research on "the social and psychological origins of needs, which generate expectations of the mass media or other sources which lead to differential patterns of media exposure (or engagement in other activities), resulting in need gratifications and other consequences, perhaps mostly unintended ones" (p. 20). In other words, this theory says that people use media in order to gratify needs. For example, people use TV for entertainment purposes. Other media, such as radio and newspapers, provide material that gratifies the need for information about the immediate and more distant social world. When in the late 20th century new communication technologies emerged, it seemed as if all knowledge with regard to how people use media was disregarded. Almost all of the attention went to the technology and the opportunities it offered. The role of the consumer using the technology was rarely highlighted. However, after a number of years of technology push thinking, U&G research has gained a renewed interest (Lin, 2002; Papacharissi & Rubin, 2000; Savolainen, 1999). There is a specific reason to believe that the U&G approach is applicable to new media, and is even better than the media it was originally developed for. Most new technologies do not simply send information to a receiver; rather, the user has to explicitly seek information and make choices as to which media fulfill his or her needs best.

The question now is how needs and media choices are linked to each other. The central issue here is whether a technology is suitable to fulfill a specific need. The *social presence* concept (Short, Williams, & Christie, 1976), media richness theory (Daft & Lengel, 1986; Trevino, Daft, & Lengel, 1990), the social influence model (Fulk, Schmitz, & Steinfield, 1990), the dual capacity model (Sitkin, Sutcliffe, & Barrios-Choplin, 1992), and media appropriateness theory (Rice, 1993) offer comparable starting points for the analysis of media choice. The basic assumptions of these theories are explained through the media richness theory. The basic assumption is that a good task-medium fit is essential for effective communication. This means that successful use is based on the user's ability to process information using media of appropriate richness to clarify ambiguity and reduce uncertainty, or equivocality, as in the media richness theory (Daft, Lengel, & Trevino, 1987). *Equivocality* refers to the assumed existence of multiple and conflicting interpretations of a specific message (Trevino et al.). *Richness* refers to the capacity of a medium to process complex and ambiguous information. A good fit between medium and task means that a lean medium is chosen for an unequivocal message and a rich medium for a more complex one. If the wrong medium is chosen to get the message across, a mismatch occurs (Daft et al.). In the social influence model, Steinfield (1986) and Fulk et al. argued that medium characteristics and attitudes are, in part, socially constructed. Medium use processes are influenced by past statements, behavior, and social norms. Consequently, in contrast to the assumptions made by more rational choice models, as presented by Trevino et al. in the media richness theory, medium choice is subject to social influence. In the social influence model, it is proposed that determinants of medium choice are medium evaluations, task evaluations, social influence, and situational factors. Social influence affects medium choice directly and also affects medium evaluations and task evaluations. Social influence is thought to consist of direct statements by relevant others, vicarious learning, group behavioral norms, and social definitions of rationality. Sitkin et al. stressed in their dual capacity model the symbolic meaning of the medium, whereas the media appropriateness model (Rice) stressed the multidimensional character of both media and tasks. Postmes, Spears, and Lea (1998) argued that, when communicators share a common social identity, they appear to be more susceptible to group influence, social attraction, stereotyping, gender typing, and discrimination in anonymous computer-mediated communication.

Summarizing, suitability can be explained by the assumption that a good task-medium fit is essential for effective communication. Media richness theory approaches this assumption from a rational perspective, whereas the social influence model states that task and media perceptions are subjective and socially constructed (Fulk et al., 1990). Webster and Trevino (1995) and Trevino et al. (2000) showed that the best way to explain media choice is to combine insights from both rational and social theories of media choice. I elaborate on the media-choice approaches.

At the end of the previous section, I concluded that physical accessibility can result in the emergence of a threshold. This section shows that suitability can also be a threshold for media use. Characteristics of the medium make it more or less suitable to perform a specific task. Moreover, social influence can be an important factor. Again, it is possible to see a demand side and a supply side that, together, play a role in the decision of whether a threshold can or will be crossed. These results are summarized in Table 13.1.

Affective Accessibility

With regard to affective accessibility, the central question is whether the nature of the technology matches the knowledge and daily life of the user. This form of accessibility again depends on both the demand side and supply side. On the demand side, for example, someone who is used to picking up a telephone in many instances will be inclined to do so when a new task emerges, whether this is a logical step or not. On the supply side, we see that certain technologies (such as DVD, UMTS, etc.) can help the user to build a young and dynamic image. User friendliness is also a characteristic of the technology that can make it more or less accessible. Furthermore, user friendliness is subjective and, as such, also depends on the demand side. Some users experience command-line tools (such as UNIX and DOS) as very user friendly, whereas others cannot use the system at all. The amount of experience a user has is decisive. Theoretical support of this notion can be found in the technology acceptance model (TAM) that was developed by Davis (1989). This model is a bridge between suitability and affective accessibility, as it explains media use according to perceived usefulness and perceived ease of use. These two factors are related to attitude toward technology and subsequently intention to use and actual use. Because the model strongly emphasizes attitudes toward technology and intention to use, it is discussed in the present section on affective accessibility. In later versions of the TAM, perceived usefulness was extended to variables like experience, subjective norm, image, job relevance, output quality, and result demonstrability (Venkatesh & Davis, 2000).

Another theoretical approach toward affective accessibility was provided by Silverstone and Haddon (1996). They described how new technologies are incorporated within the daily life of users by means of a process of domestication. In this sense, technology is not neutral. Technology influences the private area, and the domestic area influences the way in which technology is used. The central issue is the interaction between technology and the user. This process of mutual adaptation is called "domestication of technology." This process can be divided into several phases (Silverstone & Haddon): appropriation (where someone buys and accepts a new product into the domestic environment), objectification (a product is made to fit into a preexisting culture), incorporation (the routinization or embedding into social patterns), and conversion (the presentation of the constructed artifact to the world outside the domestic sphere). In order to understand the meaning of technology, it is not sufficient to look at characteristics like income, education, and age. It is more important to obtain insight into how people learn to use technologies and to master them. (See Table 13.1 for an overview of factors that influence affective accessibility.)

Again, I conclude that, also for the threshold of affective accessibility, both demand- and supply-side factors play a role and have to be matched in order to guarantee effective communication, and, furthermore, that relevant context factors have to be taken into account. In the next section I try to integrate the results of the previous theoretical exploration into the current framework.

The Analytical Framework

First of all, I concluded that all forms of accessibility have a supply side and a demand side. When the needs of a user outweigh the thresholds, it becomes possible to meet the condition of accessibility. Connecting the various forms of accessibility and relating them to supply, demand, and context, as introduced in Fig. 13.1, results in a more elaborated research model, as presented in Fig. 13.2.

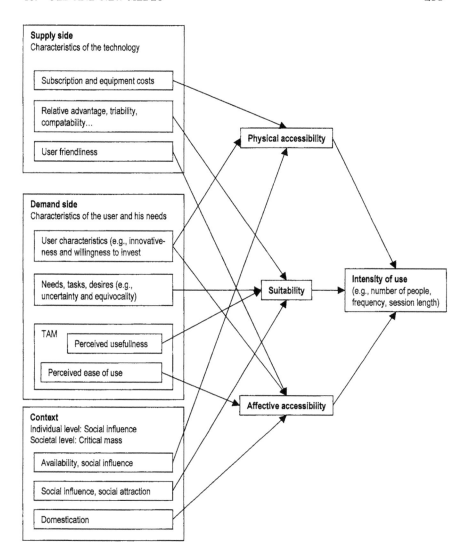

FIG. 13.2. An extended threshold model of technology use.

Figure 13.2 illustrates the results of my literature review. Media choice and use depend on the three types of accessibility. Whether a threshold can be crossed depends on user demand, technological supply, and context characteristics.

In the next section, I illustrate the model by analyzing the example of an electronic supermarket. I show how the use of a new technology relates to the framework that was presented in this section, and I also raise further research questions.

THE EXAMPLE OF THE ELECTRONIC SUPERMARKET

The internet is more and more a medium that not only allows the consumption of information, but also offers the possibility to buy products (e-commerce). For a long period of time, buying behavior was mainly aimed at durable products like music, software, and clothing. Over the past few years, fast-moving consumer goods (i.e., products sold at the supermarket) are trying to find a position in this electronic market.

Physical Access

One of the advantages of new technologies is their independency of time and place, which allows for 24-hour service. This could be an advantage, as European supermarkets have limited opening hours. A time-use survey (Breedveld & Van den Broek, 2001), however, showed that, despite the emergence of the 24-hour economy, most people still have a traditional rhythm: work on weekdays and eating, playing, and relaxation during the evening and on weekends. Although behavioral patterns are always changing, they are not changing as fast as we are led to believe by marketeers. Independency of place offers the user the opportunity to order products from any given place. For delivery of the products, a certain place is needed. Complicating things further, many groceries need cool storage. Other issues that relate to physical accessibility emerge from research by Henderson, Rickwood, and Roberts (1998), who mentioned a lack of equipment, and problems with regard to installing software and logging on. Raijas (2002) reported higher prices as a possible threshold.

    In summary, although physical accessibility is often characterized as a trivial issue, it can be an important threshold for the use of an electronic supermarket. With respect to the independency of time and place, information technology enables increased physical accessibility, but that same technology simultaneously creates new thresholds (e.g., with regard to equipment, software, and price).

Suitability

Buying behavior is generally typified as a process in several phases (Engel, Blackwell, & Miniard, 1990): need for cognition, search for information, comparison of alternatives, purchase, and outcomes. From this perspective, the electronic supermarket offers opportunities as well as limitations. Meij, Jansen, and Kersthold (2001) defined the differences between the electronic and brick-and-mortar supermarkets as follows:

- Interaction with the product: In a brick-and-mortar supermarket, consumers can feel and touch products. This is not possible in an electronic context. Consequently, users may experience difficulties in estimating the size of a package (Henderson et al., 1998).
- Strategy and efficiency: In a brick-and-mortar supermarket, consumers walk past the shelves and take what they need. In an electronic supermarket, shopping takes place by clicking on products.
- Opportunity to compare: Because products are more systematically structured in an electronic supermarket, comparison is easier than in a brick-and-mortar supermarket.

Moreover, with regard to suitability, it can be concluded that information technology for e-commerce both decreases and increases thresholds. On the one hand, electronic shopping saves time and effort, but on the other hand finding products requires a different strategy and product quality is hard to determine (Henderson et al., 1998; Raijas, 2002).

Affective Accessibility

Dahlén (1999) analyzed the adoption of online shopping, among other things, in relation to existing purchasing behavior, risk perception, innovativeness, and experience with the internet in general. Liao and Cheung (2001) confirmed Dahlén's findings. Internet buying depends on the perception of the safety of transactions, experience with online shopping, perception of quality of products offered via the internet, and prior experience with the internet. Eastin (2002) found that prior use of telephony for the same activity, perceived risk, self-efficacy, internet use, and perceived financial benefits play a role in the adoption of online shopping, banking, investing, and electronic payment of internet services. Koufaris (2002) found that shopping enjoyment and perceived usefulness have an effect on the willingness of online consumers to make unplanned purchases via the internet. Individual beliefs and attitudes toward e-commerce services, such as perceived usefulness, attitudes toward the internet, and perceived risk are determinants of the adoption decision (O'Cass & Fenech, 2003). Raijas (2002) stressed that shopping behavior in its core is a habitual activity. Grocery-shopping habits are well established, and consumers do not calculate the cost of time spent shopping or transportation. Under these circumstances, the threshold to change to a new shopping habit is high. These results indicate that for many people doing groceries is an important part of daily life. On the one hand, it is a time-consuming, repetitive activity necessary to keep the household running. In a busy time schedule, online shopping could be an effective way to obtain groceries. On the other hand, shopping for many people is a way to get out of the house, meet other people, and obtain new ideas.

Conclusion

Currently, more than two thirds of the Dutch population has internet access. However, not everyone in this group also has the right equipment to use electronic supermarkets. A user with an old computer and simple modem connection probably needs a lot of patience to use an electronic supermarket. It is only a limited part of the population that can use the electronic supermarket as a serious alternative. With regard to suitability, it is possible to say that the electronic supermarket could have a function in the day-to-day process. Eventually, everybody needs groceries. Obviously, there is a clear need for supermarkets. Busy schedules and the lack of time make the electronic supermarket very suitable. However, an electronic supermarket is not the same as a brick-and-mortar supermarket. The electronic supermarket allows for a certain type of groceries and certainly does not serve all the functions a regular supermarket has. Buying groceries is in part an experience that cannot be replaced by the electronic supermarket. Even though the electronic supermarket offers opportunities that a regular supermarket cannot offer, this does not guarantee its success. The question of whether people are interested in a personalized service should be asked. These are all issues related to affective accessibility. In summary, the electronic supermarket should be seen as an addition to the regular supermarket, with a specific function, rather than a replacement of it (Steinfield, Mahler, & Bauer, 1999).

Although this case was only an explorative illustration of the presented framework, it does show that it is useful to look at new technologies in terms of thresholds. The model allows a broad review of factors that might influence the success or failure of new technologies. In fact, much of the cited research explicitly uses the terms *threshold* and *accessibility*, but none actually integrates these concepts in its conceptual framework. Further empirical research is needed in order to validate the framework as presented in Fig. 13.2.

DISCUSSION AND LIMITATIONS

The goal of this chapter was to show the reader how the success or failure of technologies depends on the crossing of several thresholds. Thresholds have both demand and supply sides. As the supermarket case illustrates, the process of adoption does not solely depend on the ability of a technology to perform a certain task. Reality is far more complex, and context should be

TABLE 13.2
Further Research Questions

	Physical Accessibility	Suitability	Affective Accessibility
Demand side	Who has access to technologies? What is the quality of this access?	With what needs are people confronted in a home and organizational context?	How does technology use fit in daily life? How does this change?
Supply side	What is the role of alternative sources to meet user needs? How do different technologies compete?	What opportunities do new technologies have to offer?	What should services look like in order to be quick and easy to use?
Context	Should the government have an active role in the provision of universal access to technology?	How do market structures develop and what does that mean for service provision?	What is the role of other users (on a micro as well as on a macro level)?

taken into account. The relevance of the development of a conceptual framework that describes success or failure is that technology is a development that influences many aspects of modern society. However, it is very hard to predict in what direction this development can and will be most influential. The presented framework aims at grasping the complexity of technology use on the one hand and providing a comprehensive starting point for further research on the other.

With regard to the limitations of this framework, it is important to state that many of the theories that were used in the research were developed in a period when there were no "new" media. Despite the fact that it is a logical choice to use old theory to describe new phenomena, one should be careful. When one would simply transfer old theory to new media, a theoretical equivalent of the horseless carriage would emerge. That is another reason why empirical testing of this framework is very important. Further research should aim at the different areas that were described in this chapter: the three types of accessibility and the three areas of specific explanatory domains, demand, supply, and context. Table 13.2 shows a number of questions that can be raised from this perspective.

REFERENCES

Bouwman, H., Nouwens, J., Slootman, A., & Baaijens, J. (1996). *Een schat aan informatie: Een onderzoek naar de toegankelijkheid van elektronische overheidsinformatie* [The information treasure: Accessibility of governmental information]. Den Haag, The Netherlands: Rathenau Instituut.

Bouwman, H., & Van de Wijngaert, I.. (2002). Content and context: A new research approach to the basic characteristics of information needs. *New Media and Society, 4,* 329–353.

Breedveld, K., & Van den Broek, A. (2001). *Trends in de tijd. Eerste overzicht van uitkomsten* [Trends in time. An overview of the results]. Den Haag, The Netherlands: Social and Cultural Planning Office of the Netherlands.

Chen, G., & Kotz, D. (2000). *A survey of context aware mobile computing research* (Dartmouth Computer Science Tech. Rep. No. TR 2000-381). Dartmouth, England: Dartmouth College Department of Computer Science.

Daft, R. L., & Lengel, R. H. (1986). Organizational information requirements, media richness and structural design. *Management Science, 32,* 554–571.

Daft, R. L., Lengel, R. H., & Trevino, L. K. (1987). Message equivocality, media selection and manager performance: Implications for information systems. *MIS Quarterly, 11,* 354–366.

Dahlén, M. (1999). Closing in on the Web consumer. In E. Bohlin, Brodin, Lundgren, & Thorngren (Eds.), *Convergence in communications and beyond.* Amsterdam: Elsevier Science.

Davis, F. D. (1989). Perceived usefulness, perceived ease of use, and user acceptance of information technology. *MIS Quarterly, 13,* 319–341.

Eastin, M. A. (2002). Diffusion of e-commerce: An analysis of the adoption of four e-commerce activities. *Telematics and Informatics, 19,* 251–267.

Engel, J. F., Blackwell, R. D., & Miniard, P. W. (1990). *Consumer behavior.* Chicago: Dryden.

Fulk, J., Schmitz, J., & Steinfield, C. (1990). A social influence model of technology use. In J. Fulk & C. Steinfield (Eds.), *Organizations and communication technology* (pp. 117–140). Newbury Park, CA: Sage.

Henderson, R., Rickwood, D., & Roberts, P. (1998). The beta test of an electronic supermarket. *Interacting with Computers, 10,* 385–399.

Katz, E., Blumler, J., & Gurevitch, M. (1974). Uses of mass communication by the individual. In W. P. Davidson & F. Yu (Eds.), *Mass communication research: Major issues and future directions* (pp. 11–35). New York: Praeger.

Koufaris, M. (2002). Applying the technology acceptance model and flow theory to online consumer behavior. *Information Systems Research, 13,* 205–223.

Liao, Z., & Cheung, M. T. (2001). Internet-based e-shopping and consumer attitudes: An empirical study. *Information and Management, 38,* 299–306.

Lievrouw, L. A., & Livingstone, S. (2002). The social shaping and consequences of ICTs. In L. A. Lievrouw & S. Livingstone (Eds.), *The handbook of new media* (pp. 1–14). London: Sage.

Lin, C. A. (2002). Perceived gratifications of online media service use among potential users. *Telematics and Informatics, 19,* 3–19.

Markus, L. (1990). Toward a "critical mass" theory of interactive media. In J. Fulk & C. Steinfield (Eds.), *Organisations and communication technology* (pp. 117–140). Newbury Park, CA: Sage.

Marwell, G., & Oliver, P. (1993). *The critical mass in collective action: A micro-social theory.* Cambridge, England: Cambridge University Press.

McCreadie, M., & Rice, R. E. (1999). Trends in analyzing access to information. Part I: Cross-disciplinary conceptualizations of access. *Information Processing and Management, 35,* 45–76.

Meij, G., Jansen, E. M. J., & Kersthold, J. H. (2001). *Koopgedrag in supermarkt en telewinkel: Een vergelijking* [A comparison of buying behavior for on and offline shopping]. Soesterberg, the Netherlands: TNO.

O'Cass, A., & Fenech, T. (2003). Webretailing adoption: Exploring the nature of internet users' Webretailing behavior. *Journal of Retailing and Consumer Services, 10,* 81–94.

Papacharissi, Z., & Rubin, A. M. (2000). Predictors of internet use. *Journal of Broadcasting and Electronic Media, 44,* 175–197.

Postmes, T., Spears, R., & Lea, M. (1998). Breaching or building social boundaries? Side-effects of computer-mediated communication. *Communication Research, 25,* 689–716.

Raijas, A. (2002). The consumer benefits and problems in the electronic grocery store. *Journal of Retailing and Consumer Services, 9,* 107–113.

Rice, R. E. (1993). Media appropriateness: Using social presence theory to compare traditional and new organizational media. *Human Communication Research, 19,* 451–484.

Rogers, E. (1983). *Diffusion of innovations.* New York: Free Press.

Rosengren, K. E., Wenner, L. A., & Palmgreen, P. (1985). *Media gratifications research: Current perspectives.* Beverly Hills, CA: Sage.

Savolainen, R. (1999). The role of the Internet in information seeking. Putting the networked services in context. *Information Processing and Management, 35,* 765–782.

Schilit, A., Adams, N., & Want, R. (1994). Context aware computing applications. In L.-F. Cabrera & M. Satyanarayanan (Eds.), *Proceedings of IEEE Workshop on Mobile Computing Systems and Applications* (pp. 85–90). Santa Cruz, CA: IEEE Computer Society Press.

Short, J., Williams, E., & Christie, B. (1976). *The social psychology of telecommunications.* London: Wiley.

Silverstone, R., & Haddon, L. (1996). Design and the domestication of information and communication technologies: Technical change and everyday life. In R. Mansell & R. Silverstone (Eds.), *Communication by design. The politics of information and communication technologies* (pp. 44–74). Oxford, England: Oxford University Press.

Sitkin, S. B., Sutcliffe, K. M., & Barrios-Choplin, J. R. (1992). A dual capacity model of communication media choice in organizations. *Human Communication Research, 18,* 563–598.

Steinfield, C. (1986). Computer-mediated communication in an organizational setting: Explaining task-related and socio-emotional uses. In M. McLaughlin (Ed.), *Communication yearbook 9* (pp. 85–108). Beverly Hills, CA: Sage.

Steinfield, C., Mahler, A., & Bauer, J. (1999). Electronic commerce and the local merchant: Opportunities for synergy between physical and Web. *Electronic Markets, 9,* 45–50.

Trevino, L. K., Daft, R. L., & Lengel, R. H. (1990). Understanding managers' media choices: A symbolic interactionist perspective. In J. Fulk & C. Steinfield (Eds.), *Organisations and communication technology* (pp. 71–94). Newbury Park, CA: Sage.

Trevino, L. K., Webster, J., & Stein, E. W. (2000). Making connections: Complementary influences on communication media choices, attitudes, and use. *Organization Science, 11,* 163–182.

Van de Wijngaert, L. (1999). *Matching media: Information need and new media choice.* Enschede, The Netherlands: Telematica Instituut.

Venkatesh, V., & Davis, F. D. (2000). A theoretical extension of the technology acceptance model: Four longitudinal field studies. *Management Science, 46,* 186–204.

Webster, J., & Trevino, L. K. (1995). Rational and social theories as complementary explanations of communication media choices: Two policy capturing studies. *Academy of Management Journal, 38,* 1544–1572.

Chapter 14

The Diffusion and Deployment of Telework in Organizations

Ronald Batenburg
Utrecht University

Pascale Peters
Utrecht University

Since the late 1970s, teleworking has been given regular attention in many areas of media, policy, and research. Within this relatively long time period, telework as a concept has been addressed and readdressed with different terminology and definitions. In earlier days, telework was primarily associated with working at home, or working at the company's peripheral plants. Information and communication technologies provided necessary conditions for different kinds of telework practices (cf. Huws, 1996). During the 1970s the concept of telecommuting was introduced (Nilles, Carlson, Gray, & Hanneman, 1976). In the 1980s and 1990s the term *teleworking* came into vogue as a broader classification of remote work (Korte & Wynnes, 1996; Nilles, 1998). More recently, the telework concept is guided by terms like *nomadic working, hotdesking, mobile computing, working at home, hoteling,* and *home-based business.* Remote workers may be called *road warriors* or *mobile workers* (cf. Pratt, 2000).

The definition of telework remains a primary concern in the literature. A clear definition of telework is important in two respects. First, it determines the latitude of the phenomenon in society, in terms of numbers of employees, or proportion of the labor force. Second, definitions of telework determine the scope of its potential impact, such as environmental and economic effects on the societal level, labor productivity and conditions at the organizational level, and the work-life balance of employees at the individual level (Pratt, 2000). As we will elaborate, these aspects of telework are the starting points of our central research questions.

One of the largest surveys on telework was conducted in 2000 as part of the Electronic Commerce and Telework Trends project (ECaTT, 2000). This project questioned 7,700 people (employees) and over 4,100 enterprises (information technology [IT] managers) in 10 European countries. To succeed in this international and multiactor research, a clear definition of telework was naturally very important. The ECaTT researchers claimed that home-based telework is to be considered the most widely recognized type of remote work. Home-based teleworkers are defined as:

> Those who work from home (instead of commuting to a central workplace) for at least one full working day a week, use a personal computer and in the course of their work, use telecommunications links to communicate with their colleagues and supervisors during work at home and are either in salaried employment or self-employed in which case their main working place is on the contractors' premises. (ECaTT, p. 7)

For comparison, the most used and cited definition in the Netherlands is: "a teleworker is someone who works at least 20% of his or her formal working time outside the office (not necessarily from home) using information and communication technology equipment" (Klomp & Van Oosterhout, 2001, p. 32).

In both definitions, three central elements can be distinguished: (a) the work location, (b) the intensity of the worker's remote work activity (i.e., the proportion of work hours performed outside the employer's or principal's work location), and (c) the use of information and communication equipment. With regard to the first dimension, the work location, telework is usually associated with the employee's own dwelling, that is, home work. Some argue that teleworking and home working are basically the same concept and should be conceptually integrated. The current definition, however, allows teleworking also to be working from another location that is not necessarily the employee's residence. Examples of these alternative work locations are so-called satellite offices—an extra establishment created by the organization for employees living far away from the head offices—or telework hotels. The concept of the latter implies that workers (of any organization, or working for any principal) can literally plug in with the home organization, by checking into one of the hotel rooms that are facilitated with desks, telephones, and advanced connections to the outside world, in particular, the internet.

The second dimension, the intensity of the worker's remote work activity, deals with the proportion of online working away from the office. The minimum proportion is often set at one full day a week or—as in the present definition—20 or 25% of the formal working time, which is better suited to part-time labor contracts. Although this seems quite precise, it is still an arbitrary rule. At the same time, the proportion of telework during contractual labor time can also be restricted with regard to its maximum. Employees that telework 100% of their labor time will preferably be called *freelancers* or *mobile workers,* instead of *teleworkers.*

The necessary condition referring to the third dimension is the use of information and communication technology equipment. In the context of telework, equipment obviously refers to hard- and software, like network infrastructure, personal computers, modems, network protocols, shared or distributed software, databases, and so on. In its basic technological concept, telework requires some form of electronic data interchange. As is described later, the technological opportunities to enable teleworking have emerged quite rapidly.

If we take this definition of teleworking as a starting point, what can be said about the actual number of different types of teleworkers? The ECaTT survey (ECaTT, 2000) shows that the Netherlands is running in front with regard to teleworking, together with Finland and Sweden (ECaTT; European Commission, 2001). The survey reported that 8.3% of the Dutch working population in 1999 are home-based and mobile teleworkers, versus 4% of the European average. It also reported that 65% of managers judge the majority of jobs as teleworkable, whereas 75% of these respondents showed interest in practicing telework in their organizations. According to the ECaTT survey, over 35% of Dutch firms practiced telework in 1999. The survey expects a substantial growth in telework, and other sources expect about 1 million teleworkers in 2015. The ECaTT numbers are confirmed by other international research, such as the 2000 survey of the European Foundation for the Improvement of Working and Living Conditions (Paoli & Merllié, 2001) and research that compares Europe with the United States (Gareis, 2002). However, in the period from 1999 to 2001, the growth in the number of Dutch teleworkers stagnated, especially among "telehome-workers." Further growth could still be observed among mobile workers and teleworking freelancers (Van Klaveren & Van de Westelaken, 2001).

The central question we address concerns the critical conditions for the deployment of telework in organizations. This question is tackled by decomposing the opportunities and restrictions of telework from two perspectives. First, telework as a concept is related to its socioeconomic context, where we point at the macrodrivers that have led to the growing interest in telework and the teleworkability of organizations. Second, telework is analyzed from a technological perspective. Combining both approaches leads us to describe the conditions for teleworking in organizations in terms of IT alignment. To conclude, we present an integrative framework by recalling what we believe are the main managerial choices with regard to telework.

TELEWORK FROM A SOCIOECONOMIC PERSPECTIVE: MACROTRENDS AS DRIVERS

The tendency toward and need for telework are traditionally related to a number of collective societal problems. Often mentioned in this respect are traffic congestion and environmental issues. Indeed, teleworking has direct effects on the travel behavior of employees (cf. Nilles et al., 1976). Others claimed that telework can contribute to the economical development of regions that are relatively behind. Telework could also support the (re)integration of (partly) disabled people in the economic process. These drives particularly stem from public policy areas.

More recently, other relevant socioeconomic macrotrends are related to changes in the labor market and the labor relations field. It is argued that teleworking fits into the emergence of a new class of self-employed freelancers (De Vries & Weijers, 1998, p. 12). More generally, telework suits the growing number of employees that demand autonomy, time sovereignty, and professional freedom in their jobs (Powell & Maineiro, 1999). This trend is obviously related to the increase in employees' educational level and to new trends in personnel management. Instead of presenting detailed job descriptions, employers and employees increasingly negotiate the content of employees' jobs (roles), output targets, and deadlines. In line with this, new labor relations are based on decentralization of decision making and responsibilities (empowerment), broadened and deepened tasks (role defining), optimization of employees' talents (competence management), and learning and personal development (employability). In summary, telework can be easily placed within the trend toward human resource management in organizations (cf. Barney, 1991; Pfeffer, 1994).

Telework can be seen as a way to satisfy employees' growing demand to work in teams, networks, and virtual organizations (Bridges, 1994; Jackson & Van der Wielen, 1998). This is supported by the notion that teleworking has become an important part of secondary labor conditions. It enlarges the labor market potential across regions by saving travel time. Employees are better able to combine their private and working patterns and thus improve the quality of their family life (Gottlieb, Kelloway, & Braham, 1998; Kinsman, 1987). Individuals need time-saving strategies more and more, especially now that the time of a growing number of households is squeezed due to new and augmented demands from the paid and unpaid work domains (Peters, 2000). During the course of life, individuals and households are increasingly mobile, change residences more easily and often dealing with different work locations for spouses. This reason is often mentioned to explain employees' demand for telework (Van Klaveren, Tijdens, & Wetzels, 2000). Moreover, modern work trends, such as the intensification of work, seem to favor telework to give employees a moment's rest to finish reports and the like under deadline pressure (Perin, 1998).

In line with these trends, many scholars have stated that telework is an expression of a movement in which organizations, work processes, and management styles are redesigned (Daniels, Lamond, & Standen, 2000). Telework can save office space and related overhead costs. It was found that normally only 60% of the office space available is utilized, due to extending operational hours, the reduction of formal working hours, and the increase of part-time work (Klomp & Van Oosterhout, 2001). Moreover, telework was being related to the concept of the modern, post-Fordist organization. The new, flexible firm has a primary customer and process orientation that is accompanied by typical internal and external governance structures. As business activities have become more global, unpredictable, and complex, a company's ability to escape traditional restrictions on time and space with respect to labor processes has become more decisive for a successful performance (Peters, 2001; Van der Wielen, Van der Berg, & Van Diggelen, 1995). Organizational flexibility and, hence, the flexibility of workers, should be augmented because customers nowadays expect 24-hour service, especially if companies operate in global markets. Competition based on time to market and speed of transaction pushes the demands to perform in real time or, in the terminology, "any time, any place, anyhow" (Turban, MacLean, & Wetherbe, 1999). If business and information systems are able to meet these demands, employees must follow to capitalize these competitive advantages. The adagio is simply to be as flexible as the customer wants us to be. In this sense, teleworking can contribute to these developments because it allows customers to communicate with employees whenever they want. Tele(home)work may also meet predictable and unpredictable peaks in demands (De Vries & Weijers, 1998, p. 12).

So far, we have presented the reasons why telework can help organizations to improve their performance, labor market position, flexibility, and efficiency. But what determines its diffusion in practice?

THE TELEWORKABILITY OF ORGANIZATIONS

Telework as an organizational choice implies that many deliberations must be made before the intended gains are achieved. A review of the literature reveals many similar suggestions about which types of organizations (and which functions) are suitable for telework (Peters, Tijdens, & Wetzels, 2001). One important aspect in determining the teleworkability of organizations is the extent to which there is a need to be physically present at the workplace or to physically communicate with others. Another aspect is the manageability of potential teleworkers, often related to the need to control or supervise their work directly. A third, often recalled, argument concerns the intensity of complex cognitive tasks involved in jobs to be performed at home.

In a systematic overview of the Dutch literature on this topic, Lamme (2000) stressed that it should be first assessed whether the conditions for, and consequences of, telework help to meet the aims of the organization (Lamme, p. 12). Often, managers do not know whether or how telework can do so. Also, organizations should be willing to change. To understand the diffusion and consequences of teleworking, it is important to simultaneously consider the type of labor, organizational structure, and organizational culture that are potentially suited for telework. In his model, Lamme (p. 14) presents nine criteria, classified in three categories:

1. Job-related aspects, such as (a) work autonomy, (b) measurability of output, and (c) independence of locality.
2. Departmental aspects, such as (d) output orientation, (e) support of colleagues, and (f) innovative capacity.
3. Management style, such as (g) trust in employees, (h) output management, and (i) willingness to change.

In Lamme's conceptual model, these criteria converge into the latent variable "teleworkability," which consequently affects the organization's decisions with regard to the implementation of telework, the selection of employees allowed to telework, the costs and benefits of telework, and the protection or security of information flows.

From the list presented before, job-related aspects are addressed in explaining the diffusion of telework. There are several overviews of tasks and occupations that are known to be frequently performed through telework. In general, white-collar (administrative) professions at a medium or higher level are labeled as suitable for telework. Examples often named are accountants, lawyers, architects, journalists, software engineers, insurance agents, researchers, travel agents, and translators (cf. Van Klaveren et al., 2000). IT-related activities are also considered as suitable for telework, such as data entry, software development, online support, and help desk work. Remarkably, activities such as telemarketing are less often mentioned (Van Klaveren et al., p. 40).

With regard to the job-related criteria, Lamme (2000) pointed out that it is not only structured jobs and work processes whose output can be managed that are suitable for telework. In his opinion, nonstructured work may also be appropriate. Lamme distinguished also between complex and noncomplex processes. Complexity in this sense refers to the number of people needed to finish a certain task. These two dimensions can be combined, leading to a typology of structured noncomplex tasks (such as administrative tasks or data entry), structured complex tasks (such as dealing with claims or subsidy requests), nonstructured noncomplex tasks (such as writing reports), and nonstructured complex tasks (such as attending meetings). Depending on the type of tasks to be performed, the teleworkability of jobs and, hence, organizations, varies. Managers and other decision makers can benefit from a solid functional analysis in order to apply telework in an appropriate sequence within their organization and to avoid unintended implementation consequences.

Although this section covers much of the telework research, the teleworkability of organizations clearly does not depend only on job demands and human resource managerial choices. So far, the importance of information and communication technologies (ICT), as it is needed to actually facilitate remote work processes, has not been addressed. In the next section, we therefore explicitly approach teleworking from a technological perspective.

TELEWORK FROM A TECHNOLOGICAL PERSPECTIVE: OPPORTUNITIES AND CONDITIONS

In most postindustrial societies, the nature of work shifts from manual, industrial work to occupations in which the generation and processing of information plays a key role. Within the information society or digital economy, this type of work is heavily supported by ICT and dependent on it. In combination with the growing flexibility and mobility of jobs, ICT also increasingly supports the performance of work, independently of time and space. Without a doubt, the revolutionary development and diffusion of the internet neatly embodies these trends. Reading, using, presenting, spreading, publishing, and communicating metainformation through the Web (and equivalent electronic highways) is prominently time and location independent. Stimulated by fast-emerging Web-based technology and applications, employees do indeed perform their tasks and occupations at home or elsewhere without colleagues, customers, or other contacts (or even themselves) noticing it. Call centers, for instance, allow employees to perform their work within so-called virtual companies: They serve customers at different times and locations, but remain connected online to the central unit through networks of databases.

The IT industry has been permanently featured by fast-emerging technologies and accelerated capacity, availability, accessibility, performance, and speed of equipment and information systems. Interestingly enough, the consumer segment of the market appears to closely follow the business segment with regard to the adoption of new ICT inventions. In many homes, stand-alone PCs are replaced by systems with standard connections to the internet. Along with the spectacular diffusion of mobile phones and personal digital agendas, customers are expected to use mobile internet applications extensively in the near future. Nowadays, the private and mobile use of ICT seems technically limited only by the availability of bandwidth. From a technological point of view, the difference between the company and home-office environments has become significantly smaller.

At the same time, existing software is rapidly adapted and newly developed to cope with hardware inventions. Especially in the field of operating systems and communication protocols, the rewards of setting the software standard can be tremendous. Microsoft's strategy to insert its operating systems into every possible new device is a good example of exploiting the network effects of (mass) communication tools. In addition, application software and content are redesigned to connect with the mobile communication trend. E-mail and internet software are the most well-known applications that were rapidly redeveloped for the mobile device market. In particular, software that supports database management, document management, content management, and groupware applications will find new targets in the growing market for remote and mobile applications. Another reason for its potential advantages is the growing digitalization of documents and information flows in organizations. Digitalization has made organizational information accessible and exchangeable, which is particularly convenient for teleworking employees. Also in this field, we see new technological developments to optimize digitalization by standardizing document structures and content. The rapid emergence of extensible markup language (XML) is a good illustration of this.

THE TELEWORKABILITY OF ORGANIZATIONS FROM A TECHNOLOGICAL PERSPECTIVE

As mentioned earlier, the teleworkability of organizations is often analyzed according to the importance of job characteristics. Technology, or ICT, as such, is lacking in most of the academic teleworkability models. Although it seems to be covered by the criterion "innovative capacity" (see Lamme's [2000] classification), the role of ICT seems to be somewhat forgotten in most of the telework research. As we said before, however, a number of critical conditions for teleworking are explicitly related to typical technological issues. On the one hand, the availability of hardware, software, and telecommunication at the workplace is no longer a relevant barrier to teleworking. In 2001, 96% of all Dutch organizations and 75% of Dutch households used personal computers and were connected to the internet (Dutch Statistics, 2002). On the other hand, the more advanced technological issues, like security, parallel processing, distributed systems, file sharing, and data transmission have become serious conditions for teleworking. As information becomes more and more dynamic and vulnerable to misuse (think of credit card numbers and medical data), the reliability of data transfer and storage both inside and outside the organization has increased in importance.

The fast-growing field of e-business models provides one answer to these issues. With the emergence of Web-based information systems, teleworking has become more and more organized through so-called business-to-employee portals. These business portals, or enterprise information portals (EIPs), are designed to deliver organizational information to employees any time, any place, anyhow (Finkelstein, 2003; White, 2000). To put it another way: Portals can be considered as a data-management strategy that provides a window into enterprise knowledge by bringing life to data so it can be compared, analyzed, and shared by any user in the organization (Fitzloff, 1999).

From a technological perspective, EIPs are best understood as the next step after the intranet. If the intranet was developed as a place where corporate content could reside, the portal is designed to dynamically organize that information. This becomes clear if we take a look at the architecture of EIPs. The so-called multilayered data-delivery platform is designed to deliver user-specific content from different data sources (Dias, 2001). A basic component of this platform is the integration layer that integrates different data sources. Corporate information can be stored in documents, Web content, warehouse reports, groupware, or Enterprise Resource Planning (ERP) systems. The index layer describes the definition and structure of this information as metadata, usually with the aid of XML (see earlier discussion). Web crawling practically unlocks the user-specific information. This is handled by comparing the clearance level in a personal user profile with the security level of information in the metadata. At this layer, the security profile is of major importance, because it defines the access and delivery permissions of users within the EIP. Through the search layer, users are provided with regular updates of relevant information by automated search engines. In addition, users are allowed to locate and retrieve specific information from the internal business information directory and external content. Finally, the personalized layer of the EIP platform enables the user to fine-tune the presentation of his or her information and applications. At this point, there are several standard interface techniques available.

TOWARD AN INTEGRATIVE FRAMEWORK
OF TELEWORK

So far, we have focused on socioeconomic trends that have stimulated attention to telework in society on the one hand, and on technological factors that are necessary to facilitate the deployment of telework in work organizations on the other. It appears that, from both perspectives, there are many conditions that determine the actual diffusion and deployment of telework in organizations. From a managerial perspective, the general attitude of managers and employees toward labor relations and leadership appears to be a critical success factor. The complexity and structuring of work processes can strongly favor, but at the same time prevent, the introduction of telework. Moreover, from a technological perspective, the opportunities of (business-to-employee) portals seem to perfectly fit the concept of teleworking. Still, equivalent technical issues such as security and standardization add extra complexity to the deployment of this telework and its related technology.

In this section, we aim to comprise the literature and research on teleworking as described before as a system of multilevel and multiactor processes. To understand both the diffusion and deployment of telework, it is important to distinguish the position of the two major actors (employers and employees), at three levels of aggregation (micro, meso, and macro).

To start at the macrolevel, telework can be interpreted as a new technological means to organize work independently of time and space that meets societal, employers', and employees', interests. This opportunity coincides with a number of other macrodevelopments, such as individualization and empowerment. However, the mere availability of technology at the macrolevel and the interests in society as such are not sufficient conditions for a further uptake of telework.

What is important is a customized match between the management of workers and work processes and the management of technology at the mesolevel. An inventory of the work processes in the organization sheds light on which type of ICT is necessary to enable employees to telework. Next, an inventory of the availability of IT equipment in the company may give employers insight into which jobs are currently teleworkable in that particular organization. In addition, employers have to trust technology and their teleworking personnel. All in all, managers need to estimate the tangible and intangible costs and benefits of telework. Asked for the most important barriers to introducing telework, managers answered "unknown productivity/quality gains" (60%), "data security problems" (54%), "difficult management of teleworkers" (50%), and "insufficient knowledge about the relevant conditions" (51%; Dhondt & Van den Heuvel, 1998; European Commission, 2001).

At the microlevel, finally, it is shown that not all employees who have the opportunity to telework take it (Peters, Tijdens, & Wetzels, 2001). Apparently, employees are reluctant to adopt telework as a new work concept, or to adopt the technology involved. Like managers, employees need to trust their managers, coworkers, and virtual team members as well to achieve the autonomy benefits of teleworking. Research has shown that home-based telework, especially for lower skilled administrative jobs, can be applied to exploit routine workers, under bad labor conditions and with no guarantees to keep their job (Huws, Korte, & Robinson, 1990; Vlek, 1986; Weijers & Weijers, 1986). Other authors indicated that the quality of labor of this type of teleworkers is lower because employees lack social contact during their work, and feel isolated and less in the picture for promotion (e.g., De Vries & Weijers, 1998, p. 70). This implies that the motivation of teleworking employees at the microlevel has consequences for the organizational performance at the mesolevel. Next, the individual and organizational productivity influence societal and economic performance at the macrolevel.

This sketch of the adoption and deployment of telework as a system of actors interacting with each other can be summarized and visualized in Fig. 14.1, a scheme that systematically breaks down the micro-, meso-, and macrolevels involved.

As stressed before, the underlying claim behind this framework is that successful adoption and deployment of telework in organizations depends on the alignment of several technological and organizational opportunities and restrictions. This message is very much in line with the alignment perspective as developed by Henderson and Venkatraman (1993). In their in-

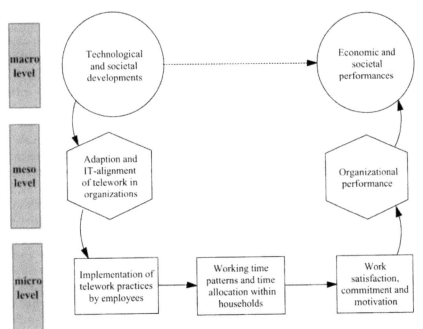

FIG. 14.1. A conceptual framework of diffusion and deployment of telework.

tensively quoted article, Venkatraman and Henderson stressed the importance of aligning technological and organizational management on both the strategic and operational levels. Their main point was that the management of technology (IT) and the management of general organizational issues are often disconnected. IT initiatives often fail because of this lack of alignment, or what is often called "mutual shaping." According to Henderson and Venkatraman, balancing IT and organizational strategy needs to be the first step, closely followed by the operational alignment of organizational processes and IT infrastructures.

With regard to telework, this implies that the goals of the organization, the managerial design of workplaces, and human resource policies need to be aligned with the IT strategy of the organization, the information infrastructure, and its IT management. All these items are similarly and highly relevant with regard to the deployment of teleworking. Governance structures in organizations traditionally determine the conditions of who has access to stored information and information flows. From a strategic point of view, an important organizational choice is about the coordination rules that are applied to teleworkers. In operational terms, organizations need to answer the question of what type of information and communication structure is needed to enable flexible workplaces outside the physical organizational boundaries while maintaining a solid security policy. In addition, as knowledge management becomes more and more important, the output and knowledge of every employee need to be captured and shared through the same type of information systems. These issues were addressed earlier in this chapter, with regard to the definition of security profile in business-to-employee portals.

To conclude, we expect that companies with strong and direct control structures provide fewer opportunities for telework. Moreover, organizations that rely on concurrent control—rather than indirect control, such as assessments or output control—will probably select fewer employees for teleworking (Hales, 1993; Nilles, 1998). In some organizations, telework will be part of the governance structure (i.e., IT firms) and presented as an explicit opportunity for employees (a fringe benefit). In other firms, employees have to negotiate their opportunities for home work or telework. Related to this process of selection and negotiations between employee and employer, human resource management again plays a central role (Daniels, Lamond, & Standen, 2000). In addition, we hypothesize that organizations with a strong tradition in outsourcing activities and flexible employment and that have the appropriate IT equipment (such as trade firms, the intermediary sector, or publishing companies) will be the early adopters of telework. In contrast, organizations that depend heavily on services and information work will have many difficulties with the alignment of the technology (i.e., ICT) and organization necessary for telework.

SUMMARY AND CONCLUSION

In this contribution, we approached the adoption, deployment, and consequences of telework in organizations from several perspectives. From a societal and employees' perspective, the advantages of telework may seem dominant. Many employees who have difficulties combining labor and domestic tasks (and especially the accompanied transportation) expect telework to be a solution to their experienced time shortage. However, less contact with colleagues and interference between home and work appear to be important disadvantages. From both technological and managerial perspectives, the list of disadvantages predominates. Uncertainty about the productivity of teleworkers and the fear of losing control over employees often restrain full adaptation and deployment of telework. In addition, a number of technological barriers are met, such as IT security, IT standardization, information sharing, and information management. In practice, managers systematically underestimate the teleworkability of their organization and employees. This explains why in many cases employees' preferences largely exceed the existing possibilities for telework in work organizations (Peters et al., 2001).

The central question remains, then, why telework as a concept has been widely embraced by some employers and employees but not by others. In many organizations, the interest in teleworking seems to have a short life cycle. Organizations that experiment with telework only evaluate the success of telework on the basis of short-term results. Unfortunately, the long-term costs and benefits (hard and soft) of teleworking are relatively unknown. The fundamental explanatory question of why organizational members differ in their teleworkability and teleworking practices has been mostly tackled in theory (cf. Lamme's [2000] model), but only partly through empirical evidence. In this chapter, we theoretically reframed the diffusion and deployment of telework as a system of choices and interactions of employees and managers. As the main matters in this system, we proposed the alignment of technology and organization, and the balance between control and trust. Still, the added value of our framework remains conceptual in terms of describing the multilevel and multiactor structure of the relationship between telework and performances (cf. Lincoln & Kalleberg, 1991). In order to apply the framework to empirical explanatory analysis, specific data is needed that measures the framework components and its relations. In practice, this means that surveys or comparative case studies are needed for samples of teleworking and nonteleworking employees and their organizations. In most cases, such as in the ECaTT (2000) project, employers and managers were surveyed separately. To actually investigate the importance of the negotiation between employers and employees with regard to teleworking, quantitative or qualitative data (or both) should cover

the decisions, behavior, and interests of both managers and (non)tele-
workers. To avoid biases as much as possible, the number of (non)tele-
workers and managers per organization should be substantial, as should
the number of organizations itself. This ambitious project is about to be executed as part of a larger research time competition project in the Netherlands (Van der Lippe & Glebbeek, 1999). As of 2003, the multiactor data
will be available to empirically test our framework. Hopefully, the results will
constitute progress beyond the existing research on teleworking and will be
supportive for practitioners and advisors in the field of teleworking.

REFERENCES

Barney, J. (1991). Firm resources and sustained competitive advantage. *Journal of Management,*
17, 99–120.
Bridges, W. (1994). *Job shift, how to prosper in a workplace without jobs.* Reading, MA: Addison-
Wesley.
Daniels, K., Lamond, D. A., & Standen, P. (Eds.). (2000). *Managing telework. Perspectives from hu-*
man resource management and work psychology. London: Thomson Learning.
De Vries, H., & Weijers, T. (1998). *Zicht op telewerken: Een studie naar de stand van zaken in de*
kennis over telewerken en de impact op de beleidsterreinen van SZW [Telework on sight: A state-of-
the-art study on the knowledge about telework and its consequences]. Den Haag, The
Netherlands: Elsevier Bedrijfsinformatie.
Dhondt, S., & Van den Heuvel, S. (1998). *Telewerken in de tweede Europese enquete naar*
arbeidsomstandigheden [Telework in the second European Survey on Labor Conditions].
Apeldoorn, The Netherlands: Nederlands Instituut voor Arbeids-omstandigheden.
Dias, C. (2001). Corporate portals: A literature review of a new concept in information man-
agement. *International Journal of Information Management, 21,* 269–287.
Dutch Statistics. (2002). *De digitale economie 2002* [The digital economy 2002]. Voorburg,
Heerlen, The Netherlands: Central Bureau voor de Statistiek.
Electronic Commerce and Telework Trends. (2000). *Benchmarking progress on new ways of work-*
ing and new forms of business across Europe. ECaTT final report. Bonn, Germany: Empirica/Eu-
ropean Commission.
European Commission. (2001). *E-inclusion. The information society's potential for social inclusion in*
Europe. Brussels: Author.
Finkelstein, C. (2003, February). The emergence and potential of enterprise information por-
tals (Eips). In *The data administration letter (TDAM.com)* [Online]. Available: http://
www.tdan.com/i010fe02.htm
Fitzloff, E. (1999). IntraNet scales up its Intra.doc system for the enterprise. *InfoWorld, 20,* 58.
Gareis, K. (2002, September). *The intensity of telework in the EU, Switzerland, and the US.* Paper
presented at the International Congress New Work "Sustainability in the new economy: Designing a new work space," Badajoz, Spain.
Gottlieb, B. H., Kelloway, E. K., & Braham, E. J. (1998). *Flexible work arrangements. Managing the*
work-family boundary. Chichester, England: Wiley.
Hales, C. (1993). *Managing through organisation: The management process, forms of organisation and*
the work of managers. London: Routledge.
Henderson, J. C., & Venkatraman, N. (1993). Strategic alignment: Leveraging information
technology for transforming organisations. *IBM Systems Journal, 32,* 4–16.
Huws, U. (1996). *Teleworking. An overview of the research.* London: Analytica.

Huws, U., Korte, W. B., & Robinson, S. (1990). *Telework: Towards the elusive office.* Chichester, England: Wiley & Sons.

Jackson, P. J., & Van der Wielen, J. M. M. (Eds.). (1998). *Teleworking: International perspectives. From telecommuting to the virtual organisation.* London: Routledge.

Kinsman, E. (1987). *The telecommuters.* Chichester, England: Wiley & Sons.

Klomp, H., & Van Oosterhout, B. (2001). Telework is unstoppable. *Intermediair, 1*, 28–33.

Korte, W. B., & Wynnes, R. (1996). *Telework: Penetration, potential and practice in Europe.* Amsterdam: IOS Press.

Lamme, E. (2000). *Telework. Towards an improvement of interaction.* Hilversum, the Netherlands: Stichting Nederlands Telewerkforum.

Lincoln, J., & Kalleberg, A. (1991). *Culture, control and commitment. A study of work organisation and work attitudes in the United States and Japan.* Cambridge, England: Cambridge University Press.

Ministry of Social Affairs. (2000). *Bereikbaarheidsscenario: verkenning van een extra optie voor taakcombineerders. Eindrapportage* [Scenarios for attainability. Exploration of options for task combination. End report]. Den Haag, The Netherlands: Ministerie van Sociale Zaken en Werkgelegenheid.

Nilles, J. M. (1998). *Managing telework. Strategies for managing the virtual workforce.* New York: Wiley & Sons.

Nilles, J. M., Carlson, F. R., Gray, P., & Hanneman, G. J. (1976). *The telecommunications-transportation trade-off.* Chichester, England: Wiley & Sons.

Paoli, P., & Merllié, D. (2001). *Third European survey on working conditions 2000.* Dublin, Ireland: European Foundation for the Improvement of Working and Living Conditions.

Perin, C. (1998). Work, space and time on the threshold of a new century. In P. J. Jackson & J. M. M. van der Wielen (Eds.), *Teleworking: International perspectives. From telecommuting to the virtual organisation* (pp. 40–55). London: Routledge.

Peters, C. P. (2000). *The vulnerable hours of leisure. New patterns of work and free time in the Netherlands, 1975–1995.* Amsterdam: Thela Thesis.

Peters, C. P. (2001). Onthaasten in het ICT-tijdperk: Utopie of werkelijkheid? [Downshifting in the ICT-area. Utopia or reality?]. In C. Hogenhuis, E. Van der Panne, & T. Hoekstra (Eds.), *A new economy, a new free time* (pp. 105–125). Kampen, The Netherlands: Uitgeverij Kok.

Peters, P., Tijdens, K., & Wetzels, C. (2001). *Factors in employees' telecommuting opportunities, preferences and practices.* Manuscript in preparation, University of Utrecht, The Netherlands.

Pfeffer, J. (1994). *Competitive advantage through people.* Boston, MA: Harvard Business School Press.

Powell, G. N., & Maineiro, L. A. (1999). Managerial decision-making regarding alternative work arrangements. *Journal of Occupational and Organisational Psychology, 72*, 41–56.

Pratt, J. (2000). Asking the right questions about telecommuting. Avoiding pitfalls in surveying homebased work. *Transportations, 27*, 99–116.

Turban, E., MacLean, E., & Wetherbe, J. (1999). *Information technology for management. Making connections for strategic advantage* (2nd ed.). New York: Wiley & Sons.

Van der Lippe, T., & Glebbeek, A. (1999). *Time competition: Disturbed balances and new options in work and care.* Utrecht, The Netherlands: Interuniversity Center for Sociology.

Van der Wielen, J. M. M., Van der Berg, P. T., & Van Diggelen, W. (1995). *Telewerk. De organisatorische aspecten* [Telework. Its organizational aspects]. Deventer, the Netherlands: Kluwer Bedrijfswetenschappen.

Van Klaveren, M., Tijdens, K., & Wetzels, C. (2000). Wie, waar en wanneer? [Who, when, and where?]. *Economisch Statistische Berichten, 85*, d22–d24.

Van Klaveren, M., & Van de Westelaken, A. (2001). *Telewerken: Het vervolg. Een onderzoek voor de FNV naar aanleiding van 10 vragen* [Teleworking: The next episode. Research on behalf of 10 questions of the FNV]. Eindhoven, The Netherlands: STZ Advies & Onderzoek.

Vlek, R. (1986). *De toekomstige betekenis en gevolgen van tele-arbeid en telethuiswerk in Nederland* [The meaning and consequences of telework and telehomework in the Netherlands]. Leiden, The Netherlands: Rijksuniversiteit Leiden.

Weijers, T., & Weijers, S. (1986). *Telewerk, een overzichtsstudie naar de recente trends en toekomstperspectieven* [Telework, an overview of recent trends and future perspectives]. Den Haag, The Netherlands: Ministerie van Sociale Zaken en Werkgelegenheid.

White, M. (2000). Enterprise information portals. *The Electronic Library, 18,* 354–362.

Chapter 15

How Do We Read Text on Screen?

Mary C. Dyson
University of Reading, United Kingdom

This chapter synthesizes experimental research on reading text from screen focusing on how reading is affected by specific typographic variables and reading speed, and how the mechanics of reading on screen (i.e., scrolling) relate to the reading task. The review evaluates the contribution that such research can make both to our understanding of how we read from screen and to informing the design of documents which support effective reading.

WHY WE NEED EXPERIMENTAL RESEARCH

Many guidelines already exist on designing material for presentation on screen, and it is not the intention of this chapter to add significantly to this volume. However, there is potential to mislead with guidelines unsupported by empirical research or based on research using a different medium or technology. If we are to design systems which optimize reading from screen, there needs to be a reliable body of knowledge of which variables are important and how they affect reading.

The guidelines for designing online displays summarized by Schriver (1997) provide an example of the implicit assumption that we can generalize from print to screen or from one technology to another. Where typographic research is cited, this is generally either based on experiments on reading from paper (e.g., Paterson & Tinker, 1940) or the results are tied to a specific outdated technology (e.g., Muter, Latrémouille, Treurniet, &

Beam, 1982). Because of the rate of technological development, studies conducted in the 1980s may have limited relevance in the 2000s. However in the context of the review, comparing results obtained from different technologies may be interesting if carried out with due regard to all factors which may vary among experiments.

Making experimental research a prerequisite in the formulation of guidelines is more contentious. In so doing, we may ignore valuable skills and knowledge acquired from design practice.

The difficulties of developing research findings into usable guidelines have also been recognized. Findings are sometimes inconclusive or provide a theoretical description which is difficult to translate to form practical guidance (Dillon, 1994). However, the questionable bases for guidelines motivates some researchers (such as the author) to conduct experiments, the results of which can be used to evaluate existing guidelines, or contribute to new ones.

DIFFERENT APPROACHES TO EXPERIMENTAL RESEARCH

A particular problem in testing variables relating to text presentation is the way in which the variables are known to interact. This was originally established with regard to print by Tinker (1963) who maintained that optimal type size depends on line length and interlinear spacing. Useful reminders are provided by Muter (1996) and Grabinger and Osman-Jouchoux (1996) when reviewing literature on reading from screen. In testing individual variables, the effects of other variables need to be considered and this can result in unmanageable numbers of experiments. However if these interactions are not explored, the generality of results may be limited.

To carry out a realistic number of comparisons, the combinations of variables tested can be determined by drawing on practical design experience, i.e. informed decisions. To complement this constrained approach, comparisons can be made of the same variable tested in different experiments. A review provides a vehicle for this and can address the possible influences of the conditions in which the experiments were conducted on the outcomes and their interpretation. If there is "robustness in variation" (Muter, 1996), i.e. separate experiments converge on similar results, there are grounds for making recommendations.

HOW THIS RESEARCH AREA HAS EVOLVED

The impetus for much of the research has been the perception that the volume of material read from screen is increasing and the process should be optimized. The natural starting point in the 1980s was comparisons of reading from screen and paper. Most studies did not attempt to identify the effects of individual variables, with the exception of Gould et al. (1987). They specifically investigated a range of variables which differ between the two, and may therefore account for performance differences. This research area is not included in the chapter as it has already been extensively reviewed (e.g., Dillon, 1992; Muter, 1996).

Other research in the 1980s looked into specific variables although Dillon, Richardson, and McKnight (1990) point out that many studies focused on the legibility of the screen image. Improvements in display technologies and the increase in capabilities for presenting text have encouraged a greater diversity of studies.

Some of these were funded by Microsoft Corporation in the mid to late 1990s. They supported two strands of research which resulted in the report of a study by Boyarski and co-workers and others by Dyson and co-workers. Having found an unexpected result in relation to line length, Dyson continued to explore this variable across a range of experiments. This work also further developed de Bruijn, de Mul, and van Oostendorp's (1992) methods for analyzing scrolling movements to supplement existing measures of reading.

Further work comes from a usability laboratory conducting controlled experiments. Bernard and co-workers provide rapid dissemination of their findings through Usability News (http://psychology.wichita.edu/surl/newsletter.htm). Another set of studies comes from Scharff and co-workers (http://hubel.sfasu.edu/research/text_display_lvs.html). The difficulty with this work is that until it is published in refereed publications, full details of the studies are not available, nor have the studies been subjected to rigorous peer review. Nevertheless, with these considerations in mind, their results can be compared with other studies to see whether there is convergence.

SCOPE OF THE REVIEW

Within this chapter, reading from screen covers the activities which readers engage in having already displayed a text on screen. In attempting to build a picture of how we read from screen, comparisons with what we know about reading from paper may be informative. For this reason, where there is a parallel literature from research on print, this is referred to in discussing the results of studies on reading from screen. Research into reading print has examined a range of typographical variables, summarized in Tinker (1963, 1965), Spencer (1968), and Zachrisson (1965).

The review focuses on very specific elements of interface design. Investigations into the legibility of fonts are included primarily because typography is commonly associated with choice of font, guidelines tend to mention fonts, and the absence of this variable might otherwise seem odd.

A positive reason for reviewing studies on fonts is that they provide a basis for comparison with other typographic variables. The effects of different fonts on reading can be compared with the effects of variables which control the amount of text on screen: line length, number of columns, and window height. The first two variables have been researched in print, but the equivalent to window height (number of lines per page) appears not to have been studied.

Other design decisions made by typographic and graphic designers in relation to pages of print are outside the scope of this review. These include the positioning of text, how elements are grouped, and the relationship of text to image. These are undoubtedly important in screen design, whether or not the same principles apply to paper and screen.

An activity that seems to be fundamentally different when reading from screen is text manipulation, moving forward or backward in the text using tools provided by the interface. This activity has no parallel in print legibility research, but forms an integral part of reading from screen. Studies which address how readers move through a document, either paging or scrolling in various ways, are covered along with investigations of scrolling patterns.

The review therefore touches upon interaction design by looking at studies that deal with manipulation at the level of individual screens. This should be seen within a broader context of research on navigation in electronic texts. This area has received a lot of attention, with studies looking at how to structure material to promote ease of navigation and enable readers to synthesize what they have read. Elements of interface design which can support navigation have also been explored by looking at the type of navigation aid (e.g., link, button, menu), their appearance and location on screen.

All the studies reviewed broadly deal with reading of continuous text. However, reading can take a different form according to the experimental task: proofreading, scanning, normal and fast reading. Some studies using proofreading have been included despite the rather different nature of the reading task. They make a general and a specific contribution by enabling comparisons with other forms of reading and supplementing, in particular, the extremely sparse number of studies which vary number of columns and window height. Fast reading appears to have particular relevance to reading from screen according to reports of a tendency to skim text on screen rather than read in detail (Horton, Taylor, Ignacio, & Hoft, 1996). More specifically, readers of academic articles on the Web may skim material to determine whether or not to print out (Rho & Gedeon, 2000).

Both outcome and process measures of reading (Dillon, 1992; Schumacher & Waller, 1985) are relevant to this chapter. Although process measures deal specifically with how readers use documents, outcomes such as reading rate and comprehension of different aspects of a text can also suggest the nature of reading.

Summary of Research Questions

The chapter looks at variables which might influence:

- how fast we can read from screen, by measuring reading rate
- how accurately we can read from screen, looking at accuracy of recall or comprehension
- how we perceive reading from screen, by asking for subjective judgments
- how we move through text on screen, recording scrolling movements

The variables explored are: reading speed; typographic presentation (fonts, line length, columns, window height); methods of movement (scrolling versus paging). Reading speed here refers to manipulations of the pace of reading, e.g. encouraging someone to read faster than normal. Reading rate is the measure of how fast they are reading.

WHAT AFFECTS HOW FAST WE CAN READ FROM SCREEN?

Fonts

Fonts designed specifically for fairly recent display technologies were introduced around 1996, but there appear to be few published studies concerning the rate at which they can be read. There are even fewer which demonstrate reliable differences in reading rates according to font. Table 15.1 summarizes the studies, listing the fonts compared and the outcomes. A difference was found between the sans serif Tahoma, intended for screen viewing, and Corsiva, an ornate font (Fig. 15.1). Some differences between more common fonts have also been found (Fig. 15.2). However, the authors themselves describe the differences in reading time as rather small and appear not to regard these results as particularly important when reading text online.

The limited amount of research may seem surprising given the apparent interest in choice of font, at least amongst developers, writers, and readers. However, the small number of published studies may be due in part to an inability to demonstrate reliable differences between reading rates for dif-

TABLE 15.1
Comparisons of Reading Rate With Different Fonts

Study	Comparisons	Results Summary
Boyarski, Neuwirth, Forizzi, & Regli (1998)	Georgia (designed for screen) Times Roman (designed for print)	No differences
	Georgia (serif) Verdana (sans serif)	No differences
	Verdana Verdana italic	No differences
Bernard, Mills, Peterson, & Storrer (2001)	Courier New Georgia Goudy Old Style Century Schoolbook Times New Roman Agency Arial Comic Sans MS Tahoma Verdana Bradley Hand ITC Monotype Corsiva	Tahoma read faster than Corsiva
Bernard, Lida, Riley, Hackler, & Janzen (2002)	Century Schoolbook Courier New Georgia Times New Roman Arial Comic Sans MS Tahoma Verdana	Times and Arial read faster than Courier, Schoolbook, and Georgia

Tahoma
Tahoma, a sans serif, intended for screen viewing is
read faster than Corsiva, an ornate font.

Monotype Corsiva
*Tahoma, a sans serif, intended for screen viewing is read faster
than Corsiva, an ornate font.*

FIG. 15.1. Examples of two of the fonts used by Bernard et al (2001):
Tahoma and Corsiva.

Times New Roman
Times New Roman and Arial are read faster

Arial
Times New Roman and Arial are read faster

Courier New
Times New Roman and Arial are read faster

Century Schoolbook
Times New Roman and Arial are read faster

Georgia
Times New Roman and Arial are read faster

FIG. 15.2.   Examples of five fonts from Bernard et al. (2002).

ferent fonts. On the other hand, researchers may have been deterred from investigating this variable because print legibility research has found very few differences in reading rate among fonts intended for reading (summarized in Tinker, 1963).

The limited evidence for reading from screen suggests that choice of font from among those designed for text (i.e., not for display at large sizes) is unlikely to affect how fast we read. Using a font specifically designed for screen may not help us read faster, but also does not slow us down: a somewhat inconsequential finding.

Line Length

Some 20 years ago comparisons of line lengths used changes in the character density (or width) to change the number of characters per line (cpl), due to the limited facilities for character display on screens. Surprisingly the resultant effects on reading rate predict some recent findings. The trend is for faster reading as line length increases, although this is not invariably the case. Table 15.2 provides a summary and examples are shown in Fig. 15.3. Fast reading of long lines is not what would be predicted from legibility of print literature, where along with very short lines, very long lines slow down reading. The advantage of longer lines on screen may be connected with the process of scrolling. Bernard, Fernandez, and Hull (2002) propose that similar reading times across line lengths may be because the benefit of reduced scrolling (with long line lengths) is offset by the difficulties of longer lines. This cannot explain the findings from Dyson and Kipping (1998a) or Dyson and Haselgrove (2001), but the range of line lengths do differ. For their longest line length, Bernard et al. use more characters per line than other studies, and a larger point size than Dyson et al. (12 point, rather than 10 point), resulting in a very long line.

TABLE 15.2
Comparisons of Reading Rate With Different Line Lengths

Study	Comparisons	Results Summary
Kolers, Duchnicky, & Ferguson (1981)	35 and 70 cpl (varying character density)	Longer lines read faster
Duchnicky & Kolers (1983)	Six lengths between 15 and 78 cpl (varying screen width and character density)	Longer lines read faster
Youngman & Scharff (1998)	4, 6, 8 inches	Fastest response with longest line
Dyson & Kipping (1998a)	25, 40, 55, 70, 85, 100 cpl (white background throughout) *(Fig. 15.3 illustrates 25 and 100 cpl)*	Longest line (100 cpl) read faster than shortest (25 cpl)
	25, 55, 100 cpl (grey background to right of text)	Longer lines read faster, but only with scrolling
Dyson & Haselgrove (2001)	25, 55, 100 cpl (2 reading speeds)	Fast: 55 and 100 cpl read faster than 25 cpl Normal: 55 cpl read faster than 25 cpl
Bernard, Fernandez, & Hull (2002)	45, 76, 132 cpl	No differences in reading times

The problem with long lines was identified by examining eye movements in reading print (Tinker & Paterson, 1955). The difficulty is locating the beginning of new lines when return sweeps are made. The upward movement of text has been suggested as a factor which may reduce the difficulties of longer lines on screen (Duchnicky & Kolers, 1983). Scrolling may therefore affect reading in ways other than how long readers spend in the activity. This explanation will be discussed further when focusing on how we move through text later in the chapter.

Some of the differences among the Dyson et al. studies may be explained by factors other than line length which vary between studies, i.e. overall speed of reading and the color of the background alongside the text. The implications of different methods of movement (scrolling vs. paging) will be covered in detail later in the chapter.

Increasing participants' speed of reading by training them to read almost twice as fast as their normal reading speed (Dyson et al., 2001) is likely to have encouraged a different type of reading (i.e., skimming rather than thorough reading). These results suggest that longer lines may facilitate skimming. Although a very different method was used, the study by Youngman and Scharff (1998) provides some support for this conclusion. Their participants scanned a text excerpt for a target word and they were fastest

On Friday doctors ruled that
President Boris Yeltsin must stay
under close medical supervision
until the end of November, denting
his foreign policy hopes and
campaign plans for the December
parliamentary elections.

Kremlin aides of Yeltsin, who
was rushed to a hospital on
Thursday after a second mild
heart attack in less than four
months, began striking a cautious
note in contrast with their earlier
optimism about his condition

Yeltsin's press secretary,
Sergei Medvedev, told the Tass
news agency that the 64-year-old
Kremlin leader was suffering from
"an unstable blood supply to the
heart " "There have been no signs
of a heart deficiency up to now,
and I stress up to now," Medvedev
added at a later news conference.
'The doctors came to the
conclusion that the president will
have to stay under their close
supervision during October and
November," he told Tass Little
real detail on the president's
condition emerged, apart from
Medvedev saying he had not lost
consciousness since falling ill. It
is however known that aides were
told to stay away from Moscow's
Central Clinic Hospital and only
doctors and security officials were
allowed near him. It was unclear if

"There was once a woman who lived in the desert." So begins, almost like a children's story, the extraordinary biography of Daisy
Bates, a woman of Irish birth who, in 1913 at the age of 54, wandered alone into the wilds of Australia. There she lived for nearly 30
years with only the Aborigines for regular companionship, a people she came to call "My People."

Through the author's eyes and voice, Bates' descriptions and tales are so vivid and powerful that the reader quickly stops
wondering, or even caring, whether it all really happened and equally quickly stops questioning whether this is Daisy speaking
now, or the book's author. What does it matter who wrote: "I am Kabbarli, the white-skinned grandmother. I am the Great White
Queen of the Never-Never and I have come from the Land of the Dead to help my people in their hour of need. I am also a lady from
a very good family, you can see that immediately of course; hear it in my voice."

The author gleaned the information for her portrait of this remarkable and unconventional woman from interviews with people who
knew Daisy Bates; from her letters, her published articles, her book, The Passing of the Aborigines -- and from her many notes
"scribbled on paper bags, old railway timetables, and even scraps of newspaper." But, as the author reminds the reader, "very little
of what this strange woman tells about herself is true. For her there were no boundaries separating experience from imagination;
she inhabited a world filled with events that could not have taken place, with people she had never met."

There are indisputable facts that the book builds on. Daisy May O'Dwyer did exist. She was born in Ireland, probably in 1860,
the child of impoverished parents; her mother died when she was young, and her whisky-guzzling father ran off with another woman
and died on the way to America. Daisy was sent to an orphanage near Dublin. Attractive and well read, at the age 18 she found
work as a governess. A scandal in the household ensued, and as a result, the young man of the house killed himself. Daisy
embarked upon her first voyage to Australia.

It didn't take long for Daisy to replace her unsavoury history with a past of her own making. She re-created in her imagination a
childhood home, "a beautiful house" that was "built of big blocks of yellow stone with deep windows and doors wide enough for
elephants."

Though Daisy painted an equally elegant world of wealth and society during her early years in Australia, the facts uncovered are
that she arrived there in 1883, basically penniless, and worked as governess on a cattle station in North Queensland. Records
show that in 1884 she was married by a Catholic priest to a stockman working at the same ranch. A month after the wedding he
was thrown in jail for stealing pigs and a saddle. The couple separated after his release, and they never saw each other again.

Apparently Daisy didn't trouble herself with an official divorce. Eleven months later, in New South Wales, she married Jack
Bates, this time declaring herself a Protestant and a spinster - a wise deception, since in Australia at the time bigamy was
punishable by several years' imprisonment.

Much of the book describes Bates' surreal life among the Aborigines, a life far from the fantasies of her fabricated upbringing.
"These ticks were revolting," she wrote about the blood-gorging insects infesting the area near one of her camps. "I once had a
whole string of them black and shining around my waist, like a belt. I tried to get them off by scorching them with a stick taken
from the fire but when that didn't work I had to wait until they were well-fed and ready to drop of their own accord."

She felt keen kinship with the Aborigines who appeared at her camps, "naked, smiling, glistening in the sunshine." She claims
to have been initiated into the ceremonies of the men and to have been almost totally accepted. "They told me that in the Old
Times I had been a man, a tribal elder . . . " Bates wrote "I have seen them dancing, dying, making love, giving birth and I have
never once been excluded from what was happening, never once made to feel like an outsider gazing into a forbidden territory."

Bates occasionally ventured back into the white world to present papers at government conferences, to argue for help for the

FIG. 15.3. Two of the line lengths used by Dyson and Kipping (1998a): 25 and 100 characters per line.

with the longest line. Skimming and scanning are not the same task, but both require rapid activity which may be where longer lines are particularly helpful.

Replacing screen areas without text with a grey rather than white background, may have removed the disadvantage of shorter line lengths by reducing glare. Whilst the size of the blank area to the right of text may have some effect on reading, this is unlikely to be the only factor. The difference in experimental design between studies may have affected reading. The first experiment in Dyson et al. (1998a) used a between subject design, with one group of participants using scrolled movement and the other paged. They also all read one document in each of the six line lengths. In the follow-up experiment scrolling and paging was a within subject variable, with each person reading only three line lengths, but using both methods of movement.

These differences may have influenced reading strategies. In the first experiment there were smaller steps between line lengths and more examples of the same method of moving through the document. This may have provided greater opportunity to modify the method of reading in response to the particular nature of the document. In contrast, the greater diversity of documents in the follow-up may have prevented participants from developing a more flexible strategy.

Combining the findings and interpretations allows two tentative conclusions:

- long lines can sometimes be read equally as fast as medium length lines but
- reading rates at different line lengths vary according to the experimental setting, such as the range of variables presented to each participant, physical characteristics of the display and the nature of the reading task
- each of the above factors may individually or together affect reading strategy and hence how fast text is read

Columns

The very limited evidence on how fast we read one or more columns is unclear, perhaps due to differences in tasks, screens, and column formats. Table 15.3 lists details of two studies which compare single and multi-column formats. The studies are separated by 10 years, they differ in the number of columns, Creed et al. measure proofreading and Dyson et al. do not, and perhaps not surprisingly, the results are different. However, if columns are considered in terms of their line lengths, the Dyson et al. study provides some confirmation that fairly long lines can be read faster than a short line.

TABLE 15.3
Comparisons of Reading Rate With Different Numbers of Columns

Study	Comparisons	Results Summary
Creed, Dennis, & Newstead (1987)	2 columns of 30 characters 1 column of 70 characters	No reliable differences
Dyson & Kipping (1997)	3 columns of 25 characters 1 column of 80 characters	1 column read faster

This research on screen has not progressed our knowledge of the relative legibility of single and multiple columns, and findings in relation to print have also been inconclusive (Foster, 1970; Hartley, Burnhill, & Fraser, 1974; Poulton, 1959). The indications are that varying the number of columns is less important than line length.

Window Height

The number of lines per screen, or window height, has been shown to affect reading rate at the extreme of very few lines. But comparisons of more likely window heights have generally failed to find differences in reading rates. Table 15.4 summarizes the main studies.

An exception to these findings (de Bruijn et al., 1992) may be attributed to using two different models of screen for the different windows. Also the measure of learning time included time spent in manipulations, making comparison with other studies problematic.

There are no clear differences between window heights beyond a few lines and no research into the number of lines per page in print with which to compare these results. On screen less area may be available to display

TABLE 15.4
Comparisons of Reading Rate With Different Numbers of Lines

Study	Comparisons	Results Summary
Duchnicky et al. (1983)	1, 2, 3, 4, 20 lines	4 & 20 lines read faster than 1, 2, 3 lines
Creed, Dennis, & Newstead (1988)	1 paragraph (4–15 lines), 25 lines 1–8 lines	Tendency for slower reading of fewer lines
Dillon, Richardson, & McKnight (1990)	20 and 60 lines	No differences
de Bruijn, de Mul, & van Oostendorp (1992)	23 and 60 lines	Longer learning times for 23 lines
Dyson & Kipping (1998b)	15, 25, 35 lines	No differences

text and transitions between screen may be more intrusive than turning pages. The contribution of manipulations to the reading task on screen should not be ignored, but is better discussed in the broader context of how we move through text on screen (a later section).

Summary of Reading Rate

Choice of font (within reason) does not affect reading rate, whereas line length does. Short lines are read more slowly than medium length lines and long lines frequently read as fast, if not faster. No conclusion can be drawn concerning columns due to the sparse and non-convergent results. With window height, going to the extreme of just a few lines may slow down reading. Beyond this threshold, there is no reliable evidence that the number of lines on screen influences reading rate.

WHAT AFFECTS HOW ACCURATELY WE CAN READ FROM SCREEN?

Unlike reading rate, which tends to be based on similar measures, accuracy can refer to detecting errors in proofing, accuracy of recall of specific or more general aspects of a text, or accuracy of comprehension. Accuracy can also be affected by reading rate, making single measures of reading rate and accuracy potentially misleading. This has been addressed in different ways across studies. Because of the diverse methods, this section starts by examining the relationship between the methods and how the text is read. The specific measures used are then evaluated.

Asking participants to scan a text to locate specific words, the method used by Youngman et al. (1998), does not require participants to read the text. This procedure measures the "reaction time" to locate the word. The target words are star, square, diamond, circle, triangle and participants click on the corresponding shape at the bottom of the screen.

Where accuracy of reading is measured, this can take various forms. Studies by Bernard and co-workers require participants to read a passage and identify words which have been substituted. This procedure is similar to the Tinker Speed of Reading Test (1947). On the surface, this also appears similar to Youngman et al.'s procedure, but in this case the text must be read for meaning to identify which words have been substituted. Another means by which a check can be made on whether the text has been read for meaning is asking participants whether a question can be answered by what they have read. Duchnicky et al. (1983) devised this method which was subsequently used by Dyson and Kipping (1997, 1998a, 1998b).

The methods described above have the advantage of being easy to score, but may not be particularly sensitive to differences in accuracy of reading. For this reason, Boyarski, Neuwirth, Forizzi, and Regli (1998) chose an established reading test with a "track record for being able to detect differences," the Nelson-Denny (1981) test. This provides passages of text with comprehension questions associated with each passage.

Using questions has the disadvantage that the specific information required by the question may be recalled, but this is not a measure of overall comprehension. This is less likely to be the case if participants are asked to summarize the text, the method used by Dillon et al. (1990). However, this technique requires extensive analyses of responses. An alternative way to broaden the measure is to probe recall of various aspects of a text (Dyson & Haselgrove, 2000, 2001). By using multiple choice questions, the data is simple to analyze and the different types of questions can address the nature of material recalled. Table 15.5 lists the question types used by Dyson et al.

Reading Speed

As might be expected, comprehension is better when reading at a normal speed compared with fast reading, induced by training participants to read at almost twice their normal speed (Dyson et al., 2000, 2001). When the two speeds are combined there are differences among question types. However, in Dyson et al. (2000) there was greater variation among question types when reading at a normal speed which may have been due to the higher level of performance. Questions on the title and main idea were better recalled than structure questions. Poor performance on structure questions was also replicated by Dyson et al. (2001).

Significantly increasing reading speed affects recall of all question types but also reduces the differences in recall among questions. However, when the two reading speeds are combined, it is evident that questions aiming to test recall of specific information are answered less accurately than those

TABLE 15.5
Six Question Types Used by Dyson et al. (2000, 2001)

Question Type	Nature of the Question
Title	Which of the alternative titles best fits the text
Main idea	Questions about one of the main themes in the text
Structure	Order of items within the text, i.e. what came before or after
Main factual	Question about a relatively important aspect of the text
Incidental	Question about a detail in the text
Recognition	Whether the extract had appeared in the text read

that are more general and based on more important parts of the text. In this instance, it is reassuring that a fundamental aspect of reading is replicated when reading from screen. Experiments testing recall when reading print have shown that the importance of text is related to its recall (Johnson, 1970).

Fonts

The few experiments that have compared fonts (see Table 15.1) report rather limited data on accuracy with only one reliable difference: Georgia is better than Verdana (Boyarski et al., 1998). Both studies by Bernard et al. fail to report accuracy data on the detection of (inappropriate) substituted words in the passages that were read. Instead the effective reading scores (accuracy divided by time) and times are given. Whilst there are differences in reading times among fonts (as described earlier), when accuracy is taken into account the differences are canceled out. There appears to be some form of trade-off between speed and accuracy.

Line Length

Table 15.6 summarizes the results of studies which have varied line length and tested recall. Two of the studies which compared line lengths (listed in Table 15.2) did not measure recall. This was not relevant to the Kolers, Duchnicky, and Ferguson (1981) study as it was designed to measure eye movements (but also included time on the task). However, Youngman et al. chose to use only correct responses, thereby losing any accuracy data and consequently evidence for a speed-accuracy trade-off.

TABLE 15.6
Comparisons of Measures Related to Accuracy
With Different Line Lengths

Study	Comparisons	Results Summary
Duchnicky et al. (1983)	Six lengths between 15 and 78 characters per line (cpl)	No differences in recall
Dyson et al. (1998a)	25, 40, 55, 70, 85, 100 cpl 25, 55, 100 cpl	No differences in recall
Dyson et al. (2001)	25, 55, 100 cpl	Better recall with 55 cpl compared to 100 cpl No speed-accuracy trade-off (see Table 15.2)
Bernard et al. (2002a)	45, 76, 132 cpl	No differences in effective reading score

Accuracy data is again not reported by Bernard et al. However, as there were no differences in reading rates across line lengths, and no differences in effective reading scores, there is no suggestion of a speed-accuracy trade-off.

The lack of differences in the first two studies may be because participants were maintaining a constant level of understanding and reading at different rates. Alternatively, this task (saying whether a question can be answered by what was read) may not be sufficiently sensitive to detect differences among line lengths. The later Dyson and Haselgrove study, which used the more sophisticated measure of comprehension described in Table 15.5, supports the explanation in terms of the sensitivity of the task.

Columns

There is little evidence to suggest that the number and therefore width of columns affects how accurately we read. Although there may be differences in the number of errors detected in proofreading (Creed, Dennis, & Newstead, 1987), this result is attributed to a speed-accuracy trade-off, as the single column was read slightly slower (see Table 15.7).

Window Height

Varying the amount of text on screen by changing the height of window seems to have less impact on reading than varying line length. Although proofreading may be more accurate with fewer lines, it is also slower (Creed, Dennis, & Newstead, 1988). However, no differences in comprehension have been found in other experiments comparing window height which have used a range of measures: a check on comprehension (Duchnicky et al., 1983; Dyson et al., 1998b); summaries (de Bruijn et al., 1992; Dillon et al., 1990) and a multiple choice test requiring detailed knowledge (de Bruijn et al., 1992).

TABLE 15.7
Comparisons of Measures Related to Accuracy
With Different Numbers of Columns

Study	Comparisons	Results Summary
Creed et al. (1987)	2 columns of 30 characters 1 column of 70 characters	Fewer errors detected in 2 columns
Dyson et al. (1997)	3 columns of 25 characters 1 column of 80 characters	No differences in recall

Summary of Accuracy

Encouraging readers to read significantly faster than their normal reading rate decreases the amount recalled in a fairly uniform way but also removes any differences between questions of different types. Recall of both general and specific information is more difficult at this fast rate. When normal variations in reading rate (across different numbers of columns and window heights) are compared with accuracy, there is a trade-off in a proof-reading task, but not when reading for comprehension. This difference may be due to the increased level of accuracy required in proofing. A moderate line length (around 55 cpl) seems to lead to better recall, but the effects of other variations in text layout (columns and window height) on recall are less clear cut, and may be dependent on readers' strategies.

These studies reinforce the need for sensitive tools when measuring accuracy (Poulton, 1965). It is also unhelpful to omit the accuracy data from reports.

WHAT AFFECTS HOW WE PERCEIVE READING FROM SCREEN?

Fonts

Table 15.8 describes the results of studies which have included various types of subjective judgments of a range of fonts. Although few, if any, performance differences are found, people's subjective judgments do discriminate between fonts in a systematic way (Bernard et al., 2001; Boyarski et al., 1998). Comparing speed of reading and judged legibility of printed fonts, Paterson and Tinker (1932) also found minor differences in performance, but marked differences in reader preferences.

On the whole, fonts which have been designed for display on screen, or are used frequently, are perceived as easier to read and preferred.

Line Length

A consistent finding across three papers and four experiments is that long line lengths are least preferred or judged as least easy to read (Bernard et al., 2002a; Dyson et al., 1998a; Youngman et al., 1998). Table 15.9 summarizes the results of paired comparisons of ease of reading carried out by Dyson et al. and the Bernard et al. study's results for general preference. Although Bernard et al. indicate that the "medium" length was most preferred, the "narrow" length was very close behind. Both of these line lengths could be considered moderate. This pattern of preferences for

TABLE 15.8
Comparative Judgments of Fonts

Study	Comparisons	Subjective Judgments
Holleran (1992)	Fonts for text on Macintosh screen	Times and Helvetica most popular
	53 fonts	Cheltenham liked most, and fonts with serifs and moderate width
Boyarski et al. (1998)	Georgia Times Roman	Georgia easier to read, more legible, has sharper characters
	Georgia Verdana	Verdana slightly easier to read
	Verdana Verdana italic	Verdana easier to read, more legible, has sharper characters
Bernard et al. (2001)	See Table 15.1	Courier, Comic, Verdana, Georgia, Times more legible than Agency, Bradley, Corsiva Arial, Comic, Tahoma, Verdana, Courier, Georgia, Century Schoolbook preferred

TABLE 15.9
Comparative Judgments of Line Lengths

Study	Comparisons	Subjective Judgments
Dyson et al. (1998a)	25, 40, 55, 70, 85, 100 cpl	55 cpl easiest to read
		100 cpl hardest to read
		85 and 25 cpl harder to read than 70 and 40 cpl
	25, 55, 100 cpl	55 cpl easiest to read
		100 cpl hardest to read
Bernard et al. (2002a)	45, 76, 132 cpl	76 cpl most preferred
		132 cpl never chosen as first choice

moderate line lengths, and dislike of long and very short lines, was also reported for print by Tinker (1963). However, in Tinker's case, preferences seem to coincide with reading rate.

There is no obvious relationship between participants' rating of ease of reading and their reading rate or comprehension when reading from screen.

Columns

The limited data on perceptions of the ease of reading columns on screen is in favor of three columns over one (Dyson et al., 1997). The single column had a longer line length, which was not perceived as easy to read. Similarly, readers' opinions of single and double column printing found a preference for two columns (Tinker, 1963). On screen, participants' subjective views are again differing from their performance.

Window Height

Preference and ease of reading judgments are not entirely consistent across studies (see Table 15.10). In proofreading and reading for comprehension, a larger window height is preferred (Creed et al., 1998; Dillon et al., 1990). However, de Bruijn et al. report no effects of screen size and Dyson et al. found less consensus on ease of reading different window heights compared to line lengths.

Summary of Perceptions of Reading

Familiarity seems to be a factor influencing our perceptions of the ease of reading or preferences. There is also a greater likelihood that subjective judgments will distinguish between different presentations than objective performance measures. This applies to fonts, in particular, where print and screen legibility research find little evidence for reading rate or comprehension differences, but consistency in judgments of what is preferred or easy to read.

A different relationship exists between judgments and performance with line length, where text that is read more efficiently is perceived in a negative way. The opinions of readers are consistent across paper and screen and over time (classic print legibility studies date from 50 or so years ago). Readers favor moderate line lengths. The interesting departure is in our apparent capacity to efficiently read longer lines on screen.

WHAT AFFECTS HOW WE MOVE THROUGH TEXT ON SCREEN?

This section addresses a rather different measure of reading compared to the previous ones (reading rate, accuracy and perceptions). The method used to progress through text is considered as an independent variable (comparing paging and scrolling) and a dependent variable (scrolling pattern).

TABLE 15.10
Comparative Judgments of Window Heights

Study	Subjective Judgments
Creed et al. (1998)	Preference for 25 lines over 1 paragraph (4–15 lines)
Dillon et al. (1990)	Desire for larger screen when reading display of 20 lines
de Bruijn et al. (1992)	Perceptions of text layout and "cognitive ergonomic" features not influenced by screen size
Dyson et al. (1998b)	15 lines not as easy to read as larger windows (25 and 35 lines)

Paging and Scrolling

In early experiments (1980s), users were restricted to continuous scrolling whereby the document scrolled at a range of prescribed rates. Greater flexibility was introduced by the late 1990s and Piolat, Roussey, and Thunin (1997) enabled scrolling by clicking on arrows within a scroll bar and Dyson and co-workers provided cursor keys for moving up and down, line-by-line, through the text. The principle underlying paging has not changed substantially over time. An action from the reader causes a new block of text to be displayed.

In terms of preference, when paging is the only means of moving through lengthy texts, some participants have suggested that a scrolling facility would improve presentation, particularly when looking at a small screen with sentences split across screens (Dillon et al., 1990). The studies by Dyson et al. (1997, 1998a, 1998b) compared judgments of the ease of reading paged and scrolled text along with other independent variables (line length, number of columns, window height). In all cases, participants did not agree as to whether paging or scrolling was easier to read, but were generally consistent in using the other variable as the criterion for their judgments.

Results of comparisons of times in paging and scrolling are summarized in Table 15.11. Under some circumstances paging results in faster reading than scrolling and this depends on line length. This interaction between movement method and line length suggests that the time spent in the physical action of scrolling accounts, at least to some extent, for the slower reading rate. When scrolling, longer line lengths are read faster. As line length increases, there are fewer lines to scroll down and the difference in times between paging and scrolling decrease with no differences at 100 cpl. However, the time spent in scrolling may not fully account for differences among line lengths.

TABLE 15.11
Comparisons of Times When Paging and Scrolling

Study	Results Summary
Schwarz, Beldie, & Pastoor (1983)	No differences in time on tasks
Piolat, Roussey, & Thunin (1997)	No differences
Dyson et al. (1997)	Paging faster than scrolling in single column of 80 cpl
Dyson et al. (1998a)	No differences regardless of line length Interaction between paging/scrolling and line length

Reading Patterns

In the first experiment reported in Dyson et al. (1998a) in which six line lengths were compared, the time spent in scrolling was calculated and removed from the total reading time. At the shortest line length (25 cpl), significantly less time was spent in pausing (i.e., the time between scrolling).

One explanation is that people can read short lines more quickly, but this is not found when paging. An alternative explanation is that participants may be reading while scrolling, making use of the extra time given to scrolling with a shorter line length. If this is the case, we would expect scrolling to be slower, which was found in this experiment. There was a slower scrolling rate at 25 cpl than longer line lengths.

Further support for reading while scrolling at shorter line lengths comes from the number of discrete scrolling movements. Participants who made a larger number of movements paused for less time in between movements than participants who made fewer movements, but this only happened with shorter lines (25, 40 and 55 cpl).

From this data, it appears that the more time spent scrolling, the more likely people will read whilst scrolling.

It was proposed earlier, when discussing reading rates and line lengths, that reading long lines on screen may not have the difficulties associated with long lines in print because of the process of scrolling. From the above discussion it can be deduced that little reading takes place whilst scrolling when lines are long. If scrolling does aid location of the next line when making a return sweep on a long line, it is therefore not when readers are actively scrolling. However, scrolling does enable readers to control the vertical positioning of the text, so this may affect accuracy of return sweeps. Without eye movement studies this issue cannot be resolved, as the many other factors which vary between paper and screen could be responsible.

The pattern of findings described above were not replicated in the second experiment reported in Dyson et al. (1998a) using a different experimental design and change in the display. In this experiment, differences in reading time across line lengths can be attributed solely to scrolling time. Two related experiments therefore appear to produce different reading patterns. The most probable explanation is that fewer line lengths and the switch between paging and scrolling prevent participants from tailoring their method of reading to the specific conditions.

Type of Scrolling Pattern

A preliminary exploration of scrolling patterns was conducted by Dyson et al. (1997) whilst comparing single and multiple columns. Two basic patterns used by participants were identified:

- infrequent long scrolling movements
- frequent very small movements

A small number of people had patterns which fell in between. These two characteristic patterns were also evident with different line lengths (Dyson et al., 1998a). Subsequent research (Dyson et al., 2001) has looked at a greater number of scrolling pattern variables and factors which may affect them. These are summarized in Table 15.12.

Relationship Between Scrolling Pattern and Reading

Dyson et al. (2000, 2001) looked at the relationship between various aspects of scrolling patterns and speed and comprehension of reading. In both studies, the time in pauses was the main determinant of reading rate, i.e. longer pauses resulted in slower reading. Table 15.13 summarizes the main findings in relation to comprehension.

TABLE 15.12
Effects of Speed of Reading and Line Length on Scrolling Patterns

Variable Measured	Effect of Faster Reading	Effect of Line Length	Effect of Faster Reading and Line Length
Length of scrolling movements	Shorter scrolling movements		Longer scrolling movements at 25 cpl
Time in pauses	Less time pausing	Longer time pausing at 100 cpl	
Pause to scroll time ratio	Relatively less time pausing compared to scrolling		
Scrolling frequency			Less frequent scrolling at 25 cpl

TABLE 15.13
Conditions in Which Scrolling Patterns Correlate
With Improved Comprehension

Study	Reading Speed	Line Length	Variables Accounting for Better Comprehension
Dyson et al. (2000)	Normal and fast	60 cpl (not varied)	Longer time pausing
Dyson et al. (2001)	Fast	25 cpl	Longer time pausing Shorter initial pause
		100 cpl	More scrolling movements

The results of the 2000 study suggest that most reading took place during pauses. Slower reading correlated with better comprehension, evidence of a speed-accuracy trade-off.

With three line lengths (Dyson et al., 2001), the factors which might account for differences in comprehension were less clear cut. Scrolling patterns appeared to have greater relevance when reading fast, but also depended on line length. In contrast to the earlier study, those who read faster did not retain less. In fact, at a normal reading speed, there was a positive correlation between reading rate and overall comprehension.

Summary of Scrolling

With current mechanisms for scrolling and paging, scrolling can sometimes be slower than paging and sometimes not. This depends on the amount of scrolling required (i.e., length of the document in lines) and whether reading takes place during scrolling.

These two factors interact as more reading appears to take place during scrolling when there is a shorter line length and more scrolling required. However, other factors which may influence when reading takes place are the scrolling pattern (e.g., number and size of discrete scrolling movements) and the context of reading (i.e., experimental design). Scrolling patterns can be affected by reading fast (skimming) and line length.

Particular aspects of scrolling patterns appear to account for reading rate and comprehension. Faster reading is correlated with less time in pauses between scrolling. Comprehension is correlated with more time in pauses between scrolling and, under certain circumstances, more scrolling movements.

SUMMARY AND CONCLUSIONS

Results

Table 15.14 summarizes the results of studies looking at the effects of typographic variables.

What the Experimental Research Can Contribute

The evidence from the experimental research reported in this chapter is that changes in typography produce small differences in performance. One explanation for this may be the versatility of readers. Participants in most experiments are skilled readers who are probably able to cope with less than optimal typographic conditions (resulting in small or non-significant

TABLE 15.14
Summary of Results Related to Typographic Variables

Measure of Reading	Typographic Variable			
	Font	Line Length	Columns	Window Height
Reading rate	Few differences	Long line lengths (80–100 cpl) sometimes read as fast as medium; short lines read slower	No consistent findings: line length more relevant	Very few lines read slower
Accuracy	Very few differences; may be trade-off with reading rate	Medium (55 cpl) better recall	No clear findings	No clear findings
Perceptions	More positive responses to fonts designed for screen and used often	Long line length viewed negatively	Limited evidence for positive view of multiple columns, but may be due to line length	No consistent findings

effects) and who may adjust their reading according to the circumstances. The lack of clear, robust findings make the development of guidelines problematic. However, this body of research indicates specific problems with current guidelines and identifies the relative importance of the variables reviewed when making design decisions.

Results from studies of line length in print appear not to apply to screen. We can therefore identify one of the problems associated with current guidelines for screen presentation, commonly packaged as Web page design guidance. Statements are based on misleading evidence from print, e.g. ". . . the lines of text on most Web pages are far too long for easy reading" (Lynch & Horton, 2002).

A second problem seems to be the prescriptive nature of recommendations for font use, which are not based on evidence of performance differences among fonts. Such differences are rarely demonstrated for print or screen, although preferences are more reliable. This tendency to rely on general assumptions, typical practices, and perhaps a belief that research has confirmed these differences, is common in guidelines on fonts.

Recommendations

Based on evidence from the studies of fonts reviewed in this chapter, choice of font is not particularly important, provided the font selected is designed as a text font for continuous reading (i.e., not an ornate font). It is sensible to use a font designed for screen and one which is reasonably familiar, as these are likely to appear to be more legible. This takes people's preferences into account, but we should be aware that these could change over time.

The number of lines on screen also seems to have little relevance to our reading performance, a reassuring finding for people using small screens.

The research does show that line length is important, and short line lengths are inadvisable when scrolling through text. A moderate length of around 55 cpl seems to optimize reading (i.e., reading rate and comprehension). Online magazines and newspapers which commonly use a moderate line length for articles, with paragraphs separated by additional space, and which require scrolling to reach the end of the text, provide a format which may well optimize reading.

However, if minimizing time in reading is the primary objective, longer lines may facilitate faster reading. Long lines can be an advantage if skimming through a text to judge whether it should be read in detail, in part because less scrolling is needed. Such screen formats are not generally used where skimming or scanning is frequently carried out, e.g. homepages of magazines or newspapers, PDFs of academic articles. In the former, multiple columns contain brief extracts of text in a short line length with links elsewhere. The PDF is often based on the printed document, which tends to have line lengths in keeping with print legibility research (i.e., not too long).

A relatively long document may be divided into chunks (e.g., creating several linked Web pages, or providing anchor points within a single page). However, enabling a form of paging may not be faster than scrolling, particularly with long lines. Small screens can mean that scrolling is still required and the way in which the text is divided into chunks needs to be considered. One situation where paging would be more efficient is with multiple columns where reading continues from the bottom of one column to the top of the next. However, the recommendation is avoid narrow columns and use single columns with longer lines.

What is more difficult to accommodate in these recommendations is readers' current dislike for long lines. If lack of familiarity is influencing people's views, exposure to longer lines may well lead to different perceptions. It is encouraging that the efficiency of less scrolling with long lines is recognized. But with current guidelines in place, exposure to longer lines may take some time to happen.

Where to Go Next

The contribution that the research has made to recommendations on the design of electronic texts has reinforced the need for experimental research in formulating guidelines, but also highlighted the difficulties of the task. More research needs to be done to further explore the circumstances and other variables which interact with line length. Returning to the classic interactions, varying type size, and interlinear spacing, along with line length might shed light on what is happening at long lines.

There is also room for further investigation of scrolling patterns. The research has identified specific methods of scrolling and pausing that are exhibited by faster readers and by those who achieve good comprehension. Research can usefully explore the effects of manipulating scrolling patterns to determine whether changing readers' patterns of pausing and scrolling can affect their reading rate or comprehension. In an experiment where scrolling rate was fixed at a rate relative to participants' preferred rates, reading was more efficient (fewer and shorter fixations) at a rate 20% faster than their preferred rate (Kolers et al., 1981).

When we know more about how we read simple blocks of text, we will be in a better position to further our investigation of reading more complex documents, which combine text, image and other media.

Final Comments

The main contribution of this chapter to user interface design is in providing some justification for making experimental research a necessary part of the formulation of guidelines. The recommendations on interface design are few, given the focus of the review, but essentially suggest that attention should be given to line length, and not choice of font. The responsibility for how such recommendations are used rests with system and standards developers. We should be cautious in implementing changes which constrain readers and undo the progress that has been made in modern user interfaces.

REFERENCES

Bernard, M., Fernandez, M., & Hull, S. (2002a). The effects of line length on children and adults' online reading performance. *Usability News, 4*, http://psychology.wichita.edu/surl/usabilitynews/42/text_length.htm

Bernard, M., Lida, B., Riley, S., Hackler, T., & Janzen, K. (2002b). A comparison of popular online fonts: Which size and type is best? *Usability News, 4*, http://psychology.wichita.edu/surl/usabilitynews/41/onlinetext.htm

Bernard, M., Mills, M., Peterson, M., & Storrer, K. (2001). A comparison of popular online fonts: Which is best and when? *Usability News, 3*, http://psychology.wichita.edu/surl/usabilitynews/3S/font.htm

Boyarski, D., Neuwirth, C., Forlizzi, J., & Regli, S. H. (1998). A study of fonts designed for screen display. In C.-M. Karat (Ed.), *CHI 98: Human Factors in Computing Systems* (pp. 87–94). Reading, MA: Addison-Wesley, ACM Press.

Creed, A., Dennis, I., & Newstead, S. (1987). Proof-reading on VDUs. *Behaviour & Information Technology, 6*, 3–13.

Creed, A., Dennis, I., & Newstead, S. (1988). Effects of display format on proof-reading with VDUs. *Behaviour & Information Technology, 7*, 467–478.

de Bruijn, D., de Mul, S., & van Oostendorp, H. (1992). The influence of screen size and text layout on the study of text. *Behaviour & Information Technology, 11*, 71–78.

Dillon, A. (1992). Reading from paper versus screens: A critical review of the empirical literature. *Ergonomics, 35*, 1297–1326.

Dillon, A. (1994). *Designing usable electronic text: Ergonomic aspects of human information usage.* London: Taylor & Francis.

Dillon, A., Richardson, J., & McKnight, C. (1990). The effects of display size and text splitting on reading lengthy text from screen. *Behaviour & Information Technology, 9*, 215–227.

Duchnicky, R. L., & Kolers, P. A. (1983). Readability of text scrolled on visual display terminals as a function of window size. *Human Factors, 25*, 683–692.

Dyson, M. C., & Haselgrove, M. (2000). The effects of reading speed and reading patterns on our understanding of text read from screen. *Journal of Research in Reading, 23*, 210–223.

Dyson, M. C., & Haselgrove, M. (2001). The influence of reading speed and line length on the effectiveness of reading from screen. *International Journal of Human–Computer Studies, 54*, 585–612.

Dyson, M. C., & Kipping, G. J. (1997). The legibility of screen formats: Are three columns better than one? *Computers & Graphics, 21*, 703–712.

Dyson, M. C., & Kipping, G. J. (1998a). The effects of line length and method of movement on patterns of reading from screen. *Visible Language, 32*, 150–181.

Dyson, M. C., & Kipping, G. J. (1998b). Exploring the effect of layout on reading from screen. In R. D. Hersch, J. André, & H. Brown (Eds.), *Electronic documents, artistic imaging and digital typography* (pp. 294–304). Berlin: Springer-Verlag.

Foster, J. J. (1970). A study of the legibility of one- and two-column layouts for BPS publications. *Bulletin of the British Psychological Society, 23,* 113–114.

Gould, J. D., Alfaro, L., Barnes, V., Finn, R., Grischkowsky, N., & Minuto, A. (1987). Reading is slower from CRT displays than from paper: Attempts to isolate a single-variable explanation. *Human Factors, 29,* 269–299.

Grabinger, R. S., & Osman-Jouchoux, R. (1996). Designing screens for learning. In H. van Oostendorp & S. de Mul (Eds.), *Cognitive aspects of electronic text processing* (pp. 181–212). Norwood, NJ: Ablex.

Hartley, J., Burnhill, P., & Fraser, S. (1974). Typographical problems of journal design. *Applied Ergonomics, 5,* 15–20.

Holleran, P. A. (1992). An assessment of font preferences for screen-based text display. In A. Monk, D. Diaper, & M. D. Harrison (Eds.), *People and Computers VII* (pp. 447–459). Cambridge: Cambridge University Press.

Horton, W., Taylor, L., Ignacio, A., & Hoft, N. L. (1996). *The Web page design cookbook.* New York: Wiley.

Johnson, R. E. (1970). Recall of prose as a function of the structural importance of the linguistic units. *Journal of Verbal Learning and Verbal Behaviour, 9,* 12–20.

Kolers, P. A., Duchnicky, R. L., & Ferguson, D. C. (1981). Eye movement measurement of readability of CRT displays. *Human Factors, 23,* 517–527.

Lynch, P. J., & Horton, S. (2002). *Web style guide: Basic design principles for creating Web sites* (2nd ed.). New Haven: Yale University Press.

Muter, P. (1996). Interface design and optimization of reading of continuous text. In H. van Oostendorp & S. de Mul (Eds.), *Cognitive aspects of electronic text processing* (pp. 161–180). Norwood, NJ: Ablex.

Muter, P., Latrémouille, S. A., Treurniet, W. C., & Beam, P. (1982). Extended reading of continuous text on television screens. *Human Factors, 24,* 501–508.

The Nelson-Denny Reading Test. (1981). Chicago: The Riverside Publishing Company.

Paterson, D. G., & Tinker, M. A. (1932). Studies of typographical factors influencing speed of reading: X. Style of type face. *Journal of Applied Psychology, 16,* 605–613.

Paterson, D. G., & Tinker, M. A. (1940). Influence of line width on eye movements. *Journal of Experimental Psychology, 27,* 572–577.

Piolat, A., Roussey, J.-Y., & Thunin, O. (1997). Effects of screen presentation on text reading and revising. *International Journal of Human–Computer Studies, 47,* 565–589.

Poulton, E. C. (1959). Effects of printing types and formats on the comprehension of scientific journals. *Nature, 184,* 1824–1825.

Poulton, E. C. (1965). On increasing the sensitivity of measures of performance. *Ergonomics, 8,* 69–76.

Rho, Y. J., & Gedeon, T. D. (2000). Academic articles on the Web: Reading patterns and formats. *International Journal of Human–Computer Interaction, 12,* 219–240.

Schriver, K. A. (1997). *Dynamics in document design.* New York: Wiley.

Schumacher, G. M., & Waller, R. (1985). Testing design alternatives: A comparison of procedures. In T. M. Duffy & R. Waller (Eds.), *Designing usable texts* (pp. 377–403). Orlando: Academic Press.

Schwarz, E., Beldie, I. P., & Pastoor, S. (1983). A comparison of paging and scrolling for changing screen contents by inexperienced users. *Human Factors, 25,* 279–282.

Spencer, H. (1968). *The visible word.* London: Royal College of Art.

Tinker, M. A. (1947). *The Tinker speed of reading test.* Minneapolis, MN: The University of Minnesota Press.

Tinker, M. A. (1963). *Legibility of print.* Iowa: Iowa State University Press.

Tinker, M. A. (1965). *Bases for effective reading.* Minneapolis: Lund Press.

Tinker, M. A., & Paterson, D. G. (1955). The effect of typographical variations upon eye movement in reading. *Journal of Educational Research, 49,* 171–184.

Youngman, M., & Scharff, L. (1998). Text width and margin width influences. http://
hubel.sfasu.edu/research/textmargin.html (Presented at South Western Psychological Association 1998)

Zachrisson, B. (1965). *Studies in the legibility of printed text.* Stockholm: Almqvist & Wiksell.

Chapter 16

Conclusion: So What Is This Thing Called *Information*?

Andrew Dillon
University of Texas

It may seem odd that, in a book examining the creation and use of digital information, the core concept of *information* is not defined. This state of affairs is not unique to the present book; it is part of the corpus of writings and discussions of information in disciplines that are now turning their attention to the emergence of new communicative forms and digital resources. This taken-for-granted nature of the information concept might not unduly worry us were it not for some important implications that surely follow from its mercurial status as a catchall.

I do not pretend to provide a solution to this problem, if it may be called one, but an exploration of it is surely of no little relevance to our concerns in the present text and I attempt to weave some of the arguments from the preceding chapters into this exploration where appropriate. If we are to wrestle with the many issues that are presented to us as we create and use digital information in new and varied forms, then an understanding of just what information is will prove useful.

A dictionary definition of the term is limited, for our purposes, but a worthwhile starting point. The *Merriam-Webster* definition covers several aspects. Information is, first and foremost, "the communication or reception of knowledge or intelligence," which leaves us with the thorny problem of defining, in turn, terms such as *communication* or *knowledge*. Information can also be "knowledge obtained from investigation, study, or instruction," which again leaves us with *knowledge* to define and really only adds to the first definition by specifying types of communicative acts underlying the gain of knowledge. *Merriam-Webster* proceeds to add to the definition by equating information with "intelligence, news, facts, data and the attribute inherent in and communicated by one of two or more alternative sequences or arrangements of something (e.g., nucleotides in DNA or binary digits in a computer program) that produce specific effects." This is far more complex and suggests attributes that stimulate a response in a recipient or perceiver, again raising the idea of intelligence as the basis for understanding information.

One could proceed along these lines, seeking further, more detailed etymological insights, but it is not clear that insight into the concept of information, as employed in the chapters of this book, will necessarily result from such definitions. Certainly, there is a common-sense meaning of the term that we can all appreciate very quickly, but even common sense indicates that the word is elusive and prone to many fuzzy interpretations. Yet information is the basis of a field of study, an academic discipline, and the name in full or part of many departments in universities such as my own (for an overview of information science as a discipline, see Williams & Carbo, 1997). So how can its definition prove so problematic?

In the present chapter I explore very briefly some of the current issues raised by the definition problem and propose a workable definition that draws a distinction between information and communication. In so doing, I emphasize the importance of representation or embodiments to any analysis of information, while arguing that representations alone cannot be understood as information in any way that offers us guidance for digital design.

INFORMATION IS MORE THAN DATA

Historically, at least within the information science field, a sharp distinction has been drawn between data and information, and this distinction has been extended further between information, knowledge, and wisdom (for a contemporary overview in practical terms, see Davenport & Prusak, 1998). I do not intend to explore this set of distinctions deeply, but it raises some issues that are worth noting to those, such as most social or computer scientists, for whom the data-information distinction is rarely made.

These distinctions reflect a line of reasoning that introduces a significant human factor into the discussion, namely, the argument that data becomes information only when a user (a sentient human) makes sense of it in some context. Thus, for example, when I am checking a Web site for weather information in a city I am about to visit, I am interrogating a database in order to gain information, the success measure of which is the satisfactory resolution of my task—knowing the weather sufficiently well. The information is not in the Web site, but in the interaction between data set and user, emerging only through the meaning I imbue given my needs and goals (leaving aside, for now, any discussion of the accuracy or validity of the meaning I establish; for more on this, see chap. 7, this volume, by Tabachneck[-Schijf]).

This distinction has a long but, sadly, less than influential history. Few writers or scholars outside of information studies or knowledge management draw this distinction so explicitly. This is a pity because the insight gained by invoking a human element in the definition and examination of information ties well with current user-centric emphases in systems design.

The everyday sense of *information*, and one that probably runs through many of the chapters here, without formal explication, is of information as object or artifact, what I term here the "embodied form" of information. In its simplest expression, information is equated to a physical or digital data set, embodied in such familiar forms as books, documents, software files, and articles. There is a certain face validity to this: After all, in common use we point to information as residing in books, in databases, in newspapers, and so on. Buckland (1991), in an insightful critique of the various interpretations of the term in use, called this view the "information-as-thing" perspective and suggested that its widespread use warrants it being taken seriously by researchers. Indeed, he argued that it is difficult to see how *any* object could not, in some sense, be information! However, face validity only goes so far. Information scientists have discussed this issue for many years and concluded that the equation of information to entities or representations alone significantly underplays the human factor. Considering information as representations alone, we might lump together all objects with the assumption of equivalent informational status, rendering the difference between, say, a rock or a tree and a book, moot.

One might ask if there is anything wrong with this, because any object might itself embody information for a particular user or group. A rock is a source of information to a geologist, a tree can provide information about weather to a biologist, and so forth. But the key here is provision. To gain information from such objects requires an understanding of how to read them. Without this understanding, there is no communication between object and human on the matter of history or climate and it is therefore difficult to conceive the object as information in any meaningful sense. It can, in context, provide information to a skilled or intelligent reader, but it does not itself embody information in any real sense; at best it can be said to serve as data.

Are such distinctions mere academic wordplay or are they important? I believe they are crucial, if only to be clear on what it means for designing and using information systems. The lumping together of every representation or artifact under the heading of "information" carries with it an implicit view of our role in creating and designing digital information as that of digitizers and navigation designers. We certainly have to contend with these issues, as they have nontrivial implications for a host of real-life applications, but they are not the limit of our work here. We are not solely in the business of taking entities in the world (rocks, books, compact discs, etc.) and finding ways of giving them to people when they ask. To do so would be to reduce us to search-engine designers of one form or other. The real value of new information technologies comes through their provision of what I will call "augmentery functions," tools that can allow us to interrogate data, manipulate it, and reorganize it to our own ends so as to enhance our capacity for intelligent thought. To do this, we have to study cognition, how people reason and think, not just as they try to locate or navigate through, but as they imagine, explore meaning, and gain understanding from the data (see, e.g., chap. 10, by Witteman & Krol, this volume). Such a perspective is not the norm, because we reside in an age that views navigation and retrieval as the core issues, but these are perspectives that reflect the narrow, embodied view of information as findable, possessable entities, rather than as the resource and enhancement of intelligence. For this reason alone, we need to move forward in our understanding of what we are dealing with when we talk of information design.

INFORMATION IS PRODUCT WITH PURPOSIVE PROCESS

So what other perspective on information can we hold that might enhance our research in this vein? Certainly there is a mathematical conceptualization that has been advanced over the years. This considers information in terms of confidence levels in receivers of the conditions that exist at the source, wherein information is considered the reduction of uncertainty (Gharhamani, 2003). Thus, information theory is the quantitative assessment of how uncertainty can be manipulated. Although this approach has had significant impact on the design of computing systems (not to be confused with information technology), and theoretically influenced classic information-processing models in psychology, it is not clear how it helps directly in digital information design. What I propose here is an alternative that builds on the data-information distinction of classical information science, outlined earlier, and what I call the "information as product with purposive process" perspective.

To make sense of the product-with-process idea, let me outline why this is more than a restatement of current ideas. First, this approach assumes that information does not reside in objects or entities. We do not have information stored on hard disks, we do not put information into words in our books, and we cannot claim that a DVD is an "information medium" in and of itself. In all these cases, information can result, it can evolve, or it can emerge, but only from the interaction of the entity with a human or intelligent agent (I allow for the latter so as to accommodate the range of life forms, physical and virtual, on the planet that can make use of information in their ecological niche).

Second, the product-with-process idea reflects the importance of intelligence in exploiting data, or the given state of affairs. The human user can exploit the data to extract information only if he or she has the intelligence or capability to read data appropriately. A book in a language you cannot read has significantly less data that you can exploit for information purposes than a book in your own language—there is less process to be found here. Less obviously, two people may make different use of exactly the same data, even when sharing the same need or performing the same task, due to their own varying intelligences. In this case, we come to realize that any one data set or object such as a book is really never equally informative to all (see, e.g., Van Oostendorp & Holzel's chap. in this volume, which shows that adding icons and chat possibilities to messages can improve problem-solving performance).

Yet, while information does not reside in the product, the necessity of product to the creation of information is a formal constraint. Without product, which I am taking here to mean a representation of the data viewable by some third party not immediately privy to the data exchange, then the process alone is not informational. For us to study information, we must be dealing with the viewable products, abstracted and embodied from these initial communicative acts, accessible to us when removed (temporally or physically) from the initial events or context that gave rise to the data. A conversation between two parties is not truly informational; it is communicational. Data may be exchanged, behaviors may result, but in the absence of a record, a product, viewable by a third party, where is the information? If the conversation is recorded, then we have product, and thus can proceed to an informational analysis, but without the record, we are not talking about information. Obviously, this leaves for further discussion the point at which we can determine what constitutes a "record viewable by some third party." It may be possible sometimes for my thought waves to be represented externally for others in a meaningful way, thus leaving forever such a record, but even now, the nature of records has changed so radically in recent years that the question of just what is or is not a record can be contested. Furthermore, the product constraint forces a distinction between information and communication technologies that is made routinely in the world, but has hardly been attended to by researchers, who conveniently lump them together.

Although this sounds extremely broad, there are some focal points that can serve as boundaries to what we study in the information field. If we are interested in designing information systems, then that places a focus on usability and ergonomics more than on hardware and software engineering. If we are applying information systems to organizational work, then we are interested in adoption and acceptance of new technologies. If education is our focus, the thrust is on how our tools impact learning outcomes, and so on. To date, such issues have almost always resided in different disciplines: Psychology underpinned usability; management information systems (in the United States) is the foundation of studies in technology adoption in organizations; education theory has driven instructional technology design. Few researchers cross these divides and cocitation rates indicate few explorations of literature outside of one's original training (Zhang & Dillon, 2003). From the information perspective outlined here, such distinctions should not be firmly drawn; instead, we should consider each of these (and the many other examples we could list) as manifestations of an underlying concern of product with process. Indeed, what is most interesting about the present book is that it collects ideas about digital-information design and use from such a diverse set of investigators across such a range of disciplinary affiliations, such as typography, psychology, classics, information science, computer science, and archaeology.

To study information, therefore, is to study human behavior in the context of data creation and use, where the data is abstracted into an examinable record. There is no meaningful study of information that is not grounded in an analysis of people communicating, solving problems, sharing ideas, and so forth. We cannot talk meaningfully of an information age or information as the basis of organizational life without invoking this human aspect. But communication alone is not sufficient. There must be records, artifacts, and products that can convey the data to people not immediately participating in the communicative act for us to enter the realm of information design and use.

DIGITAL INFORMATION ADDS ANOTHER LAYER OF COMPLEXITY

The data-laden artifacts of the predigital age tended to render themselves immediately amenable to human use. A reader could pick up a book or a newspaper, an architectural drawing or a scroll, and proceed to use it. The issue became slightly more complicated in the 20th century with the emergence of mechanical devices to "play" various data media, such as audio- and videotape, vinyl records, microfiche slides, and so on. With these technologies it became necessary to have a means of interfacing with the data-carrying component, but there was relatively fast adoption of standards that ensured, for example, that a long-playing record provided music on any turntable (within reason). This brought the software-hardware distinction vaguely to most people's consciousness. The investment of users in various media was predicated on a fairly reasonable assumption that the hardware platform was stable and an investment would last many years (indeed, advertisements for such hardware as the "last one you will need to buy" were common).

With digital systems, this distinction has now become paramount. Current software can enable data to follow us, and to be encrypted, minimized, sent wirelessly, shared, and copied effortlessly, but the software itself conveys nothing to the user without the appropriate means of decoding at the machine level. We say that one cannot judge a book by its cover, but this is false—we can and we do make such judgments, often with good reason, based on size, wear and tear, annotation, price, date of publication, and so on. Indeed, in the book world, such attributes can prove very meaningful to a reader or user (Dillon, 2004). It is hard to imagine the same being said of an e-book or floppy disk. Furthermore, the physical artifact in the book world has value above and beyond its content, as collectors vie for the limited numbers of rare books that still exist. A copy of such a book, even a high-fidelity one, would be of no interest to a collector.

At the interface level between users and data, the situation is even more complicated. A variety of operating systems, platforms, versions, and licensing agreements means that we can never guarantee that a data file you provide me can even be opened on my machine. When such transfers operate smoothly, there is no issue, but if, for example, my e-mail attachments in Microsoft Word from my Apple Macintosh turn into a series of 1s and 0s on your screen when you open them on your PC machine, then it is clear that little information is being shared. Ownership of data and concern with rights management are central to our current study of information.

Currently, I see many people with multiple pieces of what we rather casually term *information technology* in their possession. It is not unusual in early 21st-century life to have meetings where people pull out laptops, PDAs, paper and pen, and cell phones from their cases or from their pockets. Even for a person who has all of these items, it is not certain that each piece can communicate transparently with every other (my phone is independent, and I have no easy way of putting my hurriedly scrawled handwritten notes into my laptop at this time). The result, for many of us, is a complex set of interrelated but mutually uncommunicative artifacts for data collection and representation. This overload actually taxes our information-processing capabilities by requiring us to attend to matters of translation and compatibility, issues that were far less common in the predigital domain.

Even when we learn to simplify, back up, and avoid cross-platform problems, we are constantly harassed into updating our tools as new versions of applications that many of us are perfectly willing to stick with are changed for us. Microsoft Word, my text editor of default, if not of choice, to this day still offers users the chance to configure the application according to a popular old version (5.1) on the Macintosh. Part of the problem here may be consumer variability. As Rogers (1995) repeatedly noted, we do not all wish to adopt change at the same rate, a point confirmed further in chapter 13 by Van de Wijngaert, this volume.

Clearly, everyday activity with the so-called technologies of information leads us to complain of navigation problems, retrieval difficulties, or an inability to find the right kind of information. To argue that there is too much information about us is further proof of this—it is not information of which we have too much, it is data, and all data does not have equivalent value, whether we invoke contextual or economic explanations. If all data were equivalent in value, how could we invest so much effort in refining, searching, and filtering? Simple pattern matches to our task would be sufficient for us to locate something of relevance. But data differs, and its value depends on our needs and our abilities to utilize it. Hence, it is more parsimonious, when examining people's use of technologies, to consider data as a searchable terrain, with information as the goal of our journey into virtual space. If nothing else, this helps to minimize the inelegance of requiring distinctions between relevant and irrelevant information.

As we design digital-information systems, we need to attend to the layers of translation demanded by any system that brings data to humans. The ideal digital tool would be capable of reading all data and presenting it in a manner that was most appropriate for the user's need. We are a long way from such a tool at the present time, but we must learn how to break down the disciplinary divides of the preceding decades if we are to make progress here.

THE FUTURE OF INFORMATION AND ITS STUDY

History tends to be written around pivotal moments, events, battles, inventions, and legislation, as if these were cut-and-dried occurrences, points at which the status quo shifted. In that sense, it is easy to look back on the ages of information and point to the alphabet or the printing press as if they emerged fully formed, at one time, in one place. Of course, it is never so simple. The printing press, attributed to Gutenberg, is the result of centuries of refinement coupled with shifts in cultural treatments of reading. The printing press provided a massive shift in capability, just as the internet does in our time, but we should not presume that such impacts occur overnight. Just as Gutenberg's invention unleashed a potential, this was subsequently shaped by and helped shape the adoption of print culture across the world.

At the turn of the 21st century we are part of a similar revolution and we would do well to recognize that the decisions we make now will prove to have consequences beyond our imagination. More importantly, because consequences are unknowable in advance, we must enter this new information age with a commitment to explore and we must recognize that the ways we have created, used, and managed information in a paper world will not easily transfer to a digital world. Some aspects will remain: There has always been a surfeit of data, readers have always had to learn to discriminate, and for decades people have complained about the drop in literacy rates. Even the book was criticized in its early use in schools for encouraging students to believe they need not attend to teachers, because they could always read the book later. Such reactions are constants of the human society faced with invention and change. But the digital era will change the world. Publication processes that we have become used to will seem antiquated very soon. Book shops already have shifted in style and number. Text will increasingly be merged with graphics and animation. Ownership of information will take on a form different from possession of a physical artifact. As Crane puts it so well in chapter 2 (this volume), books will "talk to each other," readers will share more data among themselves, models will make accurate simulation a normal occurrence, and libraries will no longer be seen as physical buildings but as curated collections. We will create new products with attendant processes for information sharing. The impacts will be profound, precisely because information, product with process, reflects so much of human activity. Changing the information base from paper to digital will therefore have a huge impact on many human activities. The goal is to understand how this works and to learn from the past so as to shape the future.

As we enter a new information age we are challenged and yet blessed to be part of this transition. As Hobart and Schiffman (1998) noted, "our information age is but the latest of several" (p. 2). This is true and it points to need to examine our history as we plot the road ahead. But the road ahead is now likely to take us further into new territory than any changes in the information history of someone on the planet today. To be clear on the size of the challenge, we must be clear on what information truly is—a reflection of human intelligence more than a cut-and-dried data point—and design the future accordingly.

REFERENCES

Buckland, M. (1991). Information as thing. *Journal of the American Society for Information Science, 42*, 351–360.

Davenport, T., & Prusak, L. (1998). *Working knowledge: How organizations manage what they know.* Cambridge, MA: Harvard Business School Press.

Dillon, A. (2004). *Designing usable electronic text* (2nd ed.). Boca Raton: CRC Press.

Gharhamani, Z. (2003). Information theory. In *The Macmillan encyclopedia of cognitive science* (Vol. 2, pp. 551–555). London: Nature.

Hobart, M., & Schiffman, Z. (1998). *Information ages: Literacy, numeracy and the computer revolution*. Baltimore: Johns Hopkins University Press.

Rogers, E. (1995). *Diffusion of innovations*. New York: Free Press.

Williams, J., & Carbo, T. (1997). *Information science: Still an emerging discipline*. Pittsburgh, PA: Cathedral.

Zhang, P., & Dillon, A. (2003). HCI and MIS: Shared concerns. *International Journal of Human–Computer Studies, 59*, 397–522.

Author Index

Subject Index

Milton Keynes UK
Ingram Content Group UK Ltd.
UKHW022100141024
449569UK00031B/1722